7

Spelling Connections

J. Richard Gentry, Ph.D.

 **Zaner-Bloser**

Author

J. Richard Gentry, Ph. D.

Zaner-Bloser wishes to thank these educators who reviewed portions of this program and provided comments prior to publication.

Reviewers

Donetta S. Brown, Birmingham City Schools, Birmingham, AL

Kelly Caravelli, Poway Unified School District, San Diego, CA

Michelle Corsi, East Windsor Regional Schools, East Windsor, NJ

Scott J. Dan, Southwest Allen County Schools, Roanoke, IN

Naomi Drewitz, East Windsor Regional Schools, East Windsor, NJ

Karen Jackson, School District of Philadelphia, Philadelphia, PA

Liz Knowles, Ed.D., 21st Century Curriculum Designs, LLC, Del Ray Beach, FL

Nancy Mast, School City of Hobart, Hobart, IN

Geraldine A. Pappas, Detroit Public Schools, Detroit, MI

Michael Pizzingrillo, Roman Catholic Diocese of Brooklyn, NY

Deborah C. Thomas, Ed.D., Montgomery Public Schools, Montgomery, AL

Terra Trull, Salem City Schools, Salem, VA

Carrie Wells, Harding Academy, Searcy, AR

ELL and Spanish Consultants

Ellen Riojas Clark, Ph.D., Professor, College of Education and Human Development, Division of Bicultural-Bilingual Studies, The University of Texas at San Antonio, TX

Bertha Pérez, Ed.D., Professor Emeritus of Literacy, College of Education and Human Development, The University of Texas at San Antonio, TX

Rocio Reyes-Moore, Spanish Language Productions, Alexandria, OH

ISBN 978-0-7367-9476-3

Zaner-Bloser, Inc.
1-800-421-3018
www.zaner-bloser.com
Printed in the United States of America   13 14 15 25170 5 4 3 2

SUSTAINABLE FORESTRY INITIATIVE — Certified Chain of Custody — Promoting Sustainable Forestry — www.sfiprogram.org — SFI-01042

Table of Contents

Unit 1

Media Words
Connections to Thinking 14
Read • Think & Sort • Remember
Connections to Vocabulary 15
Word Meanings • Word Structure •
Use the Dictionary: Pronunciations
Connections to Reading 16
Complete the Analogies • Make Inferences •
Use Context Clues
Connections to Writing 17
Proofread an Editorial • Write an Editorial
Extend & Transfer
Word Study 18
Word Hunt: Language Arts 19

Unit 2

Syllabication Patterns: Short Vowels
Connections to Thinking 20
Read • Think & Sort • Remember
Connections to Vocabulary 21
Word Meanings • Word Analysis •
Use the Dictionary: Parts of Speech
Connections to Reading 22
Complete the Analogies • Reword the Headlines •
Complete the News Article
Connections to Writing 23
Proofread a News Story • Write a News Story
Extend & Transfer
Word Study 24
Word Hunt: Technology 25

Unit 3

Syllabication Patterns: Long Vowels
Connections to Thinking 26
Read • Think & Sort • Remember
Connections to Vocabulary 27
Word Groups • Word Structure •
Use the Dictionary: Definitions
Connections to Reading 28
Replace the Words • Complete the Analogies •
Use Context Clues
Connections to Writing 29
Proofread a Paragraph •
Write a Paragraph
Extend & Transfer
Word Study 30
Word Hunt: Science 31

Unit 4

Compound Words
Connections to Thinking 32
Read • Think & Sort • Remember
Connections to Vocabulary 33
Word Meanings • Word Replacement •
Use the Dictionary: Parts of Speech
Connections to Reading 34
Answer the Questions • Complete the Sentences •
Use Context Clues
Connections to Writing 35
Proofread a Biographical Sketch •
Write a Biographical Sketch
Extend & Transfer
Word Study 36
Word Hunt: Math 37

Unit 5

Double Consonants
Connections to Thinking 38
Read • Think & Sort • Remember
Connections to Vocabulary 39
Word Meanings • Word Structure •
Use the Dictionary: Inflected Forms
Connections to Reading 40
Complete the Analogies •
Complete the Advertisements • Use Context Clues
Connections to Writing 41
Proofread an Advertisement •
Write an Advertisement
Extend & Transfer
Word Study 42
Word Hunt: Social Studies 43

Unit 6

Assessment and Review
Assess for Transfer 44
Review Units 1–2 45
Review Units 3–4 46
Review Unit 5 47
Spelling Study Strategy 47
Word Swap
Standardized Test Practice 48
Writer's Workshop 50
Grammar, Usage, and Mechanics: Parts of a Sentence
The Writing Process: Narrative

Unit 7

Affixes

Connections to Thinking 52
  Read • Think & Sort • Remember
Connections to Vocabulary 53
  Word Meanings • Word Structure •
  Use the Thesaurus: Synonyms
Connections to Reading 54
  Solve the Analogies • Complete the Sentences •
  Use Context Clues
Connections to Writing 55
  Proofread a Journal Entry • Write a Journal Entry
Extend & Transfer
  Word Study 56
  Word Hunt: Math 57

Unit 8

Adding Suffixes to Words Ending in Silent e

Connections to Thinking 58
  Read • Think & Sort • Remember
Connections to Vocabulary 59
  Word Meanings • Word Structure •
  Use the Dictionary: Etymology
Connections to Reading 60
  Answer the Questions • Complete the Sentences •
  Use Context Clues
Connections to Writing 61
  Proofread a Speech • Write a Speech
Extend & Transfer
  Word Study 62
  Word Hunt: Science 63

Unit 9

Suffixes: -tion, -ation

Connections to Thinking 64
  Read • Think & Sort • Remember
Connections to Vocabulary 65
  Word Groups • Word Analysis •
  Use the Dictionary: Syllables and Stress
Connections to Reading 66
  Replace the Words • Use Context Clues
Connections to Writing 67
  Proofread a Paragraph • Write a Paragraph
Extend & Transfer
  Word Study 68
  Word Hunt: Language Arts 69

Unit 10

Adding Suffixes to Words Ending in Silent e

Connections to Thinking 70
  Read • Think & Sort • Remember
Connections to Vocabulary 71
  Word Meanings • Word Replacement •
  Use the Thesaurus: Synonyms
Connections to Reading 72
  Solve the Analogies • Complete the Sentences •
  Use Context Clues
Connections to Writing 73
  Proofread a Folktale • Write a Folktale
Extend & Transfer
  Word Study 74
  Word Hunt: Language Arts 75

Unit 11

Words With Silent Letters

Connections to Thinking 76
  Read • Think & Sort • Remember
Connections to Vocabulary 77
  Word Meanings • Word Groups •
  Use the Dictionary: Pronunciation
Connections to Reading 78
  Complete the Sentences • Use Context Clues
Connections to Writing 79
  Proofread a Tall Tale • Write a Tall Tale
Extend & Transfer
  Word Study 80
  Word Hunt: Health 81

Unit 12

Assessment and Review

Assess for Transfer 82
Review Units 7–8 83
Review Units 9–10 84
Review Unit 11 85
Spelling Study Strategy 85
  Sorting by Parts of Speech
Standardized Test Practice 86
Writer's Workshop 88
  Grammar, Usage, and Mechanics:
  Identifying Modifiers: Adverbs
  The Writing Process: Descriptive

Unit 13

Suffix: –ly
Connections to Thinking 90
  Read • Think & Sort • Remember
Connections to Vocabulary 91
  Word Meanings • Word Replacement •
  Use the Dictionary: Etymology
Connections to Reading 92
  Answer the Questions • Complete the Dialogue
Connections to Writing 93
  Proofread a Dialogue • Write a Dialogue
Extend & Transfer
  Word Study 94
  Word Hunt: Art 95

Unit 14

Suffixes: -able, -ible
Connections to Thinking 96
  Read • Think & Sort • Remember
Connections to Vocabulary 97
  Word Meanings • Word Analysis •
  Use the Dictionary: Parts of Speech
Connections to Reading 98
  Complete the Sentences • Draw Conclusions •
  Use Context Clues
Connections to Writing 99
  Proofread a Paragraph • Write a Paragraph
Extend & Transfer
  Word Study 100
  Word Hunt: Technology 101

Unit 15

Frequently Misspelled Words
Connections to Thinking 102
  Read • Think & Sort • Remember
Connections to Vocabulary 103
  Word Meanings • Word Structure •
  Use the Dictionary: Pronunciation
Connections to Reading 104
  Complete the Sentences • Use Context Clues
Connections to Writing 105
  Proofread a Paragraph • Write a Paragraph
Extend & Transfer
  Word Study 106
  Word Hunt: Science 107

Unit 16

Adding Suffixes That Change Stress
Connections to Thinking 108
  Read • Think & Sort • Remember
Connections to Vocabulary 109
  Word Meanings • Word Replacement •
  Use the Thesaurus: Synonyms
Connections to Reading 110
  Complete the Sentences • Use Context Clues
Connections to Writing 111
  Proofread a Paragraph • Write a Paragraph
Extend & Transfer
  Word Study 112
  Word Hunt: Social Studies 113

Unit 17

Words From Spanish
Connections to Thinking 114
  Read • Think & Sort • Remember
Connections to Vocabulary 115
  Word Meanings • Spelling Patterns •
  Use the Dictionary: Informal Language and Slang
Connections to Reading 116
  Solve the Analogies • Complete the Sentences •
  Use Context Clues
Connections to Writing 117
  Proofread a Paragraph • Write a Paragraph
Extend & Transfer
  Word Study 118
  Word Hunt: Language Arts 119

Unit 18

Assessment and Review
Assess for Transfer 120
Review Units 13–14 121
Review Units 15–16 122
Review Unit 17 123
Spelling Study Strategy 123
  Spelling Tic-Tac-Toe
Standardized Test Practice. 124
Writer's Workshop 126
  Grammar, Usage, and Mechanics: Identifying
  Modifiers: Adjectives
  The Writing Process: Informative/Explanatory

Unit 19

Plural Nouns

Connections to Thinking 128
  Read • Think & Sort • Remember
Connections to Vocabulary 129
  Word Meanings • Word Groups •
  Use the Dictionary: Plural Forms
Connections to Reading 130
  Complete the Analogies • Complete the Sentences •
  Use Context Clues
Connections to Writing 131
  Proofread a Short Story in Progress •
  Complete a Short Story
Extend & Transfer
  Word Study 132
  Word Hunt: Social Studies 133

Unit 20

Assimilated Prefix: ad-

Connections to Thinking 134
  Read • Think & Sort • Remember
Connections to Vocabulary 135
  Word Meanings • Word Structure •
  Use the Dictionary: Etymology
Connections to Reading 136
  Replace the Words • Use Context Clues
Connections to Writing 137
  Proofread a Letter • Write a Letter
Extend & Transfer
  Word Study 138
  Word Hunt: Math. 139

Unit 21

Words From Names and Places

Connections to Thinking 140
  Read • Think & Sort • Remember
Connections to Vocabulary 141
  Word Meanings • Use the Dictionary:
  Syllables and Stress
Connections to Reading 142
  Complete the Restaurant Review • Use Context Clues
Connections to Writing 143
  Proofread a Paragraph • Write a Paragraph
Extend & Transfer
  Word Study 144
  Word Hunt: Language Arts. 145

Unit 22

Frequently Misspelled Words

Connections to Thinking 146
  Read • Think & Sort • Remember
Connections to Vocabulary 147
  Word Meanings • Word Replacement •
  Use the Dictionary: Etymology
Connections to Reading 148
  Complete the Analogies • Draw Conclusions •
  Use Context Clues
Connections to Writing 149
  Proofread a Paragraph • Write a Paragraph
Extend & Transfer
  Word Study 150
  Word Hunt: Health 151

Unit 23

Latin Roots: tract, plic, sist, strict

Connections to Thinking 152
  Read • Think & Sort • Remember
Connections to Vocabulary 153
  Word Meanings • Word Structure •
  Use the Thesaurus: Synonyms
Connections to Reading 154
  Complete the Sentences • Use Context Clues
Connections to Writing 155
  Proofread a Passage • Write a Passage
Extend & Transfer
  Word Study 156
  Word Hunt: Social Studies 157

Unit 24

Assessment and Review

Assess for Transfer 158
Review Units 19–20. 159
Review Units 21–22. 160
Review Unit 23. 161
Spelling Study Strategy. 161
  Sorting by Plural Forms of Nouns
Standardized Test Practice. 162
Writer's Workshop 164
  Grammar, Usage, and Mechanics:
  Identifying Conjunctions
  The Writing Process: Argument

Unit 25

Prefixes: uni-, mono-, duo-, bi-
Connections to Thinking 166
　Read • Think & Sort • Remember
Connections to Vocabulary 167
　Word Meanings • Word Structure •
　Use the Dictionary: Guide Words
Connections to Reading 168
　Complete the Sentences • Use Context Clues
Connections to Writing 169
　Proofread a Paragraph • Write a Paragraph
Extend & Transfer
　Word Study 170
　Word Hunt: Poetry 171

Unit 26

Greek Forms: gram, chron, phon(e), scope
Connections to Thinking 172
　Read • Think & Sort • Remember
Connections to Vocabulary 173
　Word Meanings • Use the Thesaurus: Synonyms
Connections to Reading 174
　Replace the Phrases • Use Context Clues
Connections to Writing 175
　Proofread a Outline • Write a Outline
Extend & Transfer
　Word Study 176
　Word Hunt: Math 177

Unit 27

Commonly Confused Words
Connections to Thinking 178
　Read • Think & Sort • Remember
Connections to Vocabulary 179
　Word Meanings • Use the Dictionary:
　Homophones
Connections to Reading 180
　Complete the Sentences • Use Context Clues
Connections to Writing 181
　Proofread a Paragraph • Write a Paragraph
Extend & Transfer
　Word Study 182
　Word Hunt: Science 183

Unit 28

Words From French
Connections to Thinking 184
　Read • Think & Sort • Remember
Connections to Vocabulary 185
　Word Meanings • Word Replacements •
　Use the Dictionary: Etymology
Connections to Reading 186
　Complete the Analogies • Complete the Questions •
　Use Context Clues
Connections to Writing 187
　Proofread a Paragraph • Write a Mystery
Extend & Transfer
　Word Study 188
　Word Hunt: Art 189

Unit 29

Latin Forms: miss, manus, fluere, animus
Connections to Thinking 190
　Read • Think & Sort • Remember
Connections to Vocabulary 191
　Word Meanings • Word Structure •
　Use the Dictionary: Multiple Meanings
Connections to Reading 192
　Complete the Analogies • Complete the Sentences •
　Use Context Clues
Connections to Writing 193
　Proofread a Paragraph • Write a Paragraph
Extend & Transfer
　Word Study 194
　Word Hunt: Technology 195

Unit 30

Assessment and Review
Assess for Transfer 196
Review Units 25–26 197
Review Units 27–28 198
Review Unit 29 199
Spelling Study Strategy 199
　What's My Word?
Standardized Test Practice 200
Writer's Workshop 202
　Grammar, Usage, and Mechanics: Prepositions
　The Writing Process: Informative/Explanatory

Unit 31

Adding –ly to Words Ending in -ic
Connections to Thinking 204
  Read • Think & Sort • Remember
Connections to Vocabulary 205
  Word Meanings • Synonyms •
  Use the Dictionary: Entries
Connections to Reading 206
  Replace the Words • Complete the Sentences •
  Choose the Modifiers
Connections to Writing 207
  Proofread a Biographical Sketch •
  Write a Biographical Sketch
Extend & Transfer
  Word Study 208
  Word Hunt: Fine Arts 209

Unit 32

Endings: tial, cial, cious, tious
Connections to Thinking 210
  Read • Think & Sort • Remember
Connections to Vocabulary 211
  Word Meanings • Antonyms •
  Use the Thesaurus: Synonyms
Connections to Reading 212
  Solve the Analogies • Use Context Clues
Connections to Writing 213
  Proofread a Paragraph • Write a Paragraph
Extend & Transfer
  Word Study 214
  Word Hunt: Social Studies 215

Unit 33

Latin Roots: spec, volv, ver
Connections to Thinking 216
  Read • Think & Sort • Remember
Connections to Vocabulary 217
  Word Meanings • Word Structure •
  Use the Thesaurus: Synonyms
Connections to Reading 218
  Complete the Sentences • Use Context Clues
Connections to Writing 219
  Proofread a Paragraph • Write a Paragraph
Extend & Transfer
  Word Study 220
  Word Hunt: Technology 221

Unit 34

Assimilated Prefix: com-
Connections to Thinking 222
  Read • Think & Sort • Remember
Connections to Vocabulary 223
  Word Meanings • Word Structure •
  Use the Dictionary: Etymology
Connections to Reading 224
  Replace the Words • Use Context Clues
Connections to Writing 225
  Proofread a Paragraph • Write a Paragraph
Extend & Transfer
  Word Study 226
  Word Hunt: Math 227

Unit 35

Latin Roots: fic, fec, fac, fy
Connections to Thinking 228
  Read • Think & Sort • Remember
Connections to Vocabulary 229
  Word Meanings • Word Groups •
  Use the Thesaurus: Synonyms
Connections to Reading 230
  Complete the Sentences • Use Context Clues
Connections to Writing 231
  Proofread a Paragraph • Write a Paragraph
Extend & Transfer
  Word Study 232
  Word Hunt: Science 233

Unit 36

Assessment and Review
Assess for Transfer 234
Review Units 31–32 235
Review Units 33–34 236
Review Unit 35 237
Spelling Study Strategy 237
  Sorting by Word Endings
Standardized Test Practice 238
Writer's Workshop 240
  Grammar, Usage, and Mechanics:
  Subject-Verb Agreement
  The Writing Process: Argument

Writer's Handbook

Spelling and the Writing Process 242
Spelling and Writing Ideas 243
Manuscript Handwriting Models 244
Cursive Handwriting Models 245
High Frequency Writing Words 246

Spelling Dictionary

Using the Dictionary 249
Spelling Dictionary .250

Writing Thesaurus

Using the Thesaurus 297
Writing Thesaurus 298

Index

Index. 323

Word Sorting

A word sort helps you become a Word Detective. When you sort, you look for patterns in your spelling words. You see how words are the same and how they are different. Word sorting can help you remember how to spell words.

Buddy Sort using the word sort cards

Word sort on an interactive whiteboard

There are different kinds of word sorts you can use with your spelling words.

- **Individual Sort**—Use word sorting to practice your spelling words.
- **Buddy Sort**—Do a word sort with a partner.
- **Speed Sorts on Your Own**— Time yourself as you sort your spelling words. Then do it again and try to improve on the number of seconds it takes to complete the word sort.
- **Speed Sorts With a Team**— See which team can complete the sort in the shortest time and with the greatest accuracy.

Spell Check

Most computers have a spell checker. Spell check is a tool that can find many spelling mistakes, but it can't find them all!

Sometimes a writer types the wrong word. For example, if you type **there** instead of **their**, the spell checker will not catch your mistake because the word you typed is spelled correctly. The spell checker does not know you meant to write a different word.

Spell check can help you find and correct mistakes in your writing. But you still must proofread everything you write!

Look, Say

Look at the word.

Say the letters in the word. Think about how each sound is spelled.

Cover, See

Cover the word with your hand or close your eyes.

See the word in your mind. Spell the word to yourself.

Write, Check

Write the word.

Check your spelling against the spelling in the book.

Taking a Test

1. **Get** ready for the test. Make sure your paper and pencil are ready.

2. **Listen** carefully as your teacher says each word and uses it in a sentence. Don't write before you hear the word **and** the sentence.

3. **Write** the word carefully. Make sure your handwriting is easy to read. If you want to print your words, ask your teacher.

4. **Use** a pen to correct your test. Look at the word as your teacher says it.

5. **Say** the word aloud. Listen carefully as your teacher spells the word. Say each letter aloud. Check the word one letter at a time.

6. **Circle** any misspelled parts of the word.

7. **Look** at the correctly written word. Spell the word again. Say each letter out loud.

8. **Write** any misspelled words correctly.

Connections to THINKING

Compound Words

1. News|room
2. Sports|caster
3. head|line
4. News|cast
5. News|print
6. up|date
7. News|reel
8. date|line
9. Mast|head

Not Compound

10. edition
11. media
12. copy
13. editorial
14. caption
15. commentary
16. verify
17. deliver
18. footage
19. exclusive
20. coverage

Read the spelling words and sentences.

1.	newsroom	*newsroom*	The reporters waited in the **newsroom**.
2.	edition	*edition*	I read today's **edition** of the paper.
3.	sportscaster	*sportscaster*	The **sportscaster** gave the game's score.
4.	media	*media*	Will the **media** cover the story fairly?
5.	headline	*headline*	I read the **headline** above the article.
6.	copy	*copy*	He typed the **copy** for the story.
7.	editorial	*editorial*	Her **editorial** supported a dress code.
8.	newscast	*newscast*	I saw you on the six o'clock **newscast**!
9.	caption	*caption*	I read the **caption** under the photo.
10.	commentary	*commentary*	His **commentary** was informative.
11.	newsprint	*newsprint*	This thin paper is called **newsprint**.
12.	verify	*verify*	The eyewitness can **verify** what happened.
13.	deliver	*deliver*	He will **deliver** papers to earn money.
14.	footage	*footage*	We watched live **footage** of the storm.
15.	masthead	*masthead*	The editor's name is on the **masthead**.
16.	exclusive	*exclusive*	One reporter got an **exclusive** interview.
17.	update	*update*	The news gave an **update** on the story.
18.	coverage	*coverage*	All channels provided live **coverage**.
19.	newsreel	*newsreel*	Have you ever seen an old **newsreel**?
20.	dateline	*dateline*	A story's **dateline** tells when and where.

Think & Sort the spelling words.

1–9. Write the compound words. Draw a line between each word in the compound.

10–20. Write the words that are not compounds.

Remember

The English language includes many words that relate to the media. Many media words in English are compound words.

Connections to VOCABULARY

Word Meanings

Write a spelling word for each definition.

1. to prove or confirm
2. not shared by others
3. a set of explanations, interpretations, or remarks
4. a single press run or copy
5. an opinion piece
6. a short film about current events
7. to bring to a person or place
8. the extent to which something is observed and reported

Word Structure

Change the underlined part of each compound word to write a spelling word.

9. <u>bed</u>room
10. fore<u>head</u>
11. <u>under</u>line
12. up<u>stairs</u>

13. sports<u>wear</u>
14. <u>fore</u>cast
15. <u>foot</u>print
16. head<u>ache</u>

Use the Dictionary

The **pronunciation key** in the front of a dictionary matches the symbols you see in a phonetic spelling to the sounds of words you already know.

Match the vowel sound in the first syllable of each phonetic spelling in Column A with the word in Column B that has the same sound. Then write the spelling word for each phonetic spelling. Use the **Spelling Dictionary** if you need help.

A	B
17. /kŏp′ ē/	a. hat, ă
18. /mē′ dē ə/	b. pot, ŏ
19. /fŏŏt′ ĭj/	c. took, ŏŏ
20. /kăp shən/	d. be, ē

Word Meanings

1. Verify
2. exclusive
3. commentary
4. Edition
5. Editorial
6. Newsreel
7. deliver
8. Coverage

Word Structure

9. Newsroom
10. Masthead
11. Hatline
12. update
13. Sports caster
14. News cast
15. Newsprint
16. Headline

Use the Dictionary

17. _____
18. _____
19. _____
20. _____

newsroom	edition	sportscaster	media	headline
copy	editorial	newscast	caption	commentary
newsprint	verify	deliver	footage	masthead
exclusive	update	coverage	newsreel	dateline

Complete the Analogies

Write a spelling word to complete each analogy.

1. **Teacher** is to **classroom** as **reporter** is to _____ .
2. **Wool** is to **sweater** as **wood pulp** is to _____ .
3. **Printing** is to **newspaper** as **filming** is to _____ .
4. **Credits** are to **movie** as **staff list** is to _____ .
5. **Title and author** are to **bibliography** as **time and place** are to _____ .

Make Inferences

Write the spelling word that completes each sentence.

6. The person who reports athletic events will observe the teams.
7. You can listen to descriptions and explanations on the game.
8. During the game, we will give current information about the scores of games being played in other areas.
9. Computers will check the accuracy of all scores and statistics.
10. This channel will show live lengths of film of the game.
11. The extent of reporting will include postgame ceremonies.
12. During the game, we will present possessed-by-one-source-only interviews with the athletes.
13. Your local broadcast of news events will air after the game.

Use Context Clues

Write spelling words from the box to complete each sentence.

Mary Liston, a reporter for our school newspaper, was voted Reporter of the Year. She was chosen by students and teachers involved in school **14.**, including the newspaper and the school television station. Mary was recognized for her **15.** in last week's **16.** of the paper. The **17.** of her article was "School Needs Better Lunches." Under the accompanying photo was the following **18.** "Students eating in the lunchroom." Mary not only writes and edits **19.**, she is also willing to **20.** the papers to classrooms.

editorial
headline
deliver
media
edition
caption
copy

Complete the Analogies
1. Newsroom
2. Newsprint
3. Footage
4.
5. dateline

Make Inferences
6. Sports caster
7. commentary
8.
9.
10.
11.
12.
13.

Use Context Clues
14.
15.
16.
17.
18.
19.
20.

Connections to WRITING

Proofread an Editorial

Proofreading means reviewing your paper for errors in spelling, grammar, capitalization, and punctuation. To show where changes are needed, you can use **proofreading marks**. The symbol ≡ means **make a capital letter.** The symbol ╱ means **make a small letter.**

First, proofread the editorial below for ten misspelled words. Then rewrite the editorial. Write the spelling words correctly and make the corrections indicated by the proofreading marks.

SCHOOL NEWS

We need to uppdate our school's medea center. The Television Station could use computers to produce a newscaste. Reporters for the school newspaper could use computers to write copie for each edicion of the paper. The reporters could expand their coverege and commentery with the aid of computers. Computers would help students to verafy facts. Finally, teachers could use them to updait grades and to diliver e-mail to parents. ask your parents to support new computers!

Proofreading Marks

≡	Capital Letter
╱	Small Letter
∧	Add
℘	Delete
⊙	Add a Period
⌗	Indent

ARGUMENT Writing Prompt
Write an Editorial

Choose an issue that you have a strong opinion about. Write an editorial to influence others.

- Begin with a statement that states your opinion.
- Use supporting facts to persuade your readers to agree with you.
- Use as many spelling words as you can.
- Proofread for grammar, capitalization, and punctuation.
- Circle three words you are unsure about, and check their spellings in a print or online dictionary.

Transfer
Think of one way you might learn about current events; for example, radio. In your Spelling Journal, write the titles of three people who work in that medium. (For example, **DJ, producer, station manager**.)

Word Study

Pattern Power

1. _____
2. _____
3. _____
4. _____
5. _____
6. _____

Compound Words

7. _____
8. _____
9. _____
10. _____
11. _____
12. _____

Related Words

13. _____
14. _____
15. _____
16. _____
17. _____
18. _____
19. _____
20. _____

assignment	media	masthead	caption
dateline	critique	bureau	headline
exclusive	update	deliver	pagination
commerce	copy	coverage	newsprint
digital	photogenic	employee	editorial
newsroom	footage	executive	sportscaster
license	verify	narrate	commentary
gaffer	collate	edition	advertisement
newscast	newsreel	folio	photojournalism

Pattern Power

Look for words in the list that have a long vowel in the first syllable.

1. Write the word with **long i** in the first syllable.
2. Write the word with **long e** in the first syllable.
3–6. Write the words with **long o** in the first syllable.

Compound Words

When two or more words are put together to create one word, it is called a compound word.

7–10. Write the compound words from the list above that include the word **news**.

11–12. Write the compound words from the list above that include the word **line**.

Related Words

Complete the word groups.

13–14. edit, editor, _____, _____
  15. exclude, exclusion, _____
  16. critic, critical, _____
  17. employ, _____, unemployed
  18. discovery, _____, recoverable, uncover
  19. comment, commentator, _____
  20. narrator, narrative, _____

18

Language Arts
Word Hunt

Read the paragraphs below. Look for words related to the media.

At the Monday staff meeting, the newspaper editor assigns a story idea to each of her reporters. Each piece is to be researched, investigated, and documented for inclusion in the next edition of the weekly publication, and it is to be delivered by the deadline.

During the next few days, the reporters conduct interviews, verify facts, and write copy for their pieces. The reporters must also write a caption for each photo they use in their articles. After several revisions and lots of editing, the article is almost ready. It only needs a headline. If the article is especially newsworthy and interesting, it may be placed on the front page, just below the masthead.

The editor reads each article and then approves it or requests that revisions be made. The editor works with designers to place all articles and photos on each page. The pages may also have one advertisement or several. The editor may also write an editorial, which is her own commentary on a current issue.

A newspaper is just one form of news media. Other forms include television, radio, and Internet news agencies. Do you think you would like to work for a newspaper?

1. _____
2. _____
3. _____
4. _____
5. _____
6. _____
7. _____
8. _____
9. _____
10. _____

1–10. Look at the word list on page 18, and look for those words as you read the passage above. When you see a word from the list (or a form of one of the words), write it.

Connections to THINKING

Read the spelling words and sentences.

1.	transmit	*transmit*	A messenger can **transmit** your reply now.
2.	indicate	*indicate*	Signs will **indicate** the way to the party.
3.	enroll	*enroll*	Chan plans to **enroll** in that class.
4.	rustic	*rustic*	The Barrets live in a **rustic** country cabin.
5.	comfort	*comfort*	The child found **comfort** in his father's arms.
6.	enclose	*enclose*	Do not forget to **enclose** a recent snapshot.
7.	culprit	*culprit*	I will find the **culprit** who is responsible!
8.	ambition	*ambition*	My **ambition** is to play professional soccer.
9.	parachute	*parachute*	The **parachute** billowed open and floated down.
10.	elegant	*elegant*	The state dinner was very **elegant**.
11.	mistake	*mistake*	Juan rarely makes a **mistake** in grammar.
12.	campus	*campus*	The school **campus** was crowded with students.
13.	property	*property*	He planted a hedge on his **property**.
14.	support	*support*	Please **support** me for class president.
15.	witness	*witness*	A **witness** to the crash described what he saw.
16.	picnic	*picnic*	Roberta forgot the **picnic** basket.
17.	improve	*improve*	The weather should **improve** by the weekend.
18.	extreme	*extreme*	Cacti thrive in the **extreme** desert heat.
19.	dignity	*dignity*	The official greeted the guests with **dignity**.
20.	wisdom	*wisdom*	The owl is a symbol of **wisdom**.

Think & Sort the spelling words.

Write the words whose first syllable contains the following sound.

1–4. **short a** spelled **a**   **16.** **short o** spelled **o**

5–7. **short e** spelled **e**   **17–19.** **short u** spelled **o** or **u**

8–15. **short i** spelled **e** or **i**   **20.** **schwa**

Draw a vertical line between the syllables of each word. Use the **Spelling Dictionary** for help.

Remember

When a vowel is followed by a consonant in a syllable, the syllable is closed. Vowels in closed syllables are usually short.

Short a spelled a

1.

2.

3.

4.

Short e spelled e

5.

6.

7.

Short i spelled e or i

8.

9.

10.

11.

12.

13.

14.

15.

Short o spelled o

16.

Short u spelled o or u

17.

18.

19.

Schwa

20.

Connections to VOCABULARY

Word Meanings

Write a spelling word that could replace the underlined words in each sentence.

1. Some people prefer simple, country surroundings.
2. Lynnette showed good judgment in her choice of friends.
3. Students are not allowed to leave the school grounds between classes.
4. In her first speech as class president, she displayed great poise and stateliness.
5. Hurricane winds destroyed their home and possessions.
6. She is talented and has a strong desire to succeed.
7. The furniture in their home was tasteful and expensive.
8. The police arrested the person responsible for committing the theft.

Word Analysis

Write the spelling word with the same prefix as the given word.

9. transfer
10–11. engage
12. imperil
13. inspire
14. expel

Use the Dictionary

In a dictionary, the part-of-speech label follows the phonetic spelling of an entry word. When a word has more than one part of speech, the different parts of speech may be listed in separate entries.

cop•y[1] /kŏp′ ē/ *n., pl.* **-ies. a.** an imitation or reproduction of something original. **b.** a manuscript to be set in type.
cop•y[2] /kŏp′ ē/ *v.* **-ied, -y•ing, -ies. a.** to make a copy of. **b.** to imitate.

15–20. Write the spelling words that can be used as both nouns and verbs. Use the **Spelling Dictionary**.

Word Meanings	
1.	
2.	
3.	
4.	
5.	
6.	
7.	
8.	
Word Analysis	
9.	
10.	
11.	
12.	
13.	
14.	
Use the Dictionary	
15.	
16.	
17.	
18.	
19.	
20.	

transmit	indicate	enroll	rustic	comfort
enclose	culprit	ambition	parachute	elegant
mistake	campus	property	support	witness
picnic	improve	extreme	dignity	wisdom

Complete the Analogies

Write a spelling word to complete each analogy.

1. **Mansion** is to **estate** as **school** is to _____ .
2. **Deep-sea diver** is to **scuba gear** as **skydiver** is to _____ .
3. **Amaze** is to **astound** as **surround** is to _____ .
4. **Roof** is to **protect** as **foundation** is to _____ .
5. **Free** is to **freedom** as **wise** is to _____ .
6. **Commend** is to **hero** as **blame** is to _____ .

Reword the Headlines

Write the spelling word that best replaces the underlined word or words in each newspaper headline.

7. Architect makes major <u>error</u> in developing plans for new city hall
8–9. Lawyers argue as <u>observer</u> gives testimony with <u>poise</u>
10–11. Weather stations <u>send</u> reports that <u>point out</u> a serious change in weather patterns
12–13. Annual town <u>outside meal</u> to be held at <u>rural</u> site near old gristmill

Complete the News Article

Write spelling words from the box to complete the following news article.

Jon Arletta, a student at Adams Middle School, has been offered a scholarship to the Newport Summer Music Program. Jon, whose __14.__ is to play guitar in a rock band, says he will accept the award and __15.__ in the program. Jon has been taking lessons for five years, but he says he needs to __16.__ his technique if he wants to achieve __17.__ fame. Summer classes will be held in an __18.__ mansion on oceanfront __19.__ . Jon will enjoy the __20.__ and beauty of a spacious oceanside room.

| enroll |
| property |
| improve |
| ambition |
| comfort |
| elegant |
| extreme |

Complete the Analogies

1. _____
2. _____
3. _____
4. _____
5. _____
6. _____

Reword the Headlines

7. _____
8. _____
9. _____
10. _____
11. _____
12. _____
13. _____

Complete the News Article

14. _____
15. _____
16. _____
17. _____
18. _____
19. _____
20. _____

Connections to WRITING

Proofread a News Story

The symbol ∧ means **add something**. The symbol ℓ means **delete something.** First, proofread the news story below for ten misspelled words. Then rewrite the news story. Write the spelling words correctly and make the corrections indicated by the proofreading marks.

> A new parashute club in town is prepared to inroll its first students. From his rustick office in ∧ᵃ building next to stanton airport, Apollo Skydive Club founder Lewis Daniels said, "My ambishun is to have a campas in the sky where people can experience the extreem joy of skydiving. We want people to improove their skills and increase their comfurt at ∧ᵗʰᵉ idea of skydiving." Daniels speaks with the wizdom that comes from twenty-five years of experience as a skydiver. Anyone interested in taking lessons can call Daniels at 555-1234. Please indacate the date on which that you would like to skydive.

INFORMATIVE/EXPLANATORY Writing Prompt

Write a News Story

Write a news story about an actual upcoming or recent event in your school or community.

- Include details that include the five W's: Who, What, When, Where, and Why (or How).
- Be sure the facts you present are accurate.
- Follow the form used in the proofreading example.
- Use as many spelling words as you can.
- Proofread for grammar, capitalization, and punctuation.
- Circle three words you are unsure about. Check their spelling in a print or online dictionary.

Transfer

Think of five three-syllable words containing short vowel sounds. Write the words in your Spelling Journal and circle the letters that spell each short vowel sound.

Word Study

Word Usage

1. _____
2. _____
3. _____
4. _____
5. _____
6. _____
7. _____
8. _____

Syllables and Stress

9. _____
10. _____
11. _____
12. _____
13. _____
14. _____
15. _____
16. _____
17. _____
18. _____
19. _____

advance	culprit	support	comfort	dignity	helicopter
property	omelet	improve	enclose	agenda	crimson
contact	elegant	wisdom	ambition	dismal	penicillin
develop	mistake	transmit	witness	eccentric	indigestion
research	campus	enroll	picnic	victim	reception
indicate	attic	rustic	extreme	selection	parachute

Word Usage

1–8. Write the words that can be used as nouns or as verbs. Circle the word that can be pronounced in two different ways. Check a dictionary.

Syllables and Stress

9–19. Write the words that have **short i** in a stressed syllable, as it is in **hidden**. Use a dictionary to check pronunciations and stress if you are unsure.

Technology
Word Hunt

Read the paragraphs below. Look for words that have short vowels.

Now is the time to start planning for your future. What are your ambitions? What careers to you think you would like to try?

There are many resources on the Internet that can help you figure out what you want to do. Do a search for "middle school career exploration" and see what you can find. There are job descriptions and information for just about any career you can think of. Information about technical schools, apprenticeships, and internships is also available. And if you don't know what you want to do, there are activities, games, and quizzes that may help guide you on a path toward a lifetime of employment that you will love.

Preparing for a career may include earning a college degree. The Internet is also an awesome resource for discovering what college or university is best for you. As you explore university websites, you can take a virtual campus tour, read student testimonials, and learn about admission requirements.

Whether your career goals include college or not, the Internet is a great place to start collecting information. Check with your school guidance counselor or librarian for suggestions about which websites you should try out first!

1. _____
2. _____
3. _____
4. _____
5. _____
6. _____
7. _____
8. _____
9. _____
10. _____

1–10. Write the words that have three or more syllables and at least two short vowel sounds. Use an online dictionary to check pronunciations.

Connections to THINKING

Read the spelling words and sentences.

1. notify	*notify*	When will they **notify** the contest winners?
2. raven	*raven*	Is that large black bird a **raven** or a crow?
3. climate	*climate*	Our grandmother has moved to a warm **climate**.
4. vehicle	*vehicle*	We need a large **vehicle** to transport all of us.
5. alien	*alien*	Dishonesty is **alien** to her nature.
6. idol	*idol*	My uncle, a successful actor, is my **idol**.
7. trial	*trial*	Lawyers prepared evidence for the **trial**.
8. basis	*basis*	He picked players on the **basis** of their talent.
9. creature	*creature*	Every **creature** in nature has different traits.
10. motivate	*motivate*	A cheering crowd can **motivate** a team to win.
11. species	*species*	There are thousands of **species** of ants.
12. notion	*notion*	It was my **notion** that Lee should be captain.
13. prior	*prior*	Do you have **prior** experience as a lifeguard?
14. reality	*reality*	He would rather dream than face **reality**.
15. noble	*noble*	Knights performed **noble** deeds for their king.
16. idle	*idle*	While we worked hard, he was **idle**.
17. trophy	*trophy*	The winner of the tournament received a **trophy**.
18. premium	*premium*	My teacher puts a high **premium** on hard work.
19. oval	*oval*	An **oval** mirror hung over the fireplace.
20. mutual	*mutual*	They share a mutual respect for the **environment**.

Think & Sort the spelling words.

Write the words whose first syllable contains the following sound.

1–3. long a spelled **a**   **14–19. long o** spelled **o**

4–8. long e spelled **e, ea,** or **i**   **20. long u** spelled **u**

9–13. long i spelled **i**

Draw a line between the syllables of each word. Use the **Spelling Dictionary** for help.

Remember

When a vowel is not followed by a consonant in a syllable, the syllable is open. Vowels in open syllables are usually long.

Long a spelled a

1. _____
2. _____
3. _____

Long e spelled e, ea, or i

4. _____
5. _____
6. _____
7. _____
8. _____

Long i spelled i

9. _____
10. _____
11. _____
12. _____
13. _____

Long o spelled o

14. _____
15. _____
16. _____
17. _____
18. _____
19. _____

Long u spelled u

20. _____

Connections to VOCABULARY

Word Groups

Write a spelling word that is related in meaning to complete each group.

1. square, circle, triangle, _____
2. adored object, model, hero, _____
3. class, family, genus, _____
4. past, preceding, former, _____
5. crow, magpie, cowbird, _____
6. award, prize, blue ribbon, _____
7. opinion, idea, belief, _____
8. weather, atmospheric conditions, _____
9. tell, proclaim, announce, _____

Word Structure

Write a spelling word by changing the ending of each of the following base words.

10. create
11. try
12. motive
13. base
14. real

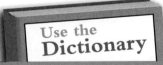

Use the
Dictionary

When an entry word has more than one meaning, the multiple definitions are listed in order, from most common to least common. Write a spelling word for each underlined word or phrase. Then use the **Spelling Dictionary** to write the letter of the definition that best fits the context.

15. Friends often have <u>common</u> interests.
16. Democracy is a <u>lofty</u> ideal.
17. He has been <u>unemployed</u> since January.
18. I put a <u>high value</u> on honesty.
19. Laziness is <u>strange</u> to him.
20. Writing is a <u>means</u> of personal expression.

Word Groups
1. _____
2. _____
3. _____
4. _____
5. _____
6. _____
7. _____
8. _____
9. _____

Word Structure
10. _____
11. _____
12. _____
13. _____
14. _____

Use the Dictionary
15. _____
16. _____
17. _____
18. _____
19. _____
20. _____

notify	raven	climate	vehicle	alien
idol	trial	basis	creature	motivate
species	notion	prior	reality	noble
idle	trophy	premium	oval	mutual

Replace the Words

1.
2.
3.
4.
5.

Complete the Analogies

6.
7.
8.
9.
10.

Use Context Clues

11.
12.
13.
14.
15.
16.
17.
18.
19.
20.

Replace the Words

Replace each underlined word or phrase by writing a spelling word.

1–2. Rashad won the <u>prize</u> in our neighborhood derby for the most original <u>structure for transporting things</u>.

3. His <u>egg-shaped</u> wagon rolled easily around the track.

4–5. We should <u>inform</u> the newspaper about the award for this unusual <u>type</u> of transportation!

Complete the Analogies

Write the spelling word that best completes each analogy.

6. Exciting is to **dull** as **busy** is to _____ .

7. Hilly is to **landscape** as **hot** is to _____ .

8. Friend is to **compassionate** as **knight** is to _____ .

9. Red is to **cardinal** as **black** is to _____ .

10. Familiar is to **usual** as **unfamiliar** is to _____ .

Use Context Clues

Write spelling words from the box to complete the paragraph.

Last week, Tino wrote a feature story about Ms. Cali, our social studies teacher. Ms. Cali, who is our __11.__, places a __12.__ on education and knows how to __13.__ us to learn. For example, last month we held a mock __14.__ to decide whether President Andrew Jackson should have been impeached for forcing Native Americans to leave their homes in the 1830s. Ms. Cali appointed a judge, two teams of lawyers, and a jury. During the week __15.__ to the mock trial, each team prepared its argument. In __16.__, we all shared the __17.__ __18.__ that Jackson was guilty, but some of us had to support Jackson. Ms. Cali reminded us to document the facts that formed the __19.__ of our arguments. In the end, the jury declared that Jackson was a heartless __20.__ and that he was guilty.

notion
mutual
creature
basis
reality
idol
trial
premium
motivate
prior

Connections to WRITING

Proofread a Paragraph

The symbol ⊙ means add a **period**. The symbol ¶ means start a new paragraph and **indent**. First, proofread the paragraph below for ten misspelled words. Then rewrite the paragraph. Write the spelling words correctly and make the corrections indicated by the proofreading marks.

Proofreading Marks

≡	Capital Letter
/	Small Letter
∧	Add
ℓ	Delete
⊙	Add a Period
¶	Indent

Standing beside her nobil horse Night Wind, Pamela Hightower had waited for her name to be called⊙As she waited, she remembered watching her idal, Joe Fargis, win the equestrian Gold Medal at the 1984 Olympics. Soon she would find out whether she and the majestic creeture beside her could make her dream of winning a realaty.¶Hightower has always placed a preimium on doing her best, even in so difficult times. When she suffered a serious fall during a tryal Competition last month, the noshen of giving up never entered her mind. "Quitting is allien to me," she said. "The desire to win a troaphy will always motavate me to compete."

INFORMATIVE/EXPLANATORY Writing Prompt

Write a Paragraph

A feature article informs, interests, and entertains readers. Write the lead paragraph for a feature article.

- Select a person or an event from sports.
- Use a catchy opening to arouse your readers' curiosity.
- Include feelings and thoughts about the subject, as well as facts.
- Use as many spelling words as you can.
- Proofread for grammar, capitalization, and punctuation.
- Circle three words you are unsure about. Check spellings in a print or online dictionary.

Transfer

Think of five three-syllable words containing long vowel sounds. Write the words in your Spelling Journal and circle the letters that spell each long vowel sound.

Word Study

bugle	vehicle	reality	motivate	mutual	visa
maintain	idol	noble	notion	chaos	vacancy
labor	trial	idle	prior	retrace	radiator
copious	basis	notify	trophy	typhoon	vial
agency	creature	raven	premium	utilize	meander
climate	species	alien	oval	violent	topiary

Phonemic Awareness

1. Write the word that begins with a long vowel sound and has a **long e** spelled with a letter other than **e**.

2–6. Write the words that begin with a long vowel sound. Circle the words that are homophones.

7–16. Write the words that have **long e** spelled with one letter (and that letter is not **e**).

Consonant Sound Spellings

17–18. Write the words in which the /ch/ sound is not spelled **ch**.

19–20. Write the words in which the /sh/ sound is not spelled **sh**. Circle the word that can pronounced more than one way.

Phonemic Awareness

1. _____
2. _____
3. _____
4. _____
5. _____
6. _____
7. _____
8. _____
9. _____
10. _____
11. _____
12. _____
13. _____
14. _____
15. _____
16. _____

Consonant Sound Spellings

17. _____
18. _____
19. _____
20. _____

Science
Word Hunt

Read the paragraphs below. Look for words that have long vowels.

Have you ever paid attention to the birds in your city, local parks, or even your own backyard? If you have, chances are you have seen a common raven. Ravens are large, black birds and can survive in almost any climate. They are widely distributed across the northern hemisphere and can be found at sea level or at high altitudes. They have even been spotted by climbers on Mount Everest in the Himalayas!

A common raven (species *Corvus corax*) normally grows to about 25 inches in length and can weigh up to 3½ pounds. The common raven has a lifespan of 15 years, although lifespans of 40 years have also been documented! The raven will eat just about anything, ranging from fruit, nuts, and grains to insects and small animals. They are known to scavenge on the carcasses of dead animals too.

There is a notion that the raven is a highly intelligent creature. Throughout recorded history, the raven has held a place in mythology and has been idolized as a spiritual symbol in many cultures. It even has a place in English literature as the subject of a famous Edgar Allen Poe poem.

1. _____
2. _____
3. _____
4. _____
5. _____
6. _____
7. _____
8. _____
9. _____
10. _____

1–5. Write the spelling words you find in the paragraphs.
  6. Write a word that is a verb form of another spelling word.
7–10. Write the four-syllable words that have a long vowel sound.

Connections to THINKING

Read the spelling words and sentences.

1.	keyboard	*keyboard*	Type on the **keyboard**.
2.	self-esteem	*self-esteem*	Everyone needs **self-esteem**.
3.	dining room	*dining room*	We ate in the **dining room**.
4.	classmate	*classmate*	Greet your new **classmate**.
5.	far-fetched	*far-fetched*	He told a **far-fetched** tale.
6.	granddaughter	*granddaughter*	Mr. An has a **granddaughter**.
7.	briefcase	*briefcase*	Put the pen in my **briefcase**.
8.	self-taught	*self-taught*	My French is **self-taught**.
9.	four-fifths	*four-fifths*	What is **four-fifths** of 20?
10.	word processing	*word processing*	Sid teaches **word processing**.
11.	newsstand	*newsstand*	Buy papers at the **newsstand**.
12.	quick-witted	*quick-witted*	I gave **quick-witted** answers.
13.	pencil sharpener	*pencil sharpener*	Use my **pencil sharpener**.
14.	well-known	*well-known*	That actor is **well-known**.
15.	thirteen-year-olds	*thirteen-year-olds*	We are **thirteen-year-olds**.
16.	textbook	*textbook*	Read the **textbook** carefully.
17.	self-employed	*self-employed*	I'm a **self-employed** writer.
18.	study hall	*study hall*	Meet me in the **study hall**.
19.	brother-in-law	*brother-in-law*	Dan is my **brother-in-law**.
20.	three-fourths	*three-fourths*	Nine is **three-fourths** of 12.

Closed compounds

1. _____
2. _____
3. _____
4. _____
5. _____
6. _____

Open compounds

7. _____
8. _____
9. _____
10. _____

Hyphenated compounds

11. _____
12. _____
13. _____
14. _____
15. _____
16. _____
17. _____
18. _____
19. _____
20. _____

Think & Sort the spelling words.

1–6. Write the closed compounds. Draw a line between the two words that form each compound.

7–10. Write the open compounds.

11–20. Write the hyphenated compounds.

Remember

A compound word may be written as one word (closed compound), two words (open compound), or a hyphenated word (hyphenated compound).

Connections to VOCABULARY

Word Meanings

Write the spelling word that matches each definition.

1. a book used for studying a subject
2. someone in the same class at school
3. pride in oneself
4. a device for putting a point on a writing instrument
5. young teenagers
6. part of a typewriter or a computer
7. a portable carrier for books and papers
8. a schoolroom or a period of time devoted to study
9. 75%

Word Replacements

Write a spelling word that could replace the underlined words in each sentence.

10. Nadia got eighty percent of the answers correct.
11. I am going fishing with my sister's husband.
12. Her son's daughter is now two years old.
13. Our new home has a large place for eating dinner.
14. They gave a very unlikely and unbelievable reason for being late.
15. The recognized and famous ballplayer will sign baseballs after the game.

Use the Dictionary

Dictionaries use abbreviations to indicate the part of speech of entry words. Look in the Spelling Dictionary for a list of part-of-speech abbreviations. Write the following words. Next to each word, write its part-of-speech label.

16. word processing
17. quick-witted
18. self-employed
19. self-taught
20. newsstand

Word Meanings	
1.	
2.	
3.	
4.	
5.	
6.	
7.	
8.	
9.	
Word Replacements	
10.	
11.	
12.	
13.	
14.	
15.	
Use the Dictionary	
16.	
17.	
18.	
19.	
20.	

keyboard	three-fourths	granddaughter	self-esteem	self-taught
briefcase	brother-in-law	word processing	far-fetched	four-fifths
study hall	quick-witted	pencil sharpener	well-known	newsstand
textbook	self-employed	thirteen-year-olds	dining room	classmate

Answer the Questions

Write the spelling word that best answers each question.

1. Where might you purchase today's paper?
2. What do you call the man married to your sister?
3. What do you study to get information on a particular subject?
4. What do you call people who learn a skill on their own?
5. What kind of worker is his or her own boss?
6. What helps people respect themselves?
7. What does a lawyer use to carry papers to court?

Complete the Sentences

Write the spelling word that best completes each sentence.

8. We painted the walls in the kitchen, bedroom, and _____.
9. This computer comes with a modem, a monitor, and a _____.
10. At work he uses an electric stapler, calculator, and _____.
11. The answer is either two-fifths, three-fifths, or _____.
12. I looked for her in the cafeteria, gym, and _____.
13. We accept eleven-year-olds, twelve-year-olds, and _____.

Use Context Clues

Write spelling words from the box to complete the paragraph.

My grandmother was born in Italy and moved here as a baby. She grew up in a community where __14.__ of the people were immigrants. Nana married right out of high school. Going to college then seemed like a __15.__ idea. Recently, Nana went back to school. First, she took a course in __16.__. Then she enrolled in college. As the oldest student on campus, she was soon __17.__ by all. A __18.__ of Nana's told me that younger students like Nana because she's funny and __19.__. I am proud to be her __20.__.

word processing
quick-witted
classmate
granddaughter
three-fourths
well-known
far-fetched

Answer the Questions
1.
2.
3.
4.
5.
6.
7.

Complete the Sentences
8.
9.
10.
11.
12.
13.

Use Context Clues
14.
15.
16.
17.
18.
19.
20.

Connections to WRITING

Proofread a Biographical Sketch

Proofread the biographical sketch below for ten misspelled words. Then rewrite the sketch. Write the spelling words correctly and make the corrections indicated by the proofreading marks.

Over the years I have grown to greatly admire my brother in law, Don. Don is a self taught man. born in New York City, he worked at a news-stand when he was very young. Most thirteen year-olds don't have that much ambition, Don did! He learned about the stock market by asking questions of businesspeople who bought papers from him every day. Naturally intelligent and quikwitted, Don wanted to learn more about finance. He couldn't afford to go to college, so he borrowed an Economics text book from a former high school class mate This may sound farfetched, but Don is now self employed as a wellknown TV personality who hosts a weekly program called "Pennies Matter."

Proofreading Marks

≡	Capital Letter
/	Small Letter
∧	Add
ℰ	Delete
⊙	Add a Period
⁋	Indent

INFORMATIVE/EXPLANATORY Writing Prompt
Write a Biographical Sketch

A **biographical sketch** is a brief summary of a person's life.

- Write a biographical sketch of an older person you know or know of.
- Choose someone who has done something new or who has approached life in an unusual way.
- Identify the person and five details about his or her birth, education, misfortunes, goals, and accomplishments.
- Use as many spelling words as you can.
- Proofread for grammar, capitalization, and punctuation.
- Circle three words you are unsure about. Check their spelling in a print or online dictionary.

Transfer

Think of four compound words that have to do with music, for example **keyboard**. Write them in your Spelling Journal and tell whether each is open, closed, or hyphenated.

Word Study

Word Meanings

1. _____
2. _____
3. _____
4. _____
5. _____
6. _____
7. _____
8. _____
9. _____
10. _____
11. _____
12. _____

Related Words

13. _____
14. _____
15. _____
16. _____
17. _____

Building Compound Words

18. _____
19. _____
20. _____

all right	self-esteem	brainstorm	granddaughter
campfire	well-known	quick-witted	word processing
daydream	four-fifths	three-fourths	brother-in-law
post office	self-taught	dining room	pencil sharpener
textbook	newsstand	far-fetched	thirteen-year-olds
keyboard	curling iron	out-of-date	radio broadcast
briefcase	stomachache	postmaster	self-addressed
classmate	best-selling	mastermind	old-fashioned
study hall	headquarters	bulletin board	self-employed

Word Meanings

1–2. Write the words that are names of family members.

3–12. Write the words that are used to describe things (adjectives).

Related Words

Complete the word groups.

13–14. mail carrier, mailbox, _____, _____

15–16. one-half, nine-tenths, _____, _____

17. campsite, sleeping bag, _____, sing-along

Building Compound Words

18–20. Create compound spelling words by combining the smaller words from the list below. Make sure to correctly write each word as an open, closed, or hyphenated compound.

storm	quarters	head
brain	esteem	self

36

Math
Word Hunt

Read the paragraphs below. Look for compound words.

When you and your classmates are in study hall and you have some extra time, look at the numerical symbol for the fraction three-fourths, or $\frac{3}{4}$. You know that the number 3 is the numerator and the number 4 is the denominator. But what do you call that line that separates them? It is most likely that you won't find the answer in your textbook!

The Babylonians used a place-value system to indicate fractions, or parts of a whole. These were actually an early form of decimals. Egyptian and Greek mathematicians used unit fractions, where 1 was always the numerator. They would write a small number 1 above a number to show that it was only part of a whole.

The Romans further developed the idea of fractions, but they wrote their fractions in words. Hindu mathematicians were the first to write a fraction as one number on top of another, but it was Arab masterminds who added the horizontal bar between numbers. The line was known as the vinculum.

As a shorthand method of writing fractions, the vinculum was later written as a diagonal line. Now, the vinculum is known by many nicknames, including *solidus, slash, virgule, virga,* and *diagonal,* among others.

1. _____
2. _____
3. _____
4. _____
5. _____
6. _____
7. _____
8. _____
9. _____

1–2. Write the open compound words.
3–7. Write the closed compound words.
8–9. Write the hyphenated compound words.

Connections to THINKING

Read the spelling words and sentences.

1.	challenge	*challenge*	First, **challenge** them to a rematch.
2.	embarrass	*embarrass*	If I act silly, will I **embarrass** you?
3.	apparent	*apparent*	It was **apparent** that he had been ill.
4.	exaggerate	*exaggerate*	Ina tends to **exaggerate** her skills.
5.	communicate	*communicate*	We **communicate** by e-mail once a week.
6.	accompany	*accompany*	Will you **accompany** Maria to the dance?
7.	unnecessary	*unnecessary*	That comment was **unnecessary**.
8.	surrender	*surrender*	They agreed to **surrender** to end the war.
9.	impression	*impression*	What is your **impression** of that movie?
10.	allegiance	*allegiance*	The knight swore **allegiance** to the king.
11.	immense	*immense*	The **immense** ship had a golf course!
12.	accomplish	*accomplish*	How much can you **accomplish** in a day?
13.	procession	*procession*	The bride and groom led the **procession**.
14.	interrupt	*interrupt*	I did not mean to **interrupt** your talk.
15.	equipped	*equipped*	The car is **equipped** with air bags.
16.	assess	*assess*	We will **assess** the damage to your home.
17.	warrant	*warrant*	We need a **warrant** to arrest the suspect.
18.	possibility	*possibility*	There is a **possibility** of rain tonight.
19.	alliance	*alliance*	The two nations formed an **alliance**.
20.	professional	*professional*	Hector is a **professional** tennis player.

Think & Sort the spelling words.

1–3. Write the words that have two sets of double consonants. Circle the double consonants.

4–20. Write the words that have one set of double consonants. Circle the double consonants.

Remember

A double consonant (the same two consonants together) can spell a single consonant sound. Some words may have two sets of double consonants.

Two sets of double consonants

1. _____
2. _____
3. _____

One set of double consonants

4. _____
5. _____
6. _____
7. _____
8. _____
9. _____
10. _____
11. _____
12. _____
13. _____
14. _____
15. _____
16. _____
17. _____
18. _____
19. _____
20. _____

Connections to VOCABULARY

Word Meanings

Write the spelling word that matches each clue.

1. loyalty
2. a group moving in a line
3. not needed
4. a person who earns money as an actress
5. to justify or call for
6. supplied with tools or provisions
7. connection, union
8. readily seen, obvious
9. a feeling that remains following an experience
10. to give up
11. huge

Word Structure

Change each of these nouns into a verb to write a spelling word.

12. interruption
13. exaggeration
14. assessment

Use the Dictionary

The **inflected forms** of an entry word in a dictionary appear after the part-of-speech label and include the irregular plurals of nouns and the principal parts of verbs. Write the entry word for each inflected form below. Use the **Spelling Dictionary** if you need help.

15. communicating
16. accompanied
17. embarrassing
18. possibilities
19. accomplished
20. challenging

Word Meanings
1.
2.
3.
4.
5.
6.
7.
8.
9.
10.
11.
Word Structure
12.
13.
14.
Use the Dictionary
15.
16.
17.
18.
19.
20.

challenge	embarrass	apparent	exaggerate	communicate
accompany	unnecessary	surrender	impression	allegiance
immense	accomplish	procession	interrupt	equipped
assess	warrant	possibility	alliance	professional

Complete the Analogies

Write a spelling word to complete each analogy.

1. **Untrained** is to **expert** as **amateur** is to _____ .
2. **Face** is to **confront** as **dare** is to _____ .
3. **Partners** are to **contract** as **nations** are to _____ .
4. **Simile** is to **compare** as **hyperbole** is to _____ .
5. **Frown** is to **smile** as **betrayal** is to _____ .
6. **Continue** is to **proceed** as **stop** is to _____ .
7. **Intrusion** is to **intrude** as **embarrassment** is to _____ .

Complete the Advertisements

Write a spelling word to replace the underlined word or words in each advertisement.

8. **For Sale:** Used car, fully <u>furnished</u> (except motor).

9–10. **Wanted:** Tuba player for <u>huge</u> Labor Day <u>parade</u>; must have own instrument.

11. **Wanted:** Experienced tutor; <u>chance</u> of travel with family.

12. **Buy Sanitize-It!** Watch germs <u>abandon</u> all hope!

13–14. **Order now!** You can <u>achieve</u> the impossible with no <u>visible</u> effort. Read whole books overnight with Sleep Tapes!

Use Context Clues

Write spelling words from the box to complete the paragraph.

Advertisements that sound too good to be true probably __15.__ a closer look. You need to __16.__ the offer. Is it true and honest? Do restrictions or hidden costs __17.__ the offer? Unless you read the fine print, you may get the wrong __18.__ . You may find yourself paying for __19.__ extras or signing up for something you neither want nor need. A smart consumer asks questions before making a purchase. And if you are not satisfied with a product, __20.__ your dissatisfaction to the company promptly.

accompany
unnecessary
assess
communicate
impression
warrant

Complete the Analogies

1. _____
2. _____
3. _____
4. _____
5. _____
6. _____
7. _____

Complete the Advertisements

8. _____
9. _____
10. _____
11. _____
12. _____
13. _____
14. _____

Use Context Clues

15. _____
16. _____
17. _____
18. _____
19. _____
20. _____

Connections to WRITING

Proofread an Advertisement

Proofread the advertisement below for ten misspelled words. Then rewrite the advertisement. Write the spelling words correctly and make the corrections indicated by the proofreading marks.

¶Are you a profesional with a busy Schedule? Do you find it a challange to acomplish all your daily chores? Does the possability of unexpected guests send you into a frenzy? Don't panic! Call Harry's helping Hands today. Let us asess your needs. We'll arrive at your door, aquipped to clean, cook, mow the lawn, and do whatever other immence chores you need to have done. Don't interupt your schedule to do chores you don't want to do! And don't let a messy house embarras you ever again. Call Harry's Helping Hands at 555-1534. We'll help you make a good impresion!

Proofreading Marks

≡	Capital Letter
/	Small Letter
∧	Add
ℰ	Delete
⊙	Add a Period
¶	Indent

INFORMATIVE/EXPLANATORY Writing Prompt
Write an Advertisement

Select a product or service you have enjoyed, such as a movie, book, or restaurant. Write an ad to promote that product or service.

- Begin with a question, a startling fact, or an endorsement by a famous person.
- Use lanuguage that will make consumers feel that they can't live without the product or service.
- Use as many spelling words as you can.
- Proofread for grammar, capitalization, and punctuation.
- Circle three words you are unsure about. Check their spelling in a print or online dictionary.

Transfer
Select a school subject and brainstorm a list of at least five words with double consonants. The words should be related to the subject you selected. Write the words in your Spelling Journal. For example, Math: **approximate**.

Word Study

banner	embarrass	equipped	immense
alliance	access	error	apparent
possibility	accomplish	accommodate	erroneous
horrible	exaggerate	professional	procession
bookkeeping	approximation	innocent	communicate
surrender	interrupt	occasional	annex
tissue	accompany	impression	assess
questionnaire	aggressive	challenge	unnecessary
allegiance	warrant	successor	connotation

Prefixes and Double Consonants

Some prefixes may be assimilated into the spelling of a base word or root. This sometimes results in a double consonant. For each item below, write the words that have the prefix or an assimilated form of it. Use a dictionary to check word etymology.

1. com-, meaning "together" or "with"

2–8. ad-, meaning "to" or "toward"

Latin Roots

Write the words with the following Latin roots.

9–11. cēdere, meaning "to go"

12–13. errāre, meaning "to err"

14. ruptūra, meaning "to break"

Consonant Sound Spellings

15–18. Write the words in which the double consonant **ss** spells a sound other than /s/.

19–20. Write the words in which the /j/ sound is spelled **g**.

Prefixes and Double Consonants

1. _____
2. _____
3. _____
4. _____
5. _____
6. _____
7. _____
8. _____

Latin Roots

9. _____
10. _____
11. _____
12. _____
13. _____
14. _____

Consonant Sound Spellings

15. _____
16. _____
17. _____
18. _____
19. _____
20. _____

Social Studies
Word Hunt

Read the paragraphs below. Look for words that have double consonants.

Around 100 BC, people from Central Asia thought it was a possibility to trade with people from all over Asia. They used the horses and camels that they had trained to carry heavy loads of goods to barter and sell. Asia is vast, so it would be a challenge to travel from one end of the continent to the other, but routes were found, and these routes became collectively known as the Silk Road.

For hundreds of years, there was a procession of European and Asian traders along the Silk Road. Among many other things, they carried cotton, cinnamon, pepper, silver, eggs, pottery, nuts, perfumes, and, of course, silk. Because the trip could be quite difficult, the travelers were equipped with enough food, water, and supplies for themselves and their animals for the entire journey.

During the time that the Silk Road was popular, there was peace in the region. Therefore, business was accomplished without any unnecessary delays due to war. It was a profitable time for the people of Central Asia. In the 14th century, however, a horrible disease, called the bubonic plague, was spreading from Europe eastward to Asia and along the Silk Road. Many travelers became ill and died. Trade along the Silk Road was interrupted by the plague and never fully recovered. Traders discovered a cheaper way to trade among Europe, India, and all of Asia—via ocean routes.

1. _____
2. _____
3. _____
4. _____
5. _____
6. _____
7. _____
8. _____
9. _____
10. _____

1–10. Write words that have three or more syllables and double consonants.

Assess for Transfer

Unit 1
1. _____

Unit 2
2. _____
3. _____
4. _____
5. _____

Unit 3
6. _____
7. _____
8. _____
9. _____
10. _____
11. _____

Unit 4
12. _____
13. _____
14. _____
15. _____
16. _____

Unit 5
17. _____
18. _____
19. _____
20. _____

Units 1–5

Assessment

Each word in the box fits one of the spelling patterns and rules you have studied over the past five weeks. Read the unit descriptions. Then write each assessment word under the unit number it fits.

Unit 1

1. The English language includes many words that relate to the media. Many media words in English are compound words.

Unit 2

2–5. When a vowel is followed by a consonant in a syllable, the syllable is closed. Vowels in closed syllables are usually short.

Unit 3

6–11. When a vowel is not followed by a consonant in a syllable, the syllable is open. Vowels in open syllables are usually long.

Unit 4

12–16. A compound word may be written as one word (closed compound), two words (open compound), or a hyphenated word (hyphenated compound).

Unit 5

17–20. A double consonant (the same two consonants together) can spell a single consonant sound. Some words may have two sets of double consonants.

Words for Assessment

patron

arrest

excess

wheelbarrow

harass

lifeguard

radiate

ammonia

expense

wholesale

stable

association

wash-and-wear

appraise

confess

cable

native

consent

turnpike

vanilla

Review

Unit 1: Media Words

edition	media	headline	copy	editorial
verify	deliver	masthead	exclusive	coverage

Write the spelling word that completes each sentence.

1. Newspaper and television are popular news _____.
2. The early _____ of the newspaper comes in the morning.
3. My brother helps to _____ papers in our neighborhood.
4. Mom reads the _____ page first.
5. Her opinion is that the *Post* has the best news _____.
6. Often the *Post* has _____ coverage.
7. Today's _____ is this: TEST SCORES ARE UP 20 PERCENT.
8. The reporter had to _____ that the information was correct.
9. Ms. Farmer sent in two pages of _____ for the article.
10. The editor and publisher are listed on the paper's _____.

Unit 2: Syllabication Patterns: Short Vowels

indicate	culprit	parachute	elegant	mistake
campus	property	support	improve	wisdom

Write the spelling word that matches the clue.

11. The first and second syllables have **short i**.
12. In the first syllable, **e** spells **short e**, but in the second syllable, **e** spells **short i**.
13–15. The first syllable of these two-syllable words has **short i**.
16. The first syllable has the **short u** sound. The second syllable has the **short i** sound.
17. The first syllable has the **short a** sound. The second syllable has the **short u** sound.
18. It has three syllables. The first syllable has the **short a** sound.
19. The first syllable has the **short o** sound.
20. The first of the two syllables has the **schwa** sound. There is a double consonant in its spelling.

Unit 1

1. _____
2. _____
3. _____
4. _____
5. _____
6. _____
7. _____
8. _____
9. _____
10. _____

Unit 2

11. _____
12. _____
13. _____
14. _____
15. _____
16. _____
17. _____
18. _____
19. _____
20. _____

45

Review

Unit 3
1.
2.
3.
4.
5.
6.
7.
8.
9.
10.

Unit 4
11.
12.
13.
14.
15.
16.
17.
18.
19.
20.

Unit 3: Syllabication Patterns: Long Vowels

climate	vehicle	idol	trial	basis
creature	species	reality	noble	idle

Write the spelling word that fits the meaning.

1. conditions that include wind, temperature, and rain
2. an image that is the object of adoration
3. the examination of evidence in court
4. grand or stately, as an idea
5. not busy; not in use
6. the quality of being actual or true
7. a device, as a car, for carrying people or goods
8. a living being
9. a group of similar animals or plants
10. foundation or supporting principle

Unit 4: Compound Words

keyboard	self-esteem	classmate	granddaughter
self-taught	word processing	well-known	textbook
	brother-in-law	three-fourths	

Write spelling words to complete the paragraph.

Elizabeth's __11.__, Ken, thought Elizabeth, his new relative, would enjoy using a computer. So he bought Elizabeth a __12.__ to study. First, Elizabeth learned how to place her hands properly on the __13.__. Then she learned __14.__ so she could write a letter to Jill, her __15.__ who lives in Germany. When Elizabeth was __16.__ of the way through the book, she realized that she was truly __17.__. Knowing that raised her __18.__ a great deal. After all, it is a __19.__ fact that computers are here to stay. Now she can even send e-mail to Jill and Margot, Jill's __20.__ and friend.

Unit 5: Double Consonants

challenge	embarrass	apparent	exaggerate	communicate
accompany	unnecessary	equipped	possibility	professional

Change the underlined part of each word to write a spelling word.

1. equip<u>ment</u>
2. embas<u>sy</u>
3. appar<u>ition</u>
4. capa<u>bility</u>
5. exact<u>ly</u>

6. <u>a</u>viary
7. accur<u>ate</u>
8. profess<u>or</u>
9. <u>champ</u>ion
10. commun<u>ity</u>

Unit 5

1. _____
2. _____
3. _____
4. _____
5. _____
6. _____
7. _____
8. _____
9. _____
10. _____

Spelling Study Strategy

Word Swap

Write words you want to study on cards—one word to a card. Put your initials on each card. Give your cards to a partner. Your partner will give you a similar set of cards.

1. Read aloud a word from your partner's stack.

2. Your partner spells the word aloud. Check to see that the word is spelled correctly. If it is, give the card back to your partner. If it is not, give the spelling and keep the card.

3. Your partner will then read one of the cards from your stack for you to spell. If you spell it correctly, you get the card. If you don't, your partner keeps the card.

4. Continue taking turns until each of you has all of your own stack of cards back.

Directions: Read the introduction and the passage that follows. Then read each question and fill in the correct answer on your answer sheet.

Zoe's teacher asked each student to write about an imaginary school field trip. As you read, look for improvements that Zoe could make.

Space Challenge

(1) My class-mate Xena was so lucky because last year her class got to take an inter-galactic field trip. (2) One purpose of the trip was to improof students' ability to get along with others during long periods spent in small spaces. (3) Certainly their tiny space vehical qualified as a "small space"! (4) A second purpose of the field trip was to deliver several important documents to an orbiting space station and make sure every crew member received a copy.

(5) The other space travelers who were to acompany Xena were her best friend Zoela, two boys, and a respected professor from the local college. (6) Having the professor with them meant there was plenty of work to do and lots to challange them. (7) The professor was well-known for being very demanding! (8) But Xena, famous for her happy nature and great self esteem, told me that she and her friends were equipped with great skill. (9) Their computer skills were largely self-taught (except for a short key board course everyone had to take in kindergarten). (10) Still, it was nice to know they had the professor's full support.

(11) The only real mistake occurred when one of the boys was doing some word-processing and accidentally entered the wrong information into the ship's log. (12) But Xena spotted the error and was able to help her classmate fix his mistake before the professor caught it. (13) Certainly nobody wanted to be the culpret responsible for sending the space-craft to the wrong place!

1 What change, if any, should be made in sentence 1?
A Change *class-mate* to **classmate**
B Change *class-mate* to **class mate**
C Change *field trip* to **fieldtrip**
D Make no change

2 What change, if any, should be made in sentence 2?
A Change *improof* to **improove**
B Change *improof* to **improve**
C Change *ability* to **abilty**
D Make no change

3 What change, if any, should be made in sentence 3?
A Change *vehical* to **vehicle**
B Change *vehical* to **vehickle**
C Change *qualified* to **quolified**
D Make no change

4 What change, if any, should be made in sentence 4?
A Change *field trip* to **fieldtrip**
B Change *deliver* to **diliver**
C Change *orbiting* to **orbitting**
D Make no change

5 What change, if any, should be made in sentence 5?
A Change *acompany* to **acommpany**
B Change *acompany* to **accompany**
C Change *professor* to **proffesor**
D Make no change

6 What change, if any, should be made in sentence 6?
A Change *professor* to **proffesor**
B Change *lots* to **alot**
C Change *challange* to **challenge**
D Make no change

7 What change, if any, should be made in sentence 8?
A Change *self esteem* to **selfesteem**
B Change *self esteem* to **self-esteem**
C Change *equipped* to **equiped**
D Make no change

8 What change, if any, should be made in sentence 9?
A Change *self-taught* to **selftaught**
B Change *key board* to **key-board**
C Change *key board* to **keyboard**
D Make no change

9 What change, if any, should be made in sentence 12?
A Change *classmate* to **class mate**
B Change *mistake* to **misstake**
C Change *error* to **erorr**
D Make no change

10 What change, if any, should be made in sentence 13?
A Change *nobody* to **no body**
B Change *culpret* to **culprit**
C Change *culpret* to **cullprit**
D Make no change

STOP

Grammar, Usage, and Mechanics

Parts of a Sentence

Every sentence has a subject and a predicate. The **simple subject** is the one noun or pronoun that tells what or whom the sentence is about. The **simple predicate** is the verb or verb phrase—the word or words telling what the subject is, has, or does.

Some <u>workers</u> on the farm <u>have used</u> a large wheelbarrow.

       ↑   ↑

   simple subject   simple predicate

Practice Activity

A. Write the simple subject of each sentence.

1. Our favorite teacher will deliver the address.
2. Was the coverage of the event fair?
3. The ripcord on the parachute opened slowly.
4. These arrows indicate where to set the boxes.
5. José supports our position.
6. This old television set is the property of our class.
7. We listed every species of plant.
8. The sad reality is that we lost the game by only one point.

B. Write the simple predicate of each sentence.

9. Chicago's climate is cooler than San Antonio's.
10. Two well-known dancers will perform at the theater tonight.
11. Marlene ate three-fourths of the pie herself.
12. She challenged us to a game of chess.
13. Please accompany me to the office now.
14. Good letter writers communicate clearly.
15. I have given you all the directions you need.

A
1.
2.
3.
4.
5.
6.
7.
8.
B
9.
10.
11.
12.
13.
14.
15.

The Writing Process: Narrative
Writing a Mystery

PREWRITING

Jamal's CD player is missing! What happened to it? In a mystery, the writer invents a story about a puzzling event or crime. How would you solve the case of Jamal's missing CD player? Think about a mystery you would like to write. You can find mysteries at the library. Or, you can get ideas about mysteries on Internet sites such as MysteryNet (http://kids.mysterynet.com). As you think about the topic, make an outline for your mystery.

DRAFTING

Use your outline to write a mystery. Begin with a topic sentence that presents the main idea. Follow your outline as you write supporting sentences. Try to write clues for the characters and readers. Use as many spelling words as possible. If you don't know how to spell a word, make your best guess. You will be able to revise your mystery later.

REVISING

When you have finished your first draft, read your mystery from beginning to end. Check to see if you have included all of the points in your outline. Did you use suspenseful words to create a feeling of mystery? Did you reveal everything at the end of your story? Now write your final draft.

EDITING

Use the editing checklist to proofread your mystery. Be sure to use proofreading marks when you make corrections. Check spellings in a print or online dictionary.

PUBLISHING

Make a copy of your mystery and share it with your readers.

EDITING CHECKLIST

Spelling

✓ Circle words that contain the spelling patterns and rules learned in Units 1–5.

✓ Check the circled words in a print or online dictionary.

✓ Check for other spelling errors.

Capital Letters

✓ Capitalize important words in the title.

✓ Capitalize the first word in each sentence.

✓ Capitalize proper nouns.

Punctuation

✓ End each sentence with the correct punctuation.

✓ Use commas, apostrophes, and quotation marks correctly.

Grammar, Usage, and Mechanics

✓ Make sure each sentence has a subject and a predicate.

Connections to THINKING

Read the spelling words and sentences.

1.	fearlessness	*fearlessness*	Her **fearlessness** was legendary.
2.	requirement	*requirement*	Some experience is a **requirement**.
3.	extremely	*extremely*	I was **extremely** happy to see him.
4.	reconsider	*reconsider*	They will **reconsider** the theory.
5.	thoughtfulness	*thoughtfulness*	We appreciate your **thoughtfulness**.
6.	inability	*inability*	I inherited an **inability** to whistle.
7.	disappointment	*disappointment*	I understood her **disappointment**.
8.	unexpected	*unexpected*	Her **unexpected** news startled us.
9.	surname	*surname*	His **surname** is Johnson.
10.	alphabetical	*alphabetical*	Are these in **alphabetical** order?
11.	reappearance	*reappearance*	We waited for his **reappearance**.
12.	surprisingly	*surprisingly*	The day was **surprisingly** cool.
13.	agreeable	*agreeable*	Is the decision **agreeable** to you?
14.	regardless	*regardless*	I will go **regardless** of the weather.
15.	unemotional	*unemotional*	Her reaction was **unemotional**.
16.	adventuresome	*adventuresome*	Skydivers are **adventuresome**.
17.	thoughtlessness	*thoughtlessness*	His **thoughtlessness** hurt me.
18.	underestimate	*underestimate*	Do not **underestimate** her strength.
19.	improvement	*improvement*	My grades show **improvement**.
20.	emotional	*emotional*	A wedding is an **emotional** event.

Prefixes and suffixes

1. _____
2. _____
3. _____
4. _____
5. _____
6. _____
7. _____
8. _____

Prefixes

9. _____
10. _____
11. _____

Suffixes

12. _____
13. _____
14. _____
15. _____
16. _____
17. _____
18. _____
19. _____
20. _____

Think & Sort the spelling words.

1–8. Write the words that have both a prefix and a suffix.
Circle all the prefixes and suffixes.

9–11. Write the words that have prefixes but not suffixes.
Circle all the prefixes.

12–20. Write the words that have suffixes but not prefixes.
Circle all the suffixes.

Remember

Words can have prefixes and suffixes.

Connections to VOCABULARY

Word Meanings

Write the spelling word that matches each definition.

1. lack of skill or talent
2. a family name
3. reemergence
4. advancement
5. think over again
6. without feeling
7. in spite of everything

Word Structure

Add one or more suffixes to each word to write a spelling word.

8. alphabet
9. agree
10. fear
11. emotion
12. surprise
13. adventure
14. extreme
15–16. thought

Use the **Thesaurus**

A thesaurus provides synonyms and antonyms for words. When you use a thesaurus, be sure that the word you choose is used in the way that you intend. Write a spelling word that is a synonym for each word below. Use the **Writing Thesaurus** if you need help.

17. undervalue
18. surprising
19. necessity
20. frustration

Word Meanings	
1.	
2.	
3.	
4.	
5.	
6.	
7.	
Word Structure	
8.	
9.	
10.	
11.	
12.	
13.	
14.	
15.	
16.	
Use the Thesaurus	
17.	
18.	
19.	
20.	

fearlessness   requirement   extremely   reconsider
thoughtfulness   inability   disappointment   unexpected
surname   alphabetical   reappearance   surprisingly
agreeable   unemotional   adventuresome   regardless
thoughtlessness   underestimate   improvement   emotional

Solve the Analogies

Write a spelling word to complete each analogy.

1. **Correct** is to **incorrect** as **ability** is to _____.
2. **Unevenly** is to **uneven** as **unexpectedly** is to _____.
3. **Dislike** is to **like** as **disagreeable** is to _____.
4. **Class** is to **classical** as **alphabet** is to _____.
5. **Count** is to **discount** as **appointment** is to _____.
6. **Care** is to **carelessness** as **thought** is to _____.
7. **Awe** is to **awesome** as **adventure** is to _____.

Complete the Sentences

Write a spelling word to complete each sentence.

8. The only _____ for joining our bike club is a love of bike riding.
9. He showed his _____ by remembering her birthday.
10. I waited quietly for the _____ of the rare bird.
11. Even though he had won, he seemed _____ .
12. Never _____ the strength of a tornado's winds.
13. After hearing the facts, I had to _____ my opinion.
14. It seemed early, but it was _____ late.

Use Context Clues

Write spelling words from the box to complete the paragraph.

My neighbors told me how they thought there would be an __15.__ in their lives if they emigrated here. It was an __16.__ dangerous journey, but they decided to set sail __17.__. I was impressed by their __18.__ and bravery. Soon after they arrived, they changed their __19.__ from Johannison to Johnson. As my neighbors spoke of friends they had left behind, they became __20.__. Although they loved life here, they yearned to see old friends once again.

surname
fearlessness
improvement
emotional
extremely
regardless

Solve the Analogies
1. _____
2. _____
3. _____
4. _____
5. _____
6. _____
7. _____

Complete the Sentences
8. _____
9. _____
10. _____
11. _____
12. _____
13. _____
14. _____

Use Context Clues
15. _____
16. _____
17. _____
18. _____
19. _____
20. _____

Connections to WRITING

Proofread a Journal Entry

First, proofread the journal entry below for ten misspelled words. Then rewrite the journal entry. Write the spelling words correctly and make the corrections indicated by the proofreading marks.

June 10, 1807. The stagecoach pumped westward⊙The
reapearance of a huge cloud convinced me that a rainstorm was
approaching. I regretted drinking all ∧my water when the cloud turned
out to be an extreamly large dust storm. I slumped in my seat with
a feeling of disapointment and began to reconcider my decision to
travel west.¶My companions, who earlier had seemed unamotinal,
came alive in the rush to close the stagecoach windows.∧Their There
adventursome spirits seemed strengthened by the unexpeckted
storm, regardliss of the dangers. I admired their fearlisness. I was
learning never to underestamate the west.

NARRATIVE Writing Prompt
Write a Journal Entry

Imagine that you are a pioneer in the Old West. Write a journal entry.

- Begin with a date to set the scene.
- Use specific details to describe your surroundings.
- Include your thoughts, opinions, and feelings.
- Proofread for grammar, capitalization, and punctuation.
- Circle three words you are unsure about and check their spellings in a print or online dictionary.

Transfer

Reread your journal entry. In your Spelling Journal, write any words from your journal entry that have an affix. Circle the affixes.

Word Study

Meaning Mastery
   1. _____
   2. _____
   3. _____
   4. _____
   5. _____
   6. _____

Multiple Suffixes
   7. _____
   8. _____
   9. _____
  10. _____

Antonyms
  11. _____
  12. _____
  13. _____
  14. _____
  15. _____
  16. _____
  17. _____
  18. _____
  19. _____
  20. _____

amendment	extremely	improvement	underestimate
unexpected	unassisted	disappointment	disagreement
regardless	surname	disappearance	disconnected
inheritance	inability	thoughtfulness	reappearance
disprove	re-elected	misunderstanding	alphabetical
fearlessness	recycle	unemotional	quarrelsome
replacement	reconsider	adventuresome	surprisingly
surcharge	agreeable	precautionary	requirement
emotional	canceling	thoughtlessness	resourcefulness

Meaning Mastery

Read the affixes and their meanings.

The prefix **re-** means "again."

The suffix **-some** means "having a specific quality."

The suffix **-ance** means "state or condition of."

Write words from the list with the following meanings.

   1. think about again
   2. having the quality of arguing a lot
   3. something received from ancestors
   4. the condition of coming into view again
   5. voted into office again
   6. having the quality of enjoying adventure

Multiple Suffixes

7–10. Write the words from the list that have at least two of the following suffixes: **less, ful, ness**.

Antonyms

Write the words that have opposite, or nearly opposite, meanings.

   11. first name   13. ability   15. expected
   12. agreement   14. appearance   16. prove

17–20. Write two sets of antonyms from the list.

Math
Word Hunt

Read the paragraphs below. Look for words that have affixes.

One unexpected place to find mathematics is right in front of us, in nature.

About 800 years ago, an Italian mathematician whose surname, Fibonacci, is still famous today, noticed that the branching of shade trees, regardless of what type they were, always followed a certain pattern. One main trunk branched into two, and then one of those branches split into two, and so on. Unassisted by anyone, Fibonacci noticed that the branching followed the counting pattern of 0, 1, 1, 2, 3, 5, 8, 13, 21 and so on. (The pattern is surprisingly simple—just add each number to the one before it to get the next number in the series.)

Many people have tried to disprove Fibonacci's theory, but they underestimated his resourcefulness. Not only do many trees follow the number sequence, but a wide variety of disconnected things in nature also follow the same pattern; the arrangement of leaves on a stem, an uncurling fern, and the spiral pattern of seeds on a sunflower.

Even sea creatures grow according to the Fibonacci series. From the outside a chambered nautilus has the familiar "horn" shape that people put to their ear to "hear the ocean." But if you were extremely careful and could slice it open horizontally, you could see that the nautilus started as a tiny dot in the center. As it grew, it built a larger "house" (or chamber) next door, and as it kept growing, the new chambers became the size of the present chamber plus the previous one. That is the famous Fibonacci series—the present one plus the previous one gives the next in the series. We can see its reappearance everywhere in nature.

1. _____
2. _____
3. _____
4. _____
5. _____
6. _____
7. _____
8. _____
9. _____
10. _____

1–5. Write words that have the suffix **-ly, -less,** or **-ness.**
6–10. Write words that have the prefix **un-** or **dis-.**

Spelling Pattern
Long a and Long e

Base words ending with -e

1. _____
2. _____
3. _____
4. _____
5. _____
6. _____

Final -e + suffix beginning with a consonant

7. _____
8. _____
9. _____
10. _____
11. _____
12. _____
13. _____
14. _____
15. _____
16. _____

ce or ge + -able or -ous

17. _____
18. _____

Base words ending with one vowel + suffix beginning with a vowel

19. _____

Base words ending with two vowels + suffix beginning with a vowel

20. _____

Connections to THINKING

Read the spelling words and sentences.

1.	encouragement	*encouragement*	Thanks for your **encouragement**.
2.	idleness	*idleness*	Wasting time shows **idleness**.
3.	canoe	*canoe*	Be careful not to tip the **canoe**!
4.	manage	*manage*	He will **manage** the entire project.
5.	forgiveness	*forgiveness*	Is **forgiveness** always easy?
6.	acreage	*acreage*	What is the **acreage** of this farm?
7.	outrageous	*outrageous*	His **outrageous** speech shocked us.
8.	management	*management*	I admire her **management** skills.
9.	forgive	*forgive*	He will **forgive** me for my mistake.
10.	canoeing	*canoeing*	I think **canoeing** is fun!
11.	inventiveness	*inventivenesss*	Her solution showed **inventiveness**.
12.	encourage	*encourage*	We **encourage** teamwork.
13.	acre	*acre*	My house sits on one **acre** of land.
14.	commencement	*commencement*	She got a degree at **commencement**.
15.	advantageous	*advantageous*	The offer was **advantageous**.
16.	commence	*commence*	When will the parade **commence**?
17.	fierceness	*fierceness*	A lion's **fierceness** is well known.
18.	amazement	*amazement*	I view his magic with **amazement**.
19.	awareness	*awareness*	His **awareness** of the issue is clear.
20.	announcement	*announcement*	Her **announcement** was a surprise.

Think & Sort the spelling words.

1–6. Write the base words that end in a silent final **e**.

7–16. Write the words with a base word ending with final **e** and a suffix beginning with a consonant.

17–18. Write the words that end with **ce** or **ge** followed by **-able** or **-ous**.

19. Write the word with a base word ending with one vowel and a suffix also beginning with a vowel.

20. Write the word with a base word ending with two vowels and a suffix also beginning with a vowel.

Remember

Some base words, particularly those ending with **ce** or **ge,** retain a final silent **e** when certain suffixes (such as **-able** and **-ous**) are added. This is done to preserve the pronunciation of the base word.

Connections to VOCABULARY

Word Meanings

Write a spelling word for each definition.

1. state of being fierce
2. state of being aware
3. traveling by canoe
4. state of being idle
5. causing outrage
6. area of land measured in acres
7. bringing or giving advantage
8. state of being inventive

Word Structure

Add a suffix to each verb to write a noun that is a spelling word.

9. manage
10. encourage
11. announce

12. forgive
13. commence
14. amaze

Use the
Dictionary

An **etymology** explains the origin and history of a word. Etymologies appear in brackets at the end of entries (following the definitions). The abbreviation **Obs.** (for "obsolete") means that the entry originated from a spelling no longer in use.

Abbreviations of Languages Used in Etymologies

<	comes from	VLat.	Vulgar Latin	OFr.	Old French
Lat.	Latin	Gk.	Greek	ME	Middle English
LLat.	Late Latin	Fr.	French	OE	Old English

Use the **Spelling Dictionary** to find the etymology of each spelling word below. Write the spelling words with the specified origins.

   acre   canoe   commence   encourage   forgive   manage

15–17. These words come from Latin.
18–19. These words come from Old English.
   20. This word has an origin that is now obsolete.

Word Meanings
1. _____
2. _____
3. _____
4. _____
5. _____
6. _____
7. _____
8. _____

Word Structure
9. _____
10. _____
11. _____
12. _____
13. _____
14. _____

Use the Dictionary
15. _____
16. _____
17. _____
18. _____
19. _____
20. _____

Connections to READING

canoe	encouragement	fierceness	acreage	awareness
forgive	management	forgiveness	outrageous	advantageous
acre	inventiveness	canoeing	idleness	commencement
manage	announcement	encourage	commence	amazement

Answer the Questions

Write the spelling word that best answers each question.

1. What characteristic are tigers known for?
2. What is a formal way that news or information can be spread?
3. With what might someone react to a spectacular sight?
4. What method of travel requires paddles?
5. How might you describe someone who causes chaos and misery?
6. In what state of activity would you accomplish nothing?
7. What do you need so you know what is going on around you?
8. What can you give someone to show your support?
9. What quality do people like Thomas Edison have?
10. What can you offer to someone who has hurt you?

Complete the Sentences

Write a spelling word to complete each sentence.

11. What is the _____ of the Zippety Ranch?
12. I hope she can _____ me for losing her sweater.
13. When you are busy, it is important to _____ your time well.
14. The fireworks display will _____ as soon as it gets dark.

Use Context Clues

Write spelling words from the box to complete the paragraph.

Attention, shoppers! The __15.__ of Chuck's Superstore is excited to announce the __16.__ of its biggest sale ever! We __17.__ you to look for __18.__ bargains in every department. For example, in our yard and garden department, we have a sale on lawn mowers. One of our models can cut an entire __19.__ of grass in less than an hour! In our sporting goods department, we have a brand-new __20.__ for half price. Included are life vests and paddles. Chuck's Superstore is a shopper's dream come true.

canoe
acre
commencement
advantageous
management
encourage

Answer the Questions

1. _____
2. _____
3. _____
4. _____
5. _____
6. _____
7. _____
8. _____
9. _____
10. _____

Complete the Sentences

11. _____
12. _____
13. _____
14. _____

Use Context Clues

15. _____
16. _____
17. _____
18. _____
19. _____
20. _____

Connections to WRITING

Proofread a Speech

Proofread the speech below for ten misspelled words. Then rewrite the speech. Write the spelling words correctly and make the corrections indicated by the proofreading marks.

Proofreading Marks

≡	Capital Letter
/	Small Letter
∧	Add
℘	Delete
⊙	Add a Period
⁋	Indent

       Ladies **and** ~~or~~ gentlemen, I will comence my speech with an announsement: Our environment needs better managment. We are ruining too much acreige of forest by cutting down trees. We are polluting the beautiful, clear waters of our ~~R~~ivers. The number of plants and ~~of~~ animals that have become extinct is outragious. We need to raise our awearness and consider the dangers of idilness.

We must encourige our government and industries to manaje the environment **more** responsibly. I will conclude my speech with another simple statement: We need to earn Mother Nature's forgivness.

ARGUMENT Writing Prompt

Write a Speech

Choose something in your neighborhood or town that requires better management. Write a speech to persuade others.

- Begin by stating your position.
- Use facts and details to support your opinion.
- Follow the form used in the proofreading sample.
- Proofread for grammar, capitalization, and punctuation.
- Circle three words you are unsure about and check their spelling in a print or online dictionary.

Transfer

In your Spelling Journal, begin a list of words with each suffix used in this lesson. Add to the list each time you encounter a new word with one of the suffixes.

Word Study

Pattern Power
1.
2.
3.
4.
5.
6.
7.
8.
9.
10.
Related Words
11.
12.
13.
14.
15.
16.
17.
18.
19.
20.

canoe	advancement	acreage	definitely
manage	awareness	discourage	excitement
forgive	advantageous	inventiveness	engagement
acre	measurement	commencement	leisurely
entirely	purposeful	encouragement	management
idleness	commence	announcement	enforcement
canoeing	wholesome	forgiveness	fierceness
mileage	peaceable	discouragement	encourage
enforce	outrageous	amazement	distasteful

Pattern Power

The suffix **-ment** means "action" or "result of an action."

1–10. Write word pairs from the list above; one word will be a base word, and its partner will have the suffix **-ment**.

Related Words

Complete the word groups.

11–12. _____, canoes, canoed, _____

13–14. _____, acres, _____

15. excite, unexcitable, _____

16. advantage, _____, disadvantage

17–18. _____, forgave, unforgiving, _____

19. fierce, fiercely, _____, fiercer

20. amaze, _____, amazingly

Science
Word Hunt

Read the paragraphs below. Look for suffixes added to base words ending in silent **e**.

Get ready to make an outrageous announcement to your friends! You can peel a hard-boiled egg without peeling it! It's a great science trick you can manage in your own kitchen, and you get to eat it!

Eggs can be hard to peel, so stop doing it. It's definitely possible to just blow them entirely out of their shells, whole. Your friends' amazement will have them talking about it to everyone they know!

Here's how. It's simple, but it requires a bit of purposeful planning and management with the help of an adult. It's advantageous to practice first at home before you try showing your friends. Make sure you have the most important ingredient, baking soda, and you're ready to commence. (Be sure it's baking soda—baking powder is definitely not the same!)

Careful measurement is important. In a small saucepan, put one teaspoon of baking soda plus three or four eggs into about two inches of water. Make sure the water covers the eggs. When the water begins to leisurely bubble, keep it at that same slow boil for about 12 minutes. Then turn it off, drain the water, and run cold water over the eggs. Add ice if you're in a hurry.

Now for the magic. Tap both ends of the egg to crack the ends, and peel away a bit of shell about the size of a pea from each end. Hold the egg up to your lips and blow hard into the narrow end. Be sure to catch it with your other hand when it pops out! Your friends will be astonished at your inventiveness!

1. _____
2. _____
3. _____
4. _____
5. _____
6. _____
7. _____
8. _____
9. _____
10. _____

1–10. Write words that have the suffix **-ous**, **-ly**, **-ment**, or **-ness**.

Connections to THINKING

Base words

1. _____
2. _____
3. _____
4. _____
5. _____
6. _____
7. _____
8. _____
9. _____
10. _____

Base words + -ition or -ation

11. _____
12. _____
13. _____
14. _____
15. _____
16. _____
17. _____
18. _____
19. _____
20. _____

Read the spelling words and sentences.

1. frustrate   *frustrate*   Math word problems **frustrate** us.
2. frustration   *frustration*   He can't hide his **frustration**.
3. decoration   *decoration*   A banner is a great party **decoration**.
4. decorate   *decorate*   Let's **decorate** the room with flags.
5. combine   *combine*   Red and blue **combine** to make purple.
6. combination   *combination*   I know the **combination** of the safe.
7. determination   *determination*   Her **determination** showed in her eyes.
8. determine   *determine*   Can you **determine** the type of insect?
9. graduation   *graduation*   I wore a blue robe on **graduation** day.
10. graduate   *graduate*   He will **graduate** from college soon.
11. hesitate   *hesitate*   Do not **hesitate** before diving in.
12. hesitation   *hesitation*   Her **hesitation** indicated her fear.
13. education   *education*   A good **education** is important in life.
14. educate   *educate*   A teacher's job is to **educate** students.
15. compete   *compete*   They will **compete** to see who is faster.
16. competition   *competition*   We watched a swimming **competition**.
17. eliminate   *eliminate*   Can I **eliminate** bugs from the garden?
18. elimination   *elimination*   We hope for the **elimination** of poverty.
19. admiration   *admiration*   A hero is worthy of **admiration**.
20. admire   *admire*   I **admire** people who do kind deeds.

Think & Sort the spelling words.

1–20. Write each base word. Then write its partner that has a **-tion** or **-ation** suffix.

Remember

Final **te** or silent **e** is dropped in words like **hesitate** and **determine** before adding the suffix **-tion** or **-ation**. These suffixes turn verbs into nouns.

Connections to VOCABULARY

Word Groups

Write a spelling word related in meaning to complete each group.

1. remove, cancel, _____
2. adorn, garnish, _____
3. decide, figure out, _____
4. battle, oppose, _____
5. put together, mix, _____
6. like, respect, _____

Word Analysis

Add a suffix to each verb to write a noun that is a spelling word.

7. decorate
8. admire
9. eliminate
10. determine
11. compete
12. combine

Use the Dictionary

The **primary stress** (′) marks the syllable in a word that receives the greatest stress. The **secondary stress** (′) marks a moderate, or lesser, stress. Write the spelling word for each phonetic spelling. Circle the syllable that has the primary stress. Underline the syllable that has a secondary stress. Use the **Spelling Dictionary** if you need help.

13. /grăj′ o͞o āt′/
14. /grăj′ o͞o ā′ shən/
15. /frŭs′ trāt′/
16. /frus′ trā′ shən/
17. /ĕj′ ə kāt′/
18. /ĕj′ ə kā′ shən/
19. /hĕz′ ĭ tāt′/
20. /hĕz′ ĭ tā′ shən/

Word Groups	
1.	
2.	
3.	
4.	
5.	
6.	
Word Anaylsis	
7.	
8.	
9.	
10.	
11.	
12.	
Use the Dictionary	
13.	
14.	
15.	
16.	
17.	
18.	
19.	
20.	

frustrate	frustration	decoration	decorate	combine
combination	determination	determine	graduation	graduate
hesitate	hesitation	education	educate	compete
competition	eliminate	elimination	admiration	admire

Replace the Words

Write a spelling word to replace the underlined word or words in each sentence.

1. I have a <u>high opinion</u> of people who help others.
2. Students can help <u>instruct</u> other students.
3. Scientists work toward the <u>complete removal</u> of disease.
4. A doctor tries to <u>figure out</u> what a person's symptoms mean.
5. I want to <u>receive a degree</u> from college someday.
6. When I had a chance to help others, I did not <u>act reluctantly</u>.
7. I helped <u>furnish</u> a senior center.
8. My sister trained a Special Olympics athlete for a gymnastics <u>contest of skill or ability</u>.
9. When asked to help, she agreed without <u>pausing</u>.
10. It is easy to <u>join together</u> hard work and good deeds.
11–12. People who enjoy helping others do not <u>contend</u> with or <u>upset</u> one another.

Use Context Clues

Write spelling words from the box to complete the paragraph.

Before the 1800s, society did not recognize the need for women to receive an __13.__. Women were appreciated for their domestic skills or their beauty, but Mary Lyon was one woman who refused to be treated as a mere __14.__. She put aside her __15.__ and put herself through school. After her __16.__, Lyon dedicated herself to educating other young women. Through a __17.__ of stubbornness and __18.__, she realized her dream. In 1837, she founded Mount Holyoke, the first women's college in America. Today, Mary Lyon receives the __19.__ she deserves for helping to __20.__ an old prejudice.

admiration
combination
decoration
eliminate
frustration
determination
graduation
education

Replace the Words
1. _____
2. _____
3. _____
4. _____
5. _____
6. _____
7. _____
8. _____
9. _____
10. _____
11. _____
12. _____

Use Context Clues
13. _____
14. _____
15. _____
16. _____
17. _____
18. _____
19. _____
20. _____

Connections to WRITING

Proofread a Paragraph

Proofread the paragraph below for ten misspelled words. Then rewrite the paragraph. Write the spelling words correctly and make the corrections indicated by the proofreading marks.

¶Without hesatation, all of her peers recognize track champion Aretha Jones as an outstanding athlete. They particularly admyre her ability to elimnate all distractions and concentrate during a compitition. After gratuation, jones must weigh a combinashun of factors to make a decision. Does she have enough love of the sport and enough determinashun to turn professional? She can always continue to compeet as an Amateur. Either way, the trophies that decorrate her room will always draw the admuration of her friends and family⊙

Proofreading Marks

≡	Capital Letter
/	Small Letter
∧	Add
ℒ	Delete
⊙	Add a Period
¶	Indent

NARRATIVE/EXPLANATORY Writing Prompt

Write a Paragraph

Choose a decision that you or someone else had to make. Write a paragraph about it.

- Describe the decision that had to be made.
- Explain the choices that were involved and the reasons for choosing one or the other.
- Follow the form used in the proofreading sample.
- Use as many spelling words as you can.
- Proofread for grammar, capitalization, and punctuation.
- Circle three words you are unsure about and check their spellings in a print or online dictionary.

Transfer

In your Spelling Journal, begin a list of words with each suffix used in this lesson. Write five words for each suffix. Add to the list each time you encounter a new word with one of the suffixes.

Word Study

Pattern Power

1. _____
2. _____
3. _____
4. _____
5. _____
6. _____
7. _____
8. _____
9. _____
10. _____
11. _____
12. _____

Meaning Mastery

13. _____
14. _____
15. _____
16. _____
17. _____
18. _____
19. _____
20. _____

introduce	combine	compete	education	defamation
expire	introduction	combination	competition	educate
expiration	initiation	complete	determination	decoration
eliminate	aspire	completion	contemplate	determine
decorate	elimination	defame	aspiration	admire
initiate	hesitate	graduation	frustration	admiration
hesitation	graduate	frustrate	contemplation	

Pattern Power

Decide whether each word below takes the **-tion** or **-ation** suffix. Then write the base word and its suffixed partner in the correct column.

hesitate	combine	expire
frustrate	determine	eliminate

-tion

1–2. _____, _____

3–4. _____, _____

5–6. _____, _____

-ation

7–8. _____, _____

9–10. _____, _____

11–12. _____, _____

Meaning Mastery

Fill in the blanks with appropriate words from the list.

13. The key to a good _____ is cooperation among teachers, students, and families.

14. Individuals are honored for military service or distinction by being given a _____, such as a ribbon or medal.

15. Video games can be used to _____ students about math.

16–18. We _____ to _____ from high school and then _____ a degree at an esteemed university.

19. When you consider something thoughtfully, you _____ it.

20. Throw the milk away if it is after its _____ date.

Language Arts
Word Hunt

Read the paragraphs below. Look for words with the suffixes **-tion** and **-ation**.

People have special admiration for famous pilots. The heroic pilot and much-loved author of *The Little Prince*, Antoine de Saint-Exupery, vanished during wartime. After 60 years of frustration spent searching for him, his plane was found in 2000 beneath the Mediterranean Sea.

Familiar to readers the world over, *The Little Prince* needs little introduction. Told by a fictional pilot who had crashed in the desert, it is a simple story of an inquisitive boy from a distant planet who lands in the same desert. His amusing determination to get some answers leads to his education about the strange ways of grown-ups. Many say that the story is not a children's book at all, for although children love it, it has long been cherished by adults who admire the questions the little prince asks with such complete seriousness.

With fresh thinking and contemplation, the tiny visitor has no hesitation about asking blunt questions many adults hesitate to discuss. "Why are adults always too busy to do the simple things? Why do grown-ups spend all their time counting things again and again? Why is the elimination of unhealthy things so difficult for people? Why do grown-ups aspire to do unimportant things? Why is it so hard to remember that you love something?"

The little space traveler's quest to find answers has been an inspiration to generations of children and adults ever since this decorated French air traveler first shared his wonderful book with the world.

1. _____
2. _____
3. _____
4. _____
5. _____
6. _____
7. _____
8. _____
9. _____
10. _____

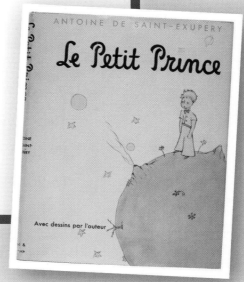

ANTOINE DE SAINT-EXUPERY

Le Petit Prince

Avec dessins par l'auteur

WORD SORT

1–3. Write the words with the suffix **-ation**.
4–10. Write the words with the suffix **-tion**.

Connections to THINKING

Read the spelling words and sentences.

1.	demonstration	*demonstration*	We saw a cooking **demonstration**.
2.	concentrate	*concentrate*	He will try harder to **concentrate**.
3.	issuing	*issuing*	The Treasury is **issuing** new coins.
4.	believable	*believable*	His books have **believable** characters.
5.	excuse	*excuse*	What is your **excuse** for being late?
6.	communication	*communication*	I received a **communication** by mail.
7.	comparable	*comparable*	These shirts are **comparable** in price.
8.	endure	*endure*	He can **endure** the heat better than I.
9.	appreciation	*appreciation*	She smiled to show her **appreciation**.
10.	ignorance	*ignorance*	My **ignorance** of the area got us lost.
11.	concentrating	*concentrating*	I am **concentrating** on my math.
12.	examination	*examination*	Our final **examination** was difficult.
13.	likable	*likable*	Anita is a sweet and **likable** child.
14.	concentration	*concentration*	Batting a ball takes **concentration**.
15.	excusable	*excusable*	Illness made her absence **excusable**.
16.	receiving	*receiving*	He will be **receiving** an award.
17.	organization	*organization*	Who founded that **organization**?
18.	endurance	*endurance*	It takes **endurance** to swim a mile.
19.	celebration	*celebration*	We attended his birthday **celebration**.
20.	achieving	*achieving*	Are you **achieving** your goals?

No suffix

1. _____
2. _____
3. _____

-tion, -ation

4. _____
5. _____
6. _____
7. _____
8. _____
9. _____
10. _____

-able

11. _____
12. _____
13. _____
14. _____

-ance

15. _____
16. _____

-ing

17. _____
18. _____
19. _____
20. _____

Think & Sort the spelling words.

1–3. Write the spelling words that do not end in a suffix.

4–10. Write the spelling words that end in the suffix **-tion** or **-ation**.

11–14. Write the spelling words that end in the suffix **-able**.

15–16. Write the spelling words that end in the suffix **-ance**.

17–20. Write the spelling words that end in the suffix **-ing**.

Remember

Final silent **e** is dropped from words like **concentrate** before adding a suffix that begins with a vowel.

Connections to VOCABULARY

Word Meanings

Write a spelling word for each definition.

1. state of being uneducated, uninformed state
2. attaining; accomplishing
3. focusing on; paying attention
4. the act of paying close attention
5. the act of celebrating
6. able to be compared
7. the result of being orderly
8. producing; distributing
9. deserving of pardon
10. can be believed

Word Replacement

Write the spelling word that could best replace each underlined word.

11. Jorge expressed his <u>gratitude</u> by sending us a thank-you note.
12. Only the sturdiest trees were able to <u>withstand</u> the storm's fury.
13–14. We should be <u>getting</u> a formal <u>message</u> about the outcome of the election any minute now.
15. Despite the conversations going on around her, she can <u>focus</u> easily.

Use the Thesaurus

Write a spelling word that is a synonym for each series of words. Use the **Writing Thesaurus** to check your answers.

16. agreeable, attractive, congenial, pleasing, popular
17. inquiry, inspection, investigation, scrutiny
18. display, exhibition, presentation
19. remove the blame from, forgive, overlook
20. perseverance, persistence, stamina, tenacity

Word Meanings
1. _____
2. _____
3. _____
4. _____
5. _____
6. _____
7. _____
8. _____
9. _____
10. _____

Word Replacement
11. _____
12. _____
13. _____
14. _____
15. _____

Use the Thesaurus
16. _____
17. _____
18. _____
19. _____
20. _____

demonstration	concentrate	issuing	believable	excuse
communication	comparable	endure	appreciation	ignorance
concentrating	examination	likable	concentration	excusable
receiving	organization	endurance	celebration	achieving

Solve the Analogies

Write a spelling word to complete each analogy.

1. Reach is to **reaching** as **achieve** is to _____.

2. Enjoyment is to **displeasure** as **knowledge** is to _____.

3. Eating is to **dining** as **distributing** is to _____.

4. Unlikely is to **improbable** as **credible** is to _____.

Complete the Sentences

Write the spelling word that best completes each sentence.

5. We will not disturb you if you are _____ on your homework.

6. Because of the storm, their delay was _____.

7. Please accept this token of _____ for a job well done.

8. She applied all her powers of _____ to learn her lines.

9. I am _____ your signal loud and clear.

10. A victory _____ was held after the game.

11. You are the most pleasant and _____ person I have ever met!

12. After a careful _____, we concluded that the refrigerator was filled with delicious leftovers.

Use Context Clues

Write spelling words from the box to complete the paragraph.

The destruction wrought by the hurricane was **13.** to nothing we had ever seen. Few of the trees and plants had been able to **14.** the storm intact. We could not in good conscience **15.** ourselves from helping out. We decided to **16.** on picking up the debris first. Working so hard all day took a lot of **17.**, but our efficient **18.** made the job much easier. A formal **19.** from the mayor a few days later mentioned our **20.** of outstanding teamwork.

endurance
concentrate
excuse
demonstration
communication
comparable
endure
organization

Solve the Analogies

1. _____
2. _____
3. _____
4. _____

Complete the Sentences

5. _____
6. _____
7. _____
8. _____
9. _____
10. _____
11. _____
12. _____

Use Context Clues

13. _____
14. _____
15. _____
16. _____
17. _____
18. _____
19. _____
20. _____

Connections to WRITING

Proofread a Folktale

First, proofread the folktale below for ten misspelled words. Then rewrite the folktale. Write the spelling words correctly and make the corrections indicated by the proofreading marks.

Proofreading Marks

=	Capital Letter
/	Small Letter
∧	Add
ℓ	Delete
⊙	Add a Period
¶	Indent

¶Anansi, a likabel spider with six sons, fell into a river. His first son, One Who Sees Troublesome, was concentrateing when he began recieving a mental communacation of Anansi in the river. Anansi's second son, Road builder, built roads to get to their father. Anansi's third son, River Dryer, gave a demenstration of his power by drying up the river, but all they found was a fish. After an examenation of the fish, they realized it had eaten Anansi. Game Skinner had to concintrate to cut open the fish to get his Father. The brothers were about to have a celibration for acheiving success when a bird swooped down and grabbed Anansi. Stone Thrower could not indure this, so he hurled a stone, making the bird drop Anansi. Then Soft-as-a-Cushion dashed to soften Anansi's fall.

NARRATIVE Writing Prompt
Write a Folktale

Rewrite a folktale or a fable in your own words.

- Add a new setting and new characters if you wish.
- Use as many spelling words as you can.
- Proofread for grammar, capitalization, and punctuation.
- Circle three words you are unsure about and check their spelling in a print or online dictionary.

Transfer

In your Spelling Journal, continue adding new words to your lists of suffixes. Add at least three new words to the **-tion, -ation, -able,** and **-ance** lists.

Word Study

Consonant Sounds

1.
2.
3.
4.
5.
6.
7.
8.
9.
10.
11.
12.

Meaning Mastery

13.
14.
15.
16.
17.
18.
19.
20.

adorable	issuing	excusable	appreciation
achieving	captivate	continuous	excuse
ignorance	organization	consolation	congregate
imaginary	celebration	communication	concentrating
observant	adversity	quotation	comparable
agile	examination	respiration	agility
sensible	likable	believable	receiving
adverse	captivating	concentrate	concentration
endure	endurance	demonstration	congregating

Consonant Sounds

Write the words with the following sound-spellings.

1–7. /s/ spelled **c**

8–10. /j/ spelled **g**

11. /sh/ spelled **ss**

12. The noun form of this word has /s/ spelled **s**, but the verb form of the same word has /z/ spelled **s**.

Meaning Mastery

Read the suffixes and their meanings.

-able and **-ible** mean "capable" or "inclined"

-tion means "result of an action or process"

Write words from the list with the following meanings.

13. inclined to be described as similar

14. the result of putting things in order

15. the result of showing gratitude

16. inclined to be forgiven

17. the result of being comforted

18. capable of being trusted or believed

19. capable of being liked a lot

20. the result of spoken words

Language Arts
Word Hunt

Read the persuasive letter below. Look for suffixes added to words ending in silent **e**.

Dear Editor Stockton:

    I wish to communicate an urgent need in our town. Our middle school has both boys' and girls' volleyball teams, but because of other schedule conflicts, the boys' team has been receiving all the remaining time slots for games. As you can imagine, this has had an adverse effect on the girls' motivation to play competitive sports. Our girls' team has fantastic agility and concentration; we just need a chance to demonstrate our skills!

    Our principal suggested I write to ask if a reporter from your newpaper could concentrate on our situation. That might correct the community's ignorance of our problem, and we wouldn't have to endure this any longer. An observant reporter could describe not only the adversity we must endure, but could suggest a sensible solution. We hope that an examination of the available buildings in town might help solve our problem.

    Our girls' volleyball team feels that once the community understands how believable our need is, they will find our story captivating, and someone might step forward and offer us a suitable building in which we can compete! Thank you very much.

With great appreciation,

Sasha Anderson
Jefferson Middle School

1. _____
2. _____
3. _____
4. _____
5. _____
6. _____
7. _____
8. _____
9. _____
10. _____

WORD SORT

Write the words from the letter that are suffixed forms of the words below.

1. believe	**3.** ignore	**5.** examine	**7.** concentrate	**9.** agile
2. adverse	**4.** compete	**6.** appreciate	**8.** motivate	**10.** observe

Connections to THINKING

Read the spelling words and sentences.

1.	wrestle	*wrestle*	I had to **wrestle** the tight lid off the jar.
2.	scenic	*scenic*	The **scenic** view from the top floor is lovely.
3.	guarantee	*guarantee*	I **guarantee** that you will enjoy this book.
4.	descendant	*descendant*	He is a **descendant** of the former president.
5.	knoll	*knoll*	We climbed the **knoll** to pick some flowers.
6.	align	*align*	Please **align** the books along the shelf.
7.	spaghetti	*spaghetti*	We had **spaghetti** and meatballs for dinner.
8.	herb	*herb*	Her secret recipe called for a rare **herb**.
9.	sought	*sought*	I **sought** them out in the crowded room.
10.	honesty	*honesty*	People respect him for his **honesty**.
11.	schedule	*schedule*	The **schedule** tells when the show will begin.
12.	thoroughly	*thoroughly*	I was **thoroughly** pleased with the results.
13.	gnarled	*gnarled*	The branches were **gnarled** and knotty.
14.	hustle	*hustle*	We had to **hustle** through the crowded shop.
15.	descend	*descend*	The stairs **descend** to the basement.
16.	scenery	*scenery*	I watched the **scenery** from my window seat.
17.	exhibition	*exhibition*	Her painting was shown at an **exhibition**.
18.	resign	*resign*	The letter explained her wish to **resign**.
19.	gauge	*gauge*	There is no way to **gauge** the damage done.
20.	jostle	*jostle*	I apologize when I **jostle** someone.

Silent h

1. _____
2. _____
3. _____
4. _____
5. _____

Silent k or g

6. _____
7. _____
8. _____
9. _____

Silent t

10. _____
11. _____
12. _____

Silent c

13. _____
14. _____
15. _____
16. _____

Silent u or gh

17. _____
18. _____
19. _____
20. _____

Think & Sort the spelling words.

1–5. Write the words with a silent **h**.

6–9. Write the words with a silent **k** or **g**.

10–12. Write the words with a silent **t**.

13–16. Write the words with a silent **c**.

17–20. Write the words with a silent **u** or **gh**.

Remember

Some words contain silent letters.

Connections to VOCABULARY

Word Meanings

Write a spelling word for each definition.

1. a small, rounded hill
2. to collide, push, or elbow
3. to arrange in a line
4. an instrument for testing or measuring
5. knotty; twisted; misshapen
6. a promise or assurance; something that ensures a particular outcome or condition

Word Groups

Write a spelling word to complete each group.

7. grandchild, offspring, _____
8. hurry, bustle, _____
9. searched, hunted, _____
10. completely, extensively, _____
11. demonstration, show, _____
12. breathtaking, picturesque, _____

Use the Dictionary

Sometimes you may know how to say a word but not know how to spell it. To find the spelling word in the dictionary, first think of the letter or different letter combinations that can spell the sounds in the word. Then look under each possible spelling until you find the entry word. Write the spelling words for the following pronunciations. Use the **Spelling Dictionary** if you need help.

13. /sē′ nə rē/
14. /dĭ sĕnd′/
15. /ûrb/
16. /ŏn′ ĭ stē/
17. /spə gĕt′ ē/
18. /rĭ zīn′/
19. /skĕj′ o͞ol/
20. /rĕs′ əl/

Word Meanings
1.
2.
3.
4.
5.
6.
Word Groups
7.
8.
9.
10.
11.
12.
Use the Dictionary
13.
14.
15.
16.
17.
18.
19.
20.

wrestle	knoll	sought	gnarled	exhibition
scenic	align	honesty	hustle	resign
guarantee	spaghetti	schedule	descend	gauge
descendant	herb	thoroughly	scenery	jostle

Complete the Sentences

Write spelling words to complete the sentences.

1–2. We have to _____ through the crowd if we want to get to the boat _____.

3–4. Carl wants to see the _____ along the coastline, so he plans to drive on the _____ route during his vacation.

5–6. For her research paper, Abby _____ facts about a direct _____ of Washington Irving.

7–8. If your new stereo came with a written _____ from the manufacturer, be sure to read it _____.

9. I have to check my _____ to see if I am busy on that day.

10. Scientists use seismographs to _____ the intensity of earthquakes.

11. I will _____ from the presidency of the debating club.

12. It is an amazing sight when the planets _____.

Use Context Clues

Write spelling words from the box to complete the paragraph.

There once was an old woman who lived on a __13.__ near a village. The townsfolk often came to her for help. With her __14.__ hands, she would apply an __15.__ to a wound, and the wound would heal. One day she hired a boy from the town as an assistant. She made him promise that he would never use her cooking pot. That night the boy heard the woman chanting a poem. Curious, he peeked through the door. The pot was magically filling with __16.__ as she spoke! When the woman went out the next day, the boy, forgetting about __17.__, repeated the poem. The pot began to fill with pasta! Word spread and the house filled with curious townsfolk. They began to __18.__ each other in a rush to eat. Soon, they were all stuffed. The pot, however, continued to cook. The boy tried to __19.__ the lid on while waves of pasta began to __20.__ on the town.

wrestle
herb
jostle
knoll
honesty
descend
gnarled
spaghetti

Complete the Sentences
1.
2.
3.
4.
5.
6.
7.
8.
9.
10.
11.
12.

Use Context Clues
13.
14.
15.
16.
17.
18.
19.
20.

Connections to WRITING

Proofread a Tall Tale

Proofread the tall tale below for ten misspelled words. Then rewrite the tall tale. Write the spelling words correctly and make the corrections indicated by the proofreading marks.

Have you heard of Pete Bunkin? he was a desendent of the giant lumberjack, Paul Bunyan. Pete Bunkin was so big that when he lay down, he used a knole as a pillow. He was so thorouly remorseful for the trees his Great-Great-Grandfather had chopped down that he saught to replace each and every one. Pete carried bundles of trees the way we might carry small piles of sticks. The trees looked like spagetti in his giant knarled hands. He would aline the trees and plant them carefully Pete wanted to garantee that future generations would have beautiful senery. Thanks to Pete Bunkin, there are senic forests all over the country.

NARRATIVE Writing Prompt
Write a Tall Tale

The **tall tale,** a form of humorous "brag" that grew out of the American frontier in the early 1800s, exaggerates elements of truth for humorous effect. Select a story from a newspaper or magazine. Retell the story as a tall tale.

- Use as many spelling words as you can.
- Proofread for grammar, capitalization, and punctuation.
- Circle three words you are unsure about and check their spelling in a print or online dictionary.

Transfer

Look again at the newspaper or magazine article and find three words that have silent letters. Write them in your Spelling Journal. Circle the silent letter or letters in each word.

Word Study

Consonant Sound-Spellings

1.

2.

3.

4.

5.

6.

7.

8.

9.

10.

11.

Meaning Mastery

12.

13.

14.

15.

16.

17.

18.

19.

20.

crumb	guarantee	scenery	align
jostle	ghastly	kneel	spaghetti
exhibition	herb	campaign	rheumatism
knob	sought	gauge	gnarled
mortgage	rhythmic	plumber	honesty
wrestle	hustle	pneumonia	answerable
solemn	schedule	descendant	descend
raspberry	rhapsody	scenic	thoroughly
knoll	resign	subtle	reminisce

Consonant Sound-Spellings

Write the words with the following sound-spellings.

1–3. /s/ spelled as it is in **mistletoe**

4–8. /s/ spelled as it is in **scientific**

9–11. /r/ spelled as it is in **rhombus**

Meaning Mastery

Write a spelling word for each definition.

12. a plant that is used in medicines and teas

13. a large, public show

14. to quit from a job or position in an organization

15. a plan of events that is followed in order to be elected to office

16. truthfulness

17. a disease affecting the lungs

18. an agenda for completing a task

19. a measuring tool

20. to rest on one's knees

Health
Word Hunt

Read the paragraphs below. Look for words that have silent letters.

My Grandpa Joe likes to reminisce about "the good old days when people didn't have to wrestle with stupid rules about what to eat and then hustle off every day to get to the gym." You can see that my Grandpa Joe wasn't very subtle!

My grandfather grew up on a farm where people worked hard all day just to keep up the mortgage payments. People in his generation seldom asked the advice of a doctor. They just suffered silently with rheumatism or arthritis or whatever else came along.

Like most people then, his daily schedule was pretty simple: after a good sleep, he'd eat a big well-balanced breakfast and work hard all day. Then he'd have a solid lunch so as to guarantee enough energy reserve to work the rest of the day. He finished the day with a hearty supper. This schedule was so tough that weight problems were virtually unheard of. There was certainly no need to go jogging or join a gym as we do today!

Grandpa Joe's generation wasn't worried about smoking or other unhealthy habits. They didn't know what we know today about such life-threatening dangers. As his descendant, I sometimes envy the simplicity of his life, but I am so glad we have the best of both worlds. It's true that we have modern medical care, but we also have a responsibility to eat healthy foods, get enough sleep, and get lots of exercise!

1. _____
2. _____
3. _____
4. _____
5. _____
6. _____
7. _____
8. _____
9. _____
10. _____

1–10. Write the words that have silent letters. Use an online dictionary to check pronunciation and underline the letters that are silent.

Unit 7	
1.	
2.	
3.	
4.	
5.	
Unit 8	
6.	
7.	
Unit 9	
8.	
9.	
10.	
11.	
Unit 10	
12.	
13.	
14.	
15.	
16.	
Unit 11	
17.	
18.	
19.	
20.	

Units 7–11

Assessment

Each word in the box fits one of the spelling patterns or rules you have studied over the past five weeks. Read the unit descriptions. Then write each assessment word under the unit number it fits.

Unit 7

1–5. Words can have prefixes and suffixes.

Unit 8

6–7. Some base words, particularly those ending with **ce** or **ge**, retain a final silent e when certain suffixes (such as **-able** and **-ous**) are added. This is done to preserve the pronunciation of the base word.

Unit 9

8–11. Final **te** or silent **e** is dropped in words like **hesitate** and **determine** before adding the suffix **-tion** or **-ation**. These suffixes turn verbs into nouns.

Unit 10

12–16. Final silent **e** is dropped in words like **concentrate** before adding a suffix that begins with a vowel.

Unit 11

17–20. Some words contain silent letters.

Words for Assessment

indefinite

grateful

preparation

curable

consign

hesitating

prearrangement

isolation

received

gnash

spiteful

indifferent

shepherd

evaporation

uselessness

severely

bristle

sincerity

evaporate

freezing

Unit 7: Affixes:

| requirement | extremely | unexpected | improvement | alphabetical |
| surprisingly | regardless | emotional | disappointment | agreeable |

Write the spelling word that is an affixed form of each of these words.

1. extreme
2. agree
3. appoint
4. require
5. prove

6. surprise
7. regard
8. expect
9. emotion
10. alphabet

Unit 8: Adding Suffixes to Words Ending in Silent e

| encouragement | manage | canoe | acreage | management |
| advantageous | encourage | acre | canoeing | announcement |

Write the word that completes each sentence.

11. Please paddle the _____ from the left side.
12. I can _____ the paddling from the right side by myself.
13. Please don't talk while we are _____ down the rapids.
14. During the race, our coach shouted words of _____ from the shore.
15. It will certainly be _____ if we practice before we begin the race.
16. We will start as soon as we hear the _____ that everything is ready.
17. I _____ you to work on your technique.
18. Ms. Amiri's style of _____ is to support everyone who tries to succeed.
19. The survey accounts for every _____ of land.
20. How much _____ has been planted in corn?

Unit 7

1. _____
2. _____
3. _____
4. _____
5. _____
6. _____
7. _____
8. _____
9. _____
10. _____

Unit 8

11. _____
12. _____
13. _____
14. _____
15. _____
16. _____
17. _____
18. _____
19. _____
20. _____

Review

Unit 9

1. _____
2. _____
3. _____
4. _____
5. _____
6. _____
7. _____
8. _____
9. _____
10. _____

Unit 10

11. _____
12. _____
13. _____
14. _____
15. _____
16. _____
17. _____
18. _____
19. _____
20. _____

Unit 9: Suffixes: -tion, -ation

| admire | combine | determination | hesitate | admiratioin |
| compete | hesitation | competition | determine | combination |

Write a spelling word and its affixed form to complete each sentence.

1–2. In a one-on-one basketball _____, two players _____ against each other.

3–4. If you _____ too long in helping someone, that _____ might result in danger.

5–6. If they _____ your acting ability, the audience will show their _____ by applauding at the end of the play.

7–8. It was the judge's _____ that the jury could _____ the damages in the court case.

9–10. If you _____ two odd numbers, the _____ will always be an even number.

Unit 10: Adding Suffixes to Words Ending in Silent e

| concentrate | issuing | excuse | communication | comparable |
| excusable | concentration | likable | organization | celebration |

Write the word that fits each clue.

11. to pardon
12. to focus
13. forgivable
14. sending out
15. an organized group

Write the spelling word that is the suffixed form of each word.

16. communicate
17. concentrate
18. celebrate
19. like
20. compare

Unit 11: Words With Silent Letters

scenic	guarantee	spaghetti	sought	honesty
schedule	thoroughly	scenery	exhibition	gauge

Write a spelling word that goes with each set.

1. pretty, picturesque
2. macaroni, linguini
3. completely, fully
4. truthfulness, integrity
5. promise, pledge

6. view, landscape
7. timetable, plan
8. display, show
9. measure, check
10. asked, requested

Unit 11

1. _____
2. _____
3. _____
4. _____
5. _____
6. _____
7. _____
8. _____
9. _____
10. _____

Spelling Study Strategy

Sorting by Parts of Speech

Sorting words is a good way to master their meanings and spellings. Here is a way to work with a partner to sort the spelling words:

1. Make a four-column chart with the headings **Noun, Verb, Adjective,** and **Adverb**.

2. Choose a partner and take turns writing a spelling word in the proper column.

3. Use the word in a sentence to demonstrate its part of speech.

4. If you can think of how the word might be used as a different part of speech, list it in that column, too.

For example, you might put **excuse** in the Noun column and also in the Verb column by giving the sentence, "I can **excuse** (verb) you for giving that poor **excuse** (noun) for being absent."

Directions: Read each item carefully. Select the best answer and fill in the circle on your answer sheet.

1. Read the following sentence.

   > The only requirement for enjoying scenic canoing is that you wear a life jacket.

   Which word in the sentence is spelled INCORRECTLY?

   A. requirement   C. canoing
   B. scenic   D. jacket

2. Read the following sentence.

   > The unexpected anouncement from the management was surprisingly brief.

   Which word in the sentence is spelled INCORRECTLY?

   A. unexpected   C. management
   B. anouncement   D. surprisingly

3. Read the following list of alphabetized words

   > acre
   > acreage
   > admire
   > advantageous
   > alphabetical

   The word **admiration** should follow the word

   A. acreage   C. advantageous
   B. admire   D. alphabetical

4. Read the following sentence.

   > The children sought to compete in the judo exibition.

   What change, if any, should be made to this sentence?

   A. Change **sought** to **sougth**
   B. Change **compete** to **conpete**
   C. Change **exibition** to **exhibition**
   D. Make no change

5. Which of the following words is spelled INCORRECTLY?

   A. determination   C. combine
   B. organisation   D. disappointment

6. Read the following sentence.

   > I'm thoroughly confused by your admiration for him. His lack of honesty is not excuseable.

   Which word in the sentence is spelled INCORRECTLY?

   A. thoroughly   C. honesty
   B. admiration   D. excuseable

7. Read the following sentence.

   > Are you able to gage whether we will be on schedule? Can you guarantee it?

   What change, if any, should be made to this sentence?

   A. Change **gage** to **gauge**
   B. Change **schedule** to **scedule**
   C. Change **guarantee** to **garantee**
   D. Make no change

8. Read the following list of alphabetized words.

> canoe
> canoeing
> combine
> compete
> competition

The word **combination** should follow the word

A. canoeing   C. compete
B. combine   D. competition

9. Read the following sentences.

> Excuse me, but tell the chef his spagetti sauce is a disappointment. The combination of tomatoes and pickles is a little strange.

Which word in these sentences is spelled INCORRECTLY?

A. Excuse   C. disappointment
B. spagetti   D. combination

10. Which of the following words is spelled INCORRECTLY?

A. emotional   C. alphabeticle
B. encouragement   D. scenic

11. Read the following sentence.

> During a chess competition, it is advantagous to make an unexpected move.

What change, if any, should be made to this sentence?

A. Change **competition** to **competetion**
B. Change **advantagous** to **advantageous**
C. Change **unexpected** to **unexpcted**
D. Make no change

12. Which of the following words is spelled INCORRECTLY?

A. reguardless   C. excusable
B. concentrate   D. schedule

13. Read the following sentences.

> Let's canoe down this scenic river and admire nature's beauty. Is that an agreable plan?

Which word in these sentences is spelled INCORRECTLY?

A. canoe   C. admire
B. scenic   D. agreable

14. Read the following sentence.

> Not surprisingly, the store management is issueing refunds for the faulty mp3 players.

What change, if any, should be made to this sentence?

A. Change **surprisingly** to **suprisingly**
B. Change **management** to **managment**
C. Change **issueing** to **issuing**
D. Make no change

15. Read the following sentences.

> Before the celabration, the president of our organization showed his admiration for all of us by praising each of us individually. He is a very likable person.

Which word in these sentences is spelled INCORRECTLY?

A. celabration   C. admiration
B. organization   D. likable

STOP

Grammar, Usage, and Mechanics
Identifying Modifiers: Adverbs

An **adverb** is a word that modifies a verb, an adjective, or another adverb. Many adverbs end in **-ly** and tell how, when, or to what extent something is done.

Fido looked up **indifferently**, although Marge spoke **loudly**.
New York has **very** tall buildings.
We reviewed the lesson **quite thoroughly**.

Practice Activity

A. Write the adverb in each sentence below.
1. We are postponing the game indefinitely.
2. "I'm sure we'll win next year," Marcus said hopefully.
3. The captains shook hands agreeably.
4. Juana tapped the empty piggy bank uselessly.
5. Ali glared severely at his opponent.
6. Carly called encouragingly to her teammates.
7. I sincerely hope that I am ready for the test.
8. Sue has completely finished the quilt.

B. Write the adverb form of the word in parentheses by adding **-ly**.
9. Please answer every question (honest).
10. I have (thorough) examined the evidence from the crime scene.
11. He cried out (emotional) at the sight.
12. The test was (surprising) easy.
13. Mr. DeNardo showed up (unexpected).
14. He handled the problem (professional).
15. The small boy ran (fearless) into the game.

A
1.
2.
3.
4.
5.
6.
7.
8.
B
9.
10.
11.
12.
13.
14.
15.

The Writing Process: Descriptive
Writing an Observation Report

PREWRITING

Stargazing can be fun. As the earth moves around the sun, different constellations are visible. For example, we can see Cygnus, or the Swan, in the morning in late summer. Writing about what you observe can be fun, too. You can describe changes that occur over time in an observation report. For ideas of things to observe, look in books at the library or on Internet sites such as Science Buddies (www.sciencebuddies.org). As you observe, take detailed notes about what you see.

DRAFTING

Use your notes to write an observation report. Begin with a topic sentence that presents the main idea. Write supporting sentences that describe what you see, hear, taste, smell, and feel. Use as many spelling words as possible. If you don't know how to spell a word, make your best guess. You will be able to revise your report later.

REVISING

When you have finished your first draft, read your report from beginning to end. Check to see if you have included all of the points in your notes. Did you describe your observations using the five senses? Does each sentence support the topic? Now write your final draft.

EDITING

Use the editing checklist to proofread your report. Be sure to use proofreading marks when you make corrections. Circle three words you are unsure about and check their spelling in a dictionary.

PUBLISHING

Make a copy of your observation report, and share it with your readers.

EDITING CHECKLIST

Spelling

✓ Circle words that contain the spelling patterns and rules learned in Units 7–11.

✓ Check the circled words in a print or online dictionary.

✓ Check for other spelling errors.

Capital Letters

✓ Capitalize important words in the title.

✓ Capitalize the first word in each sentence.

✓ Capitalize proper nouns.

Punctuation

✓ End each sentence with the correct punctuation.

✓ Use commas, apostrophes, and quotation marks correctly.

Grammar, Usage, and Mechanics

✓ Check that each sentence has a subject and a predicate.

✓ Check for proper usage of adverbs.

Connections to THINKING

Read the spelling words and sentences.

1. absolutely — *absolutely* — He is **absolutely** my favorite actor.
2. briefly — *briefly* — Since time is short, explain **briefly**.
3. vague — *vague* — He gave us only a **vague** description.
4. fortunately — *fortunately* — I was wearing a seat belt, **fortunately**.
5. urgent — *urgent* — Move fast if it is **urgent**.
6. particular — *particular* — I do not like that **particular** color.
7. instantly — *instantly* — She **instantly** knew the answer.
8. necessarily — *necessarily* — This is not **necessarily** bad news.
9. deliberate — *deliberate* — His actions were slow and **deliberate**.
10. particularly — *particularly* — I am not **particularly** fond of beets.
11. immediately — *immediately* — Please give her this note **immediately**.
12. urgently — *urgently* — We **urgently** need new uniforms.
13. accurately — *accurately* — She will relay the message **accurately**.
14. deliberately — *deliberately* — Did you **deliberately** let me win?
15. presently — *presently* — Dinner will be ready **presently**.
16. readily — *readily* — I will **readily** attend the dance.
17. approximately — *approximately* — He is **approximately** six feet tall.
18. vaguely — *vaguely* — I remember my dreams only **vaguely**.
19. positively — *positively* — He is **positively** my best friend ever!
20. absolute — *absolute* — The president's power is not **absolute**.

Think & Sort the spelling words.

1–5. Write the words that are adjectives.
6–13. Write the words that are adverbs and end in silent **e** + **-ly**.
14–18. Write the words that are adverbs and end in a **consonant** + **-ly**.
19–20. Write the adverbs that were made by changing **y** to **i** and adding **-ly**.

Remember

The suffix **-ly** may be added to adjectives such as **urgent** to form adverbs.

Adjectives
1.
2.
3.
4.
5.

Silent e + -ly
6.
7.
8.
9.
10.
11.
12.
13.

Consonant + -ly
14.
15.
16.
17.
18.

y to i + -ly
19.
20.

Connections to VOCABULARY

Word Meanings

Write a spelling word to complete each sentence. Use the underlined words to help you.

1. We will _____ get the children <u>ready</u> for the party.
2. Just add water to the <u>instant</u> soup, and we can eat it _____!
3. She will not _____ remember to bring the <u>necessary</u> items.
4. The young man inherited a <u>fortune</u>, and _____ he is using it wisely.

Word Replacement

Write a spelling word that best replaces the underlined words in each sentence.

5. Do you think you will finish your homework <u>soon after the present time</u>?
6. He spoke <u>in a positive way</u> about his teacher.
7. She will talk <u>in a brief manner</u> and then answer questions from the audience.
8. Can you tell me <u>in an approximate way</u> what time it is?
9. When a tornado comes, find shelter <u>in an immediate way</u>.
10. It is important to answer the investigator's questions <u>in an accurate way</u>.

Use the Dictionary

Write pairs of spelling words for each Latin etymology given below. Use the **Spelling Dictionary** if you need help.

11–12. **vagus,** wandering
13–14. **urgens,** pressing
15–16. **deliberatus,** considered
17–18. **absolutus,** ended
19–20. **particularis,** part

Word Meanings	
1.	
2.	
3.	
4.	

Word Replacement	
5.	
6.	
7.	
8.	
9.	
10.	

Use the Dictionary	
11.	
12.	
13.	
14.	
15.	
16.	
17.	
18.	
19.	
20.	

Connections to READING

absolutely   briefly   positively   fortunately   vague
urgent   particular   instantly   necessarily   absolute
deliberate   particularly   urgently   immediately   readily
accurately   deliberately   presently   approximately   vaguely

Answer the Questions

Write the spelling word that best answers each question.

1–2. Which two spelling words are synonyms for **definitely**?

3. Which spelling word is a synonym for **soon**?

4–5. Which two spelling words are synonyms for **now**?

6–7. Which two spelling words are antonyms for **exactly**?

8. Which spelling word is a synonym for **unclear**?

Complete the Dialogue

Write the spelling words from the box that best complete the dialogue.

Moderator: The subject for our debate is how to meet the __9.__ need for new energy sources. Are there any questions before we begin?

Carlos: Would you please fill us in on the rules of the debate? I am __10.__ curious about how much time we have to speak.

Moderator: You will have only two minutes to speak, so please present your views __11.__. This rule is __12.__; I must stop anyone from exceeding the time limit. Be sure to use supporting facts and details to state your position __13.__.

Michelle: What if the other team is __14.__ misleading the judges, and we __15.__ want to argue the point? May we interrupt?

Moderator: We will accept no __16.__ interruptions! But, __17.__, you will get time for a rebuttal.

Carlos: How is the winner chosen?

Moderator: At the end, the judges will confer and then announce the winner. The decision will not __18.__ be based on any __19.__ facts. It will include how carefully the research was prepared and how __20.__ the participants are able to respond to the opposing arguments.

readily
fortunately
deliberately
particularly
accurately
absolute
necessarily
urgent
particular
urgently
briefly
deliberate

Answer the Questions

1.
2.
3.
4.
5.
6.
7.
8.

Complete the Dialogue

9.
10.
11.
12.
13.
14.
15.
16.
17.
18.
19.
20.

Connections to WRITING

Proofread a Dialogue

First proofread the dialogue between an American colonist and a modern-day reporter for ten misspelled words. Then rewrite it. Write the spelling words correctly and make the corrections indicated by the proofreading marks.

Colonist: *Do people still read the newspaper?*

Reporter: *Many do, but it's not neccessarily the way they get news. They get news from television, too⊙*

Colonist: *That's absolutly intriguing. How does it work?*

Reporter: *I'll explain breifly. Particuler sounds and images are converted to digital signals, which are sent to satellites. The signals are immediatly returned to e̲arth, accurrately translated back to sounds and images, and sent to television sets. Urjent news∧delivered instently.* (is)

Colonist: *I do not have even a vage idea of what you mean. Digital? s̲atellites? I am posatively confused by such words!*

NARRATIVE Writing Prompt

Write a Dialogue

Write a dialogue between two imaginary characters.

- Before you begin, decide what your characters might discuss, such as politics, entertainment, transportation, or technology.
- Follow the form used in the proofreading example.
- Use as many spelling words as you can.
- Proofread for grammar, capitalization, and punctuation.
- Circle three words you are unsure about. Check their spelling in a print or online dictionary.

Transfer

Look in your Spelling Journal at your list of words with suffixes. Can you add the suffix **-ly** to any of those words? For example, you can add **-ly** to **emotional** to make the word **emotionally**. Write at least five words with **-ly**.

Word Study

Word Usage

1.
2.
3.
4.
5.
6.
7.
8.

Meaning Mastery

9.
10.
11.
12.
13.
14.
15.
16.

Word Families

17.
18.
19.
20.

intent	fortunately	immediately	instantly
positively	additionally	approximately	particular
barely	deliberate	coincidentally	previous
carefully	gradually	necessarily	urgently
absolute	diagonally	particularly	certainly
briefly	patiently	deliberately	intently
exactly	readily	strenuously	presently
strictly	previously	absolutely	accurately
urgent	vaguely	voicelessly	vague

Word Usage

Words with the suffix **-ly** are usually adverbs. In addition, they are often formed by adding **-ly** to an adjective, as with **intelligent, intelligently**. Create adverbs from the following adjectives.

1. approximate 3. certain   5. present   7. fortunate
2. voiceless   4. gradual   6. strenuous   8. ready

Meaning Mastery

Write the words from the list that are synonyms for the following word pairs. Use the **Writing Thesaurus**.

9–10. obscure, obscurely
11–12. imperative, imperatively
13–14. specific, specifically
15–16. purposeful, purposefully

Word Families

Write the missing words to complete the chart.

Noun	Verb	Adjective	Adverb
addition	add	additional	**17.**
coincidence	coincide	coincidental	**18.**
19.	intend	intentional	**20.**

Art
Word Hunt

Read the paragraphs below. Look for words with the suffix **-ly**.

1. _____
2. _____
3. _____
4. _____
5. _____
6. _____
7. _____
8. _____
9. _____
10. _____

One of the most recognizable names in art is M. C. Escher (1898–1972). This Dutch graphic artist is primarily known for creating detailed optical illusions, many of which are positively hilarious. The more intently one looks at his impossible drawings, the more they seem to be an absolute mystery and the funnier they become. Bridges and balconies deliberately end up going nowhere and waterfalls impossibly flow uphill. In other drawings, stairways seem to go up and down simultaneously. Some of the funniest drawings depict lines of people walking into a building at ground level, but somehow they end up on an entirely different level as they exit.

Escher used other types of optical illusions as well. He was particularly fond of filling the page with patterns of repetition to fool the viewer's eye. Starting in one corner and moving the eye diagonally across the page, a pattern of fish on one side gradually transforms into a pattern of birds. In another, a pattern of white lizards on a black background changes into a similar pattern of black lizards on white.

Escher's incredible volume of work was created by carving (or etching) drawings onto a flat block of wood, which was then covered with ink and transferred onto paper. He produced other prints by etching his images onto plates of glass or metal, covering it with ink and transferring the image to paper in a similar way. The process required a steady hand and a very patient and imaginative person!

1–10. Write words with the suffix **-ly**. Write other forms of the word in your Spelling Journal.

Connections to THINKING

Read the spelling words and sentences.

1. compatible   *compatible*   I have very **compatible** friends.
2. questionable   *questionable*   Were the test results **questionable**?
3. uncomfortable   *uncomfortable*   How **uncomfortable** these shoes feel!
4. eligible   *eligible*   All **eligible** voters may enter now.
5. unavoidable   *unavoidable*   We made an **unavoidable** detour.
6. accessible   *accessible*   The attic is **accessible** by ladder.
7. reasonable   *reasonable*   Make a **reasonable** offer for my bike.
8. unacceptable   *unacceptable*   Most sloppy work is **unacceptable**.
9. permissible   *permissible*   Is it **permissible** to leave early?
10. incredible   *incredible*   Her story was **incredible** but true.
11. unreasonable   *unreasonable*   Ignore any **unreasonable** requests.
12. remarkable   *remarkable*   She has had a **remarkable** career.
13. unmistakable   *unmistakable*   He speaks with **unmistakable** dignity.
14. ineligible   *ineligible*   You are **ineligible** to run for mayor.
15. considerable   *considerable*   Anna displayed **considerable** courage.
16. recognizable   *recognizable*   A duck is **recognizable** by its bill.
17. suitable   *suitable*   You have many **suitable** hats to wear.
18. admirable   *admirable*   Generosity is an **admirable** quality.
19. noticeable   *noticeable*   I made **noticeable** improvement!
20. disagreeable   *disagreeable*   The cranky child was **disagreeable**.

Think & Sort the spelling words.

1–6. Write the words that end in **-ible**.
7–9. Write the words in which silent **e** is dropped from the base word when **-able** is added. The words may also have a prefix.
10–20. Write the words in which **-able** was added to the base word without a spelling change. The words may also have a prefix.

Remember

The suffixes **-able** and **-ible** may be added to base words or word roots to form adjectives.

-ible

1.
2.
3.
4.
5.
6.

Silent e dropped and -able added

7.
8.
9.

Base word + -able

10.
11.
12.
13.
14.
15.
16.
17.
18.
19.
20.

Connections to VOCABULARY

Word Meanings

Write the spelling word that could best replace the underlined word or words.

1. The notion that dogs and cats are not capable of getting along is false.
2. Will is shy and ill at ease around strangers.
3. Only I was capable of being identified in the picture.
4. It was doubtful and debatable whether he would stay in the race after he fell.
5. Budding trees and flowering crocuses are sure and undeniable signs of spring.
6. Fog made the flight delay impossible to escape.
7. The tear in your jeans is barely evident.

Word Analysis

Change the underlined affix in each word to write a spelling word.

8. admission   9. disagreement   10. discredit   11. unaccepting

Antonyms

Write a spelling word that is an antonym for each word.

12. The antonym is **unqualified,** and the word ends in **-ible**.
13. The antonym is **sensible,** and the word begins with **un-**.
14. The antonym is **qualified,** and the word begins with **in-**.
15. The antonym is **illogical,** and the word ends in **-able**.

Use the
Dictionary

Some forms of an entry word appear before the definition of the main entry. Such **run-on entries** usually have a different part of speech from that of the entry word. Write the entry word (a spelling word) and its part of speech for each of the run-on entries below. Use the **Spelling Dictionary** if you need help.

16. considerably, *adv.*
17. suitability, *n.*
18. remarkably, *adv.*
19. admirably, *adv.*
20. accessibility, *n.*

Word Meanings
1. _____
2. _____
3. _____
4. _____
5. _____
6. _____
7. _____

Word Analysis
8. _____
9. _____
10. _____
11. _____

Antonyms
12. _____
13. _____
14. _____
15. _____

Use the Dictionary
16. _____
17. _____
18. _____
19. _____
20. _____

compatible	questionable	uncomfortable	eligible	unavoidable
accessible	reasonable	unacceptable	incredible	permissible
remarkable	unreasonable	unmistakable	ineligible	considerable
noticeable	recognizable	disagreeable	suitable	admirable

Complete the Sentences

Write a spelling word or words to complete each sentence. Use the base word indicated in parentheses.

1. Is it _____ to swim with no lifeguard present? (permit)

2. Dan's report was _____ to Ms. Lee, so he rewrote it. (accept)

3. Trahn has a _____ talent for drawing landscapes. (remark)

4. It is _____ to expect us to pay attention to a dull speech. (reason)

5–6. Because Amy was in such a _____ mood, it was _____ whether anyone would want to be her partner. (agree, question)

Draw Conclusions

Use the clue in each sentence to write a spelling word that best concludes each statement.

7. If your argument makes sense, then your argument is _____ .

8. If you would never mistake your friend's voice for someone else's, then your friend's voice is _____ .

9. If everyone observes the sign, then the sign must be _____ .

10. If a teacher is easy to approach, then the teacher is _____ .

11. If a story could not possibly be true, then the story is _____ .

12. If a dance is formal, then jeans are not _____ to wear.

13. If a room is hot and stuffy, then you may feel _____ in it.

Use Context Clues

Write spelling words from the box to complete the sentence.

The harsh taxes imposed by England on American colonists were not **14.** with the colonists' way of life. By 1774, war seemed **15.** . In April 1775, the Revolutionary War began. Every **16.** man was recruited into the colonial army. Even though women were **17.** , a few **18.** female patriots disguised themselves as men so that they would not be **19.** as they fought in the Revolutionary Army. These women displayed **20.** courage as they fought alongside their compatriots.

ineligible
considerable
unavoidable
recognizable
eligible
compatible
admirable

Complete the Sentences

1. _____
2. _____
3. _____
4. _____
5. _____
6. _____

Draw Conclusions

7. _____
8. _____
9. _____
10. _____
11. _____
12. _____
13. _____

Use Context Clues

14. _____
15. _____
16. _____
17. _____
18. _____
19. _____
20. _____

Connections to WRITING

Proofread a Paragraph

Proofread the paragraph below for ten misspelled words. Then rewrite the paragraph. Write the spelling words correctly and make the corrections indicated by the proofreading marks.

⁋ Recently, school Officials sectioned off a portion of the cafeteria for band practice. This might be a reasonible solution for the band's problem, but many students find it desagreeable and unaceptable. While there has been conciderable improvement in the quality of cafeteria food, the cafeteria is no longer suitible for the number of students who eat there. the space is crowded and uncomftable. The tables are so close together that they are barely axccessible to students in wheelchairs⊙ I suggest that the band use part of the old gym for practice. It is incredable that no one else has suggested this solutions. The new gym and part of the old gym will still be available for sports and physical education. It is unreasonible to continue with this questionible new policy.

ARGUMENT Writing Prompt
Write a Paragraph

Think about a problem in your school or community that has more than one solution. Write a paragraph about the problem. Define the problem and offer two solutions. Evaluate the pros and cons of each solution and explain which solution you think is more reasonable.

- Use as many spelling words as you can.
- Proofread for grammar, capitalization, and punctuation.
- Circle three words you are unsure about. Check their spelling in a print or online dictionary.

Transfer

Many words with **-able** are formed by adding the suffix to a verb. Using the word lists in your Spelling Journal, identify five words whose suffix you can change to **-able**. For example, **forgiveness, forgivable**. Write them in your Spelling Journal.

Word Study

edible	eligible	suitable	accessible
admirable	incapable	favorable	permissible
noticeable	reasonable	disposable	collectible
flexible	remarkable	disagreeable	unacceptable
hospitable	comfortable	notable	unmistakable
compatible	incredible	inadvisable	improbable
profitable	considerable	questionable	unreasonable
irresponsible	inseparable	uncomfortable	recognizable
unavoidable	ineligible	charitable	plausible

Antonyms

1.
2.
3.
4.
5.
6.

Pattern Power

7.
8.
9.
10.
11.
12.
13.
14.

Meaning Mastery

15.
16.
17.
18.
19.
20.

Antonyms

1–6. Write the words from the list that are antonyms.

Pattern Power

Add the suffix **-able** or **-ible** to the following words to write a word from the list above. Add a prefix, if necessary. Circle the word if a spelling change to the base word is necessary when adding the suffix.

7. dispose   **9.** avoid   **11.** recognize   **13.** collect
8. notice   **10.** mistake   **12.** admire   **14.** flex

Meaning Mastery

Write the word that best replaces the underlined word. Use a dictionary or thesaurus for help.

15. Barry and Jon are <u>always together</u>.
16. Henry and Luke are just not <u>congenial</u>.
17. Her excuse for being tardy was not <u>likely</u>.
18. Lynn is a <u>magnificent</u> pianist.
19. Chewing gum on the bus is not <u>allowable</u>.
20. We attended the <u>philanthropic</u> event.

Technology
Word Hunt

Read the paragraphs below. Look for words with the suffixes **-able** and **-ible**.

Most young computer users have heard many times how important it is to take safety precautions when using the Internet. Most of us are quite responsible when it comes to warnings about computer viruses, and we know that we should never visit questionable websites. We also know that it's advisable to install an up-to-date antivirus program that can protect against a considerable number of these destructive viruses.

But there are other notable threats to watch out for, and unfortunately, there is no anti-virus program to help us. It is probably impossible to use the Internet for long without having to give out one's name and other information. Online games and other sites often require some identifying information before you can be eligible to play. It's essential to be safe. Just as you should never share your password or credit card numbers, it is strongly discouraged to ever give out your home address and phone number online. An irresponsible person could do great harm to you or to your family's bank account.

But probably the most potentially dangerous places are also the most unavoidable. Using social networking sites and texting by cell phone are electronic means for communicating with other people. Both are valuable tools in our everyday lives. But each requires caution. It's never advisable to give out passwords, credit card numbers, or home addresses; and never, ever agree to meet new friends in person, especially alone. Networking and texting are amazing tools, but your safety is essential.

1. _____
2. _____
3. _____
4. _____
5. _____
6. _____
7. _____
8. _____
9. _____
10. _____

1–4. Write the words with the **-ible** suffix.

5–10. Write the words with the **-able** suffix. Circle the word if the spelling of the base word was changed before the suffix was added.

Connections to THINKING

Read the spelling words and sentences.

1.	breathe	*breathe*	To **breathe** fresh air is a pleasure.
2.	usually	*usually*	I **usually** eat a big meal at lunch.
3.	vacuum	*vacuum*	Please **vacuum** the rug in your room.
4.	picnicking	*picnicking*	We enjoy **picnicking** by the lake.
5.	bouquet	*bouquet*	Joe brought Mom a **bouquet** of wildflowers.
6.	annually	*annually*	The company reports its earnings **annually**.
7.	pursuit	*pursuit*	She is in **pursuit** of a gold medal.
8.	bouillon	*bouillon*	Eli had a bowl of beef **bouillon** for lunch.
9.	actual	*actual*	Is that an **actual** account of the event?
10.	league	*league*	Sasha is a member of a softball **league**.
11.	mimicking	*mimicking*	The monkey is **mimicking** human behavior.
12.	variety	*variety*	Sentence **variety** adds interest to a story.
13.	coupon	*coupon*	She has a **coupon** for a free CD.
14.	maneuver	*maneuver*	Can he **maneuver** the boat past the dock?
15.	curiosity	*curiosity*	The mysterious note aroused his **curiosity**.
16.	peculiar	*peculiar*	What is the source of that **peculiar** odor?
17.	visually	*visually*	Soft, pastel colors are **visually** soothing.
18.	courtesy	*courtesy*	It shows **courtesy** not to interrupt.
19.	initial	*initial*	He scored on the **initial** play of the game.
20.	pursue	*pursue*	Val hopes to **pursue** a career as an actress.

One or two syllables

1. _____
2. _____
3. _____
4. _____
5. _____
6. _____
7. _____
8. _____

Three syllables

9. _____
10. _____
11. _____
12. _____
13. _____
14. _____
15. _____

Four or five syllables

16. _____
17. _____
18. _____
19. _____
20. _____

Think & Sort the spelling words.

1–8. Write the words that have one or two syllables. Remember that there is a syllable for every vowel sound in a word.

9–15. Write the words that have three syllables.

16–20. Write the words that have four or five syllables.

Remember

It is important to know the spelling of words that are frequently misspelled.

Connections to VOCABULARY

Word Meanings

Write a spelling word with the same meaning as each group of words.

1. real, true, factual
2. first, beginning, introductory
3. diversity, assortment, different kinds
4. club, association, organization
5. exploration, hobby, activity
6. graciousness, politeness, refinement
7. odd, strange, different

Word Structure

Add a suffix to each word to write a spelling word. You may have to change the spelling of the word before adding the suffix.

8. usual
9. picnic
10. annual
11. visual
12. mimic
13. curious

Use the Dictionary

For entry words with more than one acceptable pronunciation, the phonetic spelling of the preferred pronunciation appears first. The alternative phonetic spelling shows only those syllables that differ from the preferred pronunciation. Look up each of the following words in the **Spelling Dictionary**. Write the word and the number (I, 2, or 3) of acceptable pronunciations given.

14. vacuum
15. coupon
16. breathe
17. bouillon
18. pursue
19. maneuver
20. bouquet

Word Meanings	
1.	
2.	
3.	
4.	
5.	
6.	
7.	
Word Structure	
8.	
9.	
10.	
11.	
12.	
13.	
Use the Dictionary	
14.	
15.	
16.	
17.	
18.	
19.	
20.	

breathe	usually	vacuum	picnicking	bouquet
annually	pursuit	bouillon	actual	league
mimicking	variety	coupon	maneuver	curiosity
peculiar	visually	courtesy	initial	pursue

Complete the Sentences

Write the spelling word that best completes each sentence.

1. Please _____ this receipt to show that you got your money back.
2. People who ask a lot of questions are often rewarded for their _____.
3. Do you understand the expression "to operate in a _____"?
4. Mountaineers find it hard to _____ above certain altitudes.
5. Adding _____ to the stew will give it the liquid it needs.
6. Thank you for remembering my birthday with this _____.
7. People became suspicious of his _____ behavior.
8. Is this the _____ cost, or are there hidden fees?
9. The dog catcher is in _____ of a stray dog.
10. He _____ walks in the park, but today he walked downtown.
11. Looking at the bright bold colors was _____ stimulating.

Use Context Clues

Write spelling words from the box to complete the announcement.

Join us this Saturday for Field Day, which is held **12.** _____ at Roland Park. Enjoy a **13.** _____ of games and activities. There will be **14.** _____ by the pond, with box lunches, **15.** _____ of Armond's Delicatessen. The town's soccer **16.** _____ and the softball club will sponsor several competitions. You can also enter a lip sync contest and have fun **17.** _____ your favorite singers. Younger children can **18.** _____ their bikes through an obstacle course as they **19.** _____ prizes, including a **20.** _____ for six free admissions to the See-It-Now Moviehouse. Be sure to come on Saturday!

league
coupon
annually
mimicking
pursue
variety
maneuver
picnicking
courtesy

Complete the Sentences

1. _____
2. _____
3. _____
4. _____
5. _____
6. _____
7. _____
8. _____
9. _____
10. _____
11. _____

Use Context Clues

12. _____
13. _____
14. _____
15. _____
16. _____
17. _____
18. _____
19. _____
20. _____

Connections to WRITING

Proofread a Paragraph

Proofread the paragraph below for ten misspelled words. Then rewrite the paragraph. Write the spelling words correctly and make the corrections indicated by the proofreading marks.

> Mr. Morris, our english teacher, has a curiousity about people who like to play with language. He likes to persue the peculier ways that people use words. People who create puns and other plays on words usully have a good understanding of grammar and vocabulary. Mr. Morris gave us a veriety of examples of language play. His inishal one was a poem title and author: "Ode To Darkness," by Sonny Day. Another example was an actuel sign he had seen in a tailor's shop: "For those in persute of the perfect fitting suit, use my couppon for $40 per suit." Our teacher's final example was a line from a book: "at court, there is often a lack of courtisy."

NARRATIVE Writing Prompt
Write a Paragraph

Choose a topic that has to do with language—puns, metaphors, similes, or alliteration, for example. Write a paragraph about it.

- Explain the topic or term you have chosen and give specific examples of the topic or term.
- Follow the form used in the proofreading example.
- Use as many spelling words as you can.
- Proofread for grammar, capitalization, and punctuation.
- Circle three words you are unsure about. Check their spelling in a print or online dictionary.

Transfer

In your Spelling Journal, list at least five troublesome words from recent spelling tests. Circle the part of the word that causes you trouble. For example, do you remember that **embarrass** has two r's and two s's?

Word Study

jewelry	usually	curiosity	pursuit
pursue	mistaken	probably	vacuum
peculiar	bouillon	committee	gratitude
restaurant	actual	courtesy	league
exhaust	maximum	rhythm	variety
picnicking	mimicking	genuine	diminish
surely	coupon	bouquet	visually
numerous	obliging	breathe	maneuver
annually	initial	maestro	accordance

Consonant Sound-Spellings

1. _____
2. _____
3. _____
4. _____
5. _____
6. _____
7. _____
8. _____
9. _____
10. _____

Pattern Power

11. _____
12. _____
13. _____
14. _____

Meaning Mastery

15. _____
16. _____
17. _____
18. _____
19. _____
20. _____

Consonant Sound-Spellings

Write the words with the sounds below. Circle the letter or letters that spell the sound.

1–2. /zh/
3–5. /sh/
6–8. /j/
9–10. /th/ as in **they**

Pattern Power

Write the spelling word or words from the box that follow the same spelling pattern as the words in each group.

11. exhibit, exhalted, exhilarating
12. dialogue, fatigued, guerrilla
13. comparably, inseparably, capably
14. spoken, beaten, forgotten

Meaning Mastery

Write the word from the box that is a synonym for each word below.

15. movement
16. emptiness
17. copying
18. yearly
19. broth
20. eatery

Science
Word Hunt

Read the paragraphs below. Look for spelling words which are frequently misspelled.

Most of us have never seen a comet, and we probably never will. But telescope photos of comets reveal dramatic long tails of gas that are genuinely beautiful. There are numerous misconceptions about comets. Perhaps the most common of these is the mistaken belief that comets are extremely hot, which is untrue. They are, in fact, made of icy gases and dust.

Like the planets in our solar system, comets orbit our sun in a regular rhythm, although not annually like our own Earth. A comet's orbital period takes many years and follows an oval-shaped orbital path, taking it far from our sun for long periods. Their initial size may be very large, but it tends to diminish every time it passes near our sun. This is because the sun's intense heat and "solar wind" melts the comet's ice and causes it to form a tail of vaporized ice crystals. The comet's tail does not stream behind the comet, but rather, always points away from the sun.

Curiously, this peculiar tail does not exist when the comet is at its maximum distance from the sun. Through a telescope one can see that the comet has a more ordinary round ball shape as it moves along its orbital path. But as it continues to maneuver nearer the sun, the heat and solar wind again begin to blast at the comet, vaporizing its ice and creating the tail. In a way, the comet's magnificent tail is a display of its own destruction.

1. _____
2. _____
3. _____
4. _____
5. _____
6. _____
7. _____
8. _____
9. _____
10. _____

1–10. This essay contains several frequently misspelled words from the list on page 100. Find ten of these words and write them. Underline the part of the word you think is most often misspelled by yourself and others.

Connections to THINKING

Read the spelling words and sentences.

1.	confer	*confer*	Krista will **confer** with her math teacher.
2.	conferred	*conferred*	The President **conferred** with his advisers.
3.	conference	*conference*	When is the parent-teacher **conference**?
4.	occur	*occur*	What time will the solar eclipse **occur**?
5.	occurred	*occurred*	The hailstorm **occurred** on our way home.
6.	occurrence	*occurrence*	Lightning is a common **occurrence** in summer.
7.	omit	*omit*	Do not **omit** your name from your test paper.
8.	omitted	*omitted*	Part of the tour was **omitted** to save time.
9.	omitting	*omitting*	He is **omitting** two chapters from his book.
10.	prefer	*prefer*	I **prefer** e-mail to handwritten notes.
11.	preferred	*preferred*	Otis **preferred** soccer to any other sport.
12.	preference	*preference*	Do you have a **preference** for red socks?
13.	infer	*infer*	I **infer** from his letter that he is homesick.
14.	inferred	*inferred*	Dad **inferred** that I did not want to leave.
15.	refer	*refer*	You may **refer** to your notes during the test.
16.	reference	*reference*	Use more than one atlas for **reference**.
17.	referring	*referring*	He is **referring** to a news article he read.
18.	compel	*compel*	What could **compel** you to wear a pink hat?
19.	compelled	*compelled*	Such kindness **compelled** us to give thanks.
20.	compelling	*compelling*	I was absorbed in a **compelling** mystery.

Think & Sort the spelling words.

1–7. Write the words that are base words.

8–17. Write the words in which the final consonant of the base word is doubled in a stressed syllable when the suffix is added.

18–20. Write the words in which the stress shifts to a different syllable when the suffix is added and the final consonant is not doubled.

Remember

A final consonant preceded by a single vowel is doubled when adding a suffix that begins with a vowel, except when the accent is on—or shifts to—the first syllable.

Base words

1. _____
2. _____
3. _____
4. _____
5. _____
6. _____
7. _____

Double final consonants before adding suffix

8. _____
9. _____
10. _____
11. _____
12. _____
13. _____
14. _____
15. _____
16. _____
17. _____

No consonant doubling; stress shifts

18. _____
19. _____
20. _____

Connections to VOCABULARY

Word Meanings

Write a spelling word for each definition.

1. to draw a conclusion on the basis of evidence
2. to take place
3. a first choice or favorite; partiality or liking
4. bestowed or consulted with
5. pressing or persuasive
6. a written statement about qualifications
7. a discussion, meeting, or session

Word Replacement

Write the spelling word that best replaces the underlined word or words.

8. Why are you <u>leaving out</u> the most exciting part of the story?
9. Do you know what actually <u>happened</u> on July 4, 1776?
10. I have always <u>favored</u> pizza over hamburgers.
11. From the early returns, the reporter <u>concluded</u> that the candidate would win the election by a landslide.
12. Was the principal <u>alluding</u> to our class in her announcement?
13. Lani's name was accidentally <u>dropped</u> from the drama club list.
14. If you do not understand the concept of flight, I can <u>direct</u> you to a good book on the subject.
15. Juana's curiosity <u>drove</u> her to ask one more question.

Use the Thesaurus

Write a spelling word that is a synonym for each group of words. Check your answers in the **Writing Thesaurus**.

16. choose, pick, select
17. eliminate, fail to include, leave out
18. coerce, force, constrain
19. advise, deliberate, discuss
20. circumstance, event, incident

Word Meanings
1.
2.
3.
4.
5.
6.
7.
Word Replacement
8.
9.
10.
11.
12.
13.
14.
15.
Use the Thesaurus
16.
17.
18.
19.
20.

confer	conferred	conference	occur	occurred
occurrence	omit	omitted	omitting	prefer
preferred	preference	infer	inferred	refer
reference	referring	compel	compelled	compelling

Complete the Sentences

Write a spelling word to complete each sentence.

1. We could not find a _____ to that author.
2. The five judges will _____ before choosing a winner.
3. Ruby has always _____ the mountains to the ocean.
4. What celebrity was that writer _____ to in her article?
5. I suspect that he is _____ several facts from the story.
6. Mom enjoys baseball, but Dad has a _____ for football.
7. When did that excellent idea _____ to you?
8. It can be _____ from the wet floor that the pipe leaks.
9. The county fair is an annual summer _____ .
10. We did not mean to _____ Cal's name from the guest list.
11. What can you _____ from her refusal to take the test?

Use Context Clues

Write spelling words from the box to complete the debate.

Topic: Should the minimum wage be lowered for persons under eighteen years of age?

Pro: We feel there should be legislation to __12.__ states to lower the minimum wage for those under eighteen. To support this view, we __13.__ to testimony given at a recent __14.__ on unemployment, indicating that there is __15.__ evidence that many small businesses would __16.__ to hire additional help but cannot afford to pay minimum wage.

Con: We are __17.__ to disagree with our colleagues. They may have __18.__ with experts, but they have __19.__ historical facts. Mistreatment of young workers __20.__ frequently in the past. By lowering wages for young persons, we would encourage similar behavior.

prefer
occurred
conferred
compelling
refer
compel
conference
compelled
omitted

Complete the Sentences
1.
2.
3.
4.
5.
6.
7.
8.
9.
10.
11.

Use Context Clues
12.
13.
14.
15.
16.
17.
18.
19.
20.

Connections to WRITING

Proofread a Paragraph

First proofread the paragraph below for ten misspelled words. Then rewrite the paragraph. Write the spelling words correctly and make the corrections indicated by the proofreading marks.

¶ *At a recent Safety conferance, students were asked if they thought that bicycle riders should be compeled by law to wear helmets. Many students said that they would preffer that the decision be left to them. I disagree. My preference is for a law that would compell bicyclists to wear helmets. according to*
head ≡
research, thousands of people suffer serious ⋀injuries from bicycle accidents each year. You can infur, therefore, that if people wear helmets, the occurance of injuries will decline. If you don't believe me, you can reffer to research that proves that wearing
by
safety helmets reduces the chance of serious head injuries⋀more
%
than 75⋀. That is a compeling statistic and should not be omited from the argument!

Proofreading Marks

≡	Capital Letter
/	Small Letter
⋀	Add
℮	Delete
⊙	Add a Period
¶	Indent

ARGUMENT Writing Prompt

Write a Paragraph

Write a paragraph supporting or challenging an issue. Choose an issue about which you have a strong opinion.

- State the issue and present your opinion.
- Use as many spelling words as you can.
- Proofread for grammar, capitalization, and punctuation.
- Circle three words you are unsure about. Check their spelling in a print or online dictionary.

Transfer

The Latin root **mit** means "to send" or "to let go." In your Spelling Journal, write two verbs with this root. Add the inflectional endings **-ed** and **-ing** to each word. For example, **commit, committed, committing**.

Word Study

Syllables and Stress			
1.			
2.			
3.			
4.			
5.			
6.			
7.			
8.			
9.			
10.			
11.			
12.			
13.			
14.			
15.			

Syllables and Stress

1.	2.	3.	4.
assume	conference	preference	omitting
compelling	remittance	autumn	occur
infer	refer	condemn	propel
autumnal	occurred	inferred	reference
condemnation	recurring	practice	occurrence
conferred	referring	resignation	remit
practical	prefer	omit	compel
recur	remitting	confer	preferred
omitted	compelled	recurrence	propelled

Syllables and Stress

The stressed syllable is underlined in each word below. Each word has at least one related word in the list above. Write the related words and underline the stressed syllable in those words. Circle the word if the stress shifts to a different syllable when the ending is added.

1–2. re<u>fer</u>	9–10. com<u>pel</u>
3–4. oc<u>cur</u>	11–12. re<u>cur</u>
5–6. pre<u>fer</u>	13–14. re<u>mit</u>
7–8. con<u>fer</u>	15. in<u>fer</u>

Silent and Sounded Consonants

Silent and Sounded Consonants			
16.			
17.			
18.			
19.			
20.			

Many words, such as **sign** and **solemn,** have silent letters. Sometimes when suffixes are added to these words, the silent letters become sounded, as in **signal** or **solemnity**. Use the list above to complete the following exercises. Circle the letter that is silent in the base word but sounded in the suffixed word.

16. Write the suffixed form of **resign**.

17–20. Write two base words that have a silent consonant and their suffixed forms.

Social Studies
Word Hunt

Read the paragraphs below. Look for words in which word stress can change when a suffix is added.

The island nation of Japan seldom occurs to people when picturing ancient castles. Most people simply assume all the world's castles were built in Europe, but actually, the ancient Japanese were highly skilled in the practice of castle building. There were many battles among neighboring warlords, and being invaded by enemies was a common occurrence.

Unlike European castles with their straight walls and tall lookout towers, the Japanese preference was for tall sloping walls which omitted all windows on the lower portion. Japanese builders were compelled to make sloping walls in order to bear the tons of weight created by thick stone walls, massive trees used in the framework inside, and heavy stone roofs. Such heavy construction proved to be very practical for basic survival, as strong typhoons and powerful earthquakes are the source of recurring disasters in mountainous Japan. Himeji Castle (hi-MAY-jee KA-sul) in central Japan has protected its people for 700 years despite devastating storms, earthquakes, and even wartime bombing.

But like castles everywhere, Japan's massive castles were superb at repelling enemies and compelling them to turn away in resignation, unable to get in. Attackers climbing the castle's sloping walls found a terrible surprise above. Himeji Castle had narrow slits at the top of each wall, through which warriors inside could shoot arrows and propel burning torches. Even worse, warriors could pour rocks and boiling oil onto the attackers below. Today, of course, we feel horror and condemnation at the idea of such brutality.

1. _____
2. _____
3. _____
4. _____
5. _____
6. _____
7. _____
8. _____
9. _____

1–6. Write the words in which the final consonant of the base word is doubled in a stressed syllable when the suffix is added.

7–9. Write the words in which the stress shifts to a different syllable when the suffix is added and the final consonant is not doubled.

113

Connections to THINKING

Read the spelling words and sentences.

1.	avocado	*avocado*	We added slices of ripe **avocado** to the salad.
2.	stampede	*stampede*	Lightning caused the cattle to **stampede**.
3.	cafeteria	*cafeteria*	Our friends eat lunch in the **cafeteria**.
4.	rodeo	*rodeo*	Dad took us to a Western **rodeo**.
5.	mustang	*mustang*	The wild **mustang** reared on its hind legs.
6.	iguana	*iguana*	An **iguana** moved slowly across the rocks.
7.	lariat	*lariat*	The cowhand used a **lariat** to rescue the calf.
8.	sierra	*sierra*	They hiked and camped in the **sierra**.
9.	tornado	*tornado*	That dark funnel cloud looks like a **tornado**.
10.	cinch	*cinch*	The **cinch** on the horse's saddle came loose.
11.	fiesta	*fiesta*	We danced and ate Spanish food at the **fiesta**.
12.	mosquito	*mosquito*	A **mosquito** was buzzing in my ear.
13.	cabana	*cabana*	You can change clothes in the beach **cabana**.
14.	bravado	*bravado*	That show of **bravado** covered up his terror.
15.	mesa	*mesa*	From afar, the **mesa** looked like a huge table.
16.	canyon	*canyon*	A stream ran along the bottom of the **canyon**.
17.	pronto	*pronto*	Please take your muddy shoes off **pronto**!
18.	siesta	*siesta*	After a short **siesta**, Jack felt rested.
19.	patio	*patio*	She sits outside on the brick **patio** to read.
20.	tortilla	*tortilla*	He wrapped the chicken mixture in a **tortilla**.

Think & Sort the spelling words.

1–7. Write the words that end with the **long o** sound.

8–15. Write the words that end with the **schwa** sound.

16. Write the word that ends in **e-consonant-e**.

17–20. Write the words that end in a consonant.

Remember

The English language includes many words from Spanish. The Spanish spelling is sometimes retained.

Ends with a long o

1.
2.
3.
4.
5.
6.
7.

Ends with schwa

8.
9.
10.
11.
12.
13.
14.
15.

Ends with e-consonant-e

16.

Ends with a consonant

17.
18.
19.
20.

Connections to VOCABULARY

Word Meanings

Write a spelling word related in meaning to complete each group.

1. festival, holiday, _____
2. plateau, tableland, _____
3. reptile, lizard, _____
4. windstorm, cyclone, _____
5. insect, bug, _____
6. courtyard, deck, _____
7. bathhouse, shelter, _____
8. restaurant, coffee shop, _____

Spelling Patterns

Write a spelling word to complete each sentence. The underlined words in the sentences are contained in the spelling words.

9. I am ill and do not feel like eating my soup or my _____ .
10. You must have gotten that tan while you were watching the _____ race across the prairie.
11. When we all stamp our feet, the noise sounds like a _____ of wild horses.
12. I can see there is not any way to climb into the _____ on horseback.
13. Paul wrote an ode to those who rode in the _____ .
14. Here is an ad for the _____ sale at the fruit market.

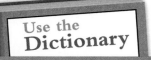

Use the
Dictionary

In a dictionary, words that are acceptable in conversation but unsuitable for formal writing are labeled *Informal* or *Slang*. The definitions below appear in the **Spelling Dictionary**. Write a spellling word for each definition.

15. *Slang.* Something easy to accomplish.
16. *Informal.* Without delay.
17. A long rope with a running noose for catching livestock.
18. A rest or nap.
19. False bravery.
20. A rugged range of mountains.

Word Meanings

1. _____
2. _____
3. _____
4. _____
5. _____
6. _____
7. _____
8. _____

Spelling Patterns

9. _____
10. _____
11. _____
12. _____
13. _____
14. _____

Use the Dictionary

15. _____
16. _____
17. _____
18. _____
19. _____
20. _____

Connections to READING

avocado	stampede	cafeteria	rodeo	mustang
iguana	lariat	sierra	tornado	cinch
fiesta	mosquito	cabana	bravado	mesa
canyon	pronto	siesta	patio	tortilla

Solve the Analogies

Write the spelling word that best completes each analogy.

1. **Red** is to **tomato** as **green** is to _____ .
2. **Woods** is to **cabin** as **beach** is to _____ .
3. **Chirp** is to **cricket** as **buzz** is to _____ .
4. **Clown** is to **circus** as **cattle roper** is to _____ .
5. **Bird** is to **hawk** as **lizard** is to _____ .

Complete the Sentences

Write the spelling word that completes each sentence.

6. We often grill chicken outside and eat it on our _____ .
7. As he prepared to rope the calf, Jim checked his _____ to be sure it was not twisted.
8. They descended into the _____ on donkeys.
9. Mom said to clean up the mess _____ !
10. A leather _____ held the saddle securely.
11. We all sometimes disguise our fear with _____ .
12. Our school _____ serves breakfast, lunch, and dinner.
13. Their camp is sponsoring a _____ with activities that will go on all weekend.

Use Context Clues

Write spelling words from the box to complete the paragraph.

Our hiking club trekked along the jagged peaks of the
14. . After a strenuous climb, we each ate a corn **15.**
with chili and cheese. Then we settled down for a **16.** .
As we rested, our guide told us about the first time he saw
a **17.** of horses. He had been traveling across a flat **18.**
when he spied a lone **19.** . It was eerily quiet. Moments
later he heard the thunderous sound of galloping horses. He
said the dust they kicked up looked like a swirling **20.** .

stampede
mesa
tornado
sierra
siesta
mustang
tortilla

Solve the Analogies
1.
2.
3.
4.
5.

Complete the Sentences
6.
7.
8.
9.
10.
11.
12.
13.

Use Context Clues
14.
15.
16.
17.
18.
19.
20.

Connections to WRITING

Proofread a Paragraph

Proofread the paragraph below for ten misspelled words. Then rewrite the paragraph. Write the spelling words correctly and make the corrections indicated by the proofreading marks.

I support the laws congress has passed to protect wild horses. Last year in New Mexico, I saw stallions and mares stampeed across a messa. I also watched a mustange climb out of a steep canion. Our Guide tried to use a lariet to pull the horse to safety, but that magnificent animal did not need help. It climbed free on its own and raced away as fast as a tornedo. I knew that its spirit should never be broken with a saddle and tightly fastened sinch. The horse reminded me of the American pioneer spirit that valued true courage and strength, not mere bravadoe. I continued to think about the horse during our afternoon seista on the pateo, and I'm sure I will always remember it!

NARRATIVE Writing Prompt

Write a Paragraph

Write a paragraph about something that symbolizes the American spirit for you. Choose an animal or object and explain why you chose it. Explain why you think it should be protected.

- Follow the form used in the proofreading example.
- Use as many spelling words as you can.
- Proofread for grammar, capitalization, and punctuation.
- Circle three words you are unsure about. Check their spelling in a print or online dictionary.

Transfer

In your Spelling Journal, write three words that come from Spanish for each of the following categories: food, animals, clothing. Use words that are not spelling words from this unit.

Word Study

alligator	stampede	fiesta	cabana	tortilla	junta
burro	cafeteria	mosquito	bravado	armadillo	gazpacho
guitar	rodeo	canyon	mesa	bonanza	serape
hammock	mustang	iguana	pronto	embargo	aficionado
plaza	sierra	lariat	siesta	guerrilla	bolero
avocado	tornado	cinch	patio	vigilante	palmetto

Spanish Spellings

Even though the English language borrows Spanish words, the spellings are sometimes different. For example, the English word **guitar** is **guitarra** in Spanish. Look at the following Spanish words below and write the English word from the box above.

1. estampida   **3.** cincha   **5.** cañón

2. hamaca   **4.** reata   **6.** lagarto

Spanish Pronunciations

When an English word is borrowed from Spanish, the spelling is often retained, but the pronunciation is different. Look at the Spanish pronunciations below. Write the corresponding English word.

7. /plä′ sä/   **9.** /prōn′ tō/   **11.** /rō dä′ ō/

8. /vē hē län′ tä/   **10.** /kä bä′ ñä/   **12.** /kä′ fĕ tĕ rĕ′ ä/

Meaning Mastery

Write a spelling word from the box that is the Spanish word for each English word below.

13. party   **17.** donkey

14. mountain   **18.** jackpot, source of great wealth

15. lizard   **19.** chilled soup

16. flatbread   **20.** an admirer, a fan

Spanish Spellings

1.

2.

3.

4.

5.

6.

Spanish Pronunciations

7.

8.

9.

10.

11.

12.

Meaning Mastery

13.

14.

15.

16.

17.

18.

19.

20.

Language Arts
Word Hunt

Read the paragraphs below. Look for words which come from Spanish.

The English language is actually a collection of words from many other languages, such as ancient Latin, Greek, French, German, and in the last few hundred years, Spanish. These borrowed words usually retain their original meaning, but only a few manage to keep their original pronunciation. For example, greetings such as *ciao* and *bon voyage* are commonly used in English, but few of them sound anything like they do back in their original countries!

Food-related words from other countries are common in English, such as *pasta, avocado, papaya, spaghetti, gazpacho, chow mein,* and *burrito*. Plants and animals are another frequent source for borrowed words, such as *palmetto, cactus, parrot, mustang, gorilla, armadillo, alligator, cougar, burro, iguana,* and *mosquito*. Many of these words seem so ordinary in English that we forget they are borrowed from other languages.

Perhaps not surprisingly, many borrowed words name things in our surroundings, both at home and in the world around us. These include words such as *sofa, veranda, garage, hammock, avenue, cafeteria, plaza, cul de sac,* and *boulevard*. Geographical examples include *plateau, mesa, canyon,* and *savannah*. Weather and environment words are another category, and include such familiar words as *typhoon, tornado, volcano,* and *blizzard*.

So many words in so many areas of our lives come to us from foreign languages. Some are clearly foreign, such as *serape, kimono,* and *beret,* but many others, like *polo, rodeo, pronto,* and *bonanza* have become so familiar to us that we no longer think of them as foreign words.

1. _____
2. _____
3. _____
4. _____
5. _____
6. _____
7. _____
8. _____
9. _____
10. _____

1–10. Write the words in the second paragraph that come from Spanish. Use an online dictionary to check word origin.

Assess for Transfer

Unit 13

1. _____
2. _____
3. _____
4. _____
5. _____

Unit 14

6. _____
7. _____
8. _____
9. _____
10. _____

Unit 16

11. _____
12. _____
13. _____
14. _____
15. _____
16. _____
17. _____

Unit 17

18. _____
19. _____
20. _____

Units 13–17

Assessment

Each word in the box fits one of the spelling patterns or rules you have studied over the past five weeks. Read the unit descriptions. Then write each assessment word under the unit number it fits.

Unit 13

1–5. The suffix **-ly** may be added to adjectives such as **urgent** to form adverbs.

Unit 14

6–10. The suffixes **-able** and **-ible** may be added to base words or word roots to form adjectives.

Unit 15

It is important to know the spelling of words that are frequently misspelled.

Unit 16

11–17. A final consonant preceded by a single vowel is doubled when adding a suffix that begins with a vowel, except when the accent is on—or shifts to—the first syllable.

Unit 17

18–20. The English language includes many words from Spanish. The Spanish spelling is sometimes retained.

Words for Assessment

defer
presentable
beautifully
enchilada
inedible
likely
preferring
referred
predictable
palomino
stirring
enormously
rapidly
guitarist
deferred
unforgivable
controllable
stirred
slightly
convertible

Review

Unit 13: Suffix: -ly

absolutely	fortunately	particular	necessarily	particularly
immediately	accurately	readily	approximately	absolute

Write the spelling words that complete the paragraph.

On one __1.__ day last October, Mario wanted to try a new chocolate cake recipe. Mario __2.__ liked chocolate cake. Since he __3.__ had everything he needed, he began __4.__ after lunch. He knew he must measure each ingredient __5.__ in order to have good results. Although Mario did not __6.__ need two cakes, he made two anyway. Then he would be able to have a party. The two cakes would be enough for __7.__ twenty friends. When the cakes were ready, Mario thought they were __8.__ delicious. He thought his friends would __9.__ agree. These cakes would be the __10.__ top of Mario's baking career.

Unit 14: Suffix: -able, -ible

uncomfortable	eligible	permissible	remarkable	unmistakable
considerable	recognizable	suitable	noticeable	disagreeable

Write the spelling word that is formed from each of these words.

11. comfort
12. consider
13. mistake

14. remark
15. notice
16. suit

Write a spelling word for each clue.

17. unpleasant
18. easily identified

19. qualified; worthy
20. allowable

Unit 13

1. _____
2. _____
3. _____
4. _____
5. _____
6. _____
7. _____
8. _____
9. _____
10. _____

Unit 14

11. _____
12. _____
13. _____
14. _____
15. _____
16. _____
17. _____
18. _____
19. _____
20. _____

Review

Unit 15

1. _____
2. _____
3. _____
4. _____
5. _____
6. _____
7. _____
8. _____
9. _____
10. _____

Unit 16

11. _____
12. _____
13. _____
14. _____
15. _____
16. _____
17. _____
18. _____
19. _____
20. _____

Unit 15: Frequently Misspelled Words

breathe	usually	vacuum	actual	variety
coupon	maneuver	curiosity	peculiar	courtesy

Write a spelling word to complete each analogy.

1. **Mouth** is to **taste** as **nose** is to _____ .
2. **Unnecessary** is to **necessary** as **unusually** is to _____ .
3. **Really** is to **real** as **actually** is to _____ .
4. **Push** is to **shove** as **move** is to _____ .
5. **Cotton** is to **shirt** as **paper** is to _____ .
6. **Wonderful** is to **marvelous** as **strange** is to _____ .
7. **Broom** is to **sweep** as **electric appliance** is to _____ .
8. **Thoughtfulness** is to **consideration** as **politeness** is to _____ .
9. **Generous** is to **generosity** as **curious** is to _____ .
10. **Heavy** is to **light** as **sameness** is to _____ .

Unit 16: Adding Suffixes That Change Stress

occur	preference	infer	occurrence	prefer
conference	preferred	occurred	confer	inferred

Write the spelling words that fit each sentence.

11–12. We will _____ at the 10:00 a.m. _____ .

13–14. The agent entered my seating _____ . I have always _____ to sit on the aisle.

15–16. As a daily _____ , we used to watch the programs that _____ between 4:30 and 5:30 p.m.

17–18. Did it ever _____ to you that I _____ not to be disturbed while I study?

19–20. Shall I _____ from the pleased look on your face that you have _____ the correct answer?

Unit 17: Words From Spanish

avocado	stampede	cafeteria	rodeo	mustang
sierra	tornado	fiesta	mosquito	canyon

Write the spelling word that replaces each underlined word or words.

1. An annoying <u>insect</u> buzzed around noisily.
2. That is a beautiful <u>wild horse</u>.
3. The building was blown down in the <u>storm</u>.
4. My salad includes sliced <u>fruit</u>.
5. Rusty will rope a horse in the <u>western show</u>.
6. Thunder echoed through the <u>gorge</u>.
7. Everyone had a great time at the <u>festival</u>.
8. We will get to camp in the high <u>rugged mountains</u>.
9. What's for lunch today in the <u>lunchroom</u>?
10. We were afraid that the cattle would <u>suddenly rush</u>.

Unit 17

1. _____
2. _____
3. _____
4. _____
5. _____
6. _____
7. _____
8. _____
9. _____
10. _____

Spelling Study Strategy

Spelling Tic-Tac-Toe

Practicing spelling words can be fun if you make it into a game. Play this game with a partner.

1. Both you and your partner write a list of spelling words. Trade lists.

2. Draw a tic-tac-toe board on a piece of paper. Decide who will use **O** and who will use **X**.

3. Ask your partner to call the first word on your spelling list to you. Spell it aloud. If you spell it correctly, make an **X** or an **O** on the tic-tac-toe board. If you misspell the word, ask your partner to spell it aloud for you. You miss your turn.

4. Now you call a word from your partner's spelling list.

5. Keep playing until one of you makes tic-tac-toe. Keep starting over until you both have practiced all your spelling words.

Directions: Read the introduction and the passage that follows. Then read each question and fill in the correct answer on your answer sheet.

1. His manuever was the actual cause of the accident.

   What change, if any, should be made to these sentences?

   (A) Change <u>manuever</u> to *maneuver*

   (B) Change <u>actual</u> to *actuel*

   (C) Change <u>accident</u> to *acident*

   (D) Make no change

2. **Hiking in the sierra requires considerable strength and a curiousity about nature and adventure.**

   Which word in the sentences is spelled **incorrectly**?

   (A) sierra

   (B) considerable

   (C) curiousity

   (D) nature

3. **You are eligible to win a remarkible prize. This chance doesn't occur every day!**

   Which word in the sentences is spelled **incorrectly**?

   (A) eligible

   (B) remarkible

   (C) occur

   (D) every day

4. **The boys usualy prefer to eat in the cafeteria.**

   What change, if any, should be made to this sentence?

   (A) Change <u>usualy</u> to *usually*

   (B) Change <u>prefer</u> to *preferr*

   (C) Change <u>cafeteria</u> to *cafitiria*

   (D) Make no change

5. **Read the following list of alphabetized words.**

   > **particular**
   > **peculiar**
   > **permissible**
   > **prefer**
   > **preferring**

   The word **preference** should follow the word

   (A) peculiar

   (B) permissible

   (C) prefer

   (D) preferring

6. **As you hike higher into the sierra, it can become uncomfortable and hard to breath.**

   What change, if any, should be made to this sentence?

   (A) Change <u>sierra</u> to *siera*

   (B) Change <u>uncomfortable</u> to *uncomfortible*

   (C) Change <u>breath</u> to *breathe*

   (D) Make no change

7. Read the following list of alphabetized words.

   > **canyon**
   > **confer**
   > **conference**
   > **coupon**
   > **curiosity**

   The word **courtesy** should follow the word

   (A) canyon

   (B) conference

   (C) coupon

   (D) curiosity

GO ON →

8. Nanny is recognizable by her peculiar laugh. Its similarity to the bray of a burro is unmistakeable.

Which word in the sentence is spelled incorrectly?

(A) recognizable

(B) peculiar

(C) burro

(D) unmistakeable

9. The tornado caused absolute destruction. Fourtunately, everyone survived.

What change, if any, should be made to these sentences?

(A) Change tornado to toronado

(B) Change absolute to abselute

(C) Change destruction to distruction

(D) Change Fourtunately to Fortunately

10. The coupon offered a considerable discount, particularly for a variaty of electronic devices, such as mp3 players and PDAs.

Which word in the sentence is spelled incorrectly?

(A) coupon

(B) considerable

(C) particularly

(D) variaty

11. Immediately after the rodeo, aproximately 4,000 people rushed to the exit. It was like a human stampede!

What change, if any, should be made to this sentence?

(A) Change Immediately to Imediately

(B) Change rodeo to roadeo

(C) Change aproximately to approximately

(D) Change stampede to stampeed

12. The housekeeper said, "I prefer this particular vaccuum cleaner."

Which word in the sentence is spelled incorrectly?

(A) housekeeper

(B) prefer

(C) particular

(D) vaccuum

13. Which of the following words is spelled incorrectly?

(A) noticable

(B) avocado

(C) courtesy

(D) fiesta

14. Jessie accurately infered from her reading that Mr. Collins was not a suitable husband for Elizabeth.

What change, if any, should be made to this sentence?

(A) Change accurately to acurately

(B) Change infered to inferred

(C) Change suitable to suiteable

(D) Make no change

15. Gravity is only noticeable in the fall. Do you think my joke is silly or absolutly hilarious?

Which word in the sentence is spelled incorrectly?

(A) Gravity

(B) noticeable

(C) absolutly

(D) hilarious

STOP

Writer's Workshop

Grammar, Usage, and Mechanics
Identifying Modifiers: Adjectives

An **adjective** is a word that modifies a noun or pronoun. Some adjectives tell what kind. Others, such as **many** and **few,** tell how many. The adjectives **this, that, these,** and **those** tell which ones. The articles **a, an,** and **the** are also adjectives.

> **These twenty** contestants will compete for **the grand** prize.
> **The clever** leader showed **remarkable** courage.
> **Some** poets use **unexpected** rhymes.

Practice Activity

A. Decide which boldfaced word is an adjective. Then write the word.

1. We **calmly** endured an **uncomfortable** silence.
2. Douye showed his **considerable** skill as he **vaulted** over the pole.
3. We thought the **movie** had a **peculiar** ending.
4. There isn't any **noticeable** difference **between** the positions of the two candidates.
5. Nellima **usually** finds a **suitable** solution.
6. Let's share this **delicious avocado**.
7. **She** is from the **great** state of Texas.
8. Her **enormous** smile made **everyone** happy.
9. What is the **approximate** distance **between** rows?
10. Ms. Pullon **needs** an **immediate** response.

B. Write the noun that is modified by the underlined adjective.

11. We took many pictures of the <u>beautiful</u> canyon.
12. Because of meteorological instruments, a tornado is <u>predictable</u>.
13. The <u>wild</u> mustang raced across the mesa.
14. That vacuum is <u>suitable</u> for commercial use.
15. The chicken enchilada she fixed is <u>inedible</u>.

A
1. _____
2. _____
3. _____
4. _____
5. _____
6. _____
7. _____
8. _____
9. _____
10. _____
B
11. _____
12. _____
13. _____
14. _____
15. _____

The Writing Process: Informative/Explanatory
Writing an E-mail

PREWRITING

E-mail is a convenient way to communicate with people all over the world. Some people have key pals, or electronic pen pals. E-mailing a key pal in another country is a great way to learn about another culture. You can find facts and details about other countries or cultures at the library or on the Internet at sites such as the Internet Public Library KidSpace (www.ipl.org/div/kidspace). As you think about your e-mail, write a list of questions you would like to ask your key pal. Ask your teacher to help you find someone to e-mail your questions to.

DRAFTING

Use your questions to write the e-mail. List your questions so they are easy to read. Use the proper Netiquette, such as typing a clear subject line, avoiding special type features, and including a detailed salutation (full name and e-mail address). Use as many spelling words as possible.

REVISING

When you have finished your first draft, read your e-mail from beginning to end. Check to see if you have included the correct e-mail address. Did you use the proper Netiquette? Did you include all of your questions? Now write your final draft.

EDITING

Print out a hard copy and use the editing checklist to proofread your e-mail. Be sure to use proofreading marks when you make corrections. Circle three words you are unsure about and check their spelling in a dictionary.

PUBLISHING

Send your e-mail to your key pal. When you receive a response, share it with your class.

EDITING CHECKLIST

Spelling

✓ Circle words that contain the spelling patterns and rules learned in Units 13–17.

✓ Check the circled words in a print or online dictionary.

✓ Check for other spelling errors.

Capital Letters

✓ Capitalize important words in the subject line.

✓ Capitalize the first word in each sentence.

✓ Capitalize proper nouns.

Punctuation

✓ End each sentence with the correct punctuation.

✓ Use commas, apostrophes, and quotation marks correctly.

Grammar, Usage, and Mechanics

✓ Use adjectives correctly to make sentences more interesting.

Connections to THINKING

Read the spelling words and sentences.

1.	activities	*activities*	We like to do craft **activities**.
2.	potatoes	*potatoes*	I love **potatoes** and gravy.
3.	mix-ups	*mix-ups*	A few **mix-ups** ruined the plan.
4.	copies	*copies*	I made four **copies** of the letter.
5.	shelves	*shelves*	We put your books on the **shelves**.
6.	spoonfuls	*spoonfuls*	I ate several **spoonfuls** of soup.
7.	mothers-in-law	*mothers-in-law*	The **mothers-in-law** sat in front.
8.	echoes	*echoes*	I yelled and listened for **echoes**.
9.	knives	*knives*	Please dry the **knives** and forks.
10.	opportunities	*opportunities*	I had two **opportunities** to play.
11.	tomatoes	*tomatoes*	He sliced **tomatoes** for the salad.
12.	cupfuls	*cupfuls*	Next, add two **cupfuls** of flour.
13.	fathers-in-law	*fathers-in-law*	The **fathers-in-law** may sit here.
14.	thieves	*thieves*	The police arrested the **thieves**.
15.	boundaries	*boundaries*	Play in the **boundaries** of our yard.
16.	volcanoes	*volcanoes*	Hawaii was formed by **volcanoes**.
17.	passersby	*passersby*	We handed the fliers to **passersby**.
18.	teaspoonfuls	*teaspoonfuls*	I added two **teaspoonfuls** of sugar.
19.	companies	*companies*	Several **companies** sell mustard.
20.	mosquitoes	*mosquitoes*	I can hear **mosquitoes** buzzing.

Think & Sort the spelling words.

1–5. Write the spelling words that end with **consonant** + **o** + **es**.

6–8. Write the spelling words in which the final **f** was changed to **v** before adding **es**.

9–13. Write the spelling words in which the final **y** was changed to **i** before adding **es**.

14–17. Write the spelling words that are compound words.

18–20. Write the spelling words that have the suffix **-ful**.

Remember

Plural nouns are formed in a variety of ways.

Consonant + o + es

1.
2.
3.
4.
5.

f to v + es

6.
7.
8.

y to i + es

9.
10.
11.
12.
13.

Compound words

14.
15.
16.
17.

Words with the suffix -ful

18.
19.
20.

Connections to VOCABULARY

Word Meanings

Write a spelling word to match each definition.

1. more than one of a plant that is a starchy, edible tuber
2. more than one of a plant that has an edible, fleshy, usually red fruit
3. more than one of a geological formation that is a crack or hole in the earth's crust through which molten lava and gases can erupt

Word Groups

Write a spelling word to complete each group.

4. reproductions, duplicates, _____
5. businesses, groups, _____
6. mayflies, gnats, _____
7. events, tasks, _____
8. robbers, burglars, _____
9. daughters, mothers, _____
10. sons, fathers, _____
11. foul-ups, mistakes, _____
12. edges, limits, _____

Use the Dictionary

An entry shows the plural form of a noun (labeled *pl.*) when the plural is **irregular** (formed other than by adding **s** or **es**). An entry also shows a regular plural when the spelling might pose a problem. Write the plural forms of the following nouns. Use the **Spelling Dictionary** if you need help.

13. passerby
14. echo
15. opportunity
16. shelf
17. spoonful
18. cupful
19. knife
20. teaspoonful

Word Meanings
1.
2.
3.
Word Groups
4.
5.
6.
7.
8.
9.
10.
11.
12.
Use the Dictionary
13.
14.
15.
16.
17.
18.
19.
20.

activities	potatoes	mix-ups	copies
shelves	spoonfuls	mothers-in-law	echoes
knives	opportunities	tomatoes	cupfuls
fathers-in-law	thieves	boundaries	volcanoes
passersby	teaspoonfuls	companies	mosquitoes

Complete the Analogies

Write a spelling word to complete each analogy.

1. **Father** is to **father-in-law** as **fathers** is to _____ .
2. **Leaf** is to **leaves** as **knife** is to _____ .
3. **Pocket** is to **pocketfuls** as **spoon** is to _____ .
4. **Sister** is to **sisters-in-law** as **mother** is to _____ .
5. **Jelly** is to **grapes** as **ketchup** is to _____ .
6. **Hobo** is to **hoboes** as **volcano** is to _____ .
7. **Hero** is to **heroes** as **echo** is to _____ .
8. **Wife** is to **wives** as **thief** is to _____ .
9. **Party** is to **parties** as **copy** is to _____ .
10. **Chin-up** is to **chin-ups** as **mix-up** is to _____ .

Complete the Sentences

Write the spelling word that best completes each sentence.

11. Which after-school _____ did you sign up for?
12. We will have many _____ to take pictures along the scenic drive.
13. This bug repellent will keep the _____ from biting you.
14. He worked for three different _____ before he started his own business.
15. We used the trees and bushes as _____ for our soccer game.

Use Context Clues

Write spelling words from the box to complete the paragraph.

The voices of farmers calling out their wares ring through the open-air market. Strolling **16.** are tempted by the colorful produce piled high on **17.** and in bins. There are green and red peppers, **18.** , melons, and oranges. As we wander, we sample **19.** of homemade jam and buy **20.** of fresh-squeezed juice.

> shelves
> teaspoonfuls
> cupfuls
> passersby
> potatoes

Complete the Analogies
1.
2.
3.
4.
5.
6.
7.
8.
9.
10.

Complete the Sentences
11.
12.
13.
14.
15.

Use Context Clues
16.
17.
18.
19.
20.

Connections to WRITING

Proofread a Short Story in Process

First proofread the short story excerpt below for ten misspelled words. Then rewrite it. Write the spelling words correctly and make the corrections indicated by the proofreading marks.

¶ Dr. kim Su recently developed a new concentrated plant food to be used by farms and other agricultural companys. Always looking for oppertunitys to get rich without working, a local band of theefs plotted to steal the miraculous plant food from the laboratory. However, through a series of mixups, the burglars took the wrong boxes from the shelfs. ¶ Alongside a nearby farm, the getaway truck suddenly overturned, and the concoction it spilled into several rows of pottatoes and tomattoes. The crooks and several passerbys immediately saw some strange activities in the field. Mounds that looked like volcanos began to form, and the echos of their rumblings could be heard from miles away ⊙

Proofreading Marks

≡	Capital Letter
/	Small Letter
∧	Add
ℰ	Delete
⊙	Add a Period
¶	Indent

NARRATIVE Writing Prompt
Complete a Short Story

Use your imagination to complete the short story in the proofreading sample above. Before you begin, think about what will happen next. You may choose to complete the mystery by explaining exactly what was happening in the field and why.

- Use as many spelling words as you can.
- Proofread for grammar, capitalization, and punctuation.
- Circle three words you are unsure about. Check their spelling in a print or online dictionary.

Transfer

Look at your spelling words from Unit 4 in this book. In your Spelling Journal, write the plural forms of the nouns on that list. Some of the words are already plural, and others (such as **self-esteem**) do not have a plural form.

Word Study

heroes	loyalties	tomatoes	mothers-in-law	passersby	shelves
knives	melodies	groceries	teaspoonfuls	boundaries	cupfuls
echoes	analyses	glossaries	opportunities	companies	thieves
loaves	centuries	spoonfuls	fathers-in-law	mosquitoes	criteria
copies	mix-ups	activities	cliffhangers	properties	abilities
data	potatoes	wharves	by-products	volcanoes	treaties

Irregular Plurals

Write the plural forms of the words below.

1. datum   2. analysis   3. criterion

Meaning Mastery

Write the word or words that belong in each group.

4–5. brothers-in-law, wives, husbands, sisters-in-law
6. dictionaries, indices, thesauri
7. foodstuffs, ingredients
8–10. bowlfuls, handfuls, tablespoonfuls
11. harmonies, lyrics, musical arrangements
12. years, decades, millennia

Pronunciations

Write the spelling words with the following pronunciations. Use your **Spelling Dictionary,** if necessary.

13. /lōvz/   14. /kŏp′ ēz/   15. /ə bĭl′ ĭ tēz/   16. /bī′ prŏd′ əkts/

Plural Possessives

The singular possessive form of each singular word is given. Write the plural possessive form.

17. the knife's blade   the _____ blades
18. the activity's goal   the _____ goals
19. the mosquito's wings   the _____ wings
20. the cliffhanger's outcome   the _____ outcomes

Irregular Plurals

1.
2.
3.

Meaning Mastery

4.
5.
6.
7.
8.
9.
10.
11.
12.

Pronunciations

13.
14.
15.
16.

Plural Possessives

17.
18.
19.
20.

Social Studies
Word Hunt

Read the paragraphs below. Look for plural nouns.

Folktales, like other stories told aloud, are handed down through families so many times that the most recent versions are mere echoes of the earliest versions. They're similar, but not exactly the same! One such folktale is the story of the young boy Epaminondas. If you were to tell the story, you could change the name, you could change the country, and you could even change the activities that take place. The important thing to keep is the funny part of the story and the mix-ups that happen.

Here's the quick version. Young Epaminondas has many opportunities to leave the boundaries of his own town to visit his aunts and his grandmothers. These relatives sometimes live in the forest, or beyond some old volcanoes, or in a nearby village. Usually these families give him a gift to share back home, such as cake, some butter, puppies, or loaves of bread.

The boy's mix-ups are the core of all these stories, and the sequence of his mistakes is what makes them funny. When the relatives give him a piece of cake to take home for his parents, he clutches it tightly in his fists and runs home. Of course it is crumbled when he arrives. He's told to wrap it carefully next time and put it under his hat. The next time, however, the gift is butter, so of course it melts under his hat! Each time, his mistakes come from trying too diligently to be obedient. He wraps puppies in cool leaves and drags loaves of bread home on a leash. And never does he even ask passersby for their advice!

1. _____
2. _____
3. _____
4. _____
5. _____
6. _____
7. _____
8. _____
9. _____
10. _____

1–5. Write the plural nouns in which the final **-y** changes to **-ies**.

6–7. Write the plural nouns in ending in consonant + **o** + **es**.

8–10. Write the plural compound nouns.

133

Connections to THINKING

Read the spelling words and sentences.

1.	application	*application*	I filled out an **application** for a job.
2.	asset	*asset*	Her experience is an **asset** to our company.
3.	affirm	*affirm*	Can you **affirm** your good intentions?
4.	according	*according*	We prepared it **according** to the recipe.
5.	attain	*attain*	Studying hard can help you **attain** success.
6.	applaud	*applaud*	The audience began to **applaud** loudly.
7.	assurance	*assurance*	I give you my **assurance** that I will attend.
8.	account	*account*	We opened a savings **account** at the bank.
9.	assortment	*assortment*	The box contained an **assortment** of nails.
10.	affix	*affix*	Please **affix** an address label to the box.
11.	appetite	*appetite*	This meal should satisfy your **appetite**.
12.	attempt	*attempt*	We will **attempt** to climb to the top.
13.	accustomed	*accustomed*	I am not yet **accustomed** to my new boots.
14.	approval	*approval*	I hope our choice meets with your **approval**.
15.	attire	*attire*	His holiday **attire** included a plaid tie.
16.	assemble	*assemble*	We need some tools to **assemble** the bike.
17.	appliance	*appliance*	A toaster is a useful **appliance** to have.
18.	afford	*afford*	If I save, I can **afford** to buy it myself.
19.	assert	*assert*	I will **assert** his right to a fair decision.
20.	attentive	*attentive*	She was **attentive** while I told my story.

Think & Sort the spelling words.

Circle the double consonants.

1–3. Write the words with the prefix **ad-** spelled **af**.

4–8. Write the words with the prefix **ad-** spelled **as**.

9–11. Write the words with the prefix **ad-** spelled **ac**.

12–15. Write the words with the prefix **ad-** spelled **at**.

16–20. Write the words with the prefix **ad-** spelled **ap**.

Remember

The prefix **ad-**, meaning "to" or "toward," may be assimilated into the spelling of the base word or word root. This will always result in a double consonant.

ad- spelled af

1. _____
2. _____
3. _____

ad- spelled as

4. _____
5. _____
6. _____
7. _____
8. _____

ad- spelled ac

9. _____
10. _____
11. _____

ad- spelled at

12. _____
13. _____
14. _____
15. _____

ad- spelled ap

16. _____
17. _____
18. _____
19. _____
20. _____

Connections to VOCABULARY

Word Meanings

Write a spelling word to match each definition.

1. paying attention; observant
2. usual; in the habit of
3. to clothe; one's clothing
4. to gain, reach, or accomplish
5. a useful or valuable quality
6–7. to declare positively; to state
8. to fasten or attach; a word part that is attached to a base word or a word root
9. a collection of various things
10. a statement that inspires confidence; a guarantee
11. to be able to meet the expense of
12. a device, usually operated by electricity and meant for household use

Word Structure

Add the missing prefixes to write spelling words.

13. -plication
14. -semble
15. -cording
16. -count

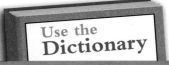

Use the Dictionary

Write a spelling word for each etymology. Use the **Spelling Dictionary** if you need help.

17. Lat. *applaudere: ad-,* to + *plaudere,* to clap
18. Lat. *appetitus,* strong desire < *appetere,* to strive after: *ad-,* toward + *petere,* to seek
19. Lat. *approbare: ad-,* to + *probare,* to test < *probus,* good
20. Lat. *attemptare: ad-,* to + *temptare,* to test

Word Meanings
1.
2.
3.
4.
5.
6.
7.
8.
9.
10.
11.
12.

Word Structure
13.
14.
15.
16.

Use the Dictionary
17.
18.
19.
20.

application	asset	affirm	according	attain
applaud	assurance	account	assortment	affix
appetite	attempt	accustomed	approval	attire
assemble	appliance	afford	assert	attentive

Replace the Words

Write a spelling word to replace the underlined word or words in each sentence.

1. What level of schooling do you plan to <u>reach</u>?
2. Give a brief <u>record</u> of your job experience.
3. Are you <u>used</u> to studying hard for tests?
4. Are you willing to <u>try</u> new tasks?
5. What is the most useful <u>valuable quality</u> you would bring to this job?
6. Are you aware that our dress code requires you to wear company <u>clothing</u> every day?
7. If you receive our <u>recommendation</u>, when can you start?
8. Please provide an <u>array or collection</u> of references from teachers and former employers.
9. Sign at the bottom to <u>assert</u> that the information is true.

10–11. You will have to <u>put together</u> the job <u>request form</u>, your references, and a cover letter.

12. Please <u>attach</u> a stamp to your envelope before mailing it.

Use Context Clues

Write spelling words from the box to complete the advertisement.

Can you __13.__ to buy new items when the old ones break? Do you have an __14.__ for greater self-reliance? Sign up for our "Repair It Right" course! We __15.__ that you will learn how to repair any small __16.__ as easily as a professional can. All of our graduates __17.__ the program, giving their __18.__ that they are now capable of making all sorts of small repairs. The only requirement for the course is an __19.__ mind; __20.__ to our satisfied graduates, you will never have to throw away a broken clock or radio again!

| appetite |
| appliance |
| according |
| assert |
| attentive |
| afford |
| assurance |
| applaud |

Replace the Words
1. _____
2. _____
3. _____
4. _____
5. _____
6. _____
7. _____
8. _____
9. _____
10. _____
11. _____
12. _____

Use Context Clues
13. _____
14. _____
15. _____
16. _____
17. _____
18. _____
19. _____
20. _____

Connections to WRITING

Proofread a Letter

Proofread the letter below for ten misspelled words. Then rewrite the letter. Write the spelling words correctly and make the corrections indicated by the proofreading marks.

Proofreading Marks	
≡	Capital Letter
/	Small Letter
∧	Add
℘	Delete
⊙	Add a Period
⌗	Indent

Frank Lee, Manager
Ed's Electronics
47 Sham Rock Ave.
Paducah, KY 42003

Dear Mr. Lee:

⌗ *Enclosed, please find my aplication for a job. Although I have an asortment of skills, my most useful asset is that I can asemble any small aplience. I also am an atentave, helpful salesperson, and I am accustumed to working efficiently and under pressure. Acording to* **my** *friends, I would be an assett to any company because I work hard to attane results. I hope my request meets with your approval.*

Yours Truly,

Sam Lorenzo

INFORMATIVE/EXPLANATORY Writing Prompt

Write a Letter

Imagine that you have invented a new appliance or piece of sports equipment. Write a letter to the U.S. Patent Office to apply for a patent.

- Explain what your invention is and the ways in which it is unique.
- Follow the form used in the proofreading example.
- Use as many spelling words as you can.
- Proofread for grammar, capitalization, and punctuation.
- Circle three words you are unsure about. Check their spelling in a print or online dictionary.

Transfer
In your Spelling Journal, brainstorm a list of three more words for each of the following **ad-** assimilated prefixes: **as, af, ac, at, ap**

Word Study

Latin Roots and Prefixes

1.
2.
3.
4.
5.
6.
7.
8.
9.
10.

Synonyms

11.
12.
13.
14.
15.
16.
17.
18.
19.
20.

accident	according	approval	assurance
attentive	accompaniment	accurate	attain
assemble	assortment	accelerate	assimilate
account	appointment	afford	affix
accolade	accountability	assistant	appetite
asset	accomplishment	attire	accumulate
attempt	attendance	affirm	appliance
affinity	appropriate	application	accustomed
applaud	assert	acclaim	attribute

Latin Roots and Prefixes

Write the spelling words with the following base words or roots. When adding the **ad-** assimilated prefix, don't forget that the new word will have a double consonant. Use a dictionary to check etymology.

1. sorte
2. compaignon
3–4. computāre
5. clāmāre
6. serere
7. petere
8. firmāre
9. tire
10. plaudere

Synonyms

For each word below, write a synonym from the word box.

11. try
12. promise
13. attach
14. honor
15. meeting
16. precise
17. mistake
18. proper
19. build up
20. quality

Math
Word Hunt

Read the paragraphs below. Look for words with the assimilated prefix **ad-**.

Just as household appliances used to be considered luxury assets, now we are so accustomed to them that they have become necessities. The same is rapidly becoming true in education. By the time young people approach high school age, it's clear that having access to a personal laptop or PC has become necessary for homework and research.

Being able to afford such expensive equipment is a problem for many young people. Fortunately, there is an assortment of financial programs available for students. According to financial-aid and admissions advisors who talk to graduating high-schoolers, colleges and banks have special loans for students who can't afford computers.

The process begins with filling in an application from the bank or college and opening one's own bank account. Both steps require approval from the student's parent or guardian, who must co-sign the application, stating that they will assume responsibility if there are any problems later.

Once these have been approved by the loan officer, it is up to the student to be attentive to his or her responsibility for making loan payments every month. These payments are not very high, but it is important to get accustomed to making regular payments every month. Usually a part-time job a few hours a week is enough. Many families affirm that a "matching funds" system works well. The parents "match" the student's payment every month. In this way, the student can have a fabulous computer and end up paying only half-price!

1. _____
2. _____
3. _____
4. _____
5. _____
6. _____
7. _____
8. _____
9. _____
10. _____

WORD SORT

Write and sort the words with the prefix **ad-** in the forms below.
- **1–2.** Write words with the prefix **ad-** spelled **af**.
- **3–5.** Write words with the prefix **ad-** spelled **as**.
- **6–9.** Write words with the prefix **ad-** spelled **ac**.
- **10.** Write the word with the prefix **ad-** spelled **at**.

Connections to THINKING

Eponyms

1. _____
2. _____
3. _____
4. _____
5. _____
6. _____

Toponyms

7. _____
8. _____
9. _____
10. _____
11. _____
12. _____
13. _____
14. _____
15. _____
16. _____
17. _____
18. _____
19. _____
20. _____

Read the spelling words and sentences.

1.	tangerine	*tangerine*	I peeled the **tangerine** and ate it.
2.	suede	*suede*	Have you seen my **suede** gloves?
3.	gardenia	*gardenia*	I placed the **gardenia** in water.
4.	calico	*calico*	The apron was made of red and blue **calico**.
5.	frankfurter	*frankfurter*	I would like mustard on my **frankfurter**.
6.	tuxedo	*tuxedo*	He wore a **tuxedo** to the wedding.
7.	angora	*angora*	My sister has a pink **angora** sweater.
8.	cardigan	*cardigan*	I got chilly, so I buttoned my **cardigan**.
9.	damask	*damask*	She bought beautiful silk **damask** curtains.
10.	cheddar	*cheddar*	I like cream cheese and **cheddar** cheese.
11.	magnolia	*magnolia*	I can smell the **magnolia** tree from here.
12.	denim	*denim*	He wore a pair of **denim** overalls.
13.	hamburger	*hamburger*	Who wants this well-done **hamburger**?
14.	cantaloupe	*cantaloupe*	My favorite melon is **cantaloupe**.
15.	satin	*satin*	The dancers wore glamorous **satin** dresses.
16.	currant	*currant*	We made homemade **currant** jelly.
17.	leotard	*leotard*	I need a new **leotard** for gymnastics class.
18.	cashmere	*cashmere*	The **cashmere** scarf kept my neck warm.
19.	hyacinth	*hyacinth*	The garden overflowed with **hyacinth** plants.
20.	camellia	*camellia*	This **camellia** looks a lot like a rose.

Think & Sort the spelling words.

1–6. Write the spelling words that are eponyms.

7–20. Write the spelling words that are toponyms.

Remember

The English language includes many words taken from names (eponyms) and places (toponyms).

Connections to VOCABULARY

Word Meanings

Write a spelling word to match each description.

1. a citrus fruit from Tangier
2. an elastic garment named after Jules Léotard
3. a patterned fabric first produced in Damascus in the Middle Ages
4. fur of a goat or a rabbit from Ankara, Turkey
5. wool from a goat; originally produced in Kashmir, India
6. a sweater that opens in the front, originally named after the Seventh Earl of Cardigan
7. a durable fabric originally from Nîmes, France (the French word for "from" is **de**)
8. a formal suit; named after Tuxedo Park, New York
9. a napped leather; from the French term **gants de Suède,** meaning "gloves from Sweden"
10. a fragrant, usually white, flower; named for Alexander Garden
11. a flower named for Hyacinthus, a figure in Greek mythology
12. a small, sour fruit; from the Middle English **raysons of coraunte,** meaning "raisins of Corinth"
13. a flower named for Pierre Magnol
14. a patterned fabric, originally from Calicut, India
15. a flower named for Georg Josef Kamel

Use the Dictionary

Write the spelling word for each respelling. In each word, circle the syllable with the primary stress. Use the **Spelling Dictionary** if you need help.

16. /kăn′ tl ōp′/
17. /chĕd′ ər/
18. /frăngk′ fər tər/
19. /hăm′ bûr′ gər/
20. /săt′ n/

Word Meanings	
1.	
2.	
3.	
4.	
5.	
6.	
7.	
8.	
9.	
10.	
11.	
12.	
13.	
14.	
15.	
Use the Dictionary	
16.	
17.	
18.	
19.	
20.	

tangerine   suede   gardenia   calico   frankfurter
tuxedo   angora   cardigan   damask   cheddar
magnolia   denim   hamburger   cantaloupe   satin
currant   leotard   cashmere   hyacinth   camellia

Complete the Restaurant Review

Write spelling words from the box to complete the restaurant review.

> calico
> cantaloupe
> cashmere
> cheddar
> currant
> denim
> frankfurter
> hamburger
> satin
> tuxedo

The Cat's Meow offers a delightful array of sights, smells, and tastes. We were greeted at the door by a friendly hostess who showed us to a table set with a cheery __1.__ tablecloth. As we read the menu, a waiter brought us a basket of fresh bread and jellies. Our favorite was the oatmeal bread with __2.__ jelly. The fruit salad of __3.__ , grapes, and bananas was delicious. The addition of a thick slice of sharp __4.__ cheese made an ordinary __5.__ extraordinary. A common __6.__ was complemented by a side order of baked beans. The restaurant offers a variety of beverages, including blended fruit juices as smooth as __7.__ . The setting is informal. Diners' attire ranged from __8.__ sweaters to __9.__ jeans. You certainly don't need a __10.__ to eat here!

Use Context Clues

Write spelling words to complete the sentences.

11. I bought a new pair of _____ shoes for the party.
12. The dancer wore a _____, tights, and ballet slippers.
13. The elegant _____ tablecloth provided the perfect background for the fine china dishes.
14. The _____ is a close relative of the orange.
15. The bottom button on her _____ was missing.
16. Camella was named after her mother's favorite flower, the _____.
17–19. She carried a bouquet of _____, _____, and _____ flowers.
20. The long fibers in her _____ sweater made her neck itch.

Complete the Restaurant Review

1.
2.
3.
4.
5.
6.
7.
8.
9.
10.

Use Context Clues

11.
12.
13.
14.
15.
16.
17.
18.
19.
20.

Connections to WRITING

Proofread a Paragraph

First, proofread the paragraph below for ten misspelled words. Then rewrite the paragraph. Write the spelling words correctly and make the corrections indicated by the proofreading marks.

Proofreading Marks

≡	Capital Letter
/	Small Letter
∧	Add
℘	Delete
⊙	Add a Period
⫲	Indent

  The sun hung low in the sky, glowing ∧like a fiery tangarine. As it slipped below the horizon, colors splashed across the clouds. It looked as if someone had thrown a piece of richly colored demask over the sea. From hysinth purple to magnollia pink to camelia red, the colors reached as far as I could have see. Bits of white flecked the edges of the magnificent sunset like tiny gardinia petals. A soft wind blew across the sand, rustling my denim skirt and rippling the water like a giant saten sheet. ⫲Savory odors drifted toward me from the food vendors. I could smell the French fries from the Frankferter stand⊙At another stand, a vendor called to passersby, tempting them to feast on a hamberger with chedar cheese. I tasted the salt air and decided there was no place else i would rather be.

DESCRIPTIVE Writing Prompt

Write a Paragraph

Choose a memorable scene, person, or event and write a descriptive paragraph.

- Make your writing vivid by using precise words that appeal to the five senses.
- Follow the form used in the proofreading example.
- Use as many spelling words as you can.
- Proofread for grammar, capitalization, and punctuation.
- Circle three words you are unsure about. Check their spelling in a print or online dictionary.

Transfer

Write the following words in your Spelling Journal, and write the name or place after which the thing was named: **odyssey, jersey, sequoia, voltage, tarantula**. Use a dictionary to help you.

Word Study

Meaning Mastery

1. _____
2. _____
3. _____
4. _____
5. _____
6. _____
7. _____
8. _____
9. _____
10. _____
11. _____
12. _____
13. _____
14. _____
15. _____
16. _____
17. _____
18. _____
19. _____
20. _____

bayonet	suede	cantaloupe	cardigan
hyacinth	madras	ampere	calico
cashmere	damask	badminton	forsythia
sardine	frankfurter	camellia	magnolia
cologne	derby	valentine	cheddar
gardenia	satin	marathon	macintosh
sandwich	denim	tuxedo	currant
tarantula	begonia	tangerine	hamburger
angora	leotard	vandalism	paisley

Meaning Mastery

A. Use a dictionary to help complete the tasks below.

1–6. Write the words from the box that name plants that produce flowers.

7. Write the word for a special food that was named after a British politician.

8–10. Write the words that were named after places in Italy.

B. Write the word that goes with each definition.

11. a heavy material used for making blue jeans

12. a soft leather used for making shoes or jackets

13. a formal suit

14. a button-down sweater

15. a sport played with a net and rackets

16. a perfume

17. a 26.2-mile foot race

18. a raincoat

19. a tight-fitting garment worn by dancers

20. a token of love

Language Arts
Word Hunt

Read the paragraphs below. Look for words that come from names and places.

Most people know that English has many words that come to us from foreign countries. We often assume that these words were simply brought here by immigrants who arrived over the centuries and became new citizens. This is certainly true of many words. There are also words that became part of English because Europeans and English-speakers went abroad and brought the words back with them from other lands.

Some words are formed from the names of actual people, such as *gardenia* (named for a Scottish biologist) and *leotard* (named for a French acrobat). Names of familiar cities like Cologne, Hamburg, Frankfurt, and Tangier give their names to everyday things in English. Most people don't realize that the word *suede* is derived from the name of Sweden, or that the word *damask* refers to the Syrian capital Damascus.

Travels to neighboring Mediterranean-region countries gave us the names for other words. The nouns *marathon* and *hyacinth* come from Greece; *denim* and *magnolia* come from France. Nearby Morocco's old port city of Tangier gives us the name of a favorite citrus fruit.

European traders and explorers travelled to many far-off lands and brought back written descriptions of the new things they'd seen, using the native words for them. Sometimes they even brought actual samples, such as calico and cashmere from India and satin from China. Many names of today's spices and types of tea and coffee came from these Asian-Pacific voyages.

1. _____
2. _____
3. _____
4. _____
5. _____
6. _____
7. _____
8. _____
9. _____
10. _____

Write and sort the words that come from names and places. Use an online dictionary to check meaning, pronunciation, and country of origin.

1–3. Write three words that name flowers.

4–10. Write seven words that name cloth or clothing.

Connections to THINKING

Read the spelling words and sentences.

1.	laboratory	*laboratory*	Chemicals are stored in the **laboratory**.
2.	auxiliary	*auxiliary*	She is an **auxiliary** firefighter.
3.	mischievous	*mischievous*	A **mischievous** kitten can be amusing.
4.	salary	*salary*	His new job included a raise in **salary**.
5.	temperature	*temperature*	The **temperature** fell below freezing.
6.	accidentally	*accidentally*	Tina **accidentally** stepped on my glasses.
7.	remembrance	*remembrance*	Joe saved the shell as a **remembrance**.
8.	veterinarian	*veterinarian*	Dr. Franco is our dog's **veterinarian**.
9.	disastrous	*disastrous*	A drought can be **disastrous** for farmers.
10.	athletic	*athletic*	That gymnast has great **athletic** ability.
11.	separately	*separately*	We arrived together but left **separately**.
12.	laundry	*laundry*	We put **laundry** in the washing machine.
13.	temperament	*temperament*	His new turtle has a calm **temperament**.
14.	principally	*principally*	She works **principally** to pay off a loan.
15.	miniature	*miniature*	Bonsai are **miniature** trees.
16.	partially	*partially*	The lake is only **partially** frozen.
17.	hindrance	*hindrance*	Icy roads are a **hindrance** to drivers.
18.	incidentally	*incidentally*	We discovered the truth **incidentally**.
19.	privilege	*privilege*	Being team captain is a **privilege**.
20.	maintenance	*maintenance*	A **maintenance** crew groomed the field.

Think & Sort the spelling words.

1–2. Write the words with two syllables.

3–10. Write the words with three syllables.

11–16. Write the words with four syllables.

17–20. Write the words with five or more syllables.

Draw a vertical line between the syllables.

Remember

It is important to know the spellings of words that are frequently misspelled.

Two syllables

1. _____

2. _____

Three syllables

3. _____

4. _____

5. _____

6. _____

7. _____

8. _____

9. _____

10. _____

Four syllables

11. _____

12. _____

13. _____

14. _____

15. _____

16. _____

Five or more syllables

17. _____

18. _____

19. _____

20. _____

Connections to VOCABULARY

Word Meanings

Write the spelling word that is the best antonym for each word.

1. together
2. intentionally
3. oversized
4. well-behaved
5. completely
6. help
7. successful

Word Replacement

Write the spelling word that best replaces the underlined word or words.

8. Every member of that family enjoys <u>muscle-strengthening</u> and intellectual activities.
9. The coach is <u>chiefly</u> interested in improving the team's speed and stamina.
10. We performed the experiment under sterile conditions in the <u>room equipped for scientific experimentation</u>.
11. Bring your bike in for <u>upkeep to keep it in good condition</u> at least three times a year.
12. As a <u>memento</u> of the winning season, the coach gave each team member an engraved plaque.
13. Oh, <u>parenthetically</u>, I met your cousin Sue yesterday.
14. My brother left his <u>dirty clothing</u> overnight at Suds and Bubbles.

Use the Dictionary

Write a spelling word for each etymology. Use the **Spelling Dictionary** if you need help.

15. ME *salarie* < Lat. *salarium*, money given to Roman soldiers to buy salt
16. Lat. *veterinarius*, pertaining to beasts of burden
17. ME < OFr. < Lat. *privilegium*, a law affecting one person: *privus*, single + *lex*, law
18. Lat. *auxiliarius* < *auxilium*, help
19. Lat. *temperatura*, composition < *temperare*, to mix
20. ME < Lat. *temperamentum* < *temperare*, to temper

Word Meanings
1.
2.
3.
4.
5.
6.
7.

Word Replacement
8.
9.
10.
11.
12.
13.
14.

Use the Dictionary
15.
16.
17.
18.
19.
20.

laboratory	auxiliary	mischievous	salary	temperature
accidentally	remembrance	veterinarian	disastrous	athletic
separately	laundry	temperament	principally	miniature
partially	hindrance	incidentally	privilege	maintenance

Complete the Analogies

Write a spelling word that best completes each analogy.

1. **Brain** is to **intellectual** as **muscles** is to _____ .
2. **Weekly** is to **annual** as **paycheck** is to _____ .
3. **Normally** is to **usually** as **mainly** is to _____ .
4. **All** is to **some** as **totally** is to _____ .
5. **Baby** is to **pediatrician** as **cat** is to _____ .
6. **Copy** is to **reproduction** as **advantage** is to _____ .
7. **Rival** is to **opponent** as **helper** is to _____ .
8. **Baker** is to **kitchen** as **scientist** is to _____ .
9. **Snapshot** is to **photograph** as **souvenir** is to _____ .

Draw Conclusions

Write a spelling word that is related to the underlined word.

10. If she tends to lose her temper, she may have an irritable _____ .
11. If he maintains his car, his car gets regular _____ .
12. If snow hinders travel, snow is a _____ .
13. If I trip by accident, I trip _____ .
14. If your puppy gets into mischief, your puppy is _____ .

Use Context Clues

Write spelling words from the box to complete the paragraph.

The first time I did my own __15.__ was __16.__ ! Dad told me to wash colors and whites __17.__ , but I threw everything in together, including my red socks and my favorite white sweatshirt. I also neglected to turn the water __18.__ down to cold. Did you know that hot water can make colors run together and can make clothes shrink to __19.__ size? My favorite white sweatshirt, which __20.__ , is now bright pink, is small enough for my baby sister!

| temperature |
| incidentally |
| laundry |
| miniature |
| disastrous |
| separately |

Complete the Analogies
1. _____
2. _____
3. _____
4. _____
5. _____
6. _____
7. _____
8. _____
9. _____

Draw Conclusions
10. _____
11. _____
12. _____
13. _____
14. _____

Use Context Clues
15. _____
16. _____
17. _____
18. _____
19. _____
20. _____

Connections to WRITING

Proofread a Paragraph

Proofread the paragraph below for ten misspelled words. Then rewrite the paragraph. Write the spelling words correctly and make the corrections indicated by the proofreading marks.

¶My first day of work at Dr. Mendez's animal hospital was disasterous. Dr. Mendez, the vetrinarian, was called away on an Emergency. While he was gone, I acidentally turned on the heating system, which went haywire⊙We were waiting for maintainence personnel to arrive when a mischivous monkey escaped from its cage and partialy destroyed the washroom. Incidentaly, a small Poodle with a nervous temprament knocked down a shelf of supplies, too. I know it is a privlidge to work for dr. Mendez, but I hope we never have a day like that again! Even so, I took a picture of the monkey covered with toilet tissue as a rememberance.

Proofreading Marks

≡	Capital Letter
/	Small Letter
∧	Add
ℓ	Delete
⊙	Add a Period
¶	Indent

NARRATIVE Writing Prompt
Write a Paragraph

Write a paragraph describing how humor helped you get through a difficult day at school.

- Describe in detail what went wrong.
- Explain how humor helped you put events in perspective.
- Follow the form used in the proofreading example.
- Use as many spelling words as you can.
- Proofread for grammar, capitalization, and punctuation.
- Circle three words you are unsure about. Check their spelling in a print or online dictionary.

Transfer

In your Spelling Journal, write five words from this list that are difficult for you. Circle the part of the word that causes you trouble. Can you think of other words with the same construction? Write them. For example, **auxiliary— peculiar, familiar.**

Word Study

Base Words and Suffixes

1. ___
2. ___
3. ___
4. ___
5. ___
6. ___
7. ___
8. ___
9. ___
10. ___

Consonant Sound-Spellings

11. ___
12. ___
13. ___
14. ___
15. ___
16. ___
17. ___
18. ___
19. ___
20. ___

amateur	salary	laundry	disastrous
menial	maintenance	athlete	temperature
hindrance	temperament	aluminum	facade
muscle	accidentally	privilege	principally
lightning	remembrance	status	pigeon
auxiliary	miniature	luxury	incognito
villain	mischievous	athletic	partially
prejudice	laboratory	verbatim	separately
veterinarian	incidentally	spontaneous	ultimatum

Base Words and Suffixes

A. Write the word that is a suffixed form of each base word. Circle the word if the spelling of the base word was changed before the ending was added.

1. disaster
2. athlete
3. separate
4. mischief
5. veterinary
6. temper

B. Write the words that are base words of the suffixed words below.

7. muscular
8. menially
9. luxurious
10. spontaneously

Consonant Sound-Spellings

11–12. Write the words that have /j/ spelled **ge**.
13–20. Write the words that have /s/ spelled **c**.

Health
Word Hunt

Read the paragraphs below. Look for spelling words that are frequently misspelled.

I am not a very athletic person. Anyone who knows me understands that I would rather be doing my laundry than participating in a sporting event. However, in order to round out my educational experience with extracurricular activities, I decided to try the school swim team. I generally like swimming, but I was worried about it. You see, I have a scary image of what a sports coach is like. Here's my crazy imagination at work:

It is obvious from his temperament that the swim team coach had been selected principally for his ability to snarl and only partially for being able to judge my swimming talent. An auxiliary job requirement for the swim coach is that he be able to yell humiliating things while clenching a whistle in his teeth. My guess is that he will receive extra salary if he can blast his whistle so sharply that it pierces our ears. It gives "pierced ears" a whole new meaning.

In the coach's view, it is my highest privilege to be chosen for this team, and whether I "enjoy" the experience is probably a hindrance to team performance. He will order me to swim lap after lap, again, faster and faster, again, until finally the coach blasts the whistle again. Whew! I'm glad to have pierced ears! My misery means nothing to him, whom I refer to as "The Poolside Dictator." It probably makes him happy that I have to suffer the icy water temperature too!

In reality, our swim coach was incredibly upbeat and encouraging. Even though I wasn't the greatest swimmer on the team, I made a lot of progress with his help. I cut my time in the 100-meter freestyle by 4 seconds! The water was still cold, but being involved with the team was so much fun. It made my dreams of doing laundry a distant memory!

1. _____
2. _____
3. _____
4. _____
5. _____
6. _____
7. _____
8. _____
9. _____
10. _____

1–10. Look at the word list on page 150. There are ten of those words in the passage above. Find and write them.

Connections to THINKING

Read the spelling words and sentences.

1.	abstract	*abstract*	An **abstract** idea may need explanation.
2.	complicate	*complicate*	Her absence will **complicate** our plans.
3.	persist	*persist*	Children may **persist** in questioning.
4.	attractive	*attractive*	That is an **attractive** pair of boots.
5.	strict	*strict*	He had **strict** orders to be on time.
6.	replica	*replica*	I bought a tiny **replica** of that statue.
7.	distract	*distract*	Will loud music **distract** the students?
8.	consist	*consist*	Dinner will **consist** of three courses.
9.	restrict	*restrict*	Will they **restrict** traffic on that road?
10.	insistence	*insistence*	At our **insistence**, prices were lowered.
11.	duplicate	*duplicate*	Keep a **duplicate** of your application.
12.	resist	*resist*	Such a generous offer is hard to **resist**.
13.	constrict	*constrict*	This cast will **constrict** arm movement.
14.	detract	*detract*	Those trash cans **detract** from the view.
15.	resistance	*resistance*	We wore down his **resistance** to hiking.
16.	complication	*complication*	The plan succeeded without **complication**.
17.	attract	*attract*	Your perfume may **attract** bees.
18.	insist	*insist*	I **insist** that you stay for supper.
19.	retract	*retract*	The paper refused to **retract** the story.
20.	consistent	*consistent*	Lee's ideas are **consistent** with ours.

Think & Sort the spelling words.

1–6. Write the spelling words with the Latin root **tract**, meaning "to pull or draw."

7–10. Write the spelling words with the Latin root **plic**, meaning "to fold."

11–17. Write the spelling words with the Latin root **sist**, meaning "to stand still."

18–20. Write the spelling words with the Latin root **strict**, meaning "to bind tightly."

Remember

Knowing Latin roots such as **tract, plic, sist**, and **strict** can give clues to the meaning and spelling of certain words.

tract
1.
2.
3.
4.
5.
6.

plic
7.
8.
9.
10.

sist
11.
12.
13.
14.
15.
16.
17.

strict
18.
19.
20.

Connections to VOCABULARY

Word Meanings
Write a spelling word to match each description.

1. to be made up of or composed of
2. a reproduction of a work of art
3. apart from concrete existence; a genre of painting
4. to draw back or take back
5. to make smaller or narrower; to restrict
6. to take away a desirable part; to diminish
7. a force that tends to oppose or retard motion
8. a firmness in a demand or a refusal to yield
9. pleasing to the eye or mind; charming
10. a factor, condition, or element that complicates

Word Structure
Write the spelling word that is derived from each Latin word and prefix.

11. **tractus** meaning "pull" + **ad-** meaning "toward"
12. **strictus** meaning "bind" + **re-** meaning "back"
13. **plicare** meaning "to fold" + **du-** meaning "twice"
14. **plicare** meaning "to fold" + **com-** meaning "together"
15. **sistere** meaning "to stand" + **per-** meaning "intensely"
16. **tractus** meaning "pull" + **dis-** meaning "apart"

Use the Thesaurus

Write spelling words that could replace the underlined words. Use the **Writing Thesaurus** to check your answers.

17. That organization has <u>inflexible</u> rules.
18. Such an adorable puppy was impossible to <u>rebuff</u>.
19. Team coaches <u>demand</u> that the athletes attend all practices.
20. Her loyalty to the team has been <u>constant</u>.

Word Meanings
1.
2.
3.
4.
5.
6.
7.
8.
9.
10.
Word Structure
11.
12.
13.
14.
15.
16.
Use the Thesaurus
17.
18.
19.
20.

abstract	complicate	persist	attractive	strict
replica	distract	consist	restrict	insistence
duplicate	resist	constrict	detract	resistance
complication	attract	insist	retract	consistent

Complete the Sentences

Write a spelling word to complete each sentence.

1. Which photocopier should I use to _____ these documents?
2. Billboards would _____ from the beauty of the landscape.
3. Will the editor _____ the statement she made about him?
4. My cousin bought a bronze _____ of an Egyptian sphinx.
5. What does the Korean dish kimchee _____ of?
6. Tie a tourniquet above the wound to _____ the blood vessels and restrict the flow of blood.
7. A _____ slowed my progress.
8. Rain will _____ all weekend, so let's rent a movie.
9. I tried, but I could not _____ a third slice of pie.
10. Try to _____ the baby's attention with this rattle.
11. I am finally beginning to understand this _____ art.
12. The smell of freshly baked bread will _____ customers to the store.

Use Context Clues

Write spelling words from the box to complete each journal entry.

March 10. My parents have worked out a **13.** _____ schedule for our trip west. However, my grandparents are showing great **14.** _____ to traveling on superhighways. They want to **15.** _____ our driving to back roads. Their **16.** _____ that we take back roads is going to **17.** _____ our plans. It's not **18.** _____ with our desire to reach the coast by Monday.

March 15. If we had not listened to my grandparents, think of all the **19.** _____ sights we would have missed. For our trip next year, I too will **20.** _____ on driving the back-roads, scenic route!

insistence
attractive
strict
insist
consistent
resistance
restrict
complicate

Complete the Sentences
1. _____
2. _____
3. _____
4. _____
5. _____
6. _____
7. _____
8. _____
9. _____
10. _____
11. _____
12. _____

Use Context Clues
13. _____
14. _____
15. _____
16. _____
17. _____
18. _____
19. _____
20. _____

Connections to WRITING

Proofread a Passage

Proofread the passage below for ten misspelled words. Then rewrite it. Write the spelling words correctly and make the corrections indicated by the proofreading marks.

Proofreading Marks

≡	Capital Letter
/	Small Letter
∧	Add
ℰ	Delete
⊙	Add a Period
¶	Indent

On a visit to an Exhibit of abstrack art, I overheard a conversation between an art critic and an eager new artist who had painted a repplica of a famous work.

"I ensist that you do review my work," the artist said. "it's almost an exact duplicat of the original." The critic tried to ressist giving an opinion. "Must I percist? I never give up, you know," continued the artist.

Finally, the critic's resistence was worn down. "It's atractive," She said, obviously trying to restrickt her comments. ¶"Can't you see the symbolism?" the artist asked.

"I prefer the strickt interpretation of the realists," the critic said. Feeling trapped, she turned to me, a total stranger, and said, "Where have you been?" Then she took my arm and escorted me around the museum ⊙

NARRATIVE Writing Prompt

Write a Passage

Imagine that you overheard a conversation between an artist and an art critic at an art exhibit. Describe the incident from your perspective.

- Use vivid verbs and adjectives, along with concrete details, to add meaning and interest to your account.
- Follow the form used in the proofreading example.
- Use as many spelling words as you can.
- Proofread for grammar, capitalization, and punctuation.
- Circle three words you are unsure about. Check their spelling in a print or online dictionary.

Transfer

Select three spelling words that are base words. In your Spelling Journal, add prefixes and/or suffixes to the words to make as many more words as you can. For example: **resist—resistant, resistor, resistance, irresistible**.

Word Study

attract	applicant	consistent	restrictive	retract	assist
strict	applicator	contractor	retraction	consist	resist
restrict	insistence	contraction	attractive	duplicate	extract
district	distraction	complication	persistent	abstract	constrict
insist	extraction	inconsistency	applicable	detract	persist
replica	complicate	persistence	resistance	distract	contract

Word Families
1.
2.
3.
4.
5.
6.
7.
8.

Latin Roots and Prefixes
9.
10.
11.
12.
13.
14.

Context Clues
15.
16.
17.
18.
19.
20.

Word Families
Write the words that are related to the following base words.

1–2. apply   **5–6.** persist
3–4. contract   **7–8.** consist

Latin Roots and Prefixes
Use prefix meanings to help you write the spelling word that goes with each meaning below.

ex-: "out of," "away from"   **con-:** "together"
dis-: "not," "apart"   **re-:** "again," "backward"
de-: "do or make the opposite of"

9. to draw or pull out of
10. to draw (something) out of
11. to be made up of (together) in one mixture
12. to bind tightly together
13. to pull or draw backward
14. to pull or draw together

Context Clues
Complete each sentence using a word from the box.
15. Don't _____ matters by asking a confusing question.
16. There was some _____ to his idea, but eventually everyone agreed.
17. Her _____ on walking caused us to arrive late for the play.
18. The playoff game was a _____ for many at the reception.
19. The newspaper printed a _____ to correct the mistake.
20. The magician asked if I would like to _____ him onstage.

Social Studies
Word Hunt

Read the paragraphs below. Look for words with Latin roots: **tract, plic, sist, strict**.

To: Student newspaper staff, Jefferson Middle School
From: Dewey C. Howe, Superintendent, Jefferson Co. School District
Re: Reminder about journalism standards

Greetings, Journalism students!

Welcome to the new school year here at Jefferson Middle School! I wish to convey my enormous pleasure that you have decided to participate in producing the journalism department's student newspaper. Bravo!

You may find the paper's strict deadlines sometimes stressful. Your instructor will help you on those occasions when you feel distracted or feel pressured by life's complications. Be persistent, and remember the Jefferson newsroom motto: "Seek out, keep going, double-check, and print on time!"

My job is to advise you of the journalistic standards we must consistently observe. Once you become accustomed to these requirements, they should neither complicate your efforts nor detract from your enthusiasm.

A reminder: District policy requires that ALL student publications eliminate the use of improper language, resist attempts to speak unkindly of people named in printed news stories, and retract wrong information promptly with a printed apology. Your instructor will explain these guidelines in more detail.

I am confident that you will enjoy your journalism experience, and I have no doubt that this year's Jefferson Middle School paper will be outstanding!

Dewey C. Howe
Superintendent, Jefferson Co. School District

1. _____
2. _____
3. _____
4. _____
5. _____
6. _____
7. _____
8. _____
9. _____
10. _____

1–10. Write spelling words with Latin roots: **tract, plic, sist, strict**. Underline the root in each word. Use an online dictionary to check for other forms of the word.

Unit 19	
1.	
2.	
3.	
4.	
5.	
6.	
Unit 20	
7.	
8.	
9.	
10.	
11.	
12.	
13.	
14.	
Unit 23	
15.	
16.	
17.	
18.	
19.	
20.	

Units 19–23

Assessment

Each word in the box fits one of the spelling patterns or rules you have studied over the past five weeks. Read the unit descriptions. Then write each assessment word under the unit number it fits.

Unit 19

1–6. Plural nouns are formed in a variety of ways.

Unit 20

7–14. The prefix **ad-,** meaning "to" or "toward," may be assimilated into the spelling of the base word or word root. This will always result in a double consonant.

Unit 21

The English language includes many words taken from names (eponyms) and places (toponyms).

Unit 22

It is important to know the spellings of words that are frequently misspelled.

Unit 23

15–20. Knowing Latin roots such as **tract, plic, sist,** and **strict** can give clues to the meaning and spelling of certain words.

Words for Assessment

restriction

brothers-in-law

accidental

utilities

desist

appall

appropriately

agencies

consistency

torpedoes

insistent

retractable

assessment

communities

resistor

authorities

attitude

attraction

accommodation

affair

Unit 19: Plural Nouns

activities	potatoes	shelves	knives	opportunities
tomatoes	volcanoes	passersby	companies	mosquitoes

Write the spelling word that is the plural form of the word in parentheses.

1. How many (activity) have you completed?
2. I have written to the presidents of five different (company).
3. The billboard caught the attention of all the (passerby).
4. Jim sharpened all the kitchen (knife).
5. You will have many (opportunity) to see that movie.
6. Put the glasses on the (shelf).
7. Hawaii has several (volcano).
8. A swarm of (mosquito) gathered around the pond.
9. Please peel these (potato) for the stew.
10. Carol picked five ripe (tomato) from the vine.

Unit 20: Assimilated Prefix: ad-

application	according	attain	account	appetite
attempt	accustomed	approval	assemble	afford

Write the spelling word that contains each word part.

11. count
12. tempt
13. custom
14. ford
15. plic

16. sem
17. prov
18. tain
19. tite
20. cord

Unit 19	
1.	
2.	
3.	
4.	
5.	
6.	
7.	
8.	
9.	
10.	
Unit 20	
11.	
12.	
13.	
14.	
15.	
16.	
17.	
18.	
19.	
20.	

Review

Unit 21: Words From Names and Places

Unit 21
1.
2.
3.
4.
5.
6.
7.
8.
9.
10.

tangerine	suede	calico	frankfurter	cheddar
denim	hamburger	cantaloupe	cashmere	camellia

Write a spelling word that gets its name from each person or place.

1. Tangier, Morocco
2. Nîmes, France
3. Cheddar, England
4. Kashmir
5. Calicut, India
6. Sweden
7. Georg Josef Kamel
8. Cantalupo, Italy
9. Hamburg, Germany
10. Frankfurt, Germany

Unit 22: Frequently Misspelled Words

Unit 22
11.
12.
13.
14.
15.
16.
17.
18.
19.
20.

laboratory	salary	temperature	accidentally	remembrance
athletic	separately	laundry	hindrance	privilege

Write a spelling word to complete each analogy.

11. **Pound** is to **weight** as **degree** is to _____.
12. **Artist** is to **studio** as **scientist** is to _____.
13. **Free** is to **expensive** as **purposefully** is to _____.
14. **Disharmony** is to **musical** as **clumsy** is to _____.
15. **Vegetable** is to **stew** as **soap** is to _____.
16. **Fair** is to **just** as **advantage** is to _____.
17. **Attached** is to **together** as **apart** is to _____.
18. **Award** is to **prize** as **pay** is to _____.
19. **Vow** is to **promise** as **keepsake** is to _____.
20. **Greeting** is to **welcome** as **obstacle** is to _____.

Unit 23: Latin Roots: tract, plic, sist, strict

insist	attractive	strict	insistence	duplicate
resist	resistance	attract	complicate	consistent

Write a spelling word to replace the underlined word or words in each sentence.

1. The secretary had to make copies of the report.
2. All of the puppies are good-looking.
3. We agreed to go at the firm suggestion of Ms. Matthews.
4. Having to get to a noon meeting will make difficult my plans.
5. The athletes had to follow a rigid diet.
6. How can you keep away from that delicious pie?
7. Is there much opposition to the new plans?
8. We will try to plan dates that are agreeable with your schedule.
9. We have to think of ways to draw in new members.
10. I really must strongly urge that you pay close attention.

Unit 23

1. _____
2. _____
3. _____
4. _____
5. _____
6. _____
7. _____
8. _____
9. _____
10. _____

Spelling Study Strategy

Sorting by Plural Forms of Nouns

One way to practice your spelling words is to place them into groups according to a spelling rule. Here is a way to organize the spelling words to practice with a partner.

1. Make columns for the plural endings: **s, es, ies,** and **ves**.

2. Have a partner choose a spelling word from Units 19 through 23 that can be a noun.

3. Agree on whether the word is singular or plural.

4. Write the plural form of the word in the proper column.

Directions: Read the introduction and the passage that follows. Then read each question and fill in the correct answer on your answer sheet.

Callie's teacher asked each student to write about something that someone lost. As you read, look for improvements that Callie could make.

Sentimental Value

(1) I recently had the privelege of sitting on the stage with our state governor and her aide during a school assembly, and afterward we went into the principal's office to talk. (2) When they left, I realized that my anggora sweater, which had been on the armrest of my chair, had disappeared. (3) It was my favorite cardigan because my mother had knitted it in remembrance of Turkey, her native country.

(4) I felt certain that the governor must have accidently picked it up when she left. (5) I telephoned her office several times, but every attempt to call took me straight to voicemail. (6) I had to perrsist because it was my most valuable piece of attire!

(7) I finally managed to speak to a secretary. (8) He affirmed that the governor had inadvertently picked up my sweater, and he gave me his assurance that the governor would telephone me later. (9) The secretary told me, incidently, that the governor had greatly admired my sweater because it was so attractive.

(10) Eventually, the governor herself returned my call and was extremely apologetic. (11) I assured her that mix-ups happen and that I was just relieved to know where it was. (12) She mailed it back to me without complication, and I couldn't ressist the spontaneous urge to send her something nice to thank her. (13) I asked my mother what we should send. (14) She insisted we knit the governor a dupliccate of my sweater, and she immediately pulled out her knitting basket and began to work!

1 What change, if any, should be made in sentence 1?

A Change *privelege* to **privilege**

B Change *governor* to **governer**

C Change *aide* to **aid**

D Make no change

2 What change, if any, should be made in sentence 2?

A Change *anggora* to **angora**

B Change *armrest* to **arm-rest**

C Change *disappeared* to **dissappeared**

D Make no change

3 What change, if any, should be made in sentence 3?

A Change *favorite* to **faverite**

B Change *cardigan* to **cardiggan**

C Change *remembrance* to **remembrence**

D Make no change

4 What change, if any, should be made in sentence 4?

A Change *governor* to **governer**

B Change *accidently* to **acciddently**

C Change *accidently* to **accidentally**

D Make no change

5 What change, if any, should be made in sentence 6?

A Change *perrsist* to **persist**

B Change *valuable* to **valueable**

C Change *attire* to **atire**

D Make no change

6 What change, if any, should be made in sentence 8?

A Change *affirmed* to **afirmed**

B Change *governor* to **governer**

C Change *assurence* to **assurance**

D Make no change

7 What change, if any, should be made in sentence 9?

A Change *incidently* to **incidentally**

B Change *admired* to **addmired**

C Change *attractive* to **atractive**

D Make no change

8 What change, if any, should be made in sentence 10?

A Change *eventually* to **eventualy**

B Change *extremely* to **exstremely**

C Change *apologetic* to **apollogetic**

D Make no change

9 What change, if any, should be made in sentence 12?

A Change *complication* to **compliccation**

B Change *ressist* to **resist**

C Change *spontaneous* to **spontanious**

D Make no change

10 What change, if any, should be made in sentence 14?

A Change *insisted* to **insissted**

B Change *dupliccate* to **duplicate**

C Change *immediately* to **imediately**

D Make no change

STOP

Grammar, Usage, and Mechanics
Identifying Conjunctions

Coordinating conjunctions, such as **and, but,** and **or,** connect words or groups of words (including independent clauses) that are similar.

Donisha **and** Kenneth will not sing, **but** they will recite poems.

Subordinating conjunctions, such as **although, as, when, because, if,** and **before,** show how one clause is related to another.

Although we were late, we didn't miss the first act.

Practice Activity

A. Write the conjunction in each sentence below. Circle each subordinating conjunction.
1. We can work together, or we can work separately.
2. Please put tomatoes and avocados on my sandwich.
3. If you come early, you can help give out programs.
4. I have asked you to help because you are so good at this.
5. Put your ballots in the box as you come in the door.
6. If you will wait a few minutes, I will go with you.
7. I wanted to get up early, but I overslept.
8. Although Jennie is accustomed to being the leader, she will give someone else the opportunity.

B. Complete each sentence with a conjunction. Circle it if it is a subordinating conjunction.
9. Set the table with knives, forks, _____ spoons.
10. Choose the red team _____ the blue team.
11. We'll watch that program _____ we get home in time.
12. I can't reach the shelves _____ I am not tall enough.
13. Turn in your papers _____ you leave the room.
14. We will finish working _____ the clock strikes six.
15. You could order two hamburgers, _____ it's not a good idea.

A
1. _____
2. _____
3. _____
4. _____
5. _____
6. _____
7. _____
8. _____

B
9. _____
10. _____
11. _____
12. _____
13. _____
14. _____
15. _____

The Writing Process: Argument
Writing an Argument Essay

PREWRITING

Computer hacking is using other computers or network resources without permission. Hacking invades people's privacy and often infects computers with viruses. Why do you think everyone should respect copyright and privacy laws? You can persuade others to agree with you by giving reasons in an essay. Look for facts about hacking at the library or on Internet sites such as the U.S. Patent and Trademark Office (www.uspto.gov/go/kids). As you think about this topic, make an outline for your essay.

DRAFTING

Use your outline to write a persuasive essay. Begin with a topic sentence that presents the main idea. Give convincing reasons that others should respect copyright and privacy laws. Use as many spelling words as possible. If you don't know how to spell a word, make your best guess. You will be able to revise your essay later.

REVISING

When you have finished your first draft, read your essay from beginning to end. Check to see if you have included all of the points in your outline. Did you achieve your purpose for writing? Does each sentence support the topic?

EDITING

Use the editing checklist to proofread your essay. Be sure to use proofreading marks when you make corrections. Circle any words you are unsure about and check their spellings in a print or online dictionary. Now write your final draft.

PUBLISHING

Make a copy of your persuasive essay and share it with your readers.

EDITING CHECKLIST

Spelling

✓ Circle words that contain the spelling patterns and rules learned in Units 19–23.

✓ Check the circled words in a print or online dictionary.

✓ Check for other spelling errors.

Capital Letters

✓ Capitalize important words in the title.

✓ Capitalize the first word in each sentence.

✓ Capitalize proper nouns.

Punctuation

✓ End each sentence with the correct punctuation.

✓ Use commas, apostrophes, and quotation marks correctly.

Grammar, Usage, and Mechanics

✓ Check that each compound sentence has a coordinating conjunction to connect independent clauses.

✓ Check that each complex sentence has a subordinating conjuction to show how clauses are related to each other.

From unus

1. _____
2. _____
3. _____
4. _____
5. _____
6. _____

From monos

7. _____
8. _____
9. _____
10. _____
11. _____
12. _____
13. _____

From duo

14. _____
15. _____
16. _____
17. _____

From bis

18. _____
19. _____
20. _____

Read the spelling words and sentences.

1.	monopoly	*monopoly*	The company has a **monopoly** on red bread.
2.	dual	*dual*	The **dual** speakers provide stereo sound.
3.	unique	*unique*	The sand and silk collage was **unique**.
4.	biennial	*biennial*	Is this the year of the **biennial** sale?
5.	monotony	*monotony*	I cannot stand the **monotony** of that song.
6.	duplication	*duplication*	We want no **duplication** of photographs.
7.	unite	*unite*	The rival teams will **unite** for a party.
8.	monocle	*monocle*	He wore a **monocle** over his left eye.
9.	unify	*unify*	How will we **unify** the arguing parties?
10.	duo	*duo*	My dachshund and I make a great **duo**.
11.	binoculars	*binoculars*	With **binoculars** I see two distant ducks.
12.	university	*university*	My ambition is to go to a **university**.
13.	monorail	*monorail*	A **monorail** may replace the subway.
14.	duplex	*duplex*	In which half of the **duplex** do you live?
15.	unison	*unison*	The members of the choir sang in **unison**.
16.	monotonous	*monotonous*	Repeating the same task is **monotonous**.
17.	biannual	*biannual*	We attend the **biannual** town meetings.
18.	monotone	*monotone*	The lecturer spoke in a droning **monotone**.
19.	universe	*universe*	Is the **universe** really expanding?
20.	monogram	*monogram*	His **monogram** was sewn onto his towel.

Think & Sort the spelling words.

1–6. Write the words that are derived from the Latin **unus**, meaning "one."

7–13. Write the words that are derived from the Greek **monos**, meaning "one" or "single."

14–17. Write the words that are derived from the Latin **duo**, meaning "two."

18–20. Write the words that are derived from the Latin **bis**, meaning "twice."

Remember

The prefixes **uni-, mono-, duo-,** and **bi-** indicate number.

Connections to VOCABULARY

Word Meanings

Write a spelling word for each definition.

1. a twosome
2. field glasses designed for use by both eyes at once
3. every two years
4. all existing things regarded as a single whole
5. singular in nature; unlike anything else
6. composed of two parts; having two uses or purposes
7. occurring twice each year
8. an institute of higher learning; a college with graduate schools
9. to consolidate, to make into a unit
10. to bring people together

Word Structure

Write the spelling word for each etymology.

11. from the Latin **unus,** "one," and **sonus,** "sound"
12. from the Latin **duo,** "two," and **-plex,** "fold"
13. from the Latin **duplicare,** "to double," and **-ion,** "the process of"

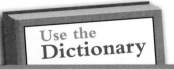

Use the
Dictionary

Guide words appear at the top of each dictionary page. They indicate the first entry word and the last entry word on the page.

14–20. Imagine that the guide words on a dictionary page are **monkey** and **monsoon.** In alphabetical order, write the spelling words that would appear between those guide words.

Word Meanings

1. _____
2. _____
3. _____
4. _____
5. _____
6. _____
7. _____
8. _____
9. _____
10. _____

Word Structure

11. _____
12. _____
13. _____

Use the Dictionary

14. _____
15. _____
16. _____
17. _____
18. _____
19. _____
20. _____

monopoly	dual	unique	biennial	monotony
duplication	unite	monocle	unify	duo
binoculars	university	monorail	duplex	unison
monotonous	biannual	monotone	universe	monogram

Complete the Sentences

Write spelling words to complete the sentences.

1. Twice a year, we march in our city's _____ parade.
2. It is often illegal in the United States for one company to have a _____ on a particular service.
3. She raised her _____ to her right eye, closed the other eye, and peered down at the opera singers.
4. You are able to _____ enthusiasm with good sense.
5. The twins seemed to read each other's mind when they gave the same response in _____.
6. My grandfather wishes his birthday could be a _____ event!
7. Batman is one-half of a famous superhero _____.
8. They bought a _____ so that they could live in one side and rent out the other side.
9. The _____ on the tie was so ornate that we could not make out the initials.
10–11. I tried to pay attention, but she spoke in a _____ that was so _____ I fell asleep.

Use Context Clues

Write spelling words from the box to complete the paragraph.

The architects of the miniature "City of the Future" had a __12.__ vision: one was to __13.__ every aspect of their city into a seamless whole; the second was to steer clear of any possibly boring __14.__ by avoiding all __15.__ of color, shape, or texture. The buildings were all connected by a tiny, operating __16.__. When I peered through my __17.__, I could see lifelike people inside every building, including students and teachers in classrooms in the __18.__. The __19.__ that the planners created was both diverse and unified: a __20.__ accomplishment!

dual
university
monorail
unique
duplication
universe
monotony
binoculars
unify

Complete the Sentences

1. _____
2. _____
3. _____
4. _____
5. _____
6. _____
7. _____
8. _____
9. _____
10. _____
11. _____

Use Context Clues

12. _____
13. _____
14. _____
15. _____
16. _____
17. _____
18. _____
19. _____
20. _____

Proofread a Paragraph

Proofread the paragraph below for ten misspelled words. Then rewrite the paragraph. Write the spelling words correctly and make the corrections indicated by the proofreading marks.

The bianual skating competition at the Univercity was to begin. In silence, the first skating duwo glided gracefully onto the ice, moving in perfect unason. The lights dimmed, the spotlight went on, and the music began. The first figure, a triple axel, was followed by a brilliant and uniqe series of spins and turns Each skater's movements were a perfect duplecation of the other's. For the finale, the skaters astonished the crowd by tracing their dool monnogram on the ice. At the end of their performance, the skaters bowed out to the audience, who could easily unyte in applauding one of the greatest skating couples in the univirse!

about (inserted after "was")

Proofreading Marks

≡	Capital Letter
/	Small Letter
∧	Add
ℒ	Delete
⊙	Add a Period
¶	Indent

INFORMATIVE/EXPLANATORY Writing Prompt

Write a Paragraph

Choose an event that you saw or in which you participated. Write a paragraph describing the event.

- Make sure your paragraph follows a logical sequence.
- Use words such as **first, next, then,** and **finally** to clearly indicate the sequence.
- Follow the form used in the proofreading example.
- Use as many spelling words as you can.
- Proofread for grammar, capitalization, and punctuation.
- Circle three words you are unsure about. Check their spelling in a print or online dictionary.

Transfer

In your Spelling Journal, begin a list of words with each prefix used in this unit. Think of two more words with each prefix. Add to the list each time you encounter a new word with one of these prefixes.

Word Study

dual	biplane	monologue	bimonthly	universe	biathlon
bisect	unique	monotonous	monorail	duplicity	unicorn
duet	duplex	monopolize	monogram	university	biennial
duo	unison	duplication	monopoly	monotony	binary
unite	uniform	bicentennial	monotone	unilateral	unicycle
unify	biceps	monosyllable	binoculars	biannual	monocle

Parts of Speech

Use words from the list above to complete these exercises. Use the **Spelling Dictionary,** if necessary.

   1–5. Write any adjectives that begin with the prefix **bi-**. Circle the two words that are easily confused.

   6–8. Write any adjectives that begin with the prefix **uni-**. One of the words is commonly used as a noun.

  9–10. Write any adjectives that begin with the prefix **mono-**.

Word Parts

Write the words from the list that have the same base word or root as the words below.

11–12. inoculate

   13. railroad

   14. tricycle

   15. century

Meaning Mastery

Write the words from the list that most closely fit the meanings below.

16–17. having to do with having complete control over the buying and selling of a product or service

   18. the muscle at the front of the upper arm

   19. to monopolize conversation by doing all the talking

   20. a mythical animal

Parts of Speech

1.

2.

3.

4.

5.

6.

7.

8.

9.

10.

Word Parts

11.

12.

13.

14.

15.

Meaning Mastery

16.

17.

18.

19.

20.

Poetry
Word Hunt

Read the selection below. Look for words with the prefixes **uni-, mono-, duo-** and **bi-**.

The monotony, of monotony, is monotonous
A monotone, the perfect tone: Monotonous!
It's lonely, it's only, a one-chorus.
So UNIFY! And here is why: there are more of us!
Ignite us, unite us, become a universe
In unison, we will be one, a One-chorus!

It's two of you, a dual you, your Inner You
Your mirror face, an easy case: Just duplicate!
I rest my case: We cannot wait, let's call it Fate.
So UNIFY! And here is why: there are more of us!
Ignite us, unite us, become a universe
In unison, we will be one, a One-chorus!

We cannot fail; we'll blaze a trail, and try to touch the stars!
In unison, we will be one, we're now binoculars.
Our eyes are shared, because we dared, we're now a One-chorus.
So UNIFY! And here is why: there are more of us!
Ignite us, unite us, become a universe
In unison, we will be one, a One-chorus!

1. _____
2. _____
3. _____
4. _____
5. _____
6. _____
7. _____
8. _____
9. _____
10. _____

Write spelling words with the prefixes **uni-, mono-, duo-** and **bi-**. Underline the prefix in each word and indicate the number it signifies.
1. Write one word with the prefix **bi-**.
2–3. Write two words with the prefix **duo-**.
4–6. Write three words with the prefix **mono-**.
7–10. Write four words with the prefix **uni-**.
Use an online dictionary to check for other forms of the words.

Connections to THINKING

Read the spelling words and sentences.

1. microscopic	*microscopic*	Scientists study **microscopic** bacteria.
2. telescope	*telescope*	We looked at stars through the **telescope**.
3. chronology	*chronology*	What was the **chronology** of the events?
4. diagram	*diagram*	I drew a **diagram** of the machine.
5. microphone	*microphone*	The mayor spoke into the **microphone**.
6. stethoscope	*stethoscope*	A nurse brought a **stethoscope** with him.
7. headphones	*headphones*	She listens with the **headphones** on.
8. telegram	*telegram*	Can you still send a **telegram** to someone?
9. chronic	*chronic*	She has a **chronic** need to tell jokes.
10. anagram	*anagram*	I can make an **anagram** with this word.
11. symphonic	*symphonic*	I enjoyed the **symphonic** performance.
12. grammatical	*grammatical*	Please correct any **grammatical** mistakes.
13. synchronize	*synchronize*	I **synchronize** my watch with the clock.
14. telephone	*telephone*	Did you get your **telephone** messages yet?
15. periscope	*periscope*	A tube and mirrors can make a **periscope**.
16. chronicle	*chronicle*	His diary is a **chronicle** of his life.
17. megaphone	*megaphone*	The coach yelled into a **megaphone**.
18. earphones	*earphones*	I cannot find the **earphones** for my radio.
19. microscope	*microscope*	The science lab needs a new **microscope**.
20. saxophone	*saxophone*	I practice my **saxophone** every day.

Think & Sort the spelling words.

1–4. Write the words that contain **gram**, from the Greek "letter."

5–8. Write the words that contain **chron**, from the Greek "time."

9–15. Write the words that contain **phon(e)**, from the Greek "sound."

16–20. Write the words that contain **scope**, from the Greek "see."

Remember

The Greek word parts **gram**, **chron**, **phon(e)**, and **scope** combine with other word parts to form new words.

gram

1. _____
2. _____
3. _____
4. _____

chron

5. _____
6. _____
7. _____
8. _____

phon(e)

9. _____
10. _____
11. _____
12. _____
13. _____
14. _____
15. _____

scope

16. _____
17. _____
18. _____
19. _____
20. _____

Connections to VOCABULARY

Word Meanings

Write spelling words to complete the sentences.

1. What is the _____ of events that led to World War I?
2. At the health fair, I used a _____ to listen to my heart.
3. My brother plays the _____ in a jazz band.
4. "Between you and I" is an example of a _____ error.
5. The crew on the submarine used the _____ to scan the ocean surface from below the water.
6. We looked through the _____ to see the tiny organisms swimming in the pond water.
7. The word **stop** is an _____ of **tops**.
8. In the past, a quick way to send a printed message was by _____.
9. Things that are too tiny to see with the naked eye are _____.
10. If you look through this _____, you can see the craters on the moon.
11–12. When you listen to the radio, you can use _____ or _____ so you do not disturb others.
13. I heard the _____ ringing, so I answered it.
14. The cheerleader yelled into the cone-shaped _____ so that the crowd could hear her.
15. The singer's _____ was not turned on, and the audience in the back row could not hear the song.
16. The choreographer will _____ the dance movements with the music.
17. Many of Beethoven's musical works are _____.

Use the Thesaurus

Write a spelling word that is a synonym for each word below. Use the **Writing Thesaurus** if you need help.

18. habitual   19. chart   20. record

Word Meanings	
1.	
2.	
3.	
4.	
5.	
6.	
7.	
8.	
9.	
10.	
11.	
12.	
13.	
14.	
15.	
16.	
17.	
Use the Thesaurus	
18.	
19.	
20.	

Connections to READING

microscopic	telescope	chronology	diagram	microphone
stethoscope	headphones	telegram	chronic	anagram
symphonic	grammatical	synchronize	telephone	periscope
chronicle	megaphone	earphones	microscope	saxophone

Replace the Phrases

Write the spelling word that best replaces each underlined phrase.

1. A Sequence of Events of the History of Tools
2. 1590: Invention of the instrument for viewing tiny objects.
3. It gives an enlarged view of very tiny objects.
4. 1668: Isaac Newton proposes design for the instrument for viewing faraway objects.
5. 1816: R. T. H. Laënnec constructs the instrument for listening to sounds within the body.
6. 1844: First message sent by telegraph sent in Morse code.
7. 1846: Adolphe Sax patents the single-reed wind instrument.
8. 1854: E. H. Marie-Davy invents the first submarine sight tube.
9. 1876: Invention of the instrument that converts sound into electric current.
10. 1876: First successful use of the instrument that transmits spoken words over a distance.
11. 1912: First attempts to operate together sound on disks and action on film.

Use Context Clues

Write spelling words from the box to complete the paragraph.

Sarah, our foreign exchange student from Poland, uses __12.__ or __13.__ to listen to English recordings at school. Her English has improved tremendously. She never makes __14.__ mistakes. She even uses the __15.__ at soccer games and helps the pep squad. Sarah loves music. She wants to conduct __16.__ music someday. Sarah is also a __17.__ puzzle maker who is always rearranging the letters in words. For example, she told me that **Chopin's** is almost an __18.__ for **phonics**. She is writing a __19.__ of her visit. She even drew a __20.__ of our neighborhood to show to her family back in Warsaw.

symphonic
anagram
earphones
diagram
megaphone
headphones
chronicle
chronic
grammatical

Replace the Phrases

1. _____
2. _____
3. _____
4. _____
5. _____
6. _____
7. _____
8. _____
9. _____
10. _____
11. _____

Use Context Clues

12. _____
13. _____
14. _____
15. _____
16. _____
17. _____
18. _____
19. _____
20. _____

Connections to WRITING

Proofread an Outline

Proofread the outline below for ten misspelled words. Then rewrite it. Write the spelling words correctly and make the corrections indicated by the proofreading marks.

Proofreading Marks

≡	Capital Letter
/	Small Letter
∧	Add
ℓ	Delete
⊙	Add a Period
¶	Indent

A Chronical of the Telaphone [Note to myself: be careful of gramatical errors when writing this essay⊙]

I. Brief description [Note to myself: include a diogram⊙]

   A. Handsets

      1. Speech converted to electrical signals by micraphone

      2. Signals converted back into sound through earphoans

II. history and Development

   A. Early telecommunications cronology

      1. Telegraph invented, 1837; first Morse code tellegram, 1844

   B. Modern advances

      1. Digital phone lines and modems; the internet

      2. Accessories (headfones, rechargers, hands-free devices)

      3. New technologies syncranize transmission of sound ∧and data

INFORMATIVE/EXPLANATORY Writing Prompt

Write an Outline

Research a communications device named in the spelling word list. Write an outline of your findings.

- Divide your outline into major topics, subtopics, and details.
- Use as many spelling words as you can.
- Proofread for capitalization and spelling.
- Circle three words you are unsure about. Check their spelling in a print or online dictionary.

Transfer

Select one of the Greek forms from the unit and brainstorm words with that root; for example, **chronic, chronicle, chronology, chronological, synchronize, synchronicity**. Write the words in your Spelling Journal.

Word Study

Word Building

1.
2.
3.
4.
5.
6.
7.
8.
9.
10.
11.

Meaning Mastery

12.
13.
14.
15.
16.
17.
18.
19.
20.

grammar	diagram	telephone	chronic
saxophone	cacophony	gramophone	microphone
earphones	anagram	gyroscope	kaleidoscope
phonics	stethoscope	microscope	symphonic
phonetic	chronological	parallelogram	telegram
microscopic	periscope	polyphonic	cardiogram
telescopic	grammatical	chronology	chronicle
symphonious	anachronism	telescope	synchronize
headphones	megaphone	epigram	synchronization

Word Building

Combine the roots and form a spelling word.

1. phon(e) meaning "sound" and **kakos** meaning "bad"

2–3. tele meaning "far" and **scope** meaning "see"

4–5. scope meaning "see" and **micro** meaning "small"

6. phon(e) meaning "sound" and **megas** meaning "great"

7. phon(e) meaning "sound" and **poly** meaning "many"

8. scope meaning "see" and **peri** meaning "around"

9. gram meaning "letter" and **epi** meaning "upon"

10–11. sym meaning "together" and **phon(e)** meaning "sound"

Meaning Mastery

Write the word from the box that best completes each sentence.

12. The word **purse** is a(n) _____ of the word **super**.

13. She has _____ bronchitis. She is always coughing.

14. The clarinet and _____ are woodwind instruments.

15. A doctor uses a(n) _____ to hear our heartbeat.

16. A square, rectangle, rhombus, and _____ are all quadrilaterals.

17. "He don't like potato chips" is an example of poor _____.

18. Practicing _____, or letter sounds, is a first step toward literacy.

19. Saying that computers existed before typewriters is a(n) _____.

20. A(n) _____ has mirrors and bits of colored glass.

Math
Word Hunt

Read the paragraphs below. Look for words with the Greek form **gram, chron, phon(e),** or **scope**.

People usually think of numbers and formulas when they think of mathematics, but our everyday lives are full of math. Look around you. The things you see are a chronology of inventions based on math. Certainly adding, subtracting, multiplying, and dividing are useful operations, but math is also spatial. This means it's concerned with size, shape, and distance. The periscope on a submarine is based on simple principles of math. Similarly, astronomers are able to see far into the universe with the telescope, and scientists can see unbelievably tiny things with microscopes. All of these devices use angles.

Math also helps us understand how things move. Sound moves across a room in a curvy pattern like ocean waves, not in a straight line. Our study of math in the physical world of sound, light, and motion—generally referred to as *physics*—has helped us invent countless things. Before the microphone was invented, for example, people had to shout or sing very loudly to be heard by an audience. Finally, someone figured out how to "aim" sound waves in the same way that we cup our hands around our mouth when shouting. The result was the megaphone, but it didn't stop there. Your doctor uses a stethoscope to focus the waves of sound from your heart to make it louder.

When people began to understand the math that made it possible to generate waves of electricity and send it through wires, we soon sent messages by telegram. Before long we had the telephone, the electric light, and even the mp3 player with tiny earphones. None of these would have been possible without math!

1. _____
2. _____
3. _____
4. _____
5. _____
6. _____
7. _____
8. _____
9. _____
10. _____

1. Write one word with the Greek form **gram**.
2. Write one word with the Greek form **chron**.
3–6. Write four words with the Greek form **phon(e)**.
7–10. Write four words with the Greek form **scope**.

Connections to THINKING

Read the spelling words and sentences.

1.	proceed	*proceed*	You may **proceed** to the next task.
2.	bazaar	*bazaar*	You can find everything at the **bazaar**.
3.	insure	*insure*	We need to **insure** our new car.
4.	formally	*formally*	We bowed **formally** to the queen.
5.	complement	*complement*	The red shoes **complement** her dress.
6.	desert	*desert*	Camels live in the **desert**.
7.	conscience	*conscience*	Her **conscience** told her she was wrong.
8.	disinterested	*disinterested*	She offered a **disinterested** opinion.
9.	marshal	*marshal*	The **marshal** rounded up the criminals.
10.	uninterested	*uninterested*	I became **uninterested** in the book.
11.	precede	*precede*	Does soup **precede** the main course?
12.	ensure	*ensure*	I can **ensure** success with hard work.
13.	martial	*martial*	Kate is a **martial** arts expert.
14.	dessert	*dessert*	We are having fresh fruit for **dessert**.
15.	bizarre	*bizarre*	Kel's behavior was **bizarre** last night.
16.	conscious	*conscious*	The man was not **conscious** after the crash.
17.	censor	*censor*	The TV **censor** bleeped out the word.
18.	formerly	*formerly*	She was **formerly** a dancer.
19.	sensor	*sensor*	That **sensor** can detect movement.
20.	compliment	*compliment*	Thank you for your kind **compliment**.

Think & Sort the spelling words.

1–20. Write each pair of commonly confused words.

Remember

When words sound similar to each other, or when they are homophones, their spellings can be easily confused.

1. _____
2. _____
3. _____
4. _____
5. _____
6. _____
7. _____
8. _____
9. _____
10. _____
11. _____
12. _____
13. _____
14. _____
15. _____
16. _____
17. _____
18. _____
19. _____
20. _____

Connections to VOCABULARY

Word Meanings

Write the correct spelling word for each meaning.

1. (conscience, conscious) awake, aware
2. (formerly, formally) previously
3. (conscious, conscience) the awareness of right and wrong
4. (precede, proceed) to go forth
5. (bizarre, bazaar) strange
6. (uninterested, disinterested) impartial
7. (insure, ensure) to arrange insurance for
8. (precede, proceed) to come before
9. (bizarre, bazaar) a street market
10. (insure, ensure) to make certain
11. (formerly, formally) ceremoniously
12. (dessert, desert) an end-of-meal treat
13. (dessert, desert) a dry area
14. (uninterested, disinterested) not interested

Word Meanings
1.
2.
3.
4.
5.
6.
7.
8.
9.
10.
11.
12.
13.
14.

Use the Dictionary
15.
16.
17.
18.
19.
20.

Use the Dictionary

Homophones are words that sound the same but have different spellings and meanings. Because they sound the same, homophones can be easily confused. Use your **Spelling Dictionary** to check the pronunciation of the words in this unit. Use the pronunciation key to practice saying the words to yourself.

15–20. Write three pairs of spelling words that are homophones.

proceed	bazaar	insure	formally	complement
desert	conscience	disinterested	marshal	uninterested
precede	ensure	martial	dessert	bizarre
conscious	censor	formerly	sensor	compliment

Complete the Sentences

Write pairs of spelling words to complete each sentence.

1–2. The woman who _____ had been ambassador to England _____ addressed our graduating class.

3–4. A _____ party has no stake in a dispute: an _____ party is indifferent to its outcome.

5–6. We received a nice _____ from our art instructor for finding the full _____ of missing sketches.

7–8. My _____ has made me _____ of the fact that I should always be honest.

9–10. The U.S. _____ is also a _____ arts expert.

11–12. To _____ that we can afford to fix our car if we are in an accident, we must _____ it.

13–14. A _____ is used to detect light, but a _____ examines books for objectionable topics.

Complete the Sentences

1. _____
2. _____
3. _____
4. _____
5. _____
6. _____
7. _____
8. _____
9. _____
10. _____
11. _____
12. _____
13. _____
14. _____

Use Context Clues

15. _____
16. _____
17. _____
18. _____
19. _____
20. _____

Use Context Clues

Write spelling words from the box to complete the paragraph.

At a street **15.** , you can find many interesting items for sale. Some items are useful, such as clothing and spices. Others are **16.** , like candied crickets. Would you like to eat a candied cricket for **17.** ? If you want to buy an item, some bargaining will often **18.** the actual sale. You will offer a price, and then the merchant will counteroffer with a higher price. Finally, you will agree on a fair amount, and you will **19.** to the transaction. Traditionally, these outdoor markets were commonly found in the Middle East in big cities and towns in the **20.** . Nowadays, they can be found in many other places, too—even near our own homes!

bazaar
bizarre
desert
dessert
precede
proceed

Connections to WRITING

Proofread a Paragraph

Proofread the paragraph below for ten misspelled words. Then rewrite the paragraph. Write the spelling words correctly and make the corrections indicated by the proofreading marks.

Proofreading Marks

☰	Capital Letter
/	Small Letter
∧	Add
℮	Delete
⊙	Add a Period
⁋	Indent

⁋The movie *The Taekwondo Master* is one of my favorites. It is about a boy named Park, who is having a hard time at school because he is bullied by bigger boys. he wants to fight back, but his conscients tells him not to do it. Park becomes unintrested in school and his friendships. Then he is formaly introduced to a marital arts master. Park is very keen to learn about Taekwondo. He plans to use to *it* enshure that he is never bullied again. Through his training, he becomes consious of his body and his mind and how they work together. I am able to identify with Park because I was formerley bullied in school too. Unlike Park, my outlet has been music⊙ I have been able to use it to compelment my education and have learned that if I follow my passion, I can procede through life with no fear. This film deserves the highest complement I can give it!

NARRATIVE Writing Prompt

Write a Paragraph

Think of a movie, play, or television program that affected you strongly. Write a paragraph about the experience.

- Briefly describe the movie, play, or TV program.
- Explain how and why it affected you.
- Use as many spelling words as you can.
- Proofread for grammar, capitalization, and punctuation.
- Circle three words you are unsure about. Check their spelling in a print or online dictionary.

Transfer

Create a list of commonly confused spelling words in your Spelling Journal, including the words in this list. Then add the following words: **accept, adapt, personnel, stationary, effect**. Can you think of any words that could be confused with these new words? Write them.

Word Study

Word Structure

1. _____
2. _____
3. _____
4. _____
5. _____
6. _____
7. _____
8. _____
9. _____
10. _____
11. _____
12. _____
13. _____
14. _____

Meaning Mastery

15. _____
16. _____
17. _____
18. _____
19. _____
20. _____

advise	formally	disinterested	bazaar	assent	elicit
advice	formerly	uninterested	persecute	bizarre	ascent
accept	precede	complement	marshal	descent	carat
except	proceed	compliment	martial	decent	illicit
ensure	desert	prosecute	conscious	censor	dissent
insure	dessert	conscience	sensor	caret	

Word Structure

1–12. Write the words that have the same number of letters and only one letter is different.

13–14. Write the words that differ by only a prefix.

Meaning Mastery

Write the correct word for each meaning.

15. (illicit, elicit)   illegal

16. (descent, dissent, decent)   a way down

17. (persecute, prosecute)   to take a legal action

18. (dissent, decent, descent)   disagreement

19. (martial, marshal)   relating to war

20. (accept, except)   to leave out, exclude

Science
Word Hunt

Read the paragraphs below. Look for words that are commonly confused with similar words.

Have you ever spotted stars moving across the night sky? These may actually have been man-made satellites orbiting Earth. Formerly, all spacecraft orbited Earth and provided valuable communication and weather links to land-based equipment. Then another type of unmanned spacecraft was developed. These spacecraft are programmed to take photos of planets, asteroids, comets, and even galaxies. They are a useful complement to Earth-based telescopes.

Galileo was one of these exploratory spacecraft. It was named for the scientist who studied Jupiter 500 years ago. Galileo was not formally credited for having discovered the giant planet. However, he did discover all four of its moons. The *Galileo* spacecraft set out to study Jupiter and its moons.

Many disinterested people were conscious of how bizarre the *Galileo* spacecraft looked. Built in three sections, it was not at all sleek and streamlined. Even so, it did what it was programmed to do. *Galileo* was launched in 1989, piggy-backing on the space shuttle *Atlantis* and proceeding from there on its path. Before heading out to space, it made a couple of "slingshot" loops around Earth to ensure that it had enough momentum. It was like swinging a yo-yo in a circle above your head.

Early explorers had to travel for months or years across deserts and oceans to reach new destinations. The spacecraft *Galileo* was no different. Its trip to Jupiter took more than six years to complete! It photographed the massive planet and its moons from very close range.

Galileo's mission was remarkable, for none of the spacecraft that preceded it had ever attempted to travel so far or teach scientists so much.

1. _____
2. _____
3. _____
4. _____
5. _____
6. _____
7. _____
8. _____
9. _____
10. _____

1–10. Look at the word list on page 182. There are ten commonly confused words in the passage above. Find and write them. Two of the words have the **-ing** or **-ed** ending.

Connections to THINKING

Read the spelling words and sentences.

1.	deluxe	*deluxe*	We stayed in a **deluxe** two-bedroom suite.
2.	carousel	*carousel*	The **carousel** turned while music played.
3.	mirage	*mirage*	Do I see water in the desert or a **mirage**?
4.	fiancé	*fiancé*	My sister will marry her **fiancé** in June.
5.	picturesque	*picturesque*	That mountain inn is very **picturesque**.
6.	masquerade	*masquerade*	Your costume for the **masquerade** is ready.
7.	corsage	*corsage*	The rose **corsage** complemented her gown.
8.	fatigue	*fatigue*	Extreme **fatigue** made him fall asleep.
9.	impasse	*impasse*	We are at an **impasse** and cannot continue.
10.	chaperone	*chaperone*	Raina's parents will **chaperone** the party.
11.	intrigue	*intrigue*	The mystery play was filled with **intrigue**.
12.	fiancée	*fiancée*	His **fiancée** will plan the entire wedding.
13.	boutique	*boutique*	I bought Mom's pin at a jewelry **boutique**.
14.	camouflage	*camouflage*	The tree branches will **camouflage** the car.
15.	expertise	*expertise*	We rely on Dr. Wing's medical **expertise**.
16.	silhouette	*silhouette*	Our art teacher cut out my **silhouette**.
17.	résumé	*résumé*	List all previous jobs on your **résumé**.
18.	souvenir	*souvenir*	We kept the ticket stub as a **souvenir**.
19.	menagerie	*menagerie*	The circus had a **menagerie** of animals.
20.	gourmet	*gourmet*	The hotel chef prepared a **gourmet** meal.

Think & Sort the spelling words. Circle the letters that spell the targeted sound.

1–4. Write the words that end in /$\bar{a}$/.

5–7. Write the words that end in /$\bar{e}$g/ or /ĕl/.

8–10. Write the words that begin with **de-, ex-,** or **im-**.

11–13. Write the words that begin with /**s**/ or /**sh**/.

14–20. Write the words in which /**zh**/ or /**j**/ is spelled **ge** or /**k**/ is spelled **que**.

Remember

The English language includes many words from French. Notice the French-influenced spellings.

/$\bar{a}$/

1.
2.
3.
4.

/$\bar{e}$g/ or /ĕl/

5.
6.
7.

de-, ex-, im-

8.
9.
10.

/s/, /sh/

11.
12.
13.

/zh/, /j/ spelled ge

14.
15.
16.
17.

/k/ spelled que

18.
19.
20.

Connections to VOCABULARY

Word Meanings

Write a spelling word for each description.

1. a summary of one's job experiences
2. one who appreciates fine food
3. luxurious, elegant
4. to conceal something by making it look like its natural surroundings
5. a collection of wild animals on exhibition
6. exhaustion; weariness
7. a dead end

Word Replacements

Write the spelling word that best replaces the underlined word or words.

8. He would soon reveal his true identity because he could not keep up the <u>pretense</u> much longer.
9. We rode up and down on the <u>merry-go-round</u> horses.
10. Cal's older sister will be a <u>supervisor</u> on the field trip.
11. They moved to a <u>charming</u> town by the seashore.
12. At their fiftieth anniversary party, Grandfather pinned a <u>small flower bouquet</u> on Grandmother's suit jacket.
13. They could use a chef with your <u>ability</u> in their restaurant.

Use the **Dictionary**

Write a spelling word for each etymology. Use the **Spelling Dictionary** if you need help.

14. Fr., memory < *souvenir*, to recall < Lat. *subvenire*, to come to mind
15. Fr. < OProv. *botica* < Lat. *apotheca*, storehouse
16. Fr. < *mirer*, to look at < Lat. *mirari*, to wonder at
17. Fr., p.part. of *fiancer*, to betroth < *fier*, to trust
18. Fr., fem. of *fiancé*, fiancé
19. Fr. < Etienne de *Silhouette* (1709–1767)
20. Fr. < Ital. *intrigo* < *intrigare*, to perplex < Lat. *intricare*

Word Meanings
1. _____
2. _____
3. _____
4. _____
5. _____
6. _____
7. _____

Word Replacements
8. _____
9. _____
10. _____
11. _____
12. _____
13. _____

Use the Dictionary
14. _____
15. _____
16. _____
17. _____
18. _____
19. _____
20. _____

deluxe	carousel	mirage	picturesque	fiancé
corsage	fatigue	chaperone	masquerade	impasse
intrigue	fiancée	boutique	camouflage	expertise
résumé	souvenir	menagerie	gourmet	silhouette

Complete the Analogies

Write the spelling word that best completes each analogy.

1. **Trophy** is to **plaque** as **memento** is to _____.
2. **Vegetables** are to **salad** as **flowers** are to _____.
3. **Reality** is to **puddle** as **illusion** is to _____.
4. **Shark** is to **aquarium** as **zebra** is to _____.
5. **Comedy** is to **humor** as **mystery** is to _____.
6. **Sunlight** is to **darkness** as **energy** is to _____.
7. **Milk** is to **supermarket** as **dress** is to _____.

Complete the Questions

Write the spelling word that best completes each question.

8. Will the artist cut out your _____ from black paper?
9. Can you afford such expensive _____ accommodations?
10. When do your sister and her _____ plan to get married?
11. Which animal's _____ makes the animal look like a leaf?
12. What information should I put on my _____?
13. How will they get beyond this _____ in their discussion and find a solution to the problem?
14. Is she a _____, or does she prefer fast food?

Use Context Clues

Write spelling words from the box to complete the paragraph.

We attended the opening of *Romeo and Juliet* at the community theater last night. My brother's **15.**, who is in the cast, got us tickets. The production was lovely! The **16.** ball was my favorite scene. The set designer had built a **17.** that rotated the sets, and the painted backdrops were charming and **18.**. The designer's **19.** showed in the detail of the period costumes. The actress who played Juliet's **20.** stole the show!

carousel
chaperone
masquerade
picturesque
fiancée
expertise

Complete the Analogies

1.
2.
3.
4.
5.
6.
7.

Complete the Questions

8.
9.
10.
11.
12.
13.
14.

Use Context Clues

15.
16.
17.
18.
19.
20.

Connections to WRITING

Proofread a Paragraph

Proofread the paragraph below for ten misspelled words. Then rewrite the paragraph. Write the spelling words correctly and make the corrections indicated by the proofreading marks.

Proofreading Marks

☰	Capital Letter
/	Small Letter
∧	Add
℘	Delete
⊙	Add a Period
⌗	Indent

⌗My partner and I were about to lock the doors to our D̶etective agency when suddenly there a stranger appeared. His sorrow and fatique were evident. He told us he was a goorme chef who had catered a fancy maskerade ball the night before⊙ He and his fiance had set up serving tables near a pictaresque menajerie of exotic animals. At midnight, his beloved had disappeared. He thought he had seen her silooette against one of the dining room walls, but it turned out to be a miraje. Now he wanted ^us to use our expertice as detectives to locate her. We enjoy intreeg, so we took the case.

NARRATIVE Writing Prompt
Write a Mystery

Write the next paragraph of this mystery story, or write the first paragraph of your own story.

- If you continue the story from above, begin by describing your actions the next day.
- If you start your own story, include the setting, the characters, and the mysterious conflict.
- Follow the form used in the proofreading example.
- Use as many spelling words as you can.
- Proofread for grammar, capitalization, and punctuation.
- Circle three words you are unsure about. Check their spelling in a print or online dictionary.

Transfer

Create a "Words from French" page in your Spelling Journal. Think of more words that have /k/ spelled **que** or end with **long a,** /ēg/ as in **fatigue,** or /ĕl/ as in **carousel.** Check a dictionary for the origin of each word. If the words come from French, write them on your journal page.

Word Study

Pronunciation

1.

2.

3.

4.

5.

6.

7.

8.

9.

10.

Meaning Mastery

11.

12.

13.

14.

15.

16.

17.

18.

19.

20.

beret	carte blanche	antique	gourmet	amateur	silhouette
fiancé	connoisseur	résumé	impasse	intrigue	chaperone
crochet	masquerade	fiancée	souvenir	etiquette	à la carte
garage	flamboyant	deluxe	boutique	corsage	chandelier
cuisine	rendezvous	fatigue	carousel	expertise	picturesque
mirage	camouflage	finesse	brochure	reservoir	menagerie

Pronunciation

Use words from the box to complete the exercises. Use a dictionary to check your answers.

1–4. Write the words in which the letters **ou** spell /o͞o/.

5–6. Write the words in which the letters **ou** spell the **schwa** sound.
Write the words that sound like the nonsense words and phrases below. The stressed syllables are in bold.

7. **shap**per own

8. di**lucks**

9. cro**shay**

10. buh**ray**

Meaning Mastery

The French are famous for their food. Write the words that match the definitions below. All of your answers will be related to food and eating.

11–12. a person who knows about fine foods and drinks

13. food, or a characteristic style of preparing food

14. a manner of ordering food where each item has a separate price on the menu

Write the words that match each definition.

15. a small flower arrangement worn on the wrist or on clothing

16. a place to park your car

17. a short report of your education and work experience

18. an item from long ago

19. a hanging light fixture

20. not professional

Art
Word Hunt

Read the paragraphs below. Look for words which come from French.

1.	
2.	
3.	
4.	
5.	
6.	
7.	
8.	
9.	
10.	

We can learn a lot about the past from art. Records of earlier lives come to us through sculpture, paintings, and written descriptions. The arts are a window into the picturesque country living in rural England and the elegance of wealthy European royalty.

Such paintings might show us the noisy fun of a town festival. In the painting we can see fancy treats, a colorful carousel, people on stilts, acrobats masquerading as clowns, and a menagerie of exotic animals. There are also villagers with expressions of amazement on their faces. Looking at such a scene, we can almost hear the laughter and music. We can also share the joy of children as they receive their souvenirs.

Other paintings reveal the formality of dating and courtship in high society. Marriages were arranged by two families. Visits between the young fiancé and fiancée were planned. A painting of this type of visit might also include a chaperone, who was often present during these visits because his or her expertise in such matters was trusted.

Elsewhere in these same mansions, quite a different atmosphere could also be found. Many paintings exist that show us what life was like in the kitchens of these estates. They depict teams of bustling cooks shouting to one another over the clang of pots and pans. There are wood stoves roaring. Counters are heaped with vegetables, bread, fish, and roast duck, and the cooks are feverishly stirring sauces for what promises to be a gourmet feast.

Such paintings give us a detailed picture of times very different from today. Through these paintings, we can begin to understand the lives of people we never met.

1–10. Look at the list of French words on page 188. There are ten of those words in the passage above. Find and write them. Two of the words have the inflectional ending **-ing** or **-s**.

Connections to THINKING

Read the spelling words and sentences.

1.	fluctuate	*fluctuate*	Her moods **fluctuate** from glad to sad.
2.	mannerism	*mannerism*	Blinking rapidly is a **mannerism**.
3.	missive	*missive*	Admiral Orr sent a **missive** to the ship.
4.	fluent	*fluent*	Diana is **fluent** in Spanish and Italian.
5.	magnanimous	*magnanimous*	It is **magnanimous** of you to pardon us.
6.	admission	*admission*	I applied for **admission** to music camp.
7.	influence	*influence*	A clever lawyer can **influence** a jury.
8.	inanimate	*inanimate*	An **inanimate** object lacks life.
9.	manicure	*manicure*	Does she **manicure** her nails often?
10.	remiss	*remiss*	It would be **remiss** of me not to help.
11.	manipulate	*manipulate*	I cannot **manipulate** the kite strings.
12.	fluency	*fluency*	His **fluency** in Chinese was a surprise.
13.	transmission	*transmission*	The old van needs a new **transmission**.
14.	emancipate	*emancipate*	Please **emancipate** me from this duty.
15.	unanimous	*unanimous*	The decision to rest was **unanimous**.
16.	manual	*manual*	The **manual** says to twist the two wires.
17.	dismiss	*dismiss*	Mr. Curtis will **dismiss** class early.
18.	animate	*animate*	An **animate** object has life.
19.	fluorescent	*fluorescent*	Dad put **fluorescent** lights in the den.
20.	intermission	*intermission*	We will now take a brief **intermission**.

Think & Sort the spelling words.

Write the spelling words that come from the following Latin words:

1–6. miss, from **missus**, past participle of **mittere**, meaning "to send" or "let go"

7–11. man, from **manus**, meaning "hand"

12–16. flu, from **fluere**, meaning "to flow"

17–20. anim, from **animus** or **anima**, meaning "soul" or "spirit"

Remember

Knowing Latin roots such as **miss, manus, fluere,** and **animus** can give clues to the meaning and spelling of certain English words.

---

miss

1. _____
2. _____
3. _____
4. _____
5. _____
6. _____

man

7. _____
8. _____
9. _____
10. _____
11. _____

flu

12. _____
13. _____
14. _____
15. _____
16. _____

anim

17. _____
18. _____
19. _____
20. _____

Connections to VOCABULARY

Word Meanings

Write a spelling word related in meaning to complete each group.

1. careless, neglectful, _____
2. undulate, sway, _____
3. ultraviolet, incandescent, _____
4. ease, ability, _____
5. characteristic, trait, _____
6. letter, note, _____

Word Structure

Write the spelling words that are formed from the following Latin words and prefixes.

7. **unus,** meaning "one" + **animus,** meaning "mind"
8. **trans-,** meaning "across" + **mittere,** meaning "to send"
9. **in-,** meaning "in" + **fluere,** meaning "to flow"
10. **in-,** meaning "not" + **anima,** meaning "spirit"
11. **ex-,** meaning "out of" + **mancipium,** meaning "ownership"
12. **inter-,** meaning "between" + **missus,** meaning "let go"
13. **magnus,** meaning "great" + **animus,** meaning "soul"

Use the Dictionary

Write a spelling word to complete each sentence. Then look up the word in the **Spelling Dictionary** and write the letter of the definition that best suits the way the word is used in the sentence.

14. Before you try to assemble the bike, read the instruction _____ carefully.
15. Tanya is _____ in French.
16. How much is the _____ fee to the planetarium?
17. Paco is getting paid to _____ his neighbor's lawn and hedges.
18. Will the principal _____ all the classes right after lunch today?
19. To land the plane in these circumstances, the pilot will have to _____ the controls skillfully.
20. Someday she hopes to _____ her own cartoons.

Word Meanings

1. _____
2. _____
3. _____
4. _____
5. _____
6. _____

Word Structure

7. _____
8. _____
9. _____
10. _____
11. _____
12. _____
13. _____

Use the Dictionary

14. _____
15. _____
16. _____
17. _____
18. _____
19. _____
20. _____

fluctuate	missive	mannerism	fluent	magnanimous
admission	influence	inanimate	manicure	transmission
fluency	remiss	manipulate	emancipate	unanimous
manual	dismiss	animate	fluorescent	intermission

Complete the Analogies

Complete the Analogies
1.
2.
3.
4.
5.
6.
7.

Write a spelling word to complete each analogy.

1. **School** is to **recess** as **theater** is to _____.
2. **Cloth** is to **damask** as **light bulb** is to _____.
3. **Notable** is to **remarkable** as **generous** is to _____.
4. **Refusal** is to **acceptance** as **denial** is to _____.
5. **Bicycle** is to **gear** as **car** is to _____.
6. **Article** is to **editorial** as **letter** is to _____.
7. **Leave out** is to **omit** as **release** is to _____.

Complete the Sentences

Complete the Sentences
8.
9.
10.
11.
12.
13.
14.

Write the spelling word that completes each sentence.

8. Our summer temperatures _____ between 80 and 90 degrees.
9. Her _____ of tossing back her hair makes her seem dramatic.
10. The vote to adopt new club rules must be _____.
11. Emilio has a positive _____ on his brother's behavior.
12. I glued tiny gold hearts on my nails after my _____.
13. We would be _____ if we did not congratulate the winners.
14. The translator's job requires _____ in Spanish.

Use Context Clues

Use Context Clues
15.
16.
17.
18.
19.
20.

Write spelling words from the box to complete the paragraph.

Animation gives the illusion of life to **15.** objects. Today filmmakers **16.**, or bring to life, everything from packages and clothes to maps and diagrams. The smooth, **17.** movement in a cartoon is not easy to achieve. Each frame requires a new drawing or model. In a sense, computers have served to **18.** filmmakers. With computers, they are now able to **19.** images in ways that were impossible when animation was a totally **20.** skill.

| animate |
| emancipate |
| manual |
| inanimate |
| manipulate |
| fluent |

Connections to WRITING

Proofread a Paragraph

Proofread the news paragraph for ten misspelled words. Then rewrite the paragraph. Write the spelling words correctly and make the corrections indicated by the proofreading marks.

> In discussing Animation, it would be rimiss not to mention Walt Disney, a man who had a tremendous influance in this fields. Before Disney, the quality of animation would often fluctuait from film to film. Then, in 1937, Disney produced the first full-length animated feature, Snow White and the Seven Dwarfs. Critics were unannimus ^in hailing Disney as a pioneer in the use of fluint motion. One cannot dismis his achievements in this field. Disney knew how to annimate and minipulate characters and inanimmate objects realistically. He often gave each characteristic a peculiar mannerizm that made him or her unique. An example is the dwarf dopey, whose absolute silence endeared him to audiences of all ages⊙

INFORMATIVE/EXPLANATORY Writing Prompt

Write a Paragraph

Write a paragraph about a person who has had a great impact on some field of entertainment.

- Write a clear topic sentence that identifies the main idea of the paragraph.
- Include details that support the main idea.
- Follow the form used in the proofreading example.
- Use as many spelling words as you can.
- Proofread for grammar, capitalization, and punctuation.
- Circle three words you are unsure about. Check their spelling in a print or online dictionary.

Transfer

Select three words from the spelling list and think of related words. Write as many words as you can think of in your Spelling Journal. For example, **admission, admit, admissible, admittance, admitted**.

Word Study

Meaning Mastery

1. _____
2. _____
3. _____
4. _____
5. _____
6. _____
7. _____

Suffixes

8. _____
9. _____
10. _____
11. _____
12. _____
13. _____
14. _____
15. _____
16. _____
17. _____
18. _____
19. _____
20. _____

admitted	admission	dismiss	fluent
animate	influenza	affluent	influence
fluorescent	manicure	animosity	manifest
manner	inanimate	intermission	remiss
commissary	animation	mission	transmission
fluctuate	manipulate	emancipation	managerial
permission	unanimous	mannerism	fluency
unanimity	commission	magnanimous	manual
missive	emancipate	superfluous	omission

Meaning Mastery

Write the word that matches each meaning.

1. consent, authorization
2. something omitted
3. a break in a musical or dramatic performance
4. the act of admitting
5. the act of sending something, such as a radio signal
6. the act of committing
7. an assigment

Suffixes

8–12. Write the words with the suffix **-ate**. When this suffix is added to a base word or root, it often creates a verb form. Circle the word with the suffix **-ate** that cannot be a verb.

13–14. Write the words with the suffix **-tion** meaning "the act of."

15–17. Write the words with the suffix **-ous** meaning "characterized by." Circle the word that means "characterized by an overflow."

18–19. Write the words with the suffix **-al** meaning "characterized by."

20. Write the word with the suffix **-ary** meaning "relating to."

Technology

Word Hunt

Read the paragraphs below. Look for spelling words with the Latin form **miss, manus, fluere,** or **animus**.

Online study can be a very rewarding way to learn. For example, students who are trying to become fluent in a foreign language can make great progress in a relatively short time. But managing one's time is crucial. Negative consequences would result if a student is lazy or becomes remiss about deadlines and online assignments.

Some students might think online study allows them to do as they wish. They might dismiss the need for self-discipline and setting schedules. They may even grow to resent the burdens of self-study. Friends and family may notice a change in mannerisms. For example, students may fluctuate between being happy and animated because they think they have so much free time. However, later they panic when the course deadline nears and they are hopelessly behind!

Most people would unanimously agree that they fall somewhere in the middle. That's understandable given all the distractions that influence us. We just need to take a good look at our use of time and make an honest admission that we need to focus and eliminate our distractions.

One way to do this is to keep track of the interruptions we have at home. Once we know that, we can manipulate our schedule a bit so that our study does not prevent us from doing the things we enjoy. Perhaps the most important thing is to work when we are most alert and when we are least likely to be interrupted.

Online study is a wonderful tool and gives us tremendous freedom. Remember, though, that it's hard to be effective unless we make studying a regular part of our routine!

1. _____
2. _____
3. _____
4. _____
5. _____
6. _____
7. _____
8. _____
9. _____
10. _____

1–2. Write two words with the Latin form **animus**.
3–4. Write two words with the Latin form **manus**.
5–7. Write three words with the Latin form **fluere**.
8–10. Write three words with the Latin form **miss**.

Assess for Transfer

Unit 25

1.

2.

3.

4.

5.

6.

Unit 26

7.

8.

9.

10.

Unit 27

11.

12.

Unit 28

13.

14.

15.

16.

Unit 29

17.

18.

19.

20.

Units 25–29

Assessment

Each word in the box fits one of the spelling patterns or rules you have studied over the past five weeks. Read the unit descriptions. Then write each assessment word under the unit number it fits.

Unit 25

1–6. The prefixes **uni-, mono-, duo-,** and **bi-** indicate number.

Unit 26

7–10. The Greek word parts **gram, chron, phon(e),** and **scope** combine with other word parts to form new words.

Unit 27

11–12. When words sound similar to each other, or when they are homophones, their spellings can be easily confused.

Unit 28

13–16. The English language includes many words from French. Notice the French-influenced spellings.

Unit 29

17–20. Knowing Latin roots such as **miss, manus, fluere,** and **animus** can give clues to the meaning and spelling of certain English words.

Words for Assessment

- unified
- censored
- phonograph
- admissible
- censured
- milligram
- sabotage
- fluorescence
- duplicator
- biyearly
- microscopically
- filet
- entourage
- universal
- chronometer
- mandatory
- mystique
- unanimously
- monopolizing
- monogrammed

Unit 25: Prefixes: uni-, mono-, duo-, bi-

monopoly	dual	unique	monotony	duplication
binoculars	unite	university	monotonous	universe

Write the spelling word that completes each sentence.

1. Each person's fingerprints are _____.
2. After hearing the same song ten times, I felt it was getting _____.
3. If the only two widget makers join, they will have a _____ on the widget market.
4. The hoozit makers do not want the widget makers to _____.
5. This clock radio has a _____ purpose, which is that of both a clock and a radio.
6. Here's a new CD to relieve the _____ of listening to the old one over and over.
7. There are many solar systems in the _____.
8. You may look through my _____ to watch the birds.
9. Check to see that there is no _____ of efforts.
10. Dr. Schnable is a professor at the _____.

Unit 26: Greek Forms: gram, chron, phon(e), scope

telescope	grammatical	earphones	stethoscope	telegram
diagram	synchronize	telephone	microphone	microscope

Write a spelling word that goes with each occupation. Use the Greek word part given in parentheses.

11. doctor (scope)
12. secretary (phone)
13. architect (gram)
14. astronomer (scope)
15. radio announcer (phone)
16. airline pilot (phones)
17. research scientist (scope)
18. telegraph operator (gram)

Write the spelling word that completes each sentence.

19. Proofread your sentences to see that they are _____.
20. We'll _____ our swimming strokes for the show.

Unit 25

1. _____
2. _____
3. _____
4. _____
5. _____
6. _____
7. _____
8. _____
9. _____
10. _____

Unit 26

11. _____
12. _____
13. _____
14. _____
15. _____
16. _____
17. _____
18. _____
19. _____
20. _____

Review

Unit 27

1. _____
2. _____
3. _____
4. _____
5. _____
6. _____
7. _____
8. _____
9. _____
10. _____

Unit 28

11. _____
12. _____
13. _____
14. _____
15. _____
16. _____
17. _____
18. _____
19. _____
20. _____

Unit 27: Commonly Confused Words

ensure	formally	complement	desert	disinterested
insure	formerly	compliment	dessert	uninterested

Write two spelling words to complete each sentence.

Coach gave me a __1.__ by telling me that my skills are a nice __2.__ to the team.

You should __3.__ your valuable jewelry in order to __4.__ you can replace it if it is lost.

Jamie, who was __5.__ our saddle club treasurer, was __6.__ introduced as the new president.

I dreamed I was eating a fruity, sweet __7.__ in the Arizona __8.__ when a lizard asked for a bite.

A(n) __9.__ party doesn't care about the outcome, but a(n) __10.__ party isn't interested at all.

Unit 28: Words From French

mirage	masquerade	picturesque	fiancé	fatigue
intrigue	camouflage	silhouette	résumé	souvenir

Write the spelling words for these clues.

11. a dark outline
12. betrothed
13. pretty as a picture
14. desert illusion
15. protective coloring
16. secret plotting

Write each spelling word by adding the missing letters.

17. fat __ __ __ __
18. s __ __ venir

19. ré __ __ mé
20. masq __ __ __ ade

Unit 29: Latin Forms: miss, manus, fluere, animus

magnanimous	dismiss	influence	inanimate	transmission
unanimous	manual	admission	fluorescent	intermission

Write the spelling word that completes each sentence.

1. There was one short _____ between acts.
2. A violent storm interrupted the radio _____.
3. A teacher has a lasting _____ on students.
4. The proposal received the _____ support of the committee.
5. The principal decided to _____ the classes early on Friday.
6. The geologist studied rocks and other _____ objects.
7. Anyone seeking _____ to this school must pass a test.
8. The new classroom will have _____ lights in the ceiling.
9. Before operating the new computer, be sure to read the _____.
10. The charity received a generous gift from a _____ citizen.

Unit 29

1. _____
2. _____
3. _____
4. _____
5. _____
6. _____
7. _____
8. _____
9. _____
10. _____

Spelling Study Strategy

What's My Word?

Practicing spelling words can be fun if you make it into a game. Prepare a list of words you want to study. Trade lists with a partner. Play "What's My Word?" with your partner.

1. Ask your partner, "What's my word?" Your partner reads one of the words from your list.

2. Write the word and then spell the word aloud. If you have spelled it correctly, your partner will say, "That's your word!" and you get two points. If you did not spell it correctly, your partner will say, "That's not your word!" and give you a clue, such as "It ends with a silent e." If you get the word right the second time, you get one point. If not, you get no points.

3. Then it's your partner's turn to ask, "What's my word?" Continue until you've gone through both lists of words.

Directions: Read each item carefully. Select the best answer and fill in the circle on your answer sheet.

1. Read the following sentence.

> With which instrument can I see the farthest: a microscope, binoculers, or a telescope?

Which word in the sentence is spelled INCORRECTLY?

A. instrument
B. microscope
C. binoculers
D. telescope

2. Read the following sentence.

> During the intermission of the university's performance, I thought I saw the silouette of an old friend.

Which word in the sentence is spelled INCORRECTLY?

A. intermission
B. university's
C. performance
D. silouette

3. In which of the following words is **bi-** a prefix meaning "twice"?

A. biennial
B. birdwatching
C. bicker
D. bizarre

4. Read the following sentence.

> The stroll through the picturesque valley did not intregue the boy.

What change, if any, should be made to this sentence?

A. Change **stroll** to **strole**
B. Change **picturesque** to **pitcheresque**
C. Change **intregue** to **intrigue**
D. Make **no** change

5. Which of the following words is spelled INCORRECTLY?

A. monopoly
B. stethescope
C. fatigue
D. admission

6. Read the following sentence.

> On their walk in the hot, dry dessert, her fiancé said he thought he saw water, but it was only a mirage.

Which word in the sentence is spelled INCORRECTLY?

A. dessert
B. fiancé
C. thought
D. mirage

7. Read the following sentence.

> The committee made a unanimous decision to offer Suzette admission to the university.

What change, if any, should be made to this sentence?

A. Change **unanimous** to **unaminous**
B. Change **admission** to **admittion**
C. Change **university** to **univeristy**
D. Make **no** change

GO ON

8. In which word do the letters **uni** NOT mean "one"?

A. unique   C. unite
B. universe   D. uninterested

9. Read the following sentence.

> To ensure her résumé is impressive, Rhonda must recheck it for misspellings and gramatical errors.

Which word in the sentence is spelled INCORRECTLY?

A. ensure   C. misspellings
B. résumé   D. gramatical

10. Which of the following words is spelled INCORRECTLY?

A. manual   C. influents
B. camouflage   D. telephone

11. Read the following sentence.

> The university president decided to dismis classes early to ensure that students could get home safely before the storm.

What change, if any, should be made to this sentence?

A. Change **univeristy** to **university**
B. Change **dismis** to **dismiss**
C. Change **ensure** to **ansure**
D. Make **no** change

12. Which of the following words is spelled INCORRECTLY?

A. syncronize   C. magnanimous
B. souvenir   D. unite

13. Read the following sentence.

> Her fiancée was a disinterested attendee at the masquerade ball, but he had the most unique costume.

Which word in the sentence is spelled INCORRECTLY?

A. fiancée   C. masquerade
B. disinterested   D. unique

14. Read the following sentences.

> I had to formerly compliment the speaker. His humor and interesting stories broke the monotony of the very dull conference.

What change, if any, should be made to these sentences?

A. Change **formerly** to **formally**
B. Change **compliment** to **complement**
C. Change **monotony** to **monotany**
D. Make **no** change

15. Read the following sentences.

> The earphones served a duel purpose. They blocked out the monotonous chatter and allowed me to listen to relaxing music.

Which word in these sentences is spelled INCORRECTLY?

A. earphones   C. monotonous
B. duel   D. relaxing

STOP

Grammar, Usage, and Mechanics
Prepositions

A **preposition** relates a word in a sentence to a noun or pronoun called the **object of the preposition**. The preposition, its object, and the words in between make up a prepositional phrase.

The pilot placed the earphones <u>over</u> his <u>ears</u>.

preposition   object

Here are some common prepositions:

above	around	between	from	near	over	into
among	behind	for	in	on	with	of

A. Write the preposition in each sentence below.

  1. Ming-Shian enrolled in the university.

  2. I wore my binoculars around my neck.

  3. Speak clearly into the microphone.

  4. What is the difference between the candidates?

  5. Place the manual on the tallest stack.

  6. Is that an admission of guilt?

  7. We bought several souvenirs from the vendor.

  8. Let's meet here during intermission.

B. Write the object of the preposition in each sentence below.

  9. Climb carefully up the ladder.

10. You might not like the effect of that advice.

11. We noticed a familiar silhouette on the wall.

12. The class looked toward the teacher.

13. The children were quiet throughout the program.

14. The team ran twice around the track.

15. The little mouse scurried down the hole.

A

1. _____

2. _____

3. _____

4. _____

5. _____

6. _____

7. _____

8. _____

B

9. _____

10. _____

11. _____

12. _____

13. _____

14. _____

15. _____

The Writing Process: Informative/Explanatory
Writing a Summary

PREWRITING

Sometimes we want to tell others about a book or article we have read. The best way to do that is to share the main points in a short piece of writing called a summary. Think of something you can summarize. You can find books and articles at the library. You can also ask your teacher to help you look on the Internet at sites such as Kids Newsroom (www.kidsnewsroom.org). As you read, take notes on the important information.

DRAFTING

Use your notes to write a summary. Begin with a topic sentence that presents the main idea. Follow your notes as you write supporting sentences. Don't give too much information in a summary. Use as many spelling words as possible. If you don't know how to spell a word, make your best guess. You will be able to revise your summary later.

REVISING

When you have finished your first draft, read your summary from beginning to end. Check to see if you have included all of the points in your notes. Did you achieve your purpose for writing? Does each sentence support the topic?

EDITING

Use the editing checklist to proofread your summary. Be sure to use proofreading marks when you make corrections. Circle any words you are unsure about and use a print or online dictionary to check spelling. Now write your final draft.

PUBLISHING

Make a copy of your summary and share it with your readers.

EDITING CHECKLIST

Spelling
- ✓ Circle words that contain the spelling patterns learned in Units 25–29.
- ✓ Check the circled words in in a print or online dictionary.
- ✓ Check for other spelling errors.

Capital Letters
- ✓ Capitalize important words in the title.
- ✓ Capitalize the first word in each sentence.
- ✓ Capitalize proper nouns.

Punctuation
- ✓ End each sentence with the correct punctuation.
- ✓ Use commas, apostrophes, and quotation marks correctly.

Grammar, Usage, and Mechanics
- ✓ Make sure each preposition relates to a noun or pronoun.

Connections to THINKING

Read the spelling words and sentences.

1.	specific	specific	Please give a **specific** description.
2.	classically	classically	The music was **classically** composed.
3.	mechanical	mechanical	His actions are **mechanical** and stiff.
4.	scientific	scientific	Her **scientific** research is famous.
5.	artistically	artistically	The image was depicted **artistically**.
6.	dynamic	dynamic	People like his **dynamic** personality.
7.	historical	historical	This is a **historical** document.
8.	drastically	drastically	She has changed **drastically**.
9.	heroic	heroic	The brave knight's deed was **heroic**.
10.	scientifically	scientifically	I approach a problem **scientifically**.
11.	artistic	artistic	His **artistic** talents are well-known.
12.	mechanically	mechanically	The robot moved **mechanically**.
13.	classic	classic	It is a **classic** piece of literature.
14.	historically	historically	This chart is **historically** incorrect.
15.	economic	economic	It was a time of **economic** prosperity.
16.	heroically	heroically	She acted **heroically** during a crisis.
17.	dynamically	dynamically	The actor performed **dynamically**.
18.	drastic	drastic	These **drastic** measures are necessary.
19.	specifically	specifically	Tell me **specifically** what happened.
20.	economically	economically	It was an **economically** unwise choice.

Think & Sort the spelling words.

1–20. Write the words that are adjectives ending with **ic** or **ical** and their adverb partners ending with **-ly**.

Remember

You must add **al** to words ending with **ic** before adding the suffix **-ly**.

Adjectives and adverbs

1. _____
2. _____
3. _____
4. _____
5. _____
6. _____
7. _____
8. _____
9. _____
10. _____
11. _____
12. _____
13. _____
14. _____
15. _____
16. _____
17. _____
18. _____
19. _____
20. _____

Connections to VOCABULARY

Word Meanings

Write the spelling word that matches each definition, using the part of speech in parentheses as an additional clue.

1. with great energy or force (adverb)
2. in a way that leaves no uncertainty (adverb)
3. relating to the study of natural phenomena (adjective)
4. showing imagination or creativity (adverb)
5. having existed in the past (adjective)
6. in an automatic or machinelike way (adverb)

Synonyms

Write the spelling word that is a synonym for each of the following words.

7. courageously
8. energetic
9. severe
10. logically
11. particular
12. cheaply
13. timeless
14. creative

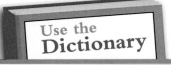

Use the
Dictionary

Look up each spelling word below in the **Spelling Dictionary**.

mechanical	drastically	heroic
classically	historically	economic

15–17. Write the words that have an individual or **separate entry**.
18–20. Write the words that have a joined or **run-on entry**.

Word Meanings

1. _____
2. _____
3. _____
4. _____
5. _____
6. _____

Synonyms

7. _____
8. _____
9. _____
10. _____
11. _____
12. _____
13. _____
14. _____

Use the Dictionary

15. _____
16. _____
17. _____
18. _____
19. _____
20. _____

Connections to READING

specific	classically	mechanical	scientific
artistically	dynamic	historical	drastically
heroic	scientifically	artistic	mechanically
classic	historically	economic	heroically
dynamically	drastic	specifically	economically

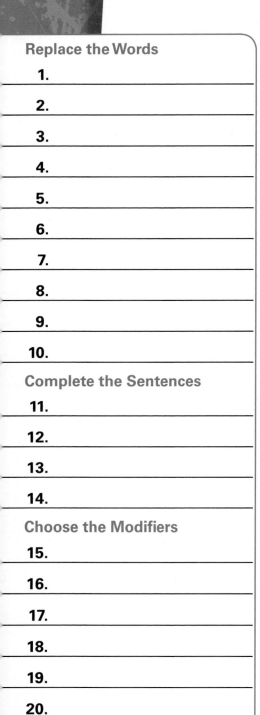

Replace the Words

1.
2.
3.
4.
5.
6.
7.
8.
9.
10.

Complete the Sentences

11.
12.
13.
14.

Choose the Modifiers

15.
16.
17.
18.
19.
20.

Replace the Words

Write the word that best replaces each underlined word or phrase.

1–2. Many inventors do not pursue their goals <u>traditionally</u>; because of this they may endure <u>monetary</u> hardships.

3. Such inventors face the challenge of poverty <u>gallantly</u>.

4–5. Inventions do not always result in <u>radical</u> changes. Often, they are <u>financially</u> impossible or impractical.

6–8. Archimedes, a citizen of ancient Greece, was one of the first inventors. His <u>lasting, significant</u> ideas changed the world radically. A true genius, he invented the <u>automatic</u> pulley.

9–10. A king once challenged him with the <u>exact</u> task of raising water from a ship's hold. The <u>noble</u> Archimedes invented a crank and screw that successfully raised the water.

Complete the Sentences

Write the spelling word that completes each sentence.

11. He decorated the room _____ with paintings and sculptures.

12. To complete this experiment _____, we should take exact measurements, observe carefully, and keep track of all details.

13. The year 1776 is _____ important for Americans.

14. The teacher was so _____ that she never sat at her desk.

Choose the Modifiers

Write the word that correctly completes each sentence.

15. Have you read any of James Michener's (**historical, historically**) novels?

16–17. Considerable (**scientific, scientifically**) research went into his books. He described times and places (**specific, specifically**).

18–19. Michener portrayed history (**dynamic, dynamically**), not (**mechanical, mechanically**).

20. He directed his (**artistic, artistically**) talent into breathing life into the past.

Connections to WRITING

Proofread a Biographical Sketch

Proofread the biographical sketch below for ten misspelled words. Then rewrite the sketch. Write the spelling words correctly and make the corrections indicated by the proofreading marks.

Leonardo da Vinci was perhaps one of the most historicly important artists of all time. Not only he was a talented and dinamic painter, but he devised many clasic inventions, including a flying machine, a parachute, and a diving bell. He succeeded in his work by using scientiffic observation and interpretation of natural and mechanicle phenomena. Amazingly, Da Vinci sketched his design of a helicopter hundreds of years before the first airplane was built! He based his invention on spesific observations of birds in flight.

This artistec genius was a product of the Italian renaissance. To aid his painting, Da Vinci scientificaly researched human anatomy. He then used his understanding of the human body to convey his subjects on canvas dynamacally and artistickly

Proofreading Marks

≡	Capital Letter
/	Small Letter
∧	Add
℘	Delete
⊙	Add a Period
¶	Indent

INFORMATIVE/EXPLANATORY Writing Prompt

Write a Biographical Sketch

Choose a famous artist, inventor, or scientist. Write a biographical sketch.

- Use both print and online resources to do your research.
- Include a specific incident, fascinating detail, or interesting story about your subject.
- Use as many spelling words as you can.
- Proofread for grammar, capitalization, and punctuation.
- Circle three words you are unsure about. Check their spelling in a print or online dictionary.

Transfer

In your Spelling Journal, write five more adjectives ending in **ic**. Then brainstorm other forms of the words, including the adverb form, and write them. For example, **fantastic, fantastically, fantasy, fantasize**.

207

Word Study

Word Usage

1.
2.
3.
4.
5.
6.
7.
8.

poetic	historical	emphatically	classically	melodic
artistic	poetically	enthusiastically	drastically	economic
drastic	automatic	economically	scientifically	dynamic
classic	enthusiastic	apologetically	mechanical	emphatic
heroic	heroically	automatically	melodically	tropically
specific	artistically	dynamically	apologetic	scientific
tropic	historically	mechanically	specifically	

Pronunciation

9.
10.
11.
12.
13.
14.
15.
16.
17.
18.
19.
20.

Word Usage

Remember that an **adjective** modifies a noun or pronoun, and an **adverb** modifies a verb, an adjective, or another adverb. For each word or phrase below, select the best modifier from the parentheses.

1. to speak (poetic, poetically)
2. a (historical, historically) accurate fact
3. a (drastic, drastically) measure
4. an (enthusiastic, enthusiastically) response
5. (mechanical, mechanically) inclined
6. to study (scientific, scientifically)
7. (automatic, automatically) renewed
8. a (specific, specifically) answer

Pronunciation

Look at the dictionary respellings below. Write the word and then write its adverb partner. Circle any words in which the stress shifts when the **-ly** suffix is added to create the adverb form.

9–10. /är tĭs′ tĭk/   15–16. /ĕm făt′ ĭk/
11–12. /hĭ rō′ ĭk/   17–18. /trŏp′ ĭk/
13–14. /klăs′ ĭk/   19–20. /me lŏd′ ĭk/

Fine Arts
Word Hunt

Read the paragraphs below.

People are often a little bewildered by the strange magic-wand movements of an orchestra conductor. The audience can see that the conductor is enthusiastic and has been classically trained. It's more difficult to understand what specific instruction the conductor's baton is telling each musician.

The audience can see that the conductor's mechanical up-and-down movements are keeping the beat. But the smaller, more artistic movements are sometimes difficult to understand. These small movements are signals to particular sections of the orchestra. The conductor may be instructing them to play more softly or to build gradually to something louder and more dramatic.

It seems as though orchestra members seldom look at the conductor. Why does the conductor bother to move about so artistically if no one is watching him or her? In actuality, the musicians can see the conductor's basic movements with their side vision, and they have practiced the music many times before. They know specifically when to watch the signals for their own parts.

The orchestra conductor is not teaching the music to the musicians. The conductor's interpretation of the piece shapes the timing. The maestro also maintains the dynamic energy and keeps all the musicians playing together. An energetic conductor may look a little crazy sometimes, but that makes the concert more fun to watch!

1. _____
2. _____
3. _____
4. _____
5. _____
6. _____
7. _____
8. _____
9. _____
10. _____

1–3. Write the words ending in **ic** to which **al** + **-ly** have been added.
4. Write the word ending in **ic** + **al** that could also take the **-ly** suffix.
5–10. Write the adjectives ending in **ic** that could also take **al** + **-ly** suffixes.

Connections to THINKING

Read the spelling words and sentences.

1.	conscientious	conscientious	A **conscientious** student works hard.
2.	crucial	crucial	The data are **crucial** to our research.
3.	substantial	substantial	A **substantial** amount is needed.
4.	spacious	spacious	Is the bedroom closet **spacious**?
5.	repetitious	repetitious	The boring speech was **repetitious**.
6.	spatial	spatial	I like the new **spatial** arrangement.
7.	confidential	confidential	The information is **confidential**.
8.	ferocious	ferocious	This tiny puppy is hardly **ferocious**.
9.	residential	residential	Drive slowly in a **residential** area.
10.	financial	financial	The **financial** impact was minimal.
11.	gracious	gracious	He was **gracious** even when he declined.
12.	impartial	impartial	A judge should be **impartial**.
13.	vicious	vicious	A hungry lion can be **vicious**.
14.	facial	facial	He has unusual **facial** features.
15.	influential	influential	She is quite an **influential** citizen.
16.	ambitious	ambitious	The **ambitious** students worked hard.
17.	glacial	glacial	The **glacial** ice melted very slowly.
18.	suspicious	suspicious	His obvious disguise was **suspicious**.
19.	potential	potential	You have **potential** for great success!
20.	superficial	superficial	The **superficial** cuts healed quickly.

Think & Sort the spelling words.

1–7. Write the words in which /shəl/ is spelled **tial**.
8–12. Write the words in which /shəl/ is spelled **cial**.
13–17. Write the words in which /shəs/ is spelled **cious**.
18–20. Write the words in which /shəs/ is spelled **tious**.

Remember

A final /shəs/ is spelled **cious** or **tious** and a final /shəl/ is spelled **tial** or **cial**.

tial
1. ___
2. ___
3. ___
4. ___
5. ___
6. ___
7. ___

cial
8. ___
9. ___
10. ___
11. ___
12. ___

cious
13. ___
14. ___
15. ___
16. ___
17. ___

tious
18. ___
19. ___
20. ___

Connections to VOCABULARY

Word Meanings

Write the spelling word that best completes each sentence.

1. Our softball team has the _____ to win the championship again this year.

2. My mother works for a bank in the _____ district.

3. The _____ relationship between the floor and the ceiling is parallel.

4. We had already heard the lecture, so hearing it again was _____.

5. Our family has just recently moved to a new home in a quiet _____ area.

6. The police artist drew a sketch based on the witness's description of the suspect's eyes, nose, and other _____ features.

7. These boulders were left here when a _____ formation moved through the area during the last ice age.

Antonyms

Write the spelling words that are antonyms for the following words.

- **8–10.** unimportant
- **11.** biased
- **12.** cramped
- **13.** trustful
- **14.** deep
- **15.** ill-mannered
- **16–17.** gentle
- **18.** publicized

Use the Thesaurus

Write a spelling word that is a synonym for each given word. Check your answers in the **Writing Thesaurus**.

19. eager   **20.** careful

Word Meanings	
1.	
2.	
3.	
4.	
5.	
6.	
7.	
Antonyms	
8.	
9.	
10.	
11.	
12.	
13.	
14.	
15.	
16.	
17.	
18.	
Use the Thesaurus	
19.	
20.	

crucial	conscientious	substantial	spacious	repetitious
spatial	confidential	ferocious	residential	financial
facial	gracious	impartial	vicious	influential
glacial	ambitious	suspicious	potential	superficial

Complete the Analogies

Write a spelling word to complete each analogy.

1. **Algebra** is to **numerical** as **geometry** is to _____.
2. **Boorish** is to **charming** as **surly** is to _____.
3. **Loving** is to **hating** as **trusting** is to _____.
4. **Lazy** is to **idle** as **fair** is to _____.
5. **Narrow** is to **wide** as **crowded** is to _____.
6. **Widespread** is to **public** as **secret** is to _____.
7. **Speech** is to **vocal** as **smile** is to _____.
8. **Exciting** is to **original** as **boring** is to _____.
9–10. **Pet** is to **gentle** as **beast** is to _____ or _____.
11. **Real** is to **actual** as **possible** is to _____.

Use Context Clues

Write the spelling words from the box to complete the paragraph.

The earth is constantly changing. Over many centuries, such seemingly **12.** changes as minor land shifts can cause **13.** changes in the earth's crust. Earthquakes, **14.** movement, volcanic eruptions, and erosion are all **15.** in the alteration of geography. Some natural forces have an immediate social and **16.** impact on business and **17.** areas. For example, the San Francisco earthquake of 1906 destroyed more than 28,000 buildings and caused 400 million dollars' worth of fire damage. It is **18.** that we continue to study the sometimes harsh, sometimes gentle forces of nature. We need to be prepared for geological changes. The **19.** and **20.** study of scientific data is a good start.

ambitious
conscientious
crucial
financial
glacial
influential
residential
substantial
superficial

Complete the Analogies

1. _____
2. _____
3. _____
4. _____
5. _____
6. _____
7. _____
8. _____
9. _____
10. _____
11. _____

Use Context Clues

12. _____
13. _____
14. _____
15. _____
16. _____
17. _____
18. _____
19. _____
20. _____

Connections to WRITING

Proofread a Paragraph

Proofread the paragraph below for ten misspelled words. Then rewrite the paragraph. Write the spelling words correctly and make the corrections indicated by the proofreading marks.

It is the Year 1,002,000. A feroshus sandstorm rages. This repeticious event happens daily since the rain stopped. Who would have thought it would never rain again? A million years ago, humans they ruined the potentiel of our environment. After eons of planetary drought, Earth is one giant desert. Oceans, lakes, and rivers are dry. Even glasial formations have melted and dried up. All wild plants have died. In spascious domes, ambicious scientists now create water, but there is not enough of the cruscial substance for everyone. Some people left Earth to live in resedential colonies in space, but only influencial people who had the finantial means could afford the trip. For those who remain, Earth is a dismal place.

DESCRIPTIVE Writing Prompt

Write a Paragraph

Write a paragraph describing what you think Earth will look like a million years from now. Compare and contrast the features of Earth today with features of Earth a million years from now.

- What will the climate be like?
- What living things will populate Earth?
- Use as many spelling words as you can.
- Proofread for grammar, capitalization, and punctuation.
- Circle three words you are unsure about. Check their spelling in a print or online dictionary.

Transfer

In your Spelling Journal, write words with **tial, cial, tious,** and **cious** that are related to the following words: **malice, benefit, superstition, fiction.** Think of three other words with each ending.

Word Study

spatial	antisocial	unconscious	ambitious	superficial	ferocious
glacial	essential	confidential	provincial	beneficial	tenacious
crucial	financial	confidentially	nutritious	residential	potential
partial	gracious	scrumptious	impartial	suspicious	spacious
vicious	precious	consequential	influential	substantial	malicious
facial	cautious	conscientious	repetitious	sequential	infectious

Synonyms and Antonyms

Use a word from the list that is a synonym or an antonym of each of the following words. Use a dictionary, if necessary.

Synonyms
- **1–2.** wary
- **3.** biased
- **4.** appreciative
- **5.** delicious

Antonyms
- **6.** biased
- **7.** aware
- **8.** publicly
- **9.** disordered
- **10.** social

Meaning Mastery

Write the word that matches each definition. Note the differences in meaning between the words that could be easily confused.

- **11.** in line with good principles
- **12.** shallow; insignificant
- **13.** easily transmitted
- **14.** providing nourishment; nourishing

Base Words and Derived Forms

Write the word that is derived from each base word.

- **15–16.** space
- **17.** consequence
- **18.** face
- **19.** tenacity
- **20.** province

Synonyms and Antonyms
1.
2.
3.
4.
5.
6.
7.
8.
9.
10.

Meaning Mastery
11.
12.
13.
14.

Base Words and Derived Forms
15.
16.
17.
18.
19.
20.

Social Studies
Word Hunt

Read the paragraphs below. Look for words with the ending **tial**, **cial**, **cious**, or **tious**.

Human beings are able to survive in the most amazing environments, from deserts to the Arctic to the highest mountains. Despite ferocious climate conditions, humans are able to feed their families, make clothing and shelter, and work together with their neighbors. Such cooperation is crucial for survival in extreme conditions.

One such harsh place where communities live is high in the Himalayas, between China and India. Surrounded by glacial ice and rocky peaks, whole families are seldom educated, but they are generous toward others and work extremely hard. The work of tending animals, gathering food, cooking meals, and mending clothes and leaky roofs is certainly repetitious. But the vicious winter weather makes it essential!

Due to financial hardship and their remote location, both men and women are conscientious about gathering food and tending the livestock. Working side-by-side is essential; after all, there are no supermarkets! But typically, the women have additional work not required of men. Women are responsible for fetching water and gathering firewood, cleaning and grinding food, cooking, and caring for children. It's a difficult life indeed, and the work is never-ending.

The hardship these gracious people endure is certainly substantial, but their ancestors have lived in these mountain communities for centuries. Their love for their world is what causes them to stay in these harsh conditions.

1. _____
2. _____
3. _____
4. _____
5. _____
6. _____
7. _____
8. _____
9. _____
10. _____

Look at the word list on page 214. There are ten of those words in the passage above. Find and write them.

1–2. Write two words ending in **tial**.

3–5. Write three words ending in **cial**.

6–8. Write three words ending in **cious**.

9–10. Write two words ending in **tious**.

Connections to THINKING

Read the spelling words and sentences.

1.	involve	*involve*	I want to **involve** you in my plans.
2.	conversation	*conversation*	We had a long **conversation** about pets.
3.	extrovert	*extrovert*	A performer is usually an **extrovert**.
4.	prospect	*prospect*	The **prospect** of your visit excites me.
5.	revolution	*revolution*	When did the computer **revolution** begin?
6.	spectacular	*spectacular*	The sunset this evening is **spectacular**.
7.	anniversary	*anniversary*	Today is my parents' wedding **anniversary**.
8.	evolve	*evolve*	Did alligators **evolve** from dinosaurs?
9.	respect	*respect*	I **respect** kind and honest people.
10.	versatile	*versatile*	He displayed his **versatile** talents.
11.	expectation	*expectation*	Our **expectation** of success has come true!
12.	advertise	*advertise*	The shop will **advertise** on television.
13.	inspect	*inspect*	Closely **inspect** the item before buying it.
14.	spectator	*spectator*	He was the loudest **spectator** at the game.
15.	converse	*converse*	We should **converse** about this decision.
16.	revolve	*revolve*	Satellites **revolve** around a planet.
17.	spectacle	*spectacle*	The parade was quite a **spectacle**.
18.	controversy	*controversy*	The new rule has caused some **controversy**.
19.	suspect	*suspect*	I **suspect** we will learn the truth shortly.
20.	introvert	*introvert*	An **introvert** tends to be quiet.

Think & Sort the spelling words.

1–4. Write the words that contain the Latin root **volv,** from the Latin verb **volvere,** meaning "to roll."

5–12. Write the words that contain the Latin root **spec,** from the Latin verb **spectare,** "to watch," or from **specere,** "to look at," "to see."

13–20. Write the words that contain the Latin root **ver,** from the Latin verb **vertere,** meaning "to turn."

Remember

Knowing Latin roots such as **spec, volv,** and **ver** can give clues to the meaning and spelling of certain words.

volv

1. _____
2. _____
3. _____
4. _____

spec

5. _____
6. _____
7. _____
8. _____
9. _____
10. _____
11. _____
12. _____

ver

13. _____
14. _____
15. _____
16. _____
17. _____
18. _____
19. _____
20. _____

Connections to VOCABULARY

Word Meanings

Write the spelling word that best completes each sentence.

1–3. If those referees do not start to _____ instead of jumping up and down, I _____ that people will begin to stare at such a _____.

4–6. Though many citizens joined in the celebration of the third _____ of the _____, others did not want to _____ themselves.

7–8. I auditioned for the play, but the _____ of a starring role was far beyond my wildest _____.

9–10. Every _____ at a tennis match ought to refrain from carrying on a loud _____ during play.

Word Structure

Write the spelling word that comes from each Latin prefix and verb.

11. ex-, out + **volvere,** to roll

12. ad-, toward + **vertere,** to turn

13. intro-, to the inside + **vertere,** to turn

14. extro-, outside + **vertere,** to turn

15. contra-, against + **versus,** to turn

Use the Thesaurus

Write a spelling word that is a synonym for each word. Check your answers in the **Writing Thesaurus**.

16. magnificent   **19.** examine

17. skillful   **20.** admire

18. turn

Word Meanings
1.
2.
3.
4.
5.
6.
7.
8.
9.
10.
Word Structure
11.
12.
13.
14.
15.
Use the Thesaurus
16.
17.
18.
19.
20.

involve	conversation	extrovert	prospect	revolution
spectacular	anniversary	evolve	respect	versatile
expectation	advertise	inspect	spectator	converse
revolve	spectacle	controversy	suspect	introvert

Complete the Sentences

Write the spelling word that best completes each sentence.

1. The _____ of a nonstop, around-the-world airplane flight did not become probable until 1981.
2. Before 1981, there was _____ among aerospace experts as to whether such a flight was possible.
3. Then Dick Rutan and Jeana Yeager had a _____ about it.
4. As they considered new, lightweight, strong materials, they began to _____ that the idea was possible.
5. Their idea started to _____ into an actual probability.
6. Soon businesses wanted to _____ themselves in the project and donated equipment and services.
7. At the 1984 test flight of *Voyager,* the sight of the aircraft slowly rising from the runway was quite a _____.
8. The success of the test flight boosted the _____ that *Voyager* would indeed succeed in an around-the-world flight.
9. The _____ record-breaking flight took place in 1986.

Use Context Clues

Write spelling words from the box to complete the paragraph.

Don't be just a __10.__! Be a part of the fitness __11.__! We are getting ready to celebrate our first __12.__! We don't usually __13.__, but we want everyone to know about our special offer. Come and __14.__ our facility. If you are an __15.__, you might like to work out by yourself. If you are an __16.__, join an aerobics class, and you will meet plenty of people with whom to __17.__. Our __18.__ instructors offer many other workout options. We __19.__ all levels of ability, and we will design a regimen to __20.__ around your needs!

| revolution |
| extrovert |
| revolve |
| inspect |
| converse |
| advertise |
| versatile |
| spectator |
| introvert |
| respect |
| anniversary |

Complete the Sentences

1. _____
2. _____
3. _____
4. _____
5. _____
6. _____
7. _____
8. _____
9. _____

Use Context Clues

10. _____
11. _____
12. _____
13. _____
14. _____
15. _____
16. _____
17. _____
18. _____
19. _____
20. _____

Connections to WRITING

Proofread a Paragraph

Proofread the paragraph below for ten misspelled words. Then rewrite the paragraph. Write the spelling words correctly and make the corrections indicated by the proofreading marks.

Proofreading Marks

	Capital Letter
/	Small Letter
∧	Add
	Delete
⊙	Add a Period
⌗	Indent

Do you take the moon for granted? Most people do not notice how specktaculer the moon is⊙Take some time as a spectater to inspeckt its fascinating craters and mountains. A contraversy once raged about whether water was present on the moon, and then ice was discovered. That led /Scientists to suspeckt that water was, and still might be, present. Thus, the prospeckt of living on the moon exists. No one ∧has been to the moon in many years, but science and technology will one day avolve so that a weekend trip to the /Moon may not envolve much trouble at all. keep in mind that the white disk in the night sky is not just a spectackle; it is a future vacation spot! Our expectacion is that it will be amazing!

ARGUMENT Writing Prompt
Write a Paragraph

Choose an item or event that is generally considered to be common. Write a paragraph about why it is extraordinary rather than commonplace.

- Use facts and details to hold the reader's attention and to support your opinion.
- Follow the form used in the proofreading example.
- Use as many spelling words as you can.
- Proofread for grammar, capitalization, and punctuation.
- Circle three words you are unsure about. Check their spelling in a print or online dictionary.

Transfer

Words that have the same root or base word can have very different meanings. Use a dictionary to discover the meanings of *a baseball* **prospect, prospecting** *for gold,* and *a* **prospective** *client*.

Word Study

Adding Suffixes

1.
2.
3.
4.
5.
6.
7.

Meaning Mastery

8.
9.
10.
11.
12.

Base Words

13.
14.
15.
16.
17.
18.
19.
20.

aspect	advertise	expectation	conversation	introvert	convert
expect	prospect	controversy	anniversary	spectator	revolve
divert	revolution	respectable	controversial	diversity	aversion
avert	reversible	spectacular	introspection	extrovert	suspect
evolve	suspected	irreversible	involvement	speculate	inspect
respect	versatile	spectacle	revolutionary	converse	involve

Adding Suffixes

Add the suffix **-ion, -tion,** or **-ation** to each word below to write a word from the list.

1. revolve
2. averse
3. converse
4. introspect
5. expect

Add the suffix **-able** or **-ible** to each word below to write a word from the list.

6. reverse
7. respect

Meaning Mastery

Write the word that best replaces the underlined word or phrase.

8. Elaine had a <u>suspicion</u> that Edward was trying to trick her.
9. She didn't know he'd planned a party for their 20th wedding <u>celebration of the day.</u>
10. Elaine tried to <u>talk</u> with her friends to find out what what going on.
11. Her friends were in on the game and tried to <u>distract</u> her attention from what Edward was doing.
12. Elaine did not <u>anticipate</u> the party, but she had so much fun!

Base Words

Write the base word for each word below. The base words are all verbs. Circle the words that changed spelling when the suffix was added.

13. revolution
14. respectable
15. convertible
16. averting
17. involvement
18. advertisement
19. inspector
20. suspicion

Technology
Word Hunt

Read the paragraphs below. Look for words with the Latin root **spec, volv,** or **ver**.

Computers have made incredible contributions to the business world. Computers do banking and billing. They make it possible to advertise online to new customers. And they operate as design and research tools. But computers have also proven extremely valuable by making online virtual meetings a truly useful tool.

In the old days, workers had to travel long distances to meet in person with clients and professional colleagues. Today it is common to converse online, using a phone, a computer, or both. This saves time and money.

Two early types of virtual meetings used phones and cameras. These are still used today. A teleconference allows many people to participate in a telephone conversation with many others. It is usually run by a leader or moderator. Videoconferences are similar, but they involve cameras and microphones. These are useful for one roomful of people who wish to talk with other people who are far away.

A third type of virtual meeting has come to evolve quite naturally to online web conferences, which use the Internet and sometimes smartphones. The real revolution of these online meetings is that people very far from one another are able to share things directly through their computers. They can discuss something as a group while everyone is able to see, hear, and inspect it at the same time.

Many people expect that in the future, greater numbers of people will work some or part of the time from home. The prospect of being able to be an active participant in long-distance virtual meetings online is exciting, and the Internet has proven to be a truly spectacular professional tool.

1. _____
2. _____
3. _____
4. _____
5. _____
6. _____
7. _____
8. _____
9. _____
10. _____

WORD SORT

1–4. Write the words with the Latin root **spec**.
5–7. Write the words with the Latin root **volv**.
8–10. Write the words with the Latin root **ver**.

Connections to THINKING

Read the spelling words and sentences.

1.	commercial	*commercial*	Gina is in that pizza **commercial**.
2.	colleague	*colleague*	A **colleague** of mine is in charge.
3.	correlate	*correlate*	His plans **correlate** with my plans.
4.	cooperation	*cooperation*	I am relying on your **cooperation**.
5.	commend	*commend*	We **commend** you for your generosity.
6.	correspondence	*correspondence*	They shared a long **correspondence**.
7.	coordinate	*coordinate*	I will **coordinate** their arrival.
8.	commuter	*commuter*	He is a **commuter** who takes the train.
9.	collaborate	*collaborate*	We will **collaborate** on a new song.
10.	corruption	*corruption*	He rid city hall of **corruption**.
11.	collide	*collide*	What happens when atoms **collide**?
12.	correction	*correction*	She made a spelling **correction**.
13.	commute	*commute*	How long is her **commute** to work?
14.	correspond	*correspond*	They **correspond** daily by e-mail.
15.	commemorate	*commemorate*	We will **commemorate** the victory.
16.	coordination	*coordination*	Party planning takes **coordination**.
17.	commodity	*commodity*	One valuable **commodity** is wheat.
18.	corrode	*corrode*	What caused the pipes to **corrode**?
19.	collapse	*collapse*	Heavy snow made the roof **collapse**.
20.	collision	*collision*	My car was damaged in a **collision**.

co-
1.
2.
3.

col-
4.
5.
6.
7.
8.

cor-
9.
10.
11.
12.
13.
14.

com-
15.
16.
17.
18.
19.
20.

Think & Sort the spelling words.

1–3. Write the words in which the assimilated prefix is spelled **co-**.

4–8. Write the words in which the assimilated prefix is spelled **col-**.

9–14. Write the words in which the assimilated prefix is spelled **cor-**.

15–20. Write the words in which the assimilated prefix is spelled **com-**.

Remember

The prefix **com-**, meaning "together" or "with," may be assimilated into the spelling of a base word or a root. If the base word begins with a consonant, this may result in a double consonant.

Connections to VOCABULARY

Word Meanings

Write a spelling word for each definition.

1. to honor the memory of
2. similarity; communication by the exchange of letters
3. having profit as a chief aim; an advertisement on radio or television
4. to be similar, parallel, equivalent, or equal; to communicate by letter, usually over a period of time
5. an article of trade or commerce, especially an agricultural or mining product
6. to substitute (one thing for another); to travel from one place to another
7. to have or to make a parallel or complementary relationship to something

Word Structure

Replace the underlined affixes with different affixes to write spelling words.

8. <u>e</u>laborate
9. <u>directed</u>
10. <u>erupted</u>
11. <u>e</u>rode

12. <u>a</u>mend
13. <u>relapse</u>
14. <u>per</u>muta<u>tion</u>

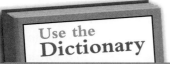

Use the
Dictionary

Write a spelling word for each etymology. Use the **Spelling Dictionary** if you need help.

15–16. Lat. **co(m)**, same + **ordinatio**, arrangement
< **ordinare**, to arrange in order < **ordo**, order.

17. Lat. **collega: co(m)**, together + **legare**, to depute (to appoint).

18. Lat. **co(m)**, same + **operari**, to work < **opus**, work.

19–20. Lat. **collidere: co(m)**, together + **laedere**, to strike.

Word Meanings
1.
2.
3.
4.
5.
6.
7.

Word Structure
8.
9.
10.
11.
12.
13.
14.

Use the Dictionary
15.
16.
17.
18.
19.
20.

colleague	correlate	commercial	cooperation	commend
commuter	coordinate	correspondence	collaborate	corruption
collide	correction	commemorate	correspond	commute
corrode	collapse	coordination	commodity	collision

Replace the Words

Write spelling words to replace the underlined words in the sentences.

1–2. A <u>traveler</u> may <u>travel</u> to work and back on the train.

3. Players wear padding to keep them safe if they <u>clash</u>.

4–6. Widespread <u>dishonesty</u> among employees can <u>wear away</u> a company from within and cause its <u>breakdown</u>.

7. Does his sudden popularity <u>have a direct relationship</u> with his winning the lottery?

8. We made a radio <u>advertisement</u> to promote our school play.

9. A gymnast needs excellent <u>balanced interaction of muscles</u>.

Use Context Clues

Write spelling words from the box to complete the letter to the editor of a newspaper.

To the Editor:

Certain groups in our community are on a __10.__ course because of town planning. Some want to __11.__ our historical heritage by saving old buildings. Others want to erect skyscrapers. If these groups would __12.__ their efforts in a spirit of __13.__, they should be able to __14.__ on town planning to link old and new. The old brownstones in our town are a precious __15.__. I, for one, __16.__ the effort to preserve them. I also recognize the need for new facilities, such as the bus terminal. I learned through written __17.__ with a former __18.__ that a major __19.__ has been made to the design of the terminal. The structure will now __20.__ to the old architecture of the town.

Angelina Perez, President
Neighborhood Associations

colleague
cooperation
commend
correspondence
coordinate
collaborate
correction
correspond
commemorate
commodity
collision

Replace the Words

1. _____
2. _____
3. _____
4. _____
5. _____
6. _____
7. _____
8. _____
9. _____

Use Context Clues

10. _____
11. _____
12. _____
13. _____
14. _____
15. _____
16. _____
17. _____
18. _____
19. _____
20. _____

Connections to WRITING

Proofread a Paragraph

Proofread the paragraph below for ten misspelled words. Then rewrite the paragraph. Write the spelling words correctly and make the corrections indicated by the proofreading marks.

Fairborough is only a short comute by comutor train to a major city, and but the town has no correspondance to the city in character. In the city, it is easy to colide with people on the crowded sidewalks. In fairborough, open space is a valued comodaty, and residents treasure the town's slow pace. At the center of Fairborough is a stone statue of a colonial soldier. It was erected to comemorate the brave people who fought in the Revolutionary War. Just beyond the statue is our new town hall, where officials collaberate on resolving issues, such as whether to allow big Companies to build comercial properties in town. Because fairborough residents care so much, town meetings are always packed. The cooperacion of the residents usually leads to the speedy corection of problems.

Proofreading Marks

	Capital Letter
	Small Letter
	Add
	Delete
	Add a Period
	Indent

DESCRIPTIVE Writing Prompt

Write a Paragraph

Write a paragraph describing your city or town.

- Think about the buildings, parks, monuments, and natural landmarks that make your hometown special.
- Use vivid words to describe in detail what makes your hometown attractive.
- Use as many spelling words as you can.
- Proofread for grammar, capitalization, and punctuation.
- Circle three words you are unsure about. Check their spelling in a print or online dictionary.

Transfer

Brainstorm five more words that begin with the assimilated prefix **com-**. Think of words that begin with **co** + double consonants, such as **connotation** and **coffee**. Then look up the new word and check that the etymology of the new word includes "Latin **com-**." (**Coffee** does not.)

225

Word Study

Word Usage

1. _____
2. _____
3. _____
4. _____
5. _____
6. _____

Base Words and Roots

7. _____
8. _____
9. _____
10. _____
11. _____
12. _____
13. _____
14. _____

Meaning Mastery

15. _____
16. _____
17. _____
18. _____
19. _____
20. _____

college	correspond	collaborate	colleague
corrode	commander	cooperation	coincide
collapse	commissioner	corroborate	colloquial
cooperate	correspondence	collision	commute
collateral	commendable	correct	coordinate
correlate	commemorate	correction	committed
commend	coordination	corruption	corruptible
collide	compensate	commercial	cooperative
commuter	commodity	correlation	corrosion

Word Usage

The word **correlate** can be used as a noun, a verb, or an adjective. Use other words from the list above to complete the tasks below.

1–3. Write the words that can be used as nouns or as verbs.

4–6. Write the words that can be used as nouns or adjectives.

Base Words and Roots

Write the words from the box that belong in the word groups below.

7–8. commendation, recommend, commended

9–10. corrosive, corroded

11–12. corrupt, corrupted

13. commission, decommission, commissary

14. coincidental, coincidence

Meaning Mastery

Fill in each blank using a word from the list above.

15. The evidence helps to _____ his story.

16–17 Synchronized swimming requires flexibility, _____, and _____.

18. Workers are paid wages to _____ them for their work.

19. How do you _____ with Mary, by text, e-mail, or snail mail?

20. Someone who works in your line of business is your _____.

Math
Word Hunt

Read the paragraphs below. Look for words with the assimilated prefix **com-**.

Air traffic controllers are a kind of modern-day mathematician. They are responsible for the safety of thousands of lives every single day. Perched high in an airport control tower, the controller may not even be able to see all the commercial jets waiting to take off and land. But it is the controller's job to know where every plane is at every moment. He or she needs to calculate exactly how fast the planes are moving and coordinate each pilot's movements so that the planes don't collide. It's a stressful job!

Air traffic controllers have many special computers and high-tech instruments in front of them. Even so, controllers need a great deal of mathematical knowledge in order to tell pilots how to make quick corrections to account for wind and airplane speed and angles. These alert professionals are to be commended. Their moment-to-moment coordination of constantly-moving planes in every direction is essential. They help planes avoid a horrible collision.

Air traffic controllers' ability to collaborate with colleagues is equally important. Controllers sit very close to each other. This way, a controller can get a second expert's quick mathematical confirmation. Such instant cooperation between experts has saved untold numbers of lives!

1. _____
2. _____
3. _____
4. _____
5. _____
6. _____
7. _____
8. _____
9. _____
10. _____

1–3. Write the words in which the assimilated prefix is spelled **co-**.

4–7. Write the words in which the assimilated prefix is spelled **col-**.

8. Write the word in which the assimilated prefix is spelled **cor-**.

9–10. Write the words in which the assimilated prefix is spelled **com-**.

Connections to THINKING

Read the spelling words and sentences.

1.	beautify	*beautify*	We planted flowers to **beautify** the park.
2.	sufficient	*sufficient*	Is there a **sufficient** amount for everyone?
3.	defective	*defective*	I returned the **defective** lamp to the store.
4.	clarify	*clarify*	I want to **clarify** what I said earlier.
5.	facsimile	*facsimile*	This is a good **facsimile** of the original.
6.	perfection	*perfection*	She always strives for **perfection**.
7.	liquefy	*liquefy*	At what temperature will ice **liquefy**?
8.	certificate	*certificate*	I asked for a copy of my birth **certificate**.
9.	defect	*defect*	Can you see the **defect** in this sweater?
10.	artificial	*artificial*	I prefer sugar to **artificial** sweeteners.
11.	effective	*effective*	This new rule is **effective** immediately.
12.	identify	*identify*	He can **identify** any bird by its call.
13.	faction	*faction*	Each **faction** argued for its own ideas.
14.	efficient	*efficient*	The new light bulb is bright and **efficient**.
15.	infection	*infection*	The doctor said I had a throat **infection**.
16.	magnify	*magnify*	A telescope can **magnify** distant objects.
17.	faculty	*faculty*	Teachers eat in the **faculty** dining room.
18.	magnificent	*magnificent*	It was a truly **magnificent** painting.
19.	certify	*certify*	Can you **certify** that the diamond is real?
20.	manufacture	*manufacture*	Does this company **manufacture** radios?

Think & Sort the spelling words.

1–5. Write the spelling words that contain the Latin root **fic**.

6–10. Write the spelling words that contain the Latin root **fec**.

11–14. Write the spelling words that contain the Latin root **fac**.

15–20. Write the spelling words that contain the Latin word part **fy**.

Remember

Knowing Latin roots such as **fic, fec, fac** and word parts such as **fy** can give clues to the meaning and spelling of certain English words.

Sidebar word list

fic
1.
2.
3.
4.
5.

fec
6.
7.
8.
9.
10.

fac
11.
12.
13.
14.

fy
15.
16.
17.
18.
19.
20.

Connections to VOCABULARY

Word Meanings

Write a spelling word to replace the underlined word or words in each sentence.

1. Cleaning a wound can prevent an invasion of microorganisms.
2. We cannot hear the radio because it has a faulty speaker.
3. Which type of heat is more able to produce a result with a minimum of waste or expense, solar or electric?
4. My older brother just received his teaching document confirming that he is competent to practice a profession.
5. A mediator might succeed in getting the members of each group of people with similar opinions to come to an agreement.
6. To apply for a passport, I need a notarized exact copy of my birth certificate.
7. Could you please make clearer what you said?
8. It is almost impossible to achieve the condition of being entirely without flaws on the first try.
9. The "Keep Off" sign was not having the intended effect in stopping people from walking on the grass.

Word Groups

Write a spelling word to complete each group.

10. melt, dissolve, _____
11. decorate, enhance, _____
12. assemble, build, _____
13. fake, phony, _____
14. prove, confirm, _____
15. define, label, _____

Use the Thesaurus

Write a spelling word that is a synonym for each word below. Check your answers in the **Writing Thesaurus**.

16. flaw
17. ability
18. exquisite
19. enlarge
20. adequate

Word Meanings	
1.	
2.	
3.	
4.	
5.	
6.	
7.	
8.	
9.	
Word Groups	
10.	
11.	
12.	
13.	
14.	
15.	
Use the Thesaurus	
16.	
17.	
18.	
19.	
20.	

beautify   sufficient   defective   clarify   facsimile
perfection   liquefy   certificate   defect   artificial
effective   identify   faction   efficient   infection
magnify   faculty   magnificent   certify   manufacture

Complete the Sentences

Write the spelling words that best complete each sentence.

1–2. Everyone should help _____ the United States by preserving its _____ trees and forests.

3–4. To get your life-saving _____, you have to be able to perform _____ respiration.

5–6. A member of one political _____ asked the senator to _____ her complex statement on nuclear disarmament.

7–8. The office copy machine can make a _____ of an original document, and it also can _____ a document to a larger size.

9–10. To fix the problem, we have to _____ the source and then repair the _____.

11–12. Ten days is usually a _____ amount of time for antibiotics to cure an ear _____.

13–14. Once we _____ that you have completed the training program, you will become a member of the school _____.

Use Context Clues

Write spelling words from the box to complete the paragraph.

Rubber is a commodity that is both __15.__ and __16.__. Yet it took Charles Goodyear many years and all of his money to find a way to make rubber usable. In the early 1800s, the rubber used to __17.__ various goods was __18.__. In the heat, it would __19.__. In the cold, it would become brittle and crack. Goodyear decided to experiment. Despite repeated failures, he continued to strive for __20.__. One day, he accidentally dropped a mixture of rubber and sulfur on a hot stove. As he cleaned it, he noticed that the rubber was firm and pliable. The heat had hardened the mixture, not melted it. In 1844, Goodyear received his patent for rubber.

liquefy
perfection
manufacture
effective
defective
efficient

Complete the Sentences

1. _____
2. _____
3. _____
4. _____
5. _____
6. _____
7. _____
8. _____
9. _____
10. _____
11. _____
12. _____
13. _____
14. _____

Use Context Clues

15. _____
16. _____
17. _____
18. _____
19. _____
20. _____

Connections to WRITING

Proofread a Paragraph

Proofread the paragraph below for ten misspelled words. Then rewrite the paragraph. Write the spelling words correctly and make the corrections indicated by the proofreading marks.

Proofreading Marks

≡	Capital Letter
/	Small Letter
∧	Add
ℰ	Delete
⊙	Add a Period
¶	Indent

¶If you follow these steps, you will make more eficient use of your time. First, identefy any defecteve behavior that causes problems. For example, perhaps you have trouble getting your homework done. Next, clarefy your goal or desired outcome. For example, maybe you want to finish your homework and still have time for afterschool activities. Define the deffect in your present system⊙ do you waste your study periods by talking to friends instead of working? If so, you need to use more efective time management. You might decide to complete at least half of your homework during your Study period. Perfecion is not necessary, but any improvement will magnefy good results. You will know you have succeeded when you complete your homework and still have suficiant time for afterschool activities. You will feel magnificient, too!

INFORMATIVE/EXPLANATORY Writing Prompt

Write a Paragraph

Think of another circumstance in which someone might need advice on managing time. Write a paragraph describing a solution.

- When you give directions or describe a process, remember to give the steps in proper order.
- Follow the form used in the proofreading example.
- Use as many spelling words as you can.
- Proofread for grammar, capitalization, and punctuation.
- Circle three words you are unsure about. Check their spelling in a print or online dictionary.

Transfer

Create a new list in your Spelling Journal for words with the Latin roots **fec, fac, fic,** and **fy**. Think of three more words with each root and write them in your new list.

Word Study

classify	perfection	affectionate	facsimile	certify	facilitate
factor	certificate	magnificent	confection	liquefy	magnify
factory	effective	manufacture	imperfect	defect	qualify
identify	beautify	beneficiary	artificial	deface	facility
satisfy	efficient	defective	efficiency	faction	disinfect
clarify	faculty	proficiency	sufficient	infection	proficient

Meaning Mastery

Words ending in **fy** are usually verbs. Write the word ending in **fy** for each meaning below.

1. to arrange according to class or category
2. to make eligible for a competition or job
3. to make clear
4. to enlarge
5. to please; to fill a need
6. to make into a liquid state
7. to make beautiful
8. to confirm as real

Words ending in **-ive** are usually adjectives. Write the words with the **-ive** suffix that matches each meaning below.

9. not in working condition
10. having the expected outcome

Parts of Speech

Write the noun form of the following words.

11. proficient
12. efficient
13. infect
14. certify
15. perfect

Write the verb form of the following words.

16. facilitator
17. manufacturer
18. defacement
19. disinfectant
20. misidentification

Meaning Mastery

1.
2.
3.
4.
5.
6.
7.
8.
9.
10.

Parts of Speech

11.
12.
13.
14.
15.
16.
17.
18.
19.
20.

Science
Word Hunt

Read the paragraphs below. Look for words with the Latin root **fic, fec, fac,** or **fy**.

Rooftop gardens are an effective way to save energy, feed people, and help the environment. It only takes a bit of preparation to certify that a building's roof has sufficient strength to carry the extra load of heavy soil and water.

With a strong roof and a good watering system, everything's in place for a magnificent rooftop vegetable garden in a crowded city. Gardens can also act as an efficient insulation layer in hot or cold climates. A rooftop patio area with chairs and a great view is another possibility. Lovely potted plants and trees can beautify the area. Each of these rooftop gardens helps the environment by adding much-needed oxygen to polluted city air.

Once a person has decided which type of garden to create, it's essential to identify which kinds of plants will best satisfy the growing conditions and produce the best results. A rooftop vegetable garden on the sunniest side of the home's roof can feed a whole family all summer. An insulation garden of wild grass can magnify the home's heat during winter and reduce its indoor temperature in the summer.

Today, many companies manufacture equipment to help build such rooftop gardens. They make and sell items, such as soil bins, watering systems, and drains. People can explore a great deal more information online, too. But perhaps the best source of information is people who have tried it!

1. _____
2. _____
3. _____
4. _____
5. _____
6. _____
7. _____
8. _____
9. _____
10. _____

1–3. Write the words with the Latin root **fic.**
4. Write the word with the Latin root **fec.**
5. Write the word with the Latin root **fac.**
6–10. Write the words with the Latin root **fy.**

Assess for Transfer

Unit 31

1.

2.

3.

4.

Unit 32

5.

6.

7.

8.

Unit 33

9.

10.

11.

12.

Unit 34

13.

14.

15.

16.

17.

Unit 35

18.

19.

20.

Units 31–35

Assessment

Each assessment word in the box fits one of the spelling patterns or rules you have studied over the past five weeks. Read the unit descriptions. Then write each assessment word under the unit number it fits.

Unit 31

1–4. You must add **al** to words ending with **ic** before adding the suffix **-ly**.

Unit 32

5–8. A final /shəs/ is spelled **cious** or **tious** and a final /shəl/ is spelled **tial** or **cial**.

Unit 33

9–12. Knowing Latin roots such as **spec, volv,** and **ver** can give clues to the meaning and spelling of certain words.

Unit 34

13–17. The prefix **com-,** meaning "together" or "with," may be assimilated into the spelling of a base word or a root. If the base word begins with a consonant, this may result in a double consonant.

Unit 35

18–20. Knowing Latin roots such as **fic, fec, fac** and word parts such as **fy** can give clues to the meaning and spelling of certain English words.

Words for Assessment

correspondent

scholastic

compassionate

respectful

atrocious

basically

gratify

authentically

uncoordinated

insufficient

deferential

authentic

superstitious

disrespectful

solidify

collaboration

revolving

preferential

speculation

corrosive

Unit 31: Adding -ly to Words Ending in ic

mechanical	scientific	historical	drastically	scientifically
mechanically	historically	economic	economically	drastic

Write the related spelling words that complete each sentence. First use the adjective form, then the adverb form.

1–2. That so-called _____ account of the Civil War is not considered _____ accurate by historians.

3–4. The emergency forced us to take _____ measures that were _____ different from those we had taken before.

5–6. Because of our treasurer's smart _____ policies in the past, our company is now _____ sound.

7–8. "Although I have some _____ skills, I am not _____ inclined," he said as he changed the light bulb.

9–10. Although he claimed it was a _____ study of pollution, most scientists felt his methods were not _____ sound.

Unit 32: Endings: tial, cial, cious, tious

facial	substantial	confidential	financial	gracious
vicious	ambitious	conscientious	suspicious	potential

Change the underlined part of each word to write a spelling word.

11. contentious
12. consequential
13. factual
14. ambidextrous
15. pretentious

16. substantive
17. gravity
18. victory
19. finances
20. suspicion

Unit 31

1. _____
2. _____
3. _____
4. _____
5. _____
6. _____
7. _____
8. _____
9. _____
10. _____

Unit 32

11. _____
12. _____
13. _____
14. _____
15. _____
16. _____
17. _____
18. _____
19. _____
20. _____

Review

Unit 33
1. _____
2. _____
3. _____
4. _____
5. _____
6. _____
7. _____
8. _____
9. _____
10. _____

Unit 34
11. _____
12. _____
13. _____
14. _____
15. _____
16. _____
17. _____
18. _____
19. _____
20. _____

Unit 33: Latin Roots: spec, volv, ver

involve	conversation	prospect	revolution	spectacular
suspect	controversy	respect	advertise	anniversary

Write spelling words to complete the paragraph.

The Clover Club is planning a terrific fifth __1.__ celebration. It is to be a __2.__ event with music and delicious food. The planners have had a long phone __3.__ with __4.__ to the guest list and entertainment. They plan to __5.__ the event through the newspaper and television. The many tasks to be done __6.__ such duties as making phone calls, decorating, collecting money, and printing programs. We __7.__ that this will be the biggest celebration ever. The __8.__ of such a successful event has everyone excited. It will truly be a __9.__ in the way Clover Club anniversaries are celebrated. The only problem so far is a little __10.__ over the location.

Unit 34: Assimilated Prefix: com-

commercial	colleague	cooperation	correspondence	coordinate
corruption	collide	correspond	collapse	collision

Write the spelling word that rhymes with each word below.

11. intrigue
12. abide
13. relapse
14. precision
15. despondence
16. calibration
17. beyond
18. disruption
19. controversial
20. subordinate

Unit 35: Latin Roots: fic, fec, fac, fy

sufficient	perfection	certificate	magnificent	identify
efficient	infection	magnify	manufacture	effective

Write the spelling word that belongs with each pair of words.

1. enough, adequate
2. document, award
3. sickness, disease

4. make, create
5. enlarge, increase
6. recognize, distinguish

Add the missing letters to write a spelling word.

7. p__rf__ __ __ion
8. magnif__ __ __nt

9. e__ __ __cient
10. ef__ __ct__ve

Unit 35

1. _____
2. _____
3. _____
4. _____
5. _____
6. _____
7. _____
8. _____
9. _____
10. _____

Spelling Study Strategy

Sorting by Word Endings

Sorting words is a good way to help you practice your spelling words. Here is a way to sort the spelling words with a partner.

1. Make columns on a piece of paper and write these endings as column heads: **-fy, -ly, -ious,** and **-ial.** Write a sample word in each column. For example, you might write **magnify** under **-fy, drastically** under **-ly, gracious** under **-ious,** and **commercial** under **-ial.**

2. Ask a partner to write another spelling word in one of the columns. Work together to check the spelling.

3. Take turns filling the columns.

4. Place other words you want to study in a separate column.

Directions: Read each item carefully. Select the best answer and fill in the circle on your answer sheet.

1. During this difficult economic time, many families have to drasticly reduce the amount of money that they spend.

   What change should be made to this sentence?

   (A) Change <u>economic</u> to *economik*

   (B) Change <u>families</u> to *familys*

   (C) Change <u>drasticly</u> to *drastically*

   (D) Make no change

2. My collegue did a spectacular job presenting our scientific research. She was so effective that the university decided to continue to fund our work.

   Which word in these sentences is spelled **incorrectly**?

   (A) collegue

   (B) spectacular

   (C) scientific

   (D) effective

3. Which word contains a Latin root that means "together" or "with"?

   (A) suspicious

   (B) magnificent

   (C) mechanical

   (D) cooperation

4. For their anniversary, he took her to a fancy restaurant with a magnifisent view of the city.

   What change, if any, should be made to this sentence?

   (A) Change <u>anniversary</u> to *anniversery*

   (B) Change <u>restaurant</u> to *resturant*

   (C) Change <u>magnfisent</u> to *magnificent*

   (D) Make no change

5. The factory employees must earn a certificate that proves they know how to fix the machines when they experience mechanicle problems.

   Which word in the sentence is spelled **incorrectly**?

   (A) employees   (C) machines

   (B) certificate   (D) mechanicle

6. Contraversy often surrounds ideas that have not been scientifically proven to be fact.

   What change, in any, should be made to this sentence?

   (A) Change <u>Contraversy</u> to *Controversy*

   (B) Change <u>surrounds</u> to *surounds*

   (C) Change <u>scientifically</u> to *scientificaly*

   (D) Make no change

7. Which of the following words is spelled incorrectly?

   (A) economic

   (B) certifcate

   (C) collision

   (D) magnificent

8. The company is going to advertize the product in such a spectacular way that everyone will want to own one.

   Which word in the sentence is spelled **incorrectly**?

   (A) company

   (B) advertize

   (C) product

   (D) spectacular

GO ON →

9. Which word contains an assimilated prefix that means "to turn"?

(A) collision

(B) magnify

(C) drastically

(D) anniversary

10. When the man did not give the police his full cooperation, they became suspiscious that he was involved in the crime.

Which word in the sentence is spelled incorrectly?

(A) police

(C) suspiscious

(B) cooperation

(D) involved

11. You cannot present a balanced report of the controversy if you magnify one side of the issue.

What change, if any, should be made to this sentence?

(A) Change present to *prezent*

(B) Change controversy to *contraversy*

(C) Change magnify to *magnufy*

(D) Make no change

12. If we cordinate our efforts, our search to find the missing dog will be more effective.

What change, if any, should be made to this sentence?

(A) Change cordinate to *coordinate*

(B) Change search to *serch*

(C) Change effective to *affective*

(D) Make no change

13. The newspaper reported that the details of the police chase are confidential, but they could share that it ended in a colision.

Which word in the sentence is spelled **incorrectly**?

(A) reported

(B) details

(C) confidential

(D) colision

14. Which of the following words is spelled incorrectly?

(A) conscientious

(B) scientificly

(C) effective

(D) coordinate

15. Everyone enjoys working with my colleague because she is a conscientious worker who rarely makes mistakes.

What change, if any, should be made to this sentence?

(A) Change colleague to *coleague*

(B) Change conscientious to *conshentious*

(C) Change mistakes to *misstakes*

(D) Make no change

STOP

239

Writer's Workshop

Grammar, Usage, and Mechanics

Subject-Verb Agreement

The subject of a sentence and the verb must agree in number. When the subject of a sentence is singular, it takes a singular verb. When the subject is plural, it takes a plural verb.

Amy hopes to join the softball team. (singular)

The **boys think** Amy will make a great player. (plural)

Practice Activity

A. Write the subject of each sentence. Write **S** if the subject is singular. Write **P** if the subject is plural.

1. The fall leaves are spectacular this year.
2. This building is in a commercial zone.
3. The controversy revolves around the eligibility of players.
4. That commercial shows a ridiculous situation.
5. Potentially dangerous storms are on their way.
6. Comic strips provide many laughs.
7. Every word is spelled correctly.

B. Write the verb that agrees with the subject and correctly completes the sentence.

8. The leaders (hope, hopes) for cooperation.
9. Mom (respect, respects) our decision.
10. Suddenly the speeding cars (collide, collides).
11. Ms. Elizario (advertise, advertises) in our paper.
12. Jean and a colleague (has, have) football tickets.
13. Their wedding anniversary (was, were) last week.
14. Your answer (affect, affects) our decision.
15. If the boxes (collapse, collapses), the toys will be ruined.

A

1. _____
2. _____
3. _____
4. _____
5. _____
6. _____
7. _____

B

8. _____
9. _____
10. _____
11. _____
12. _____
13. _____
14. _____
15. _____

The Writing Process: Argument
Writing an Editorial

PREWRITING

What would the world be like without books, magazines, or newspapers? Many things that we read are now online. What would happen if books weren't printed anymore? What are the advantages of electronic books? Which are better: printed books or electronic ones? A good way to express your opinions about this topic is to write an editorial for a school or class newspaper. As you think about this debate, make an outline for your editorial.

DRAFTING

Use your outline to write an editorial. Begin with a topic sentence that presents the main idea. Follow your outline as you write supporting sentences. Make sure to give several reasons to support your opinion. Use as many spelling words as possible. If you don't know how to spell a word, make your best guess. You will be able to revise your editorial later.

REVISING

When you have finished your first draft, read your editorial from beginning to end. Check to see if you have included all of the points in your outline. Does each sentence support the topic?

EDITING

Use the editing checklist to proofread your editorial. Be sure to use proofreading marks when you make corrections. Circle any words you are unsure about. Check their spelling in an online dictionary. Now write your final draft.

PUBLISHING

Make a copy of your editorial and share it with your readers. You can also have it published in your school or class newspaper.

EDITING CHECKLIST

Spelling
- ✓ Circle words that contain the spelling patterns and rules learned in Units 31–35.
- ✓ Check the circled words in a print or online dictionary.
- ✓ Check for other spelling errors.

Capital Letters
- ✓ Capitalize important words in the title.
- ✓ Capitalize the first word in each sentence.
- ✓ Capitalize proper nouns.

Punctuation
- ✓ End each sentence with the correct punctuation.
- ✓ Use commas, apostrophes, and quotation marks correctly.

Grammar, Usage, and Mechanics
- ✓ Make sure each subject and verb agree in number.

Spelling and the Writing Process

Writing anything—a friendly letter, a paper for school—usually follows a process. The writing process has five steps. It might look like this if you tried to draw a picture of it:

Part of the writing process forms a loop. That is because not every writing task is the same. It is also because writers often jump back and forth between the steps as they change their minds and think of new ideas.

Here is a description of each step:

PREWRITING This is thinking and planning ahead to help you write.

DRAFTING This means writing your paper for the first time. You usually just try to get your ideas down on paper. You should spell correctly those words that you do know. Attempt to spell those that you don't. You can fix them later.

REVISING This means fixing your final draft. Here is where you rewrite, change, and add words.

EDITING This is where you feel you have said all you want to say. Now you proofread your paper for spelling errors and errors in grammar and punctuation. Be sure to use a print or online dictionary to check your spelling.

PUBLISHING This is making a copy of your writing and sharing it with your readers. Put your writing in a form that your readers will enjoy.

Confident spellers are better writers. Confident writers understand their own writing process better. Know how the five steps best fit the way you write.

Spelling and
Writing Ideas

Being a good speller can help make you a more confident writer. Writing often can make you a better writer. Here are some ideas to get you started.

Descriptive writing describes something.
You might...
- describe your most prized possession.
- describe your favorite holiday or season.
- describe an unusual or beautiful landscape. Take a photo or sketch the place and use the image to help you describe it.

Narrative writing tells a story.
You might...
- write a story about your first visit to someplace new.
- write a story about your neighborhood.
- write a story about an experience you've had in seventh grade that you could share with a sixth grader.

Argument writing tries to persuade the reader to think or do something.
You might...
- try to persuade your parents to let you purchase a CD, DVD, or smart phone.
- try to persuade your friends to start a neighborhood recycling program.
- try to persuade your school administrators to abolish a rule you disagree with.

Informative/Explanatory writing explains something.
You might...
- write a report about the effect of daily exercise on health.
- write to a local sports figure about a career in professional sports.
- inform your classmates how to ride a bicycle safely.

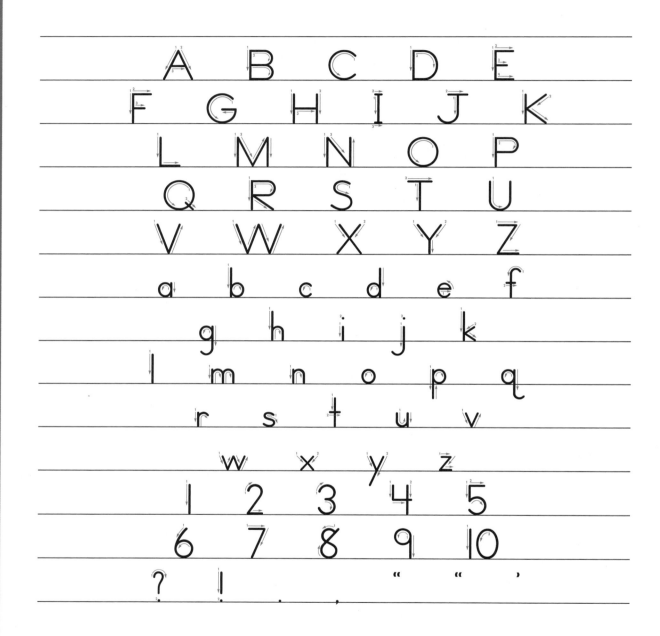

Handwriting Models

A B C D E
F G H I J
K L M N O
P Q R S T
U V W X Y Z

a b c d e
f g h i j
k l m n o p
q r s t u
v w x y z

1 2 3 4 5
6 7 8 9 10

? ! . , " " '

High Frequency Writing Words

A

a
about
afraid
after
again
air
all
almost
also
always
am
America
an
and
animal
animals
another
any
anything
are
around
as
ask
asked
at
ate
away

B

baby
back
bad
ball
balloons
baseball

basketball
be
bear
beautiful
because
become
bed
been
before
being
believe
best
better
big
bike
black
boat
book
books
both
boy
boys
bring
broke
brother
build
bus
but
buy
by

C

call
called
came
can
candy

can't
car
care
cars
cat
catch
caught
change
charge
children
Christmas
circus
city
class
clean
clothes
come
comes
coming
could
couldn't
country
cut

D

Dad
day
days
decided
did
didn't
died
different
dinner
do
does
doesn't

dog
dogs
doing
done
don't
door
down
dream

E

each
earth
eat
eighth
else
end
enough
even
every
everybody
everyone
everything
except
eyes

F

family
fast
father
favorite
feel
feet
fell
few
field
fight

finally
find
fire
first
fish
five
fix
food
football
for
found
four
free
Friday
friend
friends
from
front
fun
funny
future

G

game
games
gas
gave
get
gets
getting
girl
girls
give
go
God
goes
going

good
got
grade
grader
great
ground
grow

 H

had
hair
half
happened
happy
hard
has
have
having
he
head
heard
help
her
here
he's
high
hill
him
his
hit
home
homework
hope
horse
horses
hot
hour
house

how
hurt

 I

I
I'd
if
I'm
important
in
into
is
it
its
it's

 J

job
jump
just

 K

keep
kept
kids
killed
kind
knew
know

 L

lady
land
last
later
learn
leave

left
let
let's
life
like
liked
likes
little
live
lived
lives
long
look
looked
looking
lost
lot
lots
love
lunch

 M

mad
made
make
making
man
many
math
may
maybe
me
mean
men
might
miss
Mom
money

more
morning
most
mother
mouse
move
Mr.
Mrs.
much
music
must
my
myself

 N

name
named
need
never
new
next
nice
night
no
not
nothing
now

 O

of
off
oh
OK
old
on
once
one

only
or
other
our
out
outside
over
own

 P

parents
park
party
people
person
pick
place
planet
play
played
playing
police
president
pretty
probably
problem
put

 R

ran
read
ready
real
really
reason
red
responsibilities

rest
ride
riding
right
room
rules
run
running

S

said
same
saw
say
scared
school
schools
sea
second
see
seen
set
seventh
she
ship
shot
should
show
sick
since
sister
sit
sleep
small
snow
so

some
someone
something
sometimes
soon
space
sport
sports
start
started
states
stay
still
stop
stopped
store
story
street
stuff
such
sudden
suddenly
summer
sure
swimming

T

take
talk
talking
teach
teacher
teachers
team
tell
than

Thanksgiving
that
that's
the
their
them
then
there
these
they
they're
thing
things
think
this
thought
three
through
throw
time
times
to
today
together
told
too
took
top
tree
trees
tried
trip
trouble
try
trying
turn
turned

TV
two

U

united
until
up
upon
us
use
used

V

very

W

walk
walked
walking
want
wanted
war
was
wasn't
watch
water
way
we
week
weeks
well
went
were
what
when

where
which
while
white
who
whole
why
will
win
winter
wish
with
without
woke
won
won't
work
world
would
wouldn't

Y

yard
year
years
yes
you
your
you're

Using the
Dictionary

Guide Words

The **guide words** at the top of each dictionary page can help you find the word you want quickly. The first guide word tells you the first word on that page. The second guide word tells you the last word on that page. The entries on the page fall in alphabetical order between these two guide words.

Entries

Words you want to check in the dictionary are called **entries**. Entries provide a lot of information besides the correct spelling. Look at the sample entry below.

Tips for Finding a Word in a Dictionary

- Practice using guide words in a dictionary. Think of words to spell. Then use the guide words to find each word's entry. Do this again and again until you can use guide words easily.

- Some spellings are listed with the base word. To find **easiest,** you would look up **easy**. To find **remaining,** you would look up **remain**. To find **histories,** you would look up **history**.

- If you do not know how to spell a word, guess the spelling before looking it up. Try to find the first three letters of the word. (If you use just the first letter, it will probably take too long to find the word.)

- If you can't find a word, think of how else it might be spelled. For example, if a word starts with the /**k**/ sound, the spelling might begin with **k, c,** or even **ch**.

entry the correct spelling, sometimes broken into syllables

pronunciation

other spellings other word forms, including plurals, that change the spelling of the base word

mem•o•ry /mĕm′ ə rē/ *n.* (**mem•o•ries** *pl.*) **a.** the power or the ability to remember things. *She has a great memory for names.* **b.** anything that is remembered. *Seeing our old house again brought back happy memories.*

definition to be sure you have the correct entry word

sample sentence to make the definition clearer

a•bil•i•ties /ə **bĭl′** ĭ tēz/ *n. pl.* (**a•bil•i•ty** *sing.*) special talents or skills. *The test was designed to check our math and science abilities.*

-able a suffix, used to form adjectives, that means: **a.** capable or worthy of: *eatable.* **b.** tending toward: *sizable.*

ab•so•lute¹ /**ăb′** sə lōōt′/ *adj.* **a.** perfect in quality or nature; complete. **b.** not mixed; pure. **c.1.** not limited by restrictions or exceptions: *absolute trust.* **c.2.** unqualified in extent or degree; total: *absolute silence.* **d.** not to be doubted or questioned; positive: *absolute proof.* [ME *absolut* < Lat. *absolutus,* ended < *absoluere,* to finish: *ab,* from + *solvere,* to loose.]

ab•so•lute² /**ăb′** sə lōōt′/ *n.* something that is absolute.

ab•so•lute•ly /**ăb′** sə lōōt′ lē/ *adv.* definitely and completely; unquestionably.

ab•stract /ăb′ **străkt′**, ăb′ străkt′/ *adj.* **a.** considered apart from concrete existence: *an abstract concept.* **b.** not applied or practical. **c.** thought of or stated without reference to a specific instance: *abstract words like "truth" and "justice."* **d.** designating a genre of painting or sculpture whose intellectual and affective content depends solely on intrinsic form. **—idiom. in the abstract.** apart from actual substance or experience.

ac•cel•er•ate /ăk **sĕl′** ə rāt′/ *v.* (**-ates, -at•ed, -at•ing**). **a.** to increase the speed of. **b.** to move or act faster.

ac•cept /ăk **sĕpt′**/ *v.* **a.** to receive, especially with gladness or approval: *accept an apology.* **b.** to regard as proper or right: *widely accepted beliefs.* **c.** to endure resignedly or patiently: *accept their punishment.* **d.** to answer affirmatively: *accept an invitation.*

ac•cess /**ăk′** sĕs/ *n.* the right to enter or to use. *We were able to gain access to the stadium's private club.*

ac•ces•si•ble /ăk sĕs′ ə bəl/ *adj.* (**ac•ces•si•bil•i•ty** *n.*) (**ac•ces•si•bly** *adv.*) **a.** easily approached or entered. **b.** easily obtained. **c.** easy to communicate or get along with. **d.** open to: *accessible to flattery.*

ac•ci•dent /**ăk′** sĭ dənt/ *n.* **a.** a harmful or unexpected event. *Ali had an accident on his bike.* **b.** something that occurs without being planned for. *The cure for the disease was discovered by accident.*

ac•ci•den•tal /ăk sĭ **dĕn′** tl/ *adj.* (**ac•ci•den•tal•ly** *adv.*) **a.** occurring unexpectedly and unintentionally; by chance. **b.** not part of the real or essential nature of a thing.

ac•claim /ə **klām′**/ *v.* to welcome with praise. *The students will acclaim the arrival of the new computers.*

ac•co•lade /**ăk′** ə lād′/ or /**ăk′** ə lăd′/ *n.* an expression of approval. *When the queen tapped him on the shoulder with a sword, he was proud of the accolade.*

ac•com•mo•date /ə **kŏm′** ə dāt/ *v.* (**-dates, -dat•ed, -dat•ing**) **a.** to do a favor or service for; oblige. **b.** to provide for; supply with. **c.** to contain comfortably; have space for.

ac•com•pa•ni•ment /ə **kŭm′** pə nē mənt/ or /ə **kŭmp′** nē mənt/ *n.* an instrumental or vocal part that supports or complements a principal voice or instrument. *The audience roared with approval for the vocalist and her accompaniment.*

ac•com•pa•ny /ə **kŭm′** pə nē, ə **kŭmp′** nē/ *v.* (**-nies, -nied, -ny•ing**) **a.** to go along with; join in company. **b.** to supplement; add to. **c.** to coexist or occur with.

ac•com•plish /ə **kŏm′** plish/ *v.* (**ac•com•plished, ac•com•plishing**) **a.** to succeed in doing; bring to pass. **b.** to reach the end of; complete.

ac•com•plish•ment /ə **kŏm′** plish mənt/ *n.* an achievement; a performance. *When he finished the essay, he was proud of his accomplishment.*

ac•cor•dance /ə **kôr′** dns/ *n.* agreement; harmony. *Because we all agreed, we voted in accordance with one another.*

ac•cord•ing to *prep.* **a.** as stated or indicated by; on the authority of: *according to historians.* **b.** in keeping with; in agreement with: *according to instructions.* **c.** as determined by: *a list arranged according to the alphabet.*

ac•count /ə **kount′**/ *n.* **a.** a narrative or record of events; a written or oral explanation, as of blame or cause. **b.** a precise list or enumeration of monetary transactions. **c.** a business relationship involving the exchange of money or credit: *a charge account.*

ac•count•a•bil•i•ty /ə koun′ tə **bĭl′** ĭ tē/ *n.* (**-ties** *pl.*) responsibility.

ac•cu•mu•late /ə **kyōom′** yə lāt′/ *v.* (**-lates, -lat•ed, -lat•ing**) **a.** to amass or gather; pile up; collect. **b.** to grow or increase; mount up.

ac•cu•rate /ăk′ yər ĭt/ *adj.* (**ac•cu•rate•ly** *adv.*) **a.** in exact conformity to fact; errorless. **b.** deviating only slightly or within acceptable limits from a standard.

ac•cus•tomed /ə kŭs′ təmd/ *adj.* **a.** usual, characteristic, or normal: *worked with her accustomed thoroughness.* **b.** in the habit of: *accustomed to sleeping late.*

a•chieve /ə chēv′/ *v.* (**a•chieves, a•chieved, a•chiev•ing**) **a.** to do or finish with success. **b.** to attain or get with effort: *finally achieved mastery of the piano.*

a•cre /ā′ kər/ *n.* **a.** a unit of area used in land measurement and equal to 160 square rods, 4,840 square yards, or 43,560 square feet. **b.** *Archaic.* a field or plot of land. [ME *aker* < OE *œcer*.]

a•cre•age /ā′ kər ĭj, ā′ krĭj/ *n.* area of land in acres.

ac•tiv•i•ty /ăk tĭv′ ĭ tē/ *n.* (**-ties** *pl.*) **a.** energetic action or movement. **b.** a specified form of supervised action or field of action.

ac•tu•al /ăk′ chōō əl/ *adj.* **a.** existing in fact or reality. **b.** current. **c.** based on fact: *an actual account.*

ad- or **ac-** or **af-** or **ag-** or **al-** or **ap-** or **as-** or **at-** a prefix that means toward, to: *adapt.*

ad•di•tion•al•ly /ə dĭsh′ ə nə lē/ *adv.* also; moreover; in addition. *Additionally, the movie has won international awards.*

ad•mi•ra•ble /ăd′ mər ə bəl/ *adj.* (**ad•mi•ra•bly** *adv.*) deserving admiration; excellent.

ad•mi•ra•tion /ăd′ mə rā′ shən/ *n.* a feeling of pleasure, wonder, and approval.

ad•mire /ăd mīr′/ *v.* (**-mires, -mired, -mir•ing**) **a.** to regard with pleasure, wonder, and approval. **b.** to have a high opinion of; esteem or respect.

ad•mis•si•ble /ăd mĭs′ ə bəl/ *adj.* **a.** allowable. **b.** worthy of admission.

ad•mis•sion /ăd mĭsh′ ən/ *n.* **a.1.** the act of admitting or allowing to enter. **a.2.** the state of being allowed to enter. **b.** the right to enter; access. **c.** the price required or paid for entering; entrance fee. **d.** a voluntary acknowledgment that something is true.

ad•mit•ted /ăd′ mĭt′ id/ *v.* (**ad•mit, ad•mits, ad•mit•ted, ad•mit•ting**) acknowledged; confessed.

a•dor•a•ble /ə dôr′ ə bəl/ or /ə dōr′-/ *adj.* lovable; charming. *The stuffed animals were cuddly and adorable.*

ad•vance /ăd văns′/ *n.* a payment of money before it is due. *The worker asked the contractor for an advance of the funds, so he could order supplies.*

Pronunciation Key

ă	pat	ŏ	pot	th	thin
ā	pay	ō	toe	*th*	this
âr	care	ô	paw, for	hw	which
ä	father	oi	noise	zh	vision
ĕ	pet	ou	out	ə	about,
ē	be	ŏŏ	took		item,
ĭ	pit	ōō	boot		pencil,
ī	pie	ŭ	cut		gallop,
îr	pier	ûr	urge		circus

---

ad•vance•ment /ăd văns′ mənt/ *n.* improvement; progress; promotion. *They dedicated their new club to the advancement of poetry.*

ad•van•ta•geous /ăd′ văn tā′ jəs, -vən-/ *adj.* affording benefit or gain; useful.

ad•ven•ture[1] /ăd vĕn′ chər/ *n.* (**ad•ven•ture•some** *adj.*) **a.** an undertaking or enterprise of a hazardous nature. **b.** an unusual experience or course of events marked by excitement and suspense. **c.** participation in hazardous or exciting experiences.

ad•ven•ture[2] /ăd vĕn′ chər/ *v.* (**-tures, -tured, -tur•ing**) to venture; risk; dare.

ad•verse /ăd vûrs′/ or /ăd′ vûrs′/ *adj.* harmful; hostile. *The roaring storm had an adverse effect on the trees in the park.*

ad•ver•si•ty /ăd vûr′ sĭ tē/ *n.* (**-ties** *pl.*) misfortune; hardship. *The hurricane victims suffered much adversity.*

ad•ver•tise /ăd′ vər tīz′/ *v.* (**-tis•es, -tised, -tis•ing**) (**ad•ver•tis•er** *n.*) **a.** to make public announcement of, especially to proclaim the qualities or advantages of (a product or business) so as to increase sales. **b.** to call the attention of the public to a product or business. **c.** to inquire or seek in a public notice, as in a newspaper: *advertise for an apartment.* [ME *advertisen,* to notify < OFr. *avertir, avertiss-,* to notice < Lat. *advertere,* to turn toward: *ad-,* toward + *vertere,* to turn.]

ad•ver•tise•ment /ăd′ vər tīz′ mənt, ăd vûr′ tĭs-, -tĭz-/ *n.* a notice designed to attract public attention or patronage.

ad•vice /ăd vīs′/ *n.* opinion about what could or should be done about a problem; counsel.

ad•vise /ăd vīz′/ *v.* (**-vis•es, -vised, -vis•ing**) **a.** to offer advice to; counsel. **b.** to recommend; suggest. **c.** to inform; notify: *advise a person of a decision.*

af•fair /ə **fâr′**/ *n.* **a.** something done or to be done; business. **b.** an occurrence, event, or matter. **c.** a matter of personal concern. **d.** a matter causing public scandal and controversy.

af•fec•tion•ate /ə **fĕk′** shə nĭt/ *adj.* showing affection; loving. *The affectionate little boy gave me a big hug.*

af•fin•i•ty /ə **fĭn′** ĭ tē/ *n.* (**-ties** *pl.*) an attraction. *Because we enjoy it so much, we have an affinity for chocolate.*

af•firm /ə **fûrm′**/ *v.* (**af•fir•ma•tion** *n.*) **a.** to declare positively or firmly; maintain to be true. **b.** to confirm.

af•fix[1] /ə **fĭks′**/ *v.* **a.** to secure (an object) to another; attach: *affix a label to a package.* **b.** to attribute: *affix blame to him.* **c.** to place at the end; append: *affix a postscript.*

af•fix[2] /**ăf′** ĭks′/ *n.* **a.** something that is attached, joined, or added. **b.** a word element, such as a prefix or suffix, that can only occur attached to a base, stem, or root.

af•flu•ent /**ăf′** lōō ənt/ *or* /ə **flōō′** ənt/ *adj.* rich in material goods; wealthy.

af•ford /ə **fôrd′**, ə **fōrd′**/ *v.* (**af•ford•a•ble** *adj.*) **a.** to have the financial means for; be able to meet the expense of. **b.** to be able to spare or give up: *could afford an hour for lunch.* **c.** to be able to do or perform (something) without incurring harm or criticism, or with benefit to oneself: *can afford to be tolerant.*

a•fi•cio•na•do /ə fĭsh′ ē ə **nä′** dō/, /ə fĭs′ ē ə **nä′** dō/ *or* /ə fē′ sē ə **nä′** dō/ *n.* (**-dos** *pl.*) fan; a devotee. *After adopting the two kittens, he became a cat aficionado.*

-age a suffix, used to form nouns, that means: **a.** collectively; in general: *mileage.* **b.** condition; state: *marriage.* **c.** charge or fee: *postage.* **d.** residence or place: *orphanage.* **e.** act or result: *spoilage.*

a•gen•cy /**ā′** jən sē/ *n.* (**-cies** *pl.*) a service or business set up to act for or in place of others. *An employment agency helped him find a new job.*

a•gen•da /ə **jĕn′** də/ *n.* a list of things to be done, especially the program for a meeting.

ag•gres•sive /ə **grĕs′** ĭv/ *adj.* forceful. *The firefighters used aggressive techniques to fight the huge blaze.*

ag•ile /**ăj′** əl/ *or* /**ăj′** īl′/ *adj.* nimble; able to move easily or quickly. *Our agile cat jumped on top of the refrigerator.*

a•gil•i•ty /ə **jĭl′** ĭ tē/ *n.* the condition of being able to move easily or quickly. *Good dancers show great agility.*

a•gree•a•ble /ə **grē′** ə bəl/ *adj.* **a.** to one's liking; pleasing. **b.** ready to consent or submit.

-al[1] a suffix that forms adjectives from nouns: *postal.*

-al[2] a suffix that forms nouns from verbs: *arrival.*

à la carte /ä′ lə **kärt′**/ *or* /äl′ ə′ **kärt′**/ *adj.* having a separate price for each item on the menu. *The prices are for whole, not à la carte, meals.*

a•li•en[1] /**ā′** lē ən, **āl′** yən/ *adj.* **a.** owing political allegiance to another country or government; foreign. **b.** belonging to, characteristic of, or derived from another country, place, society, or person; strange. **c.** being inconsistent or opposed; repugnant. *Lying is alien to his nature.*

a•li•en[2] /**ā′** lē ən, **āl′** yən/ *n.* **a.** an unnaturalized foreign resident of a country. **b.** an outsider. **c.** *Slang.* a creature from outer space.

a•lign /ə **līn′**/ *v.* **a.** to arrange in a line. **b.** to adjust to produce a proper relationship or condition. **c.** to ally with one side of an argument or cause.

al•le•giance /ə **lē′** jəns/ *n.* loyalty or the obligation of loyalty, as to nation or cause.

al•li•ance /ə **lī′** əns/ *n.* **a.** a formal pact of union or confederation between nations in a common cause. **b.** a union, relationship, or connection by kinship, marriage, or common interest.

al•li•ga•tor /**ăl′** ĭ gā′ tər/ *n.* a large reptile with a narrow body, short legs, long tail, and thick skin. [Spanish *el lagarto,* the lizard.]

all right /ôl′ **rīt′**/ *adv.* **a.** yes; very well. *All right, I'll come home early.* **b.** in a satisfactory way. *Is everything going all right?*

al•pha•bet•i•cal /ăl′ fə **bĕt′** ĭ kəl/ *adj.* (**al•pha•bet•i•cal•ly** *adv.*) **a.** arranged in the customary order of the letters of a language. **b.** of, pertaining to, or expressed by an alphabet.

a•lu•mi•num /ə **lōō′** mə nəm/ *n. Symbol* **Al.** a silvery-white, ductile metallic element, the most abundant in the earth's crust, but found only in combination, chiefly in bauxite. It is used to form many hard, light, corrosion-resistant alloys.

am•a•teur /**ăm′** ə tûr′/ *or* /**ăm′** ə chŏŏr′/ *adj.* having the status or quality of being for fun, not for money. *The amateur athletes won trophies and ribbons instead of earning money.*

a•maze•ment /ə **māz′** mənt/ *n.* a state of extreme surprise or wonder; astonishment.

am•bi•tion /ăm bĭsh′ ən/ *n.* **a.** an eager or strong desire to achieve something. **b.** the object or goal desired.

am•bi•tious /ăm bĭsh′ əs/ *adj.* **a.** full of, characterized by, or motivated by ambition. **b.** greatly desirous; eager. **c.** showing or requiring much effort.

a•mend•ment /ə mĕnd′ mənt/ *n.* a formal change in a law or a bill. *An amendment to the Constitution gave women the right to vote.*

am•mon•ia /ə mōn′ yə/ *n.* a colorless gas with a sharp smell used to manufacture fertilizers and a wide variety of chemicals.

am•pere /ăm′ pîr′ / *n.* the unit used in measuring the strength of an electric current. *How many amperes does a light bulb use?* [After the French scientist, André Maria Ampère, 1775–1836.]

ana- a prefix that means **a.** upward; up. **b.** backward; back. **c.** again; anew.

a•nach•ro•nism /ə năk′ rə nĭz′ əm/ *n.* something placed out of its historical order and into another time period. *A covered wagon is an anachronism on modern highways.*

an•a•gram /ăn′ ə grăm′/ *n.* a word or phrase formed by reordering the letters of another word or phrase.

a•nal•y•ses /ə năl′ ĭ sēz′/ *n., pl.* (**a•nal•y•sis** *sing.*) systematic, careful examinations, usually of information.

-ance a suffix that forms nouns from verbs: *resemblance.*

an•go•ra also **An•go•ra** /ăng gôr′ ə, -gōr′ ə/ *n.* **a.** the long, silky hair of the Angora goat. **b.** the fine, light hair of the Angora rabbit, sometimes blended with wool in fabrics. **c.** a yarn or fabric made from either of these fibers. [after *Angora* (Ankara), Turkey.]

an•i•mate[1] /ăn′ ə māt′/ *v.* (**-mates, -mat•ed, -mat•ing**) **a.** to give life to; fill with life. **b.** to impart interest or zest to; enliven. **c.** to impart motion or activity to. **d.** to make, design, or produce (a cartoon, for example) so as to create the illusion of motion.

an•i•mate[2] /ăn′ ə mĭt′/ *adj.* **a.** possessing life; living. **b.** of or relating to animal life as distinct from plant life.

an•i•ma•tion /ăn′ ə mā′ shən/ *n.* liveliness. *When excited, he talked with great animation.*

an•i•mos•i•ty /ăn′ ə mŏs′ ĭ tē/ *n.* (**-ties** *pl.*) an intense, hostile feeling; hatred.

Pronunciation Key

ă	pat	ŏ	pot	th	thin
ā	pay	ō	toe	*th*	this
âr	care	ô	paw, for	hw	which
ä	father	oi	noise	zh	vision
ĕ	pet	ou	out	ə	about,
ē	be	ŏŏ	took		item,
ĭ	pit	ōō	boot		pencil,
ī	pie	ŭ	cut		gallop,
îr	pier	ûr	urge		circus

an•nex /ăn′ ĕks′/ or /ăn′ ĭks/ *n.* (**an•nex•es** *pl.*) a room or building added to a building that is already there. *The store added an annex to hold the plants and garden supplies.*

an•ni•ver•sa•ry /ăn′ ə vûr′ sə rē/ *n.* (**-ries** *pl.*) the annual recurrence of an event that took place in some preceding year: *a wedding anniversary.*

an•nounce•ment /ə nouns′ mənt/ *n.* **a.** something that has been announced. **b.** a printed or published statement or notice.

an•nu•al /ăn′ yŏŏ əl/ *adj.* (**an•nu•al•ly** *adv.*) **a.** recurring, done, or performed every year; yearly. **b.** of or pertaining to a year; determined by a year's time: *an annual income.*

an•swer•a•ble /ăn′ sər ə bəl/ *adj.* responsible. *I am answerable for doing my homework.*

-ant a suffix that forms nouns and adjectives: *resultant.*

an•tique /ăn tēk′/ *n.* an object having special value because of its age, especially a work of art or handicraft that is more than 100 years old. [Fr.]

an•ti•so•cial /ăn′ tē sō′ shəl/ *adj.* avoiding the company of others. *It is a mistake to assume that a shy person is deliberately antisocial.*

a•pol•o•get•ic /ə pŏl′ ə jĕt′ ĭk/ *adj.* regretful; expressing regret. *She was apologetic after accidentally bumping into the other woman.*

a•pol•o•get•i•cal•ly /ə pŏl′ ĭ jĕt′ ə kəl ē/ *adv.* in a regretful way. *When the assembly had to be canceled, the principal made the announcement apologetically.*

ap•pall /ə pôl′/ *v.* to fill with dismay.

ap•par•ent /ə păr′ ənt, ə pâr′-/ *adj.* **a.** readily seen; open to view; visible. **b.** readily understood or perceived; plain or obvious. **c.** appearing as such but not necessarily so: *an apparent advantage.*

ap•pe•tite /ăp′ ĭ tīt′/ *n.* **a.** a desire for food or drink. **b.** a physical desire. **c.** a strong wish or urge: *an appetite for learning.* [ME *appetit* < OFr. < Lat. *appetitus,* strong desire < *appetere,* to strive after: *ad-,* toward + *petere,* to seek.]

ap•plaud /ə plôd′/ *v.* **a.** to express approval, especially by clapping the hands. **b.** to praise; approve. [Lat. *applaudere: ad-,* to + *plaudere,* to clap.]

ap•pli•ance /ə plī′ əns/ *n.* a device or instrument, especially one operated by electricity and designed for household use.

ap•pli•ca•ble /ăp′ lĭ kə bəl/ or /ə plĭk′ ə bəl/ *adj.* proper; appropriate; set apart for special use. *The teacher's criticism was not applicable to my assignment.*

ap•pli•cant /ăp′ lĭ kənt/ *n.* a person applying for a job or position. *There were many applicants for the after-school job.*

ap•pli•ca•tion /ăp′ lĭ kā′ shən/ *n.* **a.** a request, as for assistance, employment, or admission to a school. **b.** the form or document upon which such a request is made.

ap•pli•ca•tor /ăp′ lĭ kā′ tər/ *n.* a tool, such as a brush; a sponge-tipped device used for application. *The artist needed a tiny applicator to paint the miniature design.*

ap•point•ment /ə point′ mənt/ *n.* an arrangement to meet someone at a certain time. *I have a two o'clock appointment.*

ap•praise /ə prāz′/ *v.* (**ap•prais•es, ap•praised, ap•prais•ing**) **a.** to evaluate. **b.** to estimate the quality, amount, size, and other features of; judge.

ap•pre•ci•a•tion /ə prē shē ā′ shən/ *n.* **a.** recognition of the quality, value, or significance of people and things. **b.** an expression of gratitude. **c.** a rise in value or price.

ap•pro•pri•ate /ə prō′ prē ĭt / *adj.* suitable for a particular person, condition, occasion, or place; proper; fitting.

ap•prov•al /ə prō͞o′ vəl/ *n.* **a.** the act of approving. **b.** favorable regard; commendation. [ME *approven* < OFr. *aprover* < Lat. *approbare: ad-,* to + *probare,* to test < *probus,* good.]

ap•prox•i•mate /ə prŏk′ sə mĭt/ *adj.* (**ap•prox•i•mate•ly** *adv.*) **a.** almost exact, correct, complete, or perfect. **b.** very similar; closely resembling.

ap•prox•i•ma•tion /ə prŏk′ sə mā′ shən/ *n.* a close estimate. *Her approximation was nearest the true cost of the project.*

ar•ma•dil•lo /är′ mə dĭl′ ō/ *n.* an animal covered with a hard, plated shell. [Sp., dim. of *armado,* armored, p.part. of *armar,* to arm < Lat. *armare* < *arma,* arms.]

ar•rest[1] /ə rĕst′/ *v.* **a.** to stop; check. **b.** to seize and hold under the authority of law. **c.** to capture and hold briefly.

ar•rest[2] /ə rĕst′/ *n.* **a.** the act of detaining in legal custody: *the arrest of a suspect.* **b.** the state of being so detained: under arrest. **c.** The act of stopping or the condition of being stopped: *cardiac arrest.*

ar•ti•fi•cial /är′ tə fĭsh′ əl/ *adj.* **a.** made by man rather than occurring in nature: *an artificial sweetener.* **b.** made in imitation of something natural: *artificial flowers.*

ar•tis•tic /är tĭs′ tĭk/ *adj.* (**ar•tis•ti•cal•ly** *adv.*) **a.** of or relating to art or artists. **b.** appreciative of or sensitive to art or beauty.

as•cent /ə sĕnt′/ *n.* **a.** the act or process of rising or going upward: *the hiker's ascent up the hill.* **b.** an upward slope or incline. *The hiker had difficulty climbing the ascent.*

> **Ascent** sounds like **assent.**

as•pect /ăs′ pĕkt / *n.* an element or facet of something. *Most problems have more than one aspect to them.*

as•pi•ra•tion /ăs′ pə rā′ shən/ *n.* **a.** a strong desire for high achievement. **b.** an object of such desire; ambitious goal. [Lat. *aspirare, aspirat-,* to breathe on: *ad-,* to + *spirare,* to breathe.]

as•pire /ə spīr′/ *v.* (**as•pires, as•pired, as•pir•ing**) to have a great ambition or ultimate goal; strongly desire. *The lead actress in our school musical aspires to a singing career.*

as•sem•ble /ə sĕm′ bəl/ *v.* (**-bles, -bled, -bling**) **a.** to bring or gather together into a group or whole. **b.** to fit or join together the parts of.

as•sent /ə sĕnt′/ *v.* to express agreement; concur: assented to his plan.

> **Assent** sounds like **ascent.**

as•sert /ə sûrt′/ *v.* **a.** to state or express positively; affirm. **b.** to defend or maintain. **c.** assert oneself. to express oneself forcefully or boldly.

as•sess /ə sĕs′/ *v.* to evaluate; appraise.

as•sess•ment /ə sĕs′ mənt/ *n.* **a.** the act of assessing; appraisal. **b.** an amount assessed.

as•set /ăs′ ĕt′/ *n.* a useful or valuable quality or thing.

as•sign•ment /ə sīn′ mənt/ *n.* a thing assigned. *It took me three hours to complete my homework assignments.*

as•sim•i•late /ə sĭm′ ə lāt′/ *v.* (**as•sim•i•lates, as•sim•i•lat•ed, as•sim•i•lat•ing**) to take something in and cause it to blend indistinguishably. *Some early explorers tried to assimilate the local cultures into their own.*

as•sist /ə sĭst′/ *v.* to help; to aid. *I assisted Mother in preparing dinner.*

as•sis•tant /ə sĭs′ tənt/ *n.* a person who assists another; a helper. *We need an assistant to help with the project.*

as•so•ci•a•tion /ə sō′ sē ā′ shən, -shē-/ *n.*
a. an organized body of people who have some interest, activity, or purpose in common; society; league. **b.** a mental connection or relation between thoughts, feelings, ideas, or sensations.

as•sort•ment /ə sôrt′ mənt/ *n.* a collection of various things; variety.

as•sume /ə sōō m′/ *v.* (**as•sumes, as•sumed, as•sum•ing**) **a.** to accept as true; to take for granted. *People once assumed the earth was flat.* **b.** to accept; to take upon oneself. *Megan assumed the job of decorating the room.*

as•sur•ance /ə shŏŏr′ əns/ *n.* **a.** a statement or indication that inspires confidence; guarantee. **b.1.** freedom from doubt; certainty. **b.2.** self-confidence.

-ate¹ a suffix that forms adjectives: *affectionate.*

-ate² a suffix that forms verbs: *pollinate.*

ath•lete /ăth′ lēt′/ *n.* a person who performs in competitive sports. *An athlete trains daily.*

ath•let•ic /ăth lĕt′ ĭk/ *adj.* **a.** of or for athletics or athletes. **b.** physically strong; muscular.

-ation a suffix that forms nouns from verbs: *civilization.*

a•tro•cious /ə trō′ shəs/ *adj.* **a.** extremely evil or cruel: *an atrocious crime.* **b.** exceptionally bad; abominable. *Doctors are known for having atrocious handwriting.*

at•tain /ə tān′/ *v.* to gain, reach, or accomplish by mental or physical effort.

at•tempt¹ /ə tĕmpt′/ *v.* to try to do, make, or achieve. [ME *attempten* < OFr. *attempter* < Lat. *attemptare: ad-,* to + *temptare,* to test.]

at•tempt² /ə tĕmpt′/ *n.* **a.** an effort or try. **b.** an attack; assault: *an attempt on one's life.*

at•ten•dance /ə tĕn′ dəns/ *n.* the act of being present. *His attendance at school has been perfect all year.*

at•ten•tive /ə tĕn′ tĭv/ *adj.* **a.** paying attention; observant. **b.** mindful of the well-being of others; considerate.

Pronunciation Key

ă	pat	ŏ	pot	th	**thin**
ā	pay	ō	toe	*th*	**this**
âr	care	ô	paw, for	hw	**which**
ä	father	oi	noise	zh	vision
ĕ	pet	ou	**out**	ə	about,
ē	be	ŏŏ	took		item,
ĭ	pit	ōō	boot		pencil,
ī	pie	ŭ	cut		gallop,
îr	pier	ûr	**urge**		circus

at•tic /ăt′ ĭk/ *n.* a room just below the roof of a house. *We found a big box up in our attic.*

at•tire¹ /ə tīr′/ *v.* (**-tires, -tired, -tir•ing**) to dress or clothe, especially in elaborate or splendid garments.

at•tire² /ə tīr′/ *n.* clothing; array.

at•ti•tude /ăt′ ĭ tōōd′/ *or* /ăt′ ĭ tyōōd′/ *n.* **a.** a state of mind or a feeling; disposition: *has a positive attitude about work.* **b.** an arrogant or hostile state of mind or disposition.

at•tract /ə trăkt′/ *v.* **a.** to cause to draw near. **b.** to evoke by arousing interest or admiration; allure. [ME *attracten* < Lat. *attrahere: ad-,* to + *trahere,* to draw.]

at•trac•tion /ə trăk′ shən/ *n.* **a.** the act or capability of attracting. **b.** the quality of attracting; charm. **c.** a person, place, thing, or event that attracts. **d.** *Science.* the gravitational force exerted by one body on another.

at•trac•tive /ə trăk′ tĭv/ *adj.* **a.** having the power to attract. **b.** pleasing to the eye or mind; charming.

at•tri•bute /ăt′ rə byōō t′/ *n.* a quality belonging to a particular person or thing. *Kindness is an attribute of a good friend.*

au•then•tic /ô thĕn′ tĭk/ *adj.* (**au•then•ti•cal•ly** *adv.*) **a.** conforming to fact and therefore worthy of trust, reliance, or belief. **b.** having a verifiable origin; not counterfeit or copied.

au•thor•i•ty /ə thôr′ ĭ tē/, /ə thŏr′ ĭ tē/, /ô thôr′ ĭ tē/, *or* /ô-thŏr′ ĭ tē/ *n.* (**au•thor•i•ties** *pl.*) **a.** the power to enforce laws, command, determine, or judge. **b.** one that is invested with this power, especially a government or body of government officials. **c.** an accepted source of expert information or advice. **d.** power to influence or persuade resulting from knowledge or experience.

au•to•mat•ic /ô′ tə **măt′** ĭk/ *adj.* mechanical; moving or acting by itself. *Some banks allow for the automatic payment of bills for their account holders.*

au•to•mat•i•cal•ly /ô′ tə **măt′** ĭ kəl ē/ *adv.* in a mechanical way. *When we stepped up to the door, it opened automatically.*

au•tumn /ô′ təm/ *n.* the season that comes after summer and before winter; fall. *In autumn, many leaves turn beautiful colors.*

au•tum•nal /ô tŭm′ nəl/ *adj.* having to do with the fall season. *We love to see the autumnal colors in the countryside.*

aux•il•ia•ry[1] /ôg zĭl′ yə rē, -zĭl′ ə rē/ *adj.* **a.** giving assistance or support; helping. **b.** held in or used as a reserve: *auxiliary troops.*

aux•il•ia•ry[2] /ôg zĭl′ yə rē, -zĭl′ ə rē/ *n.* (**-ries** *pl.*) an individual or group that assists or functions in an auxiliary capacity. [Lat. *auxiliarius* < *auxilium,* help.]

a•ver•sion /ə vûr′ zhən/ or /ə vûr′ shən/ *n.* an extreme dislike. *I have an aversion to dirt and sweat.*

a•vert /ə vûrt′/ *v.* to turn away; to prevent. *She swerved the car to avert hitting the huge pothole.*

av•o•ca•do /ăv′ ə kä′ dō, ä′ və-/ *n.* (**-dos** *pl.*) **a.** a tropical American tree, cultivated for its edible fruit. **b.** the oval or pear-shaped fruit of the avocado, having leathery green or blackish skin, a large seed, and bland, greenish-yellow pulp. [Mex. Sp. *aguacate* < Nahuatl *ahuactl.*]

a•ware /ə wâr′/ *adj.* (**a•ware•ness** *n.*) having knowledge or cognizance.

bad•min•ton /băd′ mĭn tən/ *n.* a game played by hitting a shuttlecock back and forth over a high net by means of a light racket. [After *Badminton,* the Duke of Beaufort's country seat in western England.]

ban•ner /băn′ ər/ *n.* **a.** a flag. *"The Star-Spangled Banner"* is a song about the American flag. **b.** a piece of cloth with a picture, design, or writing on it. *The owners hung a banner for the grand opening.*

bare•ly /bâr′ lē/ *adv.* hardly; scarcely. *We could barely see the cars because of the fog.*

ba•si•cal•ly /bā′ sĭ kə lē/ or/ **bā′** sĭ klē/ *adv.* **a.** in a basic way; fundamentally or essentially. **b.** for the most part.

ba•sis /bā′ sĭs/ *n.* (**-ses** /-sēz/ *pl.*) **a.** a supporting element; foundation. **b.** the chief component of something. **c.** the essential principle.

bay•o•net /bā′ ə nĭt/ or /bā′ ə nĕt/ or /bā′ ə nĕt′/ *n.* a special blade or knife attached to the front end of a rifle. [*baïonnette,* after *Bayonne,* a town in SW France.]

ba•zaar /bə zär′/ *n.* **a.** a Middle Eastern market consisting of a street lined with shops and stalls. **b.** a fair or sale at which miscellaneous articles are sold, often for charitable purposes.

beau•ti•ful /byoō t′ ə fəl/ *adj.* (**beau•ti•ful•ly** *adv.*) **a.** having qualities that delight the senses, especially the sense of sight. **b.** Excellent; wonderful.

beau•ti•fy /byoō′ tə fī′/ *v.* (**-fies, -fied, -fy•ing**) to make or become beautiful.

be•go•nia /bĭ gōn′ yə/ *n.* a kind of plant with bright flowers and waxy leaves. *She planted a begonia in one pot and a violet in another pot.*

be•lieve /bĭ lēv′/ *v.* (**-lieves, -lieved, -liev•ing**) (**be•liev•a•ble** *adj.*) **a.** to accept as true or real. **b.** to expect or suppose; think. *I believe he will come shortly.*

ben•e•fi•cial /bĕn′ ə fĭsh′ əl/ *adj.* promoting a favorable result; enhancing well-being; advantageous. [Fr. *bé né ficial* < LLat. *beneficialis* < Lat. *beneficium,* benefit < *bene facere,* to do well.]

ben•e•fi•ci•ar•y /bĕn′ ə fĭsh′ ē ĕr ē, -fĭsh′ ə rē/ *n.* (**-ies** *pl.*) **a.** one that receives a benefit. **b.** *Law.* the recipient of funds, property, or other benefits, as from an insurance policy or will.

be•ret /bə rā′/ *n.* a round, soft, flat cap of wool or felt. *She wore her beret tilted at a jaunty angle.* [French *béret.*]

best-sell•ing /bĕst-sĕl′ ing/ *adj.* of or pertaining to something that is the most popular with buyers.

bi- a prefix meaning two or twice: *bimonthly, bisect.*

bi•an•nu•al /bī ăn′ yoō əl/ *adj.* (**bi•an•nu•al•ly** *adv.*) happening twice each year; semiannual.

bi•ath•lon /bī ăth′ lən/ or /bī ăth′ lŏn′/ *n.* an athletic contest made of two separate events. *An Olympic biathlon requires skis and a rifle.*

bi•cen•ten•ni•al /bī′ sĕn tĕn′ ē əl/ *adj.* relating to a 200th anniversary. *The United States' bicentennial celebration was in 1976.*

bi•ceps /bī′ sĕps′/ *n.* (**bi•ceps** or **bi•ceps•es** /-sĕp′ sĭz/ *pl.*) the large muscle in the front of the upper arm. *The athletes used dumbbells to firm their biceps.*

bi•en•ni•al¹ /bī ĕn′ ē əl/ *adj.* (**bi•en•ni•al•ly** *adv.*) **a.** lasting or living for two years. **b.** happening every second year.

bi•en•ni•al² /bī ĕn′ ē əl/ *n.* **a.** an event that occurs once every two years. **b.** a plant that normally requires two years to reach maturity, producing leaves in the first year, blooming and producing fruit in the second year, and then dying.

bi•month•ly¹ /bī mŭnth′ lē / *adj.* **a.** occurring once every two months: *a bimonthly magazine.* **b.** occurring twice a month: *bimonthly meetings.*

bi•month•ly² /bī mŭnth′ lē/ *adv.* **a.** every two months. *Issues appear bimonthly.* **b.** twice a month. *We meet bimonthly.*

bi•na•ry /bī′ nə rē/ *adj.* made up of two things or parts. *Because it had only two stars, the scientist called it a binary system.*

bin•oc•u•lar /bə nŏk′ yə lər, bī-/ *n.* (often **binoculars**) an optical device, especially a pair of field glasses, designed for use by both eyes at once.

bi•plane /bī′ plān′/ *n.* a plane having two sets of wings, usually on different levels above and below the body of the plane.

bi•sect /bī sĕkt′/ or /bī′ sĕkt/ *v.* to divide into two equal parts. *Use your compass to bisect this angle.*

bi•year•ly¹ /bī yîr′ lē/ *adj.* **a.** occurring once every two years. **b.** occurring twice a year; semiyearly.

bi•year•ly² /bī yîr′ lē/ *adv.* **a.** every two years. **b.** twice a year; semiyearly.

bi•zarre /bī zär′/ *adj.* strikingly unconventional or far-fetched, as in style or appearance; odd.

bo•le•ro /bō lâr′ ō/ or /bə lâr′ ō/ *n.* (**bo•le•ros** *pl.*) **a.** a short, open vest or jacket. *The red bolero looked nice with the tan pants.* **b.** a dance. *The dancer couldn't stop tapping her toes during the lively bolero.*

bo•nan•za /bə nǎn′ zə/ *n.* **a.** a rich mine, vein, or pocket of ore. **b.** a source of great wealth or prosperity. [Sp. exaggerated good, aug. of *bueno*, good < Lat. *bonus.*]

book•keep•ing /bŏŏk′ kē′ pĭng/ *n.* the art or practice of recording the accounts and transactions of a business.

bouil•lon /bŏŏl′ yŏn′, -yən, bŏŏ′ yŏn′/ *n.* a clear, thin broth made typically by simmering beef or chicken in water with seasonings.

bound•a•ry /boun′ də rē , -drē/ *n.* (**-ries** *pl.*) something that indicates a border or limit.

bou•quet /bō kā′, bŏŏ -/ *n.* a cluster of flowers; nosegay.

Pronunciation Key

ă	pat	ŏ	pot	th	**th**in
ā	pay	ō	toe	*th*	**th**is
âr	care	ô	paw, for	hw	**wh**ich
ä	father	oi	n**oi**se	zh	vi**s**ion
ĕ	pet	ou	**ou**t	ə	**a**bout,
ē	be	ŏŏ	t**oo**k		item,
ĭ	pit	ōō	b**oo**t		pencil,
ī	pie	ŭ	c**u**t		gall**o**p,
îr	pier	ûr	**ur**ge		circ**u**s

---

bou•tique /bŏŏ tēk′/ *n.* a small retail shop that specializes in gifts, fashionable clothes, and accessories. [Fr. < OProv. *botica* < Lat. *apotheca*, storehouse.]

brain•storm /brān′ stôrm′/ *n.* a sudden inspiration or clever idea. *Their combined thoughts created a great brainstorm.*

bra•va•do /brə vä′ dō/ *n.* (**-dos** or **-does** *pl.*) a pretense of courage; false bravery. [Sp. *bravada* < *bravo*, brave.]

breathe /brē*th*/ *v.* **a.** to inhale and exhale air. **b.** to be alive; live. **c.** to pause to rest or regain breath. *Give me a moment to breathe.*

brief /brēf/ *adj.* (**brief•ly** *adv.*) **a.** short in time or duration. **b.** short in length or extent.

brief•case /brēf′ kās′/ *n.* a portable rectangular case used for carrying books or papers.

bris•tle¹ /brĭs′ əl/ *n.* **a.** a stiff hair. **b.** a stiff hairlike structure: *bristles on a brush.*

bris•tle² / brĭs′ əl/ *v.* (**bris•tles, bris•tled, bris•tling**) **a.** to stand on end like bristles; stiffen: *The hair on my neck bristled.* **b.** to raise the bristles: *The dog bristled at the sight of the hissing cat.* **c.** to react in an angry or offended manner: *The man bristled at being told what to do.*

bro•chure /brō shŏŏr′/ *n.* a small booklet or pamphlet. *Zachary sent for a brochure on soccer camps.*

broth•er-in-law /brŭ*th*′ ər ĭn lô′/ *n.* (**broth•ers-in-law** *pl.*) **a.** the brother of one's husband or wife. **b.** the husband of one's sister. **c.** the husband of the sister of one's husband or wife.

bu•gle /byŏŏ′ gəl/ *n.* a brass instrument similar to a trumpet, used for military signals. *The soldiers woke up to a bugle call.*

bul•le•tin board /bŏŏl′ ĭ tn bôrd/ or /bŏŏl′ ĭ tĭn bōrd/ *n.* a board or wall on which notices or signs are put up. *The students displayed their work on the class bulletin board.*

bu•reau /byŏŏr′ō/ *n.* (**-reaus** or **-reaux** /ōz/ *pl.*) an office for a special kind of business.

bur•ro /bûr′ ō/ or /bŏŏr′ ō/ *n.* a small donkey. *Burros can carry heavy packs.*

by-prod•ucts /bī′ prŏd′ əkts/ *n. pl.* (**by-prod•uct** *sing.*) secondary results; bonuses. *Penicillin was a by-product of a bread mold experiment.*

C

ca•ban•a also **ca•ba•ña** /kə băn′ ə, -băn′ yə/ *n.* a shelter on a beach or at a swimming pool used as a bathhouse. [Sp. *cabaña* < LLat. *capanna,* hut.]

ca•ble¹ /kā′ bəl/ *n.* **a.** a strong, thick, heavy steel or fiber rope. **b.** something that resembles such a rope. **c.** a cablegram. **d.** cable television.

ca•ble² /kā′ bəl/ *v.* (**ca•bles, ca•bled, ca•bling**) **a.** to transmit a message by telegraph. **b.** to fasten with a cable or cables.

ca•coph•o•ny /kə kŏf′ ə nē/ *n.* (**-nies** *pl.*) a harsh or unpleasant sound. *The cacophony of screaming fans jangled our nerves.*

caf•e•te•ri•a /kăf ĭ tîr′ ē ə/ *n.* a restaurant in which the customers are served at a counter and carry their meals on trays to tables. [Sp. *cafeteria,* coffee shop < *café,* coffee < Turk. *kahve.*]

cal•i•co /kăl′ ĭ kō′/ *n.* (**-coes** or **-cos** *pl.*) a coarse cloth, usually printed with bright designs. [after *Calicut* (Kozhikode), India.]

ca•mel•lia /kə mēl′ yə/ *n.* **a.** any of several shrubs or trees of the genus *Camellia,* native to Asia, having shiny evergreen leaves and showy, variously colored flowers. **b.** the flower of a camellia. [NLat. *Camellia,* genus name, after Georg Josef *Kamel* (1661–1706).]

cam•ou•flage¹ /kăm′ ə fläzh′, -fläj′/ *n.* the method or result of concealing personnel or material from an enemy by making them appear to be part of the natural surroundings. [Fr. < *camoufler,* to disguise < Ital. *camuffare.*]

cam•ou•flage² /kăm′ ə fläzh′, -fläj′/ *v.* (**-flag•es, -flaged, -flag•ing**) to conceal by or use camouflage.

cam•paign /kăm pān′/ *adj.* of or having to do with an operation for achieving a specific purpose. *We need a campaign motto for the election.*

camp•fire /kămp′ fīr′/ *n.* a fire in a camp, for keeping warm or for cooking. *It is fun to sit around a campfire at night and sing songs.*

cam•pus /kăm′ pəs/ *n.* (**-pus•es** *pl.*) the grounds of a school, college, or university.

can•cel /kăn′ səl/ *v.* (**can•cels, can•celed, can•cel•ing**) put an end to; stop. *Because of the bad storm, they are canceling the picnic.*

ca•noe¹ /kə nŏŏ′/ *n.* a light, slender boat with pointed ends propelled by paddles.

ca•noe² /kə nŏŏ′/ *v.* (**-noes, -noed, -noe•ing**) (**ca•noe•ist** *n.*) **a.** to travel in a canoe. **b.** to propel a canoe. [Obs. *canoa* < Sp. of Cariban orig.]

can•ta•loupe /kăn′ t lōp′/ *n.* **a.** a variety of melon, having fruit with a ribbed, rough rind and aromatic orange flesh. **b.** the fruit of a cantaloupe. [Fr. *cantaloup* < Ital. *cantalupo* < *Cantalupo,* a former papal villa near Rome.]

can•yon /kăn′ yən/ *n.* a narrow chasm with steep cliff walls, formed by running water; gorge. [Sp. *cañon,* aug. of *caña,* tube < Lat. *canna,* reed < Gk. *kanna.*]

cap•tion¹ /kăp′ shən/ *n.* a title, short explanation, or description accompanying an illustration or photograph.

cap•tion² /kăp′ shən/ *v.* to furnish a caption for.

cap•ti•vate /kăp′ tə vāt′/ *v.* (**cap•ti•vates, cap•ti•vat•ed, cap•ti•vat•ing**) to attract the attention or affection of. *The lights and music captivate everyone in the audience.*

cap•ti•vat•ing /kăp′ tə vāt′ ĭng/ *adj.* attracting the attention or affection of. *The dance performance was captivating.*

car•at /kăr′ ət/ *n.* a measure of weight for precious stones. *The ring held a ruby that was one carat in size.*

car•di•gan /kär′ dĭ gən/ *n.* a sweater or knitted jacket opening down the front. [after the Seventh Earl of *Cardigan;* James Thomas Brudenell (1797–1868).]

car•di•o•gram /kär′ dē ə grăm′ / *n.* a printed record of a special test of a patient's heart. *The doctor studied the cardiogram to see if there were any problems with the patient's heart.*

care•ful•ly /kâr′ fə lē/ *adv.* with care; cautiously or thoroughly. *Peter dusted the tiny figurines carefully.*

car•et /kăr′ it/ *n.* a special mark used in editing to show where something needs to be put in. *I put a caret between the two words, to show where I wanted to add an adjective.*

car•ou•sel /kăr′ ə sĕl′, -zĕl′/ *n.* a merry-go-round. [Fr. *carrousel* < Ital. *carosello,* a kind of tournament.]

carte blanche /kärt **blänsh′**/, /kärt′ **blänch′**/, or /kart **blänch′**/ *n.* (**cartes blanches** *pl.*) the freedom to do whatever one wants. *The students were given carte blanche in choosing the topics for their science fair projects.*

cash•mere /kăzh′ mîr′, kăsh′-/ *n.* a soft fabric made of wool from the Cashmere goat or of similar fibers. [after *Kashmir,* a region in India.]

cau•tious /kô′ shəs/ *adj.* careful; keeping away from danger.

cel•e•brate /sĕl′ ə brāt / *v.* (**-brates, -brat•ed, -brat•ing**) (**cel•e•bra•tion** *n.*) **a.** to observe (a day or event) with ceremonies of respect, festivity, or rejoicing: *celebrated their anniversary.* **b.** to praise publicly; honor: *a sonnet that celebrates love.*

cen•sor[1] /sĕn′ sər/ *n.* a person who looks for objectionable material and deletes it. *The censor deleted several words in the new movie.*

➤ **Censor** sounds like **sensor.**

cen•sor[2] /sĕn′ sər/ *v.* to examine and delete something considered objectionable.

cen•sure[1] /sĕn′ shər/ *n.* an expression of disapproval.

cen•sure[2] /sĕn′ shər/ *v.* to criticize harshly; blame.

cen•tu•ries /sĕn′ chə rēz/ *n. pl.* (**cen•tu•ry** *sing.*) sections of time equal to one hundred years. *It has been several centuries since the invention of the printing press.*

cer•tain•ly /sûr′ tn lē/ *adv.* definitely; surely. *Your grades will certainly improve if you study hard.*

cer•tif•i•cate /sər tĭf′ ĭ kĭt / *n.* **a.** a document testifying to the factuality or truth of something: *a birth certificate.* **b.** a document certifying that a person may officially practice in certain professions.

cer•ti•fy /sûr′ tə fī′/ *v.* (**-fies, -fied, -fy•ing**) **a.** to confirm formally as true, accurate, or genuine, especially in writing. **b.** to guarantee as meeting a standard.

chal•lenge[1] /chăl′ ənj/ *n.* **a.** a demand for an explanation. **b.** the quality of requiring full use of one's abilities, energy, or resources: *a career that offers a challenge.*

chal•lenge[2] /chăl′ ənj/ *v.* (**-leng•es, -lenged, -leng•ing**) **a.** to call to engage in a contest or fight. **b.** to take exception to; dispute: *challenged the statements.* **c.** to summon to action, effort, or use; stimulate: *a problem that challenges the imagination.*

Pronunciation Key

ă	pat	ŏ	pot	th	thin
ā	pay	ō	toe	*th*	this
âr	care	ô	paw, for	hw	which
ä	father	oi	noise	zh	vision
ĕ	pet	ou	out	ə	about,
ē	be	ŏŏ	took		item,
ĭ	pit	ōō	boot		pencil,
ī	pie	ŭ	cut		gallop,
îr	pier	ûr	urge		circus

chan•de•lier /shăn′ də **lîr′**/ *n.* an ornate, decorative lighting fixture that hangs from the ceiling. *Mom ordered a new chandelier to hang over the dining room table.*

cha•os /**kā′** ŏs′/ *n.* a condition or place of total disorder or confusion.

chap•er•one[1] also **chap•er•on** /shăp′ ə rōn′/ *n.* **a.** a person, especially an older or married woman, who accompanies a young unmarried woman in public. **b.** an older person who attends and supervises a social gathering for young people. [Fr. < *chaperon,* hood < OFr. < *chape,* covering.]

chap•er•one[2] also **chap•er•on** /shăp′ ə rōn′/ *v.* (**-ones, -oned, -on•ing**) to act as chaperone to or for.

char•i•ta•ble /**chăr′** ĭ tə bəl/ *adj.* generous; unselfish. *A charitable person enjoys helping others.*

ched•dar also **Ched•dar** /**chĕd′** ər/ *n.* any of several types of smooth, hard cheese varying in flavor from mild to extra sharp. [after *Cheddar,* England.]

chron•ic /**krŏn′** ĭk/ *adj.* **a.** of long duration; continuing; constant. **b.** prolonged; lingering, as certain diseases. **c.** subject to a disease or habit for a long time.

chron•i•cle[1] /**krŏn′** ĭ kəl/ *n.* a chronological record of historical events.

chron•i•cle[2] /**krŏn′** ĭ kəl/ *v.* (**-cles, -cled, -cling**) to record in or in the form of a chronicle.

chrono- or **chron-** a prefix meaning time: *chronometer.* [< Gk. *khronos,* time.]

chron•o•log•i•cal /krŏn′ ə **lŏj′** ĭ kəl/ or /krō′ nə **lŏj′** ĭ kəl/ *adj.* listed in order of time. *The history book explained events in chronological order.*

chro•nol•o•gy /krə **nŏl′** ə jē/ *n.* (**-gies** *pl.*) **a.** the determination of dates and the sequence of events. **b.** the arrangement of events in time. **c.** a chronological list or table.

chro•nom•e•ter /krə **nŏm′** ĭ tər/ *n.* an exceptionally precise timepiece.

cinch¹ /sĭnch/ *n.* **a.** a girth for a pack or saddle. **b.** *Slang.* something easy to accomplish. [Sp. *cincha* < Lat. *cingula* < *cingere,* to gird.]

cinch² /sĭnch/ *v.* **a.** to put a saddle girth on. **b.** *Slang.* to make certain of: *cinch a victory.*

clar•i•fy /klăr′ ə fī′/ *v.* (**-fies, -fied, -fy•ing**) to make clear or easier to understand.

clas•sic¹ /klăs′ ĭk/ *adj.* **a.** serving as an outstanding representative of its kind; model. **b.** having lasting significance or recognized worth. **c.** of or pertaining to ancient Greek or Roman literature or art; classical.

clas•sic² /klăs′ ĭk/ *n.* an artist, author, or work generally considered to be of the highest rank or excellence.

clas•si•cal /klăs′ ĭ kəl/ *adj.* (**clas•si•cal•ly** *adv.*) **a.** of or pertaining to the culture of ancient Greece and Rome, especially the art, architecture, and literature. **b.** standard and authoritative rather than new or experimental.

clas•si•fy /klăs′ ə fī′/ *v.* to sort; to arrange according to category or class. *Librarians do not classify fairy tales with other fiction.*

class•mate /klăs′ māt′/ *n.* a member of the same academic class.

cliff•hang•er /klĭf′ hăng′ ər/ *n.* mysteries that end in suspense. *Reading cliffhangers can leave you in real suspense!*

cli•mate /klī′ mĭt/ *n.* **a.** the meteorological conditions, including temperature, precipitation, and wind, that characteristically prevail in a particular region. **b.** a prevailing condition or atmosphere: *a climate of hope.*

co•in•cide /kō′ ĭn sīd′/ *v.* (**co•in•cides, co•in•cid•ed, co•in•cid•ing**) to take place at the same time. *I hope that my baseball practice does not coincide with my soccer practice.*

co•in•ci•den•tal•ly /kō ĭn′ sĭ dĕn′ tl lē/ *adv.* happening at the same time, seemingly accidentally.

col•lab•o•rate /kə lăb′ ə rāt′/ *v.* (**-rates, -rat•ed, -rat•ing**) to work together, especially in a joint intellectual effort. [LLat. *collaborare, collaborat-:* Lat. *com-,* together + Lat. *laborare,* to work < *labor,* work.]

col•lapse¹ /kə lăps′/ *v.* (**-laps•es, -lapsed, -laps•ing**) **a.** to fall down or inward suddenly; cave in. **b.** to cease to function; break down suddenly in strength or health. **c.** to fold compactly.

col•lapse² /kə lăps′/ *n.* the act of falling down or inward, as from loss of supports.

col•lat•er•al /kə lăt′ ər əl/ *n.* something of value given to a lender of money as a guarantee that the loan will be repaid. *The bank used our car as collateral for the loan.*

col•league /kŏl′ ēg′/ *n.* a fellow member of a profession, staff, or academic faculty; associate. [OFr. *collegue* < Lat. *collega: com-,* together + *legare,* to depute.]

col•lect•i•ble /kə lĕk′ tə bəl/ *n.* anything, valuable or not, that can be gathered together as a hobby. *That old coin is a collectible.*

col•lege /kŏl′ ĭj/ *n.* a school that is more advanced than a high school. *Students who plan to go to college often study a foreign language.*

col•lide /kə līd′/ *v.* (**-lides, -lid•ed, -lid•ing**) **a.** to come together with violent, direct impact. **b.** to meet in opposition; clash; conflict. [Lat. *collidere: com-,* together + *laedere,* to strike.]

col•li•sion /kə lĭzh′ ən/ *n.* the act or process of colliding; crash. [ME < Lat. *collisio* < *collidere,* to strike: *com-,* together + *laedere,* to strike.]

col•lo•qui•al /kə lō′ kwē əl/ *adj.* characteristic of or appropriate to the spoken language or to writing that seeks the effect of speech; informal.

co•logne /kə lōn′/ *n.* a light perfume. [Short for *cologne (water),* translation of Fr. (*eau de*) *Cologne,* after Cologne, a city in Germany.]

com- a prefix meaning together, with, joint, or jointly: *compress.* Before **l** or **r, com-** becomes **col-** or **cor-**. Before vowels, **h,** or **gn,** it is reduced to **co-**. Before all other consonants except **p, b,** or **m,** it becomes **con-**. [ME < OFr. < Lat.]

com•bi•na•tion /kŏm′ bə nā′ shən/ *n.* **a.** the act of combining or state of being combined. **b.** something resulting from combining two or more things.

com•bine /kəm bīn′/ *v.* (**-bines, -bined, -bin•ing**) **a.** to bring into a state of unity. **b.** to join (two or more substances) to make a single substance; mix.

com•fort¹ /kŭm′ fərt/ *v.* **a.** to soothe in time of grief or fear; console. **b.** to ease physically; relieve.

com•fort² /kŭm′ fərt/ *n.* **a.** a condition of ease or well-being. **b.** solace in time of grief or fear.

com•fort•a•ble /kŭm′ fər tə bəl/, /kŭmf′ tə bəl/, or /kŭmf′ tər bəl/ *adj.* cozy; at ease. *I am comfortable in my old sneakers.*

com•mand•er /kə măn′ dər/ *n.* a person who commands. *The superintendent of police is the commander of the police force.*

com•mem•o•rate /kə **měm′** ə rāt′/ v. (**-rates, -rat•ed, -rat•ing**) **a.** to honor the memory of with a ceremony. **b.** to serve as a memorial to.

com•mence /kə **měns′**/ v. (**-menc•es, -menced, -menc•ing**) **a.** to begin; start. **b.** to come into existence; have a beginning. [ME *commencen* < OFr. *comencier* < VLat. *cominitiare:* Lat. *com-* (intensive) + LLat. *initiare,* to begin < Lat. *initium,* beginning.]

com•mence•ment /kə **měns′** mənt/ n. **a.** a beginning; start. **b.** a ceremony at which academic degrees or diplomas are conferred.

com•mend /kə **měnd′**/ v. **a.** to represent as worthy, qualified, or desirable; recommend. **b.** to express approval of; praise.

com•mend•a•ble /kə **měnd′** ə bəl/ adj. worthy; desirable.

com•men•tar•y /**kŏm′** ən tĕr′ ē/ n. (**-ies** pl.) **a.** a series of explanations or interpretations. **b.** something that explains or illustrates.

com•merce /**kŏm′** ərs/ n. the buying and selling of goods, especially on a large scale, as between cities or nations.

com•mer•cial[1] /kə **mûr′** shəl/ adj. **a.** of or pertaining to commerce. **b.** having profit as a chief aim. **c.** sponsored by an advertiser or supported by advertising.

com•mer•cial[2] /kə **mûr′** shəl/ n. an advertisement on radio or television.

com•mis•sar•y /**kŏm′** ĭ sĕr′ ē/ n. (**-ies** pl.) a supermarket, usually on a military base, where military personnel buy groceries.

com•mis•sion /kə **mĭsh′** ən/ n. a percentage or fee paid to someone for sales or services rendered. *Salespeople often earn a commission as well as a salary.*

com•mis•sion•er /kə **mĭsh′** ə nər/ n. a person in charge of a governmental department. *After the flood, the health commissioner issued a warning that the people should boil their water before drinking it.*

com•mit /kə **mĭt′**/ v. (**com•mits, com•mit•ted, com•mit•ting**) to do; perform; perpetrate.

com•mit•tee /kə **mĭt′** ē/ n. a group of people officially delegated to perform a function, as investigating, considering, reporting, or acting on a matter.

Pronunciation Key

ă	pat	ŏ	pot	th	thin
ā	pay	ō	toe	*th*	this
âr	care	ô	paw, for	hw	which
ä	father	oi	noise	zh	vision
ĕ	pet	ou	out	ə	about,
ē	be	o͞o	took		item,
ĭ	pit	o͞o	boot		pencil,
ī	pie	ŭ	cut		gallop,
îr	pier	ûr	urge		circus

com•mod•i•ty /kə **mŏd′** ĭ tē/ n. (**-ties** pl.) **a.** something that is useful or can be turned to commercial or other advantage. **b.** an article of trade or commerce, especially an agricultural or mining product, that can be transported.

com•mu•ni•cate /kə **myo͞o′** nĭ kāt′/ v. (**-cates, -cat•ed, -cat•ing**) **a.** to have an interchange, as of ideas. **b.** to express oneself in such a way that one is readily and clearly understood. [Lat. *communicare, communicat-* < *communis,* common.]

com•mu•ni•ca•tion /kə **myo͞o′** nĭ **kā′** shən/ n. **a.** the act of communicating; transmission. **b.** the exchange of thoughts, messages, or information, as by speech, signals, or writing. **c.** something communicated; message.

com•mu•ni•ty /kə **myo͞o′** nĭ tē/ n. (**com•mu•ni•ties** pl.) **a.** a group of people living in the same locality and under the same government. **b.** the district or locality in which such a group lives. **c.** a group of people having common interests.

com•mute[1] /kə **myo͞ot′**/ v. (**-mutes, -mut•ed, -mut•ing**) **a.** to substitute. **b.** to make substitution; exchange. **c.** to travel as a commuter.

com•mute[2] /kə **myo͞ot′**/ n. Informal. the trip made by a commuter: *a 22-mile commute.*

com•mut•er /kə **myo͞ot′** tər/ n. a person who travels regularly from one place to another, as from suburb to city and back.

com•pa•ny /**kŭm′** pə nē/ n. (**-nies** pl.) **a.** a group; gathering: *the whole company of Nobel Prize winners.* **b.** a business enterprise; firm.

com•pa•ra•ble /**kŏm′** pər ə bəl/ adj. **a.** capable of being compared. **b.** similar or equivalent.

com•pas•sion /kəm **păsh′** ən/ n. sympathy for the problems of others. *When her dog died, her friends showed her great compassion.*

com•pas•sion•ate /kəm **păsh'** ə nĭt/ *adj.* feeling or showing compassion; sympathetic. *She gave the sick child a compassionate smile.*

com•pat•i•ble /kəm **păt'** ə bəl/ *adj.* capable of living or performing in harmonious, agreeable, or congenial combination with another or others.

com•pel /kəm **pĕl'**/ *v.* (**-pels, -pelled, -pel•ling**) to force, drive, or constrain.

com•pel•ling /kəm **pĕl'** ĭng/ *adj.* pressing; persuasive; needing attention.

com•pen•sate /**kŏm'** pĕn sāt'/ *v.* (**com•pen•sates, com•pen•sat•ed, com•pen•sat•ing**) to pay someone, as for a service. *If you help us, we will compensate you for your troubles.*

com•pete /kəm **pēt'**/ *v.* to strive or contend with another or others, as for profit or a prize; vie.

com•pe•ti•tion /kŏm' pĭ **tĭsh'** ən/ *n.* **a.** the act of competing, as for profit or a prize; rivalry. **b.** a contest or similar test of skill or ability.

com•ple•ment[1] /**kŏm'** plə mənt/ *n.* **a.** something that completes, makes up a whole, or brings to perfection. **b.** the quantity or number needed to make up a whole: *shelves with a full complement of books.* **c.** either of two parts that complete the whole or mutually complete each other.

➤ **Complement** sounds like **compliment**.

com•ple•ment[2] /**kŏm'** plə mĕnt'/ *v.* to add or serve as a complement to.

com•plete[1] /kəm **plēt'**/ *adj.* **a.** having all necessary or normal parts, components, or steps; entire: *a complete set.* **b.** having come to an end; concluded. **c.** absolute; total: *a complete mess.*

com•plete[2] / kəm **plēt'**/ *v.* (**com•pletes, com•plet·ed, com•plet•ing**) **a.** to bring to a finish or an end: *completed his homework.* **b.** to make whole, with all necessary elements or parts. *This piece will complete the puzzle.*

com•ple•tion /kəm **plē'** shən/ *n.* a making or being completed; finishing. *The completion of a job gives one a feeling of accomplishment.*

com•pli•cate /**kŏm'** plĭ kāt'/ *v.* (**-cates, -cat·ed, -cat•ing**) **a.** to make or become complex, intricate, or perplexing. **b.** to twist or become twisted together. [Lat. *complicare, complicat-*, to fold up: *com-*, together + *plicare*, to fold.]

com•pli•ca•tion /**kŏm'** plĭ **kā'** shən/ *n.* **a.** the act of complicating. **b.** a confused or intricate relationship of parts. **c.** a factor, condition, or element that complicates.

com•pli•ment[1] /**kŏm'** plə mənt/ *n.* **a.** an expression of praise, admiration, or congratulation. **b.** a formal act of courtesy, or respect.

➤ **Compliment** sounds like **complement**.

com•pli•ment[2] /**kŏm'** plə mənt/ *v.* **a.** to pay a compliment to. **b.** to show fondness, regard, or respect for by giving a gift or performing a favor.

con•cen•trate /**kŏn'** sən trāt'/ *v.* (**-trates, -trat·ed, -trat•ing**) **a.** to direct or draw toward a common center; focus. **b.** to converge toward or meet in a common center. **c.** to direct one's thoughts or attention.

con•cen•tra•tion /kŏn' sən **trā'** shən/ *n.* the act or process of concentrating, especially close, undivided attention.

con•demn /kən **dĕm'**/ *v.* to strongly disapprove of someone or something. *The city may condemn the old library because part of the floor fell through.*

con•dem•na•tion /kŏn' dĕm **nā'** shən/ *n.* an act of severe reproof; an expression of strong disapproval.

con•fec•tion /kən **fĕk'** shən/ *n.* a sweet preparation, such as candy.

con•fer /kən **fûr'**/ *v.* (**-fers, -ferred, -fer•ring**) **a.** to bestow (an honor, for example): *conferred a medal on the hero.* **b.** to hold a conference; consult together.

con•fer•ence /**kŏn'** fər əns, -frəns/ *n.* **a.** a meeting for consultation or discussion. **b.** an exchange of views. **c.** a meeting of committees to settle differences between two legislative bodies.

con•fess /kən **fĕs'**/ *v.* (**con•fess•es, con•fessed, con•fess•ing**) **a.** to acknowledge belief or faith in; profess: *He confessed his love for her.* **b.** to admit or acknowledge something damaging or inconvenient to oneself: *The suspect confessed to the crime.*

con•fi•den•tial /kŏn' fĭ **dĕn'** shəl/ *adj.* done or communicated in confidence; secret.

con•fi•den•tial•ly /kŏn' fĭ **dĕn'** shĕl lē/ *adv.* secretly.

con•gre•gate /**kŏng'** grĭ gāt'/ *v.* (**con•gre•gates, con•gre•gat•ed, con•gre•gat•ing**) to gather together. *The children like to congregate in the toy area.*

con•nois•seur /kŏn' ə **sûr'**/ or /kŏn' ə **soor'**/ *n.* an expert who judges art or food. *The food editor of the large newspaper had become a respected connoisseur in local restaurants.*

con•no•ta•tion /kŏn′ ə tā′ shən/ *n.* the image or idea a word suggests in addition to its exact meaning. *The word* winter *may have a connotation of snow, ice, and cold temperatures.*

con•science /kŏn′ shəns/ *n.* the faculty of recognizing the distinction between right and wrong in regard to one's conduct coupled with a sense that one should act accordingly. —*idiom.* **in (all) conscience.** in all truth or fairness.

con•sci•en•tious /kŏn′ shē ĕn′ shəs/ *adj.* thorough and painstaking; careful: *a conscientious worker.*

con•scious /kŏn′ shəs/ *adj.* having an awareness of one's own existence, sensations, and thoughts and of one's environment.

con•sent¹ /kən sĕnt′/ *v.* (**con•sents, con•sent•ed, con•sent•ing**) to give assent, as to the proposal of another; agree.

con•sent² /kən sĕnt′/ *n.* **a.** acceptance or approval of what is planned or done by another. **b.** *agreement as to opinion or a course of action.*

con•se•quen•tial /kŏn′ sĭ kwĕn′ shəl/ *adj.* important; meaningful. *The consequential results of the study brought about changes in the company's procedures.*

con•sid•er•a•ble /kən sĭd′ ər ə bəl/ *adj.* (**con•sid•er•a•bly** *adv.*) **a.** large in amount, extent, or degree. **b.** worthy of consideration; important; significant.

con•sign /kən sīn′/ *v.* (**con•signs, con•signed, con•sign•ing**) **a.** to give over to the care of another; entrust. **b.** to deliver for custody or sale: *She hopes to make some money by consigning the clothes she no longer wears.*

con•sist /kən sĭst′/ *v.* to be made up or composed.

con•sis•ten•cy /kən sĭs′ tən sē/ *n.* (**con•sis•ten•cies,** *pl.*) **a.** agreement or logical coherence among things or parts: *The chapters of the book lacked consistency.* **b.** reliability or uniformity of successive events: *You must exercise with consistency to get results.* **c.** degree of density, firmness, or viscosity: *The cookie batter will have a lumpy consistency.*

con•sis•tent /kən sĭs′ tənt/ *adj.* (**con•sis•tent•ly** *adv.*) in agreement; compatible.

con•so•la•tion /kŏn′ sə lā′ shən/ *adj.* of or related to a prize given to a competitor who loses or who does not win first prize. *We were surprised that the consolation prizes were almost as nice as the first prize.*

Pronunciation Key

ă	pat	ŏ	pot	th	thin
ā	pay	ō	toe	th	this
âr	care	ô	paw, for	hw	which
ä	father	oi	noise	zh	vision
ĕ	pet	ou	out	ə	about,
ē	be	o͞o	took		item,
ĭ	pit	o͞o	boot		pencil,
ī	pie	ŭ	cut		gallop,
îr	pier	ûr	urge		circus

con•strict /kən strĭkt′/ *v.* **a.** to make smaller or narrower, as by shrinking or contracting. **b.** to squeeze or compress by or as if by narrowing or tightening.

con•tact /kŏn′ tăkt/ *v.* to communicate with. *The pilot contacted the control tower for landing instructions.*

con•tem•plate /kŏn′ təm plāt′ / *v.* to think deeply about. *I like to contemplate beautiful things.*

con•tem•pla•tion /kŏn′ təm plā′ shən/ *n.* deep thinking; pondering. *He was in deep contemplation as he watched the blazing sunset.*

con•tin•u•ous /kən tĭn′ yo͞o əs/ *adj.* going on without stopping; unbroken; connected. *A continuous line of people passed the window.*

con•tract /kŏn′ trăkt′/ *n.* a legal agreement. *The striking workers finally accepted the new contract.*

con•trac•tion /kən trăk′ shən/ *n.* the shortened form of a word or phrase; a reduction in wording. *Won't is the contraction of will not.*

con•trac•tor /kŏn′ trăk′ tər/ or /kən trăk′ tər/ *n.* a person who makes an agreement to do a job.

con•trol¹ /kən trōl′/ *v.* (**con•trols, con•trolled, con•trol•ling**) **a.** to exercise authoritative or dominating influence over; direct. **b.** to regulate. **c.** to hold in restraint; check.

con•trol² /kən trōl′/ *n.* **a.** authority or ability to manage or direct. **b.** an instrument or set of instruments used to operate, regulate, or guide a machine or vehicle. **c.** a standard of comparison for checking or verifying the results of an experiment.

con•trol•la•ble /kən trōl′ ə bəl/ *adj.* responsive to direction or authority.

263

con•tro•ver•sial /kŏn′ trə **vûr′** shəl/ or / kŏn′ trə **vûr′** sē əl/ *adj.* causing conflict or disagreement. *City council was preparing to vote on the controversial motion.*

con•tro•ver•sy /**kŏn′** trə vûr′ sē/*n.* (**-sies** *pl.*) a dispute, especially a lengthy and public one, between sides holding opposing views. [ME *controversie* < Lat. *controversia* < *controversus,* disputed < *contro-,* against (var. of *contra-*) + *versus,* p.part. of *vertere,* to turn.]

con•ver•sa•tion /kŏn′ vər **sā′** shən/ *n.* a spoken exchange of thoughts, opinions, and feelings; talk.

con•verse¹ /kən **vûrs′**/ *v.* (**-vers•es, -versed, -vers•ing**) to engage in spoken exchange of thoughts and feelings; talk.

con•verse² /**kŏn′** vûrs′/ *n.* spoken interchange of thoughts and feelings; conversation.

con•verse³ /kən **vûrs′**, kŏn′ vûrs′/ *adj.* reversed, as in position, order, or action; contrary.

con•vert /kən **vûrt′**/ *v.* to change into another form, substance, or condition. *Jim's dad converted their unfinished basement into a playroom.*

con•vert•i•ble /kən **vûr′** tə bəl/ *adj.* **a.** able to be converted: *a convertible sofa.* **b.** having a top that can be folded back or removed: *a convertible car.*

co•op•er•ate /kō ŏp′ ə rāt′/ *v.* (**-ates, -at•ed, -at•ing**) to work together toward a common end.

co•op•er•a•tion /kō ŏp′ ə **rā′** shən/ *n.* an act of cooperating. [Lat. *co(m)-,* same + *operari,* to work < *opus,* work.]

co•op•er•a•tive /kō ŏp′ ər ə tĭv, -ŏp′ rə-, ə rā′ tĭv/ *adj.* **a.** done in cooperation with others: *a cooperative effort.* **b.** marked by willingness to cooperate: *a cooperative patient.*

co•or•di•nate¹ /kō **ôr′** dn āt′, -ĭt/ *n.* **a.** one that is equal in importance, rank, or degree. **b.** *Math.* one of a set of numbers that determines the location of a point in a space of a given dimension.

co•or•di•nate² /kō ôr′ dn **āt′**/ *v.* (**-nates, -nat•ed, -nat•ing**) **a.** to place in the same rank. **b.** to work well together; to harmonize.

co•or•di•na•tion /kō ôr′ dn **ā′** shən/ *n.* **a.** the state of being coordinate; harmonious interaction. **b.** *Physiol.* the coordinated functioning of muscles in the execution of a complex task. [Fr. or < LLat. *coordinatio: co(m)-,* same + *ordinatio,* arrangement < *ordinare,* to arrange in order < *ordo,* order.]

co•pi•ous /**kō′** pē əs/ *adj.* a large supply; more than enough. *The farmer was pleased with his copious harvest.*

cop•y¹ /**kŏp′** ē/ *n.* (**-ies** *pl.*) **a.** an imitation or reproduction of something original; duplicate. **b.** one specimen or example of a printed text or picture. **c.** a manuscript or other material to be set in type.

cop•y² /**kŏp′** ē/ *v.* (**-ies, -ied, -y•ing**) **a.** to make a copy of. **b.** to follow as a model or pattern; imitate.

cor•rect /kə **rĕkt′**/ *v.* to remove errors from; to make right. *Please correct the spelling on your papers.*

cor•rec•tion /kə **rĕk′** shən/ *n.* **a.** the act or process of correcting. **b.** something offered or substituted for a mistake or fault.

cor•re•late /**kôr′** ə lāt′, kŏr′-/ *v.* (**-lates, -lat•ed, -lat•ing**) **a.** to put or bring into complementary, parallel, or reciprocal relation. **b.** to establish or demonstrate as having a relationship.

cor•re•la•tion /kôr′ ə **lā′** shən/ or /kŏr′ ə **lā′** shən/ *n.* a relationship; a systematic connection; a correspondence.

cor•re•spond /kôr′ ĭ **spŏnd′**, kŏr′-/ *v.* **a.** to be similar, parallel, equivalent, or equal in character, quantity, origin, structure, or function. **b.** to communicate by letter, usually over a period of time.

cor•re•spon•dence /kôr′ ĭ **spŏn′** dəns, kŏr′-/ *n.* **a.** similarity. **b.1.** communication by the exchange of letters. **b.2.** the letters written or received.

cor•re•spon•dent /kôr′ ĭ **spŏn′** dənt/ or /kŏr′ ĭ **spŏn′** dənt/ *n.* **a.** one who communicates by means of letters. **b.** one employed by the print or broadcast media to supply news stories or articles: *a foreign correspondent.* **c.** something that corresponds; a correlative.

cor•rob•o•rate /kə **rŏb′** ə rāt′/ *v.* (**cor•rob•o•rates, cor•rob•o•rat•ed, cor•rob•o•rat•ing**) to confirm as true; to support with facts. *The detective separated the two men before they could corroborate their alibis.*

cor•rode /kə **rōd′**/ *v.* (**-rodes, -rod•ed, -rod•ing**) **a.** to dissolve or wear away gradually, especially by chemical action. **b.** to be eaten or worn away; become corroded.

cor•ro•sion /kə **rō′** zhən/ *n.* a gradual rusting. *Because of the corrosion, the worker was not able to loosen the nut from the bolt.*

cor•ro•sive¹ /kə **rō′** sĭv/ or /kə **rō′** zĭv/ *adj.* **a.** capable of causing corrosion. **b.** gradually destructive; steadily harmful.

cor•ro•sive² /kə **rō′** sĭv/ or / kə **rō′** zĭv/ *n.* a substance capable of causing corrosion.

cor•rupt•i•ble /kə **rŭp′** tə bəl/ *adj.* able to be made dishonest; prone to be influenced by bribery.

cor•rup•tion /kə **rŭp'** shən/ *n.* **a.** the act or result of corrupting. **b.** the state of being corrupt.

cor•sage /kôr **säzh'**, -säj'/ *n.* a small bouquet of flowers worn by a woman at the shoulder or waist or on the wrist. [ME, torso < OFr. < *cors*, body < Lat. *corpus*.]

cou•pon /**kōō'** pŏn, **kyōō'**-/ *n.* **a.** a negotiable certificate attached to a bond that represents a sum of interest due. **b.** a detachable part, as of a ticket or advertisement, that entitles the bearer to certain benefits, such as a cash refund or a gift.

cour•te•sy /**kûr'** tĭ sē/ *n.(-sies pl.)* **a.** polite behavior; gracious manner or manners. **b.** a polite gesture or remark.

cov•er•age /**kŭv'** ər ĭj/ *n.* the extent or degree to which something is observed, analyzed, and reported.

crea•ture /**krē'** chər/ *n.* **a.** something created. **b.** a living being, especially an animal. **c.** a human being.

crim•son /**krĭm'** zən/ *n.* a rich red color. *The players chose crimson and gold as their team colors.*

cri•te•ri•on /krī **tîr'** ē ən/ *n.* (**cri•te•ri•a** *pl.*) measure, rule, or standard on which a judgment or decision is based.

cri•tique /krĭ **tēk'**/ *n.* a review of a literary or artistic work. *The reporter wrote a critique of the play for the newspaper.*

cro•chet /krō **shā'**/ *v.* to make by looping yarn or thread into links with a hooked needle. *My aunt crocheted a sweater for the baby.* [French *crochet*, a hook.]

cru•cial /**krōō'** shəl/ *adj.* of supreme importance; critical: *a crucial election.*

crumb /krŭm/ *n.* a small piece or fragment, especially of bread or cake. *We fed crumbs to the birds during the winter.*

cui•sine /kwĭ **zēn'** / *n.* a style of cooking. *His favorite cuisine is Italian.*

cul•prit /**kŭl'** prĭt/ *n.* **a.** one charged with an offense or crime. **b.** one guilty of a fault or crime.

cup•ful /**kŭp'** fōŏl'/ *n.* (**-fuls** *pl.*) **a.** the amount a cup will hold. **b.** a measure of capacity equal to ½ pint, 8 ounces, or 16 tablespoons.

cur•a•ble /**kyōŏr'** ə bəl/ *adj.* capable of curing or healing: *curable illness.*

cu•ri•os•i•ty /kyōŏr' ē **ŏs'** ĭ tē/ *n.* (**-ties** *pl.*) **a.** a desire to know or learn. **b.** a desire to know about people or things that do not concern one; nosiness. **c.** something that arouses interest, as by being novel or extraordinary. **d.** a strange or odd aspect.

curl•ing i•ron /**kûr'** lĭng ī' ərn/ *n.* a device used when heated to style hair. *She used a curling iron to make soft curls around her face.*

cur•rant /**kûr'** ənt, **kŭr'**-/ *n.* **a.** the small, sour fruit of any of the currant plants, used chiefly for making jelly. **b.** a small, dried seedless grape of the Mediterranean region, used in cooking. [ME *(raysons of) coraunte*, (raisins of) Corinth.]

dam•ask /**dăm'** əsk/ *n.* **a.** a rich patterned fabric of cotton, linen, silk, or wool. **b.** a fine, twilled table linen. [ME < Med. Lat. *(pannus de) damasco*, (cloth of) *Damascus*.]

da•ta /**dā'** tə, **dăt'** ə, **dä'** tə/ *n. pl.* (used with a *sing.* or *pl. verb*). information, especially organized for analysis or used as the basis for a decision. [Lat., pl. of *datum*.]

date•line /**dāt'** līn'/ *n.* a phrase at the beginning of a newspaper or magazine article that gives the date and place of its origin.

day•dream[1] /**dā'** drēm'/ *n.* a pleasant, dreamy thought. *She has daydreams about being a famous poet.*

day•dream[2] /dā' drēm'/ *v.* to have pleasant, dreamy thoughts. *Try not to daydream in class.*

de•cent /**dē'** sənt/ *adj.* **a.** characterized by conformity to recognized standards. **b.** morally upright; respectable. **c.** kind or obliging: *very decent of them to help a stranger.*

dec•o•rate /**dĕk'** ə rāt'/ *v.* (**-rates, -rat•ed, -rat•ing**) to furnish or adorn with fashionable or beautiful things.

dec•o•ra•tion /děk′ ə rā′ shən/ *n.* **a.** the act, process, technique, or art of decorating. **b.** an object or group of objects used to decorate. **c.** a medal, badge, or other emblem of honor.

de•face /dĭ fās′/ *v.* (**de•fac•es, de•faced, de•fac•ing**) to spoil the appearance of; to disfigure.

def•a•ma•tion /děf ə mā′ shən/ *n.* the act of slandering; the oral or written abuse of someone's character.

de•fame /dĭ fām′/ *v.* (**de•fames, de•famed, de•fam•ing**) to damage the reputation, character, or good name of.

de•fect /dē′ fěkt′, dĭ fěkt′/ *n.* **a.** the lack of something necessary or desirable for completion or perfection; deficiency. **b.** an imperfection; fault.

de•fec•tive /dĭ fěk′ tĭv/ *adj.* having a defect; faulty.

de•fer /dĭ fûr′/ *v.* (**de•fers, de•ferred, de•fer•ring**) **a.** to put off; postpone. **b.** to submit to the opinion, wishes, or decision of another through respect or in recognition of his or her authority, knowledge, or judgment.

de•fer•en•tial /děf′ ə rěn′ shəl/ *adj.* marked by or exhibiting deference.

def•i•nite•ly /děf′ ə nĭt lē/ *adv.* certainly; indisputably. *The strong breeze definitely enhanced our kite-flying success.*

de•lib•er•ate /dĭ lĭb′ ər ĭt/ *adj.* (**de•lib•er•ate•ly** *adv.*) **a.** done or said on purpose; intentional. **b.** careful and thorough in deciding or determining: *a deliberate choice.* [Lat. *deliberatus,* resolved, p.part. of *deliberare,* to consider: *de-,* thoroughly + *librare,* to balance < *libra,* a balance, scales.]

de•liv•er /dĭ lĭv′ ər/ *v.* to take to the intended recipient: *deliver groceries.*

de•luxe¹ also **de-luxe** /dĭ lŭks′, -lŏŏks′/ *adj.* particularly elegant and luxurious; sumptuous. [Fr., of luxury.]

de•luxe² also **de-luxe** /dĭ lŭks′, -lŏŏks′/ *adv.* in an elegant and luxurious manner; sumptuously.

dem•on•stra•tion /děm′ ən strā′ shən/ *n.* **a.** the act of making evident or proving. **b.** conclusive evidence; proof. **c.** an illustration or explanation, as of a theory or product, by practical application. **d.** a public display of group opinion, as by a rally or march.

den•im /děn′ ĭm/ *n.* **a.** a coarse twilled cloth used for jeans, overalls, and work uniforms. **b. denims.** garments made of coarse denim. [Fr. *(serge) de Nîmes,* (serge) of Nîmes, a city in southern France.]

der•by /dûr′ bē/ *n.* (**-bies** *pl.*) a man's round felt hat with a small brim. *The gentleman topped off his new suit with a stylish brown derby.*

de•scend /dĭ sěnd′/ *v.* **a.** to move from a higher to a lower place. **b.** to come down from a source; derive: *descended from an old New England family.*

de•scen•dant /dĭ sěn′ dənt/ *n.* **a.** an individual descended from another. **b.** something derived from a prototype or earlier form.

de•scent /dĭ sěnt′/ *n.* **a.** the act or an instance of descending. **b.** downward incline or passage; a slope. **c.** hereditary derivation; lineage: *a person of Italian descent.*

➤ **Descent** sounds like **dissent**.

de•sert¹ /děz′ ərt/ *n.* **a.** a dry, often sandy region of little rainfall, extreme temperatures, and sparse vegetation. **b.** an empty or forsaken place; a wasteland.

de•sert² /děz′ ərt/ *adj.* **a.** of, relating to, characteristic of, or inhabiting a desert: *desert wildlife.* **b.** barren and uninhabited; desolate: *a desert island.*

de•sert³ /dĭ zûrt′/ *n.* something that is deserved or merited, especially a punishment: *They got their just deserts when they were caught cheating.*

de•sert⁴ /dĭ zûrt′/ *v.* (**de•serts, de•sert•ed, de•sert•ing**) **a.** to leave empty or alone; abandon. **b.** to forsake one's duty or post.

➤ **Desert** can sound like **dessert**.

de•sist /dĭ sĭst′/ or /dĭ zĭst′/ *v.* (**de•sists, de•sist•ed, de•sist•ing**) to stop doing something; cease.

des•sert /dĭ zûrt′/ *n.* a usually sweet course or dish, such as fruit, ice cream, or pastry, served at the end of a meal.

➤ **Dessert** can sound like **desert**.

de•ter•mi•na•tion /dĭ tûr′ mə nā′ shən/ *n.* **a.** the act of making or arriving at a decision. **b.** the quality of being resolute or firm in purpose; resoluteness.

de•ter•mine /dĭ tûr′ mĭn/ *v.* (**-mines, -mined, -min•ing**) **a.** to decide or settle (a dispute, for example) conclusively and authoritatively. **b.** to establish or ascertain definitely, as after consideration, investigation, or calculation.

de•tract /dĭ trăkt′/ *v.* **a.** to take away a desirable part; diminish. **b.** to distract.

de•vel•op /dĭ věl′ əp/ *v.* to grow; to come into being. *The bud developed into a blossom.*

dia- a prefix meaning through or across: *diagonal.*

di•ag•o•nal•ly /dī ăg′ ə nəl lē/ *adv.* in a way that is across, from corner to corner.

di•a•gram /dī′ ə grăm′/ *n.* **a.** a plan, sketch, drawing, or outline designed to demonstrate or explain how something works or to clarify the relationship between the parts of a whole. **b.** a chart or graph.

dig•i•tal /dĭj′ ĭ tl/ *adj.* **a.** of, relating to, or resembling a digit, especially a finger. **b.** expressed in digits, especially for use by a computer.

dig•ni•ty /dĭg′ nĭ tē/ *n.* (**-ties** *pl.*) **a.** poise and self-respect. **b.** stateliness and reserve in deportment and appearance.

di•min•ish /dĭ mĭn′ ĭsh/ *v.* (**di•min•ish•es, di•min•ished, di•min•ish•ing**) to lessen, reduce, or make smaller. *We can diminish the sound of traffic by closing the windows.*

din•ing room /dī′ nĭng rōōm′/ *n.* a room in which meals are served.

dis- a prefix meaning: **a.** not: *dissimilar.* **b.1.** absence of: *disinterest.* **b.2.** opposite of: *disfavor.* **c.** undo; do the opposite of: *disarrange.* **d.** used as an intensive.

dis•a•gree•able /dĭs′ ə grē′ ə bəl/ *adj.* **a.** not to one's liking; unpleasant or offensive. **b.** characterized by a quarrelsome manner; bad-tempered.

dis•a•gree•ment /dĭs ə grē′ mənt / *n.* a dispute; a difference of opinion. *We had a disagreement over whose turn it was.*

dis•ap•pear•ance /dĭs′ ə pîr′ ənce/ *n.* state or condition of having passed out of sight; the act of passing out of sight.

dis•ap•point•ment /dĭs′ ə point′ mənt / *n.* the act, condition, or feeling of being disappointed.

dis•as•trous /dĭ zăs′ trəs, -săs′-/ *adj.* causing disaster.

dis•con•nect /dĭs′ kə nĕkt′/ *v.* **a.** to sever or interrupt a connection. **b.** to shut off by removing the connection to a power source. *When we moved out of our old house, our telephone was disconnected.*

dis•con•nect•ed /dĭs′ kə nĕk′ tĭd/ *adj.* not connected; separate or detached.

dis•cour•age /dĭ skûr′ ĭj/ or /dĭ skŭr′ ĭj/ *v.* (**dis•cour•ag•es, dis•cour•aged, dis•cour•ag•ing**) to persuade against something. *We tried to discourage her from playing in the mud.*

dis•cour•age•ment /dĭ skûr′ ĭj mənt/ or /dĭ skŭr′ ĭj mənt/ *n.* the condition of having lost confidence or hope. *The constant rain brought on discouragement about the camping trip.*

dis•in•fect /dĭs′ ĭn fĕkt′/ *v.* to cleanse away germs. *The students had to disinfect the testing supplies before beginning their experiment.*

dis•in•ter•est•ed /dĭs ĭn′ trĭ stĭd, -ĭn′ tə rĕs′ tĭd/ *adj.* free of bias and self-interest; impartial.

Pronunciation Key

ă	pat	ŏ	pot	th	thin
ā	pay	ō	toe	*th*	this
âr	care	ô	paw, for	hw	which
ä	father	oi	noise	zh	vision
ĕ	pet	ou	out	ə	about,
ē	be	ōō	took		item,
ĭ	pit	ōō	boot		pencil,
ī	pie	ŭ	cut		gallop,
îr	pier	ûr	urge		circus

dis•mal /dĭz′ məl/ *adj.* **a.** causing gloom or depression; dreary. **b.** characterized by lack of hope.

dis•miss /dĭs mĭs′/ *v.* **a.** to discharge, as from employment. **b.** to direct or allow to leave: *dismiss troops.* **c.** to discontinue consideration of; drop.

dis•pos•a•ble /dĭ spō′ zə bəl/ *adj.* designed to be disposed of after use.

dis•prove /dĭs prōōv′/ *v.* (**dis•proves, dis•proved, dis•prov•ing**) to show for certain to be false.

dis•re•spect•ful /dĭs′ rĭ spĕkt′ fəl/ *adj.* having or showing a lack of respect; rude.

dis•sent[1] /dĭ sĕnt′/ *v.* (**dis•sents, dis•sent•ed, dis•sent•ing**) **a.** to differ in opinion or feeling; disagree. **b.** to withhold assent or approval.
　➤ **Dissent** sounds like **descent**.

dis•sent[2] /dĭ sĕnt′/ *n.* difference of opinion or feeling; disagreement.

dis•taste•ful /dĭs′ tāst′ fəl/ *adj.* rude, unpleasant, or offensive. *We agreed that calling people names is distasteful.*

dis•tract /dĭ străkt′/ *v.* to cause to turn away from the original focus of attention or interest; divert. [ME *distracten* < Lat. *distractus*, p.part. of *distrahere*, to pull away: *dis-*, apart + *trahere*, to draw.]

dis•trac•tion /dĭ străk′ shən/ *n.* something that draws attention away from a target or a focus.

dis•trict /dĭs′ trĭkt / *n.* a part of a country, state, or county that has certain duties or functions. *We have school districts and voting districts.*

di•ver•si•ty /dĭ vûr′ sĭ tē/ or /dĭ vûr′ sĭ tē/ *n.* (**di•ver•si•ties** *pl.*) variety; difference.

di•vert /dĭ vûrt′/ or /dĭ vûrt′/ *v.* to turn from one course to another; to change the path of. *They plan to divert the traffic during construction.*

dras•tic /drăs′ tĭk/ *adj.* (**dras•ti•cal•ly** *adv.*) **a.** taking effect violently or rapidly. **b.** quite severe or radical in nature; extreme: *took drastic steps.*

dual /dōō′ əl, dyōō′-/ *adj.* **a.** composed of two parts; double; twofold. **b.** having a double characater, nature, or purpose.

du•et / dōō ĕt′/ or / dyōō ĕt′/ *n.* a piece of music written for two singers or two musicians.

duo /dōō′ ō, dyōō′ ō/ *n.* (**-os** *pl.*) **a.** *Mus.* **a.1.** a duet. **a.2.** two performers singing or playing together. **b.** two people in close association.

duo- a prefix meaning two.

du•plex¹ /dōō′ plĕks′, dyōō′-/ *adj.* twofold or double. [Lat. *duplex,* twofold.]

du•plex² /dōō′ plĕks′, dyōō′-/ *n.* a duplex apartment or house.

du•pli•cate¹ /dōō′ plĭ kĭt, dyōō′-/ *adj.* **a.** identically copied from an original. **b.** existing or growing in two corresponding parts; double.

du•pli•cate² /dōō′ plĭ kĭt, dyōō′-/ *n.* **a.** an identical copy; facsimile. **b.** something that corresponds exactly to something else, especially an original.

du•pli•cate³ /dōō′ plĭ kāt′/ *v.* (**-cates, -cat•ed, -cat•ing**) **a.** to make an identical copy of. **b.** to double; make twofold.

du•pli•ca•tion /dōō′ plĭ kā′ shən, dyōō′-/ *n.* **a.** the act, procedure, or condition of being duplicated. **b.** a duplicate; replica.

du•pli•ca•tor /dōō′ plĭ kā′ tər/ or /dyōō′ plĭ kā′ tər/ *n.* a machine that makes copies of printed or graphic material. *He used a duplicator to make multiple copies of the document.*

du•pli•ci•ty /dōō plĭs′ ĭ tē/ or /dyōō plĭs′ ĭ tē/ *n.* (**-ties** *pl.*) deceit; dishonesty.

dy•nam•ic /dī năm′ ĭk/ *adj.* (**dy•nam•i•cal•ly** *adv.*) characterized by vigor and energy; forceful: *a dynamic personality.*

ear•phone /îr′ fōn′/ *n.* a device that converts electric signals, as from a telephone or radio receiver, to audible sound and that fits over or in the ear.

ec•cen•tric /ĭk sĕn′ trĭk/ *adj.* departing or deviating from the conventional or established norm; odd or unusual in appearance, behavior, etc.; strange, peculiar.

ech•o /ĕk′ ō/ *n.* (**-oes** *pl.*) **a.1.** repetition of sound by reflection of sound waves from a surface. **a.2.** the sound produced in this manner.

ec•o•nom•ic /ĕk′ ə nŏm′ ĭk, ē′ kə-/ *adj.* (**ec•o•nom•i•cal•ly** *adv.*) not wasteful or extravagant; prudent and thrifty in management; financially rewarding.

ed•i•ble /ĕd′ ə bəl/ *adj.* capable of being eaten. *Many wild berries are not edible.*

e•di•tion /ĭ dĭsh′ ən/ *n.* **a.1.** the entire number of copies of a publication printed from a single typesetting or other form of reproduction. **a.2.** a single copy from this group. **b.** one closely similar to an original; version. *The boy was a smaller edition of his father.* **c.** all the copies of a single press run of a newspaper: *the morning edition.*

ed•i•to•ri•al /ĕd′ ĭ tôr′ ē əl, -tōr′-/ *n.* **a.** an article in a publication expressing the opinion of its editors or publishers. **b.** a commentary on radio or television expressing the opinion of the station or network.

ed•u•cate /ĕj′ ə kāt′/ *v.* (**-cates, -cat•ed, -cat•ing**) **a.** to provide with knowledge or training, especially through formal schooling; teach. **b.** to provide with information; inform. **c.** to teach or instruct a person or group.

ed•u•ca•tion /ĕj′ ə kā′ shən/ *n.* **a.** the knowledge or skill obtained or developed by a learning process. **b.** the field of study that is concerned with teaching and learning.

ef•fec•tive /ĭ fĕk′ tĭv/ *adj.* **a.** having an intended or expected effect. **b.** producing or designed to produce the desired impression or response: *an effective speech.* **c.** operative; in effect. *The law is effective immediately.*

ef•fi•cien•cy /ĭ fĭsh′ ən sē/ *n.* (**-cies** *pl.*) the quality or property of being efficient.

ef•fi•cient /ĭ fĭsh′ ənt/ *adj.* (**ef•fi•cient•ly** *adv.*) **a.** acting directly to produce an effect: *an efficient cause.* **b.** acting or producing effectively with a minimum of waste, expense, or unnecessary effort. [ME < OFr. < Lat. *efficiens,* pr.part. of *efficere,* to effect.]

el•e•gant /ĕl′ ĭ gənt/ *adj.* **a.** characterized by or exhibiting elegance. **b.** excellent.

e•lic•it /ĭ lĭs′ ĭt/ *v.* a. to bring or draw out: *elicit information.* b. to arrive at by logic: *elicit the truth.* c. to call forth, draw out, or pro-voke: *elicit a reaction.*

➤ **Elicit** sounds like **illicit**.

el•i•gi•ble /ĕl′ ĭ jə bəl/ *adj.* **a.** qualified, as for an office or position. **b.** desirable and worthy of choice, especially for marriage.

e•lim•i•nate /ĭ lĭm′ ə nāt′/ *v.* (**-nates, -nat•ed, -nat•ing**) (**e•lim•i•na•tion** *n.*) **a.** to get rid of; remove. **b.1.** to leave out or omit from consideration; reject. **b.2.** to remove from consideration by defeating, as in a contest.

e•man•ci•pate /ĭ măn′ sə pāt′/ *v.* (**-pates, -pat•ed, -pat•ing**) to free from oppression, bondage, or restraint; liberate. [Lat. *emancipare, emancipat-: ex-*, out of, + *mancipium*, ownership < *manceps*, purchaser.]

e•man•ci•pa•tion /ĭ măn′ sə pā′ shən/ *n.* a release from slavery.

em•bar•go /ĕm bär′ gō/ *n.* (**-goes** *pl.*) a government order that forbids ships from leaving or entering the country's ports.

em•bar•rass /ĕm băr′ əs/ *v.* (**-rass•es, -rassed, -rass•ing**) **a.** to cause to feel self-conscious or ill at ease; disconcert. **b.1.** to beset with difficulties. **b.2.** to hinder; impede. **c.** to complicate.

e•mo•tion•al /ĭ mō′ shə nəl/ *adj.* **a.** readily affected with or stirred by emotion. **b.** marked by or exhibiting emotion.

em•phat•ic /ĕm făt′ ĭk/ *adj.* expressed with force or strength. *We knew she meant what she said when she was so emphatic.*

em•phat•i•cal•ly /ĕm făt′ ĭk ə lē/ *adv.* forcefully or strongly expressed. *The innocent man emphatically denied knowing anything about the crime.*

em•ploy•ee /ĕm ploi′ ē/, /ĭm ploi′ ē /, or /ĕm′ ploi ē′/ *n.* a person who works for another in return for compensation.

en- a prefix that forms verbs: *endanger.* When **en-** is followed by **b**, **m**, or **p**, it becomes **em-**.

-en¹ a suffix that forms verbs from adjectives: *cheapen.*

-en² a suffix that forms adjectives from nouns: *wooden.*

-ence a suffix that forms nouns from verbs: *reference.*

en•chi•la•da /ĕn′ chə lä′ də/ *n.* a tortilla rolled and stuffed usually with a mixture containing meat or cheese and served with a sauce spiced with chili.

en•close /ĕn klōz′/ *v.* (**-clos•es, -closed, -clos•ing**) **a.** to surround on all sides; close in. **b.1.** to place within a container. **b.2.** to insert in the same envelope or package. **c.** to fence in or place an enclosure around so as to prevent common use. [ME *enclosen* < OFr. *enclos*, p.part. of *enclore* < Lat. *includere*, to include: *in-*, in + *claudere*, to close.]

ă	pat	ŏ	pot	th	thin
ā	pay	ō	toe	th	this
âr	care	ô	paw, for	hw	which
ä	father	oi	noise	zh	vision
ĕ	pet	ou	out	ə	about,
ē	be	ŏŏ	took		item,
ĭ	pit	ōō	boot		pencil,
ī	pie	ŭ	cut		gallop,
îr	pier	ûr	urge		circus

en•cour•age /ĕn kûr′ ĭj, -kŭr′-/ *v.* (**-ag•es, -aged, -ag•ing**) **a.** to inspire with hope, courage, or confidence; hearten. **b.** to give support to; foster. **c.** to stimulate. [ME *encouragen* < OFr. *encoragier: en-* (causative) < Lat. *in-*, in + *corage*, courage < Lat. *cor*, heart.]

en•cour•age•ment /ĕn kûr′ ĭj mənt, -kŭr′-/ *n.* the act of encouraging.

en•dur•ance /ĕn dŏŏr′ əns, -dyŏŏr′-/ *n.* the act, quality, or power of withstanding hardship or stress.

en•dure /ĕn dŏŏr′, -dyŏŏr′/ *v.* (**-dures, -dured, -dur•ing**) **a.** to carry on through, despite hardships; undergo. **b.** to suffer patiently without yielding.

en•force /ĕn fôrs′/ or /ĕn fōrs′/ *v.* (**en•forc•es, en•forced, en•forc•ing**) to demand obedience to. *When Mom makes a rule, we know she will enforce it.*

en•force•ment /ĕn fôrs′ mənt/ or /ĕn fōrs′ mənt / *n.* a forcing of obedience. *The police officer's job is the enforcement of laws.*

en•gage•ment /ĕn gāj′ mənt / *n.* a promise or agreement to marry. *They had a short engagement before the wedding.*

e•nor•mous /ĭ nôr′ məs/ *adj.* (**e•nor•mous•ly** *adv.*) very great in size, extent, number, or degree.

en•roll /ĕn rōl′/ *v.* **a.** to enter the name of in a register, record, or roll. **b.** to roll or wrap in.

en•sure /ĕn shŏŏr′/ *v.* (**en•sures, en•sured, en•sur•ing**) to make sure or certain; insure.
➤ **Ensure** sounds like **insure**.

-ent a suffix that forms adjectives and nouns: *effervescent; resident.*

en•thu•si•as•tic /ĕn thŏŏ′ zē ăs′ tĭk/ *adj.* eager; excited. *She was enthusiastic about my idea of going to the park.*

en•thu•si•as•ti•cal•ly /ĕn thoō′ zē ăs′ tĭ′ kə lē/ *adv.* eagerly, excitedly. *When preparing for a party, everyone pitches in enthusiastically.*

en•tire•ly /ĕn tīr′ lē/ *adv.* wholly; completely.

en•tou•rage /ŏn′ toō räzh′/ *n.* a group of attendants or associates. [French < *entourer,* to surround, < Old French *entour,* surroundings: *en-, in.*]

ep•i•gram /ĕp′ ĭ grăm′/ *n.* a short, witty saying. *The author ended each chapter with a relevant epigram.*

e•quip /ĭ kwĭp′/ *v.* (**e•quips, e•quipped, e•quip•ping**) **a.** to supply with necessities such as tools or provisions. **b.** to furnish with the qualities necessary for performance.

er•ro•ne•ous /ĭ rō′ nē əs/ *adj.* incorrect; mistaken. *The candidate admitted that he had made several erroneous statements.*

er•ror /ĕr′ ər/ *n.* a mistake. *I was happy because my spelling test had no errors.*

es•sen•tial /ĭ sĕn′ shəl/ *adj.* **a.** constituting or part of the nature of something; inherent. **b.** basic or indispensable; necessary: *essential ingredients.*

et•i•quette /ĕt′ ĭ kĕt′, -kĭt/ *n.* the practices and forms prescribed by social convention or by authority.

e•vap•o•rate /ĭ văp′ ə rāt/ *v.* (**e•vap•o•rates, e•vap•o•rat•ed, e•vap•o•rat•ing**) (**e•vap•o•ra•tion** *n.*) **a.** to convert or change into a vapor. **b.** to draw moisture from, as by heating, leaving only the dry solid portion. **c.** to disappear; vanish: *Our fears evaporated.*

e•volve /ĭ vŏlv′/ *v.* (**-volves, -volved, -volv•ing**) **a.1.** to develop or achieve gradually. **a.2.** to work out; devise. **b.** *Biol.* to develop by evolutionary processes from a primitive to a more highly organized form. **c.** to experience evolutionary change. **d.** to undergo change or development.

ex- a prefix meaning: **a.** out; out of. **b.** former.

ex•act•ly /ĭg zăkt′ lē/ *adv.* **a.** precisely; without any change. *Do exactly as the teacher says.* **b.** true; quite so. *"Exactly!" exclaimed George in agreement.*

ex•ag•ger•ate /ĭg zăj′ ə rāt′/ *v.* (**-ates, -at•ed, -at•ing**) **a.** to enlarge or increase to an abnormal degree. **b.** to make greater than is actually the case; overstate: *exaggerated his own importance.*

ex•am•i•na•tion /ĭg zăm′ ə nā′ shən/ *n.* **a.** the act of examining or the state of being examined. **b.** an exercise testing knowledge or skill.

ex•cept¹ /ĭk sĕpt′/ *prep.* with the exclusion of; other than; but.

ex•cept² /ĭk sĕpt′/ *conj.* **a.** if it were not for the fact that: *I would own a cat except that I am allergic to them.* **b.** otherwise than: *They didn't stop working except to eat and sleep.*

ex•cept³ /ĭk sĕpt′/ *v.* to leave out; exclude.

ex•cess¹ /ĭk sĕs′/ or /ĕk′ sĕs/ *n.* **a.** the state of exceeding what is normal or sufficient. **b.** an amount or quantity beyond what is normal or sufficient; a surplus. **c.** overindulgence: *ate to excess.*

ex•cess² /ĭk sĕs′/ or /ĕk′ sĕs/*adj.* being more than is usual, required, or permitted. —*idiom:* **in excess of.** greater than; more than: *spent in excess of my budget.*

ex•cite•ment /ĭk sīt′ mənt / *n.* an excited condition; the state of being stirred up. *The entrance of the tigers created great excitement among the circus crowd.*

ex•clu•sive /ĭk skloō′ sĭv/ *adj.* not divided or shared with others.

ex•cuse¹ /ĭk skyoōz′/ *v.* (**-cus•es, -cused, -cus•ing**) (**ex•cus•a•ble** *adj.*) **a.1.** to apologize for. **a.2.** to seek to remove the blame from. **b.1.** to grant pardon to; forgive: *excuse him for his clumsiness.* **b.2.** to make allowance for; overlook.

ex•cuse² /ĭk skyoōs′/ *n.* **a.** an explanation offered to elicit forgiveness. **b.** a note explaining an absence.

ex•ec•u•tive /ĭg zĕk′ yə tĭv/ *n.* a person or group having administrative or managerial authority in an organization. *The president is the country's chief executive.*

ex•haust /ĭg zôst′/ *v.* **a.** to use up; consume. **b.** to wear out completely; tire. **c.** to deal with comprehensively: *exhaust a topic.*

ex•hi•bi•tion /ĕk′ sə bĭsh′ ən/ *n.* a display for the public, as of art objects, industrial achievements, or agricultural products.

ex•pect /ĭk spĕkt′/ *v.* **a.** to look for something to happen; to look forward to. *We expected rain, but the sky was clear.* **b.** to require. *My parents expect me to study hard in school.*

ex•pec•ta•tion /ĕk′ spĕk tā′ shən/ *n.* **a.** the act or state of expecting. **b.** eager anticipation.

ex•pense¹ /ĭk spĕns′/ *n.* **a.** something spent to attain a goal or accomplish a purpose. **b.** a loss for the sake of something gained; a sacrifice. **c.** an expenditure of money; a cost. —*idiom:* **at (one's) expense.** to one's detriment: *laugh at my expense.*

ex•pense² / ĭk spĕns′/ *v.* (**ex•pens•es, ex•pensed, ex•pens•ing**) **a.** to charge with expenses. **b.** to write off as an expense.

ex•per•tise /ĕk′ spûr **tēz**′/ *n.* **a.** expert advice or opinion. **b.** specialized knowledge or skill. [Fr. < OFr. < *expert*, experienced < Lat. *expertus*, p.part. of *experiri*, to try.]

ex•pi•ra•tion /ĕk′ spə **rā**′ shən/ *n.* the act of coming to a close; termination.

ex•pire /ĭk **spīr**′/ *v.* (**ex•pires, ex•pired, ex•pir•ing**) **a.** to come to an end; terminate. **b.** to breathe one's last breath; die. **c.** to exhale; breathe out.

ex•tract /ĭk **străkt**′/ *v.* to obtain or to derive information from. *I could not extract information from the document because it was in a foreign language.*

ex•trac•tion /ĭk **străk**′ shən/ *n.* the act of pulling or drawing out. *I went to the dentist for a filling and an extraction.*

ex•treme /ĭk **strēm**′/ *adj.* (**ex•treme•ly** *adv.*) **a.** being in or attaining the greatest or highest degree; very intense. **b.** of the greatest severity; drastic. [ME < OFr. < Lat. *extremus.*]

ex•tro•vert also **ex•tra•vert** /ĕk′ strə vûrt′/ *n.* an individual who is socially outgoing.

fa•cade /fə **säd**′/ *n.* a false appearance. *We knew her smile was a facade for how she really felt.*

fa•cial¹ /**fā**′ shəl/ *adj.* of or concerning the face.

fa•cial² /**fā**′ shəl/ *n.* a treatment for the face, usually consisting of a massage and the application of cosmetic creams.

fa•cil•i•tate /fə **sĭl**′ ĭ tāt′/ *v.* (**fa•cil•i•tates, fa•cil•i•tat•ed, fa•cil•i•tat•ing**) to make easier. *These folders facilitate keeping our papers in order.*

fa•cil•i•ty /fə **sĭl**′ ĭ tē/ *n.* (**-ties** *pl.*) something built for a particular function. *Our community has a great recreational facility.*

fac•sim•i•le /făk **sĭm**′ ə lē/ *n.* an exact copy or reproduction, as of a document.

fac•tion /**făk**′ shən/ *n.* a group of persons forming a united, usually troublesome minority within a larger group.

fac•tor /**făk**′ tər/ *n.* **a.** any of the things that cause a certain result. *Time is an important factor to consider in cooking.* **b.** any of the numbers multiplied to obtain a product. *Two factors of 21 are 3 and 7.*

fac•to•ry /**făk**′ tə rē/ *n.* (**-ries** *pl.*) a building or plant in which goods are manufactured. *When the factory closed down, many people were out of work.*

fac•ul•ty /**făk**′ əl tē/ *n.* (**-ties** *pl.*) **a.** a special ability or skill. **b.** a body of teachers as distinguished from their students.

far-fetched /fär′ fĕcht′/ *adj.* strained or improbable.

fa•ther-in-law /**fä**′ *th*ər ĭn lô′/ *n.* (**fa•thers-in-law** *pl.*) **a.** the father of one's husband or wife. **b.** *Archaic.* a stepfather.

fa•tigue /fə **tēg**′/ *n.* **a.** physical or mental weariness resulting from exertion. **b.** tiring effort or activity; labor. [Fr. < OFr. < *fatiguer*, to fatigue < Lat. *fatigare.*]

fa•vor•a•ble /**fā**′ vər ə bəl/ or /**fāv**′ rə-/ *adj.* (**fa•vor•a•bly** *adv.*) **a.** encouraging: *a favorable answer.* **b.** helpful: *favorable winds.*

fear•less /**fîr**′ lĭs/ *adj.* (**fear•less•ly** *adv.*) (**fear•less•ness** *n.*) having no fear; brave.

fe•ro•cious /fə **rō**′ shəs/ *adj.* **a.** extremely savage; fierce. **b.** marked by unrelenting intensity; extreme: *a ferocious blizzard.*

fi•an•cé /fē′ än **sā**′, fē **än**′ sā′/ *n.* a man engaged to be married. [Fr., p.part. of *fiancer*, to betroth < OFr. *fiancier* < *fiance*, trust < *fier* to trust < Lat. *fidere.*]

fi•an•cée /fē′ än **sā**′, fē **än**′ sā′/ *n.* a woman engaged to be married. [Fr., fem. of *fiancé*, fiancé.]

fierce /fîrs/ *adj.* (**fierc•er, fierc•est**) (**fierce•ly** *adv.*) (**fierce•ness** *n.*) **a.** having a savage and violent nature; ferocious. **b.** extremely severe or violent; terrible.

fi•es•ta /fē ĕs′ tə/ *n.* **a.** a festival or religious holiday, especially a saint's day celebrated in Spanish-speaking countries. **b.** any celebration or festive occasion. [Sp. < Lat. *festa,* neuter pl. of *festus,* joyous.]

filet¹ /fĭl′ ĭt/ *n.* a narrow strip of ribbon or similar material, often worn as a headband. [Middle English *filet* < Old French, diminutive of *fil, thread* < Latin *fīlum.*]

filet² also **fil·let** /fĭ lā′, fĭl′ ā/ *n.* **a.** a strip or compact piece of boneless meat or fish, especially the beef tenderloin. **b.** a boneless strip of meat rolled and tied, as for roasting.

filet³ also **fil·let** /fĭ lā′, fĭl′ ā/ *v.* to cut into strips.

fi•nan•cial /fə năn′ shəl, fī-/ *adj.* (**fi•nan•cial•ly** *adv.*) of, pertaining to, or involving finance, finances, or financiers.

fi•nesse /fə nĕs′/ *n.* subtle, skillful handling of a delicate or sensitive situation. *The teacher used great finesse in judging the students' work for display.*

flam•boy•ant /flăm boi′ ənt/ *adj.* showy; elaborate. *The comedienne likes to wear flamboyant clothing when she is performing.*

flex•i•ble /flĕk′ sə bəl/ *adj.* capable of being bent. *The clay figures were still flexible enough to shape.*

fluc•tu•ate /flŭk′ chōō āt′/ *v.* (**-ates, -at•ed, -at•ing**) to vary irregularly: *prices fluctuating dramatically.*

flu•ent /flōō′ ənt/ *adj.* (**flu•en•cy** *n.*) (**flu•ent•ly** *adv.*) **a.** having facility in the use of language: *fluent in three languages.* **b.1.** flowing effortlessly; polished. **b.2.** flowing smoothly; graceful: *fluent curves.*

flu•o•res•cence /flōō′ rĕs′ əns, flô-, flō-/ *n.* the emission of electromagnetic radiation, especially of visible light, resulting from the absorption of incident radiation and persisting only as long as the stimulating radiation is continued.

flu•o•res•cent /flōō′ rĕs′ ənt, flô-, flō-/ *adj.* exhibiting or capable of exhibiting fluorescence.

fo•li•o /fō′ lē ō′/ *n.* (**fo•li•os** *pl.*) a page number in a book. *The page with an odd-numbered folio always appears on the right.*

foot•age /fŏot′ ĭj/ *n.* a portion of motion-picture film, especially an amount of film depicting a specified event or kind of action: *news footage.*

for•give /fər gĭv′, fôr-/ *v.* (**-gives, -gave, -giv•en, -giv•ing**) to excuse for a fault or offense; pardon. [ME *forgiven* < OE *forgifan.*]

for•give•ness /fər gĭv′ nĭs, fôr-/ *n.* the act of forgiving; pardon.

for•mal /fôr′ məl/ *adj.* (**for•mal•ly** *adv.*) **a.** relating to form or structure. **b.** done in proper form. **c.** stiffly ceremonious.

for•mer•ly /fôr′ mər lē/ *adv.* at a former time; once.

for•syth•i•a /fôr sĭth′ ē ə/, /fôr sĭ′ thē ə/, or /fər sĭth′ ē ə/ *n.* a kind of bush with yellow flowers that bloom in the spring.

for•tu•nate /fôr′ chən ĭt/ *adj.* (**for•tu•nate•ly** *adv.*) **a.** bringing something good and unforeseen. **b.** having unexpected good fortune; lucky.

four-fifths /fôr fifths/ *n. pl.* four parts of something that has been divided into five equal parts. *Marcie ate nearly four-fifths of the pie.*

frank•furt•er /frăngk′ fər tər/ *n.* a smoked sausage of beef or beef and pork made in long, reddish links. [after *Frankfurt am Main,* Germany.]

freeze¹ /frēz/ *v.* (**freez•es, froze, fro•zen, freez•ing**) **a.** to convert into ice. **b.** to cause to congeal or stiffen from extreme cold. **c.** to preserve by subjecting to freezing temperatures. **d.** to damage or kill by cold or the formation of ice. **e.** to make very cold; chill. **f.** to immobilize, as with fear or shock. **g.** to stop the motion or progress of.

freeze² /frēz/ *n.* **a.** the act of freezing. **b.** the state of being frozen. **c.** a spell of cold weather; a frost. **d.** a restriction that forbids a quantity from rising above a certain level.

frus•trate /frŭs′ trāt/ *v.* (**frus•trates, frus•trat•ed, frus•trat•ing**) to cause to thwart or prevent plans. *Wind and rain always frustrate plans for a picnic.*

frus•tra•tion /frŭ strā′ shən/ *n.* the state of feeling that efforts or plans seem thwarted or prevented. *We felt frustration about all the work that had to be done.*

-ful a suffix meaning: **a.** full of: *eventful.* **b.** characterized by: *boastful.* **c.** having a specified tendency or capability: *mournful.* **d.** an amount or quantity that will fill: *cupful.*

-fy a suffix that forms verbs: *simplify.*

gaf•fer /găf′ ər/ *n.* the person in charge of lighting on a television or a movie set.

ga•rage /gə räzh′/ or /-räj′/ *n.* **a.** a building in which cars are kept. **b.** a place where vehicles are repaired or stored. [French *garer,* to shelter.]

gar•de•nia /gär **dēn′** yə/ *n.* a shrub having glossy evergreen leaves and large, fragrant, usually white flowers. [NLat., genus name, after Alexander *Garden* (1731–1790).]

gauge[1] /gāj/ *n.* **a.1.** a standard or scale of measurement. **a.2.** a standard dimension, quantity, or capacity. **b.** an instrument for measuring or testing. **c.** a means of estimating or evaluating; test: *a gauge of character.*

gauge[2] /gāj/ *v.* (**gaug•es, gauged, gaug•ing**) **a.** to measure precisely. **b.** to determine the capacity, volume, or contents of. **c.** to evaluate or judge: *gauge a person's ability.*

gaz•pa•cho /gə **spä′** chō′/ or /gəz **pä′** chō′ / *n.* (**gaz•pa•chos** *pl.*) a chilled, spicy soup. *We wanted to taste something different on that hot day, so we tried the gazpacho.*

gen•u•ine /**jĕn′** yo͞o ĭn/ *adj.* not false; real; true.

ghast•ly /**găst′** lē/ *adj.* (**ghast•li•er, ghast•li•est**) horrible; awful; terrible. *Everyone wore ghastly masks to the party.*

gla•cial /**glā′** shəl/ *adj.* **a.** of, pertaining to, or derived from a glacier. **b.** extremely cold; icy: *glacial waters.* **c.** having the appearance of ice. **d.** lacking warmth and friendliness: *a glacial stare.*

glos•sa•ry /**glô′** sə rē/ or /**glŏs′** ə rē/ *n.* (**glos•sa•ries** *pl.*) alphabetical lists of special or difficult words, often with explanations or definitions. *All of our class history books have glossaries.*

gnarled /närld/ *adj.* **a.** having gnarls; knotty or misshapen: *gnarled branches.* **b.** rugged and roughened, as from old age or work: *the gnarled hands of a carpenter.*

gnash /năsh/ *v.* (**gnash•es, gnashed, gnash•ing**) **a.** to grind or strike together. **b.** to bite by grinding the teeth.

gour•met[1] /goͦor **mā′**, goͦor′ mā′/ *n.* a connoisseur of fine food and drink. [Fr. < OFr., wine merchant's servant.]

gour•met[2] /goͦor **mā′**, goͦor′ mā′/ *adj.* of or relating to fine food: *a gourmet meal.*

gra•cious /**grā′** shəs/ *adj.* **a.** characterized by kindness and warm courtesy. **b.** characterized by charm and beauty; graceful. **c.** characterized by elegance and good taste: *a gracious dinner.*

grad•u•al•ly /**grăj′** oͦo ə lē/ *adv.* slowly; little by little. *The recipe said to gradually add the milk to the batter.*

grad•u•ate[1] /**grăj′** oͦo āt′/ *v.* (**-ates, -at•ed, -at•ing**) **a.** to be granted an academic degree or diploma. **b.** to grant an academic degree or diploma to.

Pronunciation Key

ă	pat	ŏ	pot	th	thin
ā	pay	ō	toe	*th*	this
âr	care	ô	paw, for	hw	which
ä	father	oi	noise	zh	vision
ĕ	pet	ou	out	ə	about,
ē	be	oͦo	took		item,
ĭ	pit	oͦo	boot		pencil,
ī	pie	ŭ	cut		gallop,
îr	pier	ûr	urge		circus

grad•u•ate[2] /**grăj′** oͦo ĭt / *n.* one who has received an academic degree or diploma.

grad•u•ate[3] /**grăj′** oͦo ĭt / *adj.* of, for, or relating to studies beyond a bachelor's degree: *graduate courses.*

grad•u•a•tion /**grăj′** oͦo ā′ shən/ *n.* **a.** the conferring or receipt of an academic degree or diploma marking completion of studies. **b.** a ceremony at which degrees or diplomas are conferred; commencement.

gram•mar /**grăm′** ər/ *n.* the study of how words are arranged in sentences. *A knowledge of grammar helps us write effectively.*

gram•mat•i•cal /grə **măt′** ĭ kəl/ *adj.* **a.** of or relating to grammar. **b.** conforming to the rules of grammar.

gram•o•phone /**grăm′** ə fōn′/ *n.* original name for a record player.

grand•daugh•ter /**grăn′** dô′ tər/ *n.* the daughter of one's son or daughter.

grate•ful /**grāt′** fəl/ *adj.* appreciative; thankful; expressing gratitude.

grat•i•fy /**grăt′** ə fī′/ *v.* (**grat•i•fies, grat•i•fied, grat•i•fy·ing**) **a.** to please or satisfy. **b.** to give what is desired to; indulge.

grat•i•tude /**grăt′** ĭ toͦod′/ or /**grăt′** ĭ tyoͦod′/ *n.* thankfulness. *After we raked the neighbor's leaves, he showed his gratitude by offering us hot cocoa.*

gro•cer•ies /**grō′** sə rēz/ *n. pl.* anything sold by a grocer. *We carried two bags of groceries home from the store.*

guar•an•tee[1] /găr′ ən **tē′**/ *n.* **a.** something that ensures a particular outcome or condition. **b.** a promise or assurance, especially as to the quality or durability of a product or service. **c.** something given or held as security; pledge.

guar•an•tee² /găr′ ən tē′/ *v.* **a.** to assume responsibility for the debt, default, or miscarriage of. **b.** to assume responsibility for the quality or execution of. **c.** to give a guarantee for.

guer•ril•la /gə rĭl′ ə/ *n.* a person who belongs to a band of fighters who are not part of a regular army. [Sp., raiding party, dim. of *guerra,* war, of Gmc. orig.]

gui•tar /gĭ tär′/ *n.* a musical instrument having strings that are played with the fingers or with a pick. *The entertainer sat in a chair and played her guitar as she sang.* [Spanish *guitarra.*]

gy•ro•scope /jī′ rə skōp′/ *n.* a device with an axis that can turn or spin in one or more directions.

ham•burg•er /hăm′ bûr′ gər/ *n.* **a.1.** ground meat, usually beef. **a.2.** a patty of such meat. **b.** a sandwich made with a hamburger patty, usually in a roll or bun. [short for *Hamburger steak,* after *Hamburg,* Germany.]

ham•mock /hăm′ ək/ *n.* a kind of hanging bed or couch made of cloth, canvas, or cords. [Spanish *hamaca.*]

ha•rass /hə răs′/ or / hăr′ əs/ *v.* (**ha•rass•es, ha•rassed, ha•rass•ing**) **a.** to irritate or torment persistently. **b.** to wear out; exhaust.

head•line /hĕd′ līn/ *n.* **a.** the title or caption of a newspaper article, usually set in large type. **b.** a line at the head of a page or passage giving information such as the title, author, and page number.

head•phone /hĕd′ fōn′/ *n.* a receiver, as for a radio, held to the ear by a headband.

head•quar•ters /hĕd′ kwôr′ tərz/ *n.* (*used with sing. or pl. verb*) the main office of a company. *The president of the company sent out orders from headquarters to all the workers.*

hel•i•cop•ter /hĕl′ ĭ kŏp′ tər/ *n.* a kind of aircraft without wings, powered by a rotating, horizontal blade. *People can fly by helicopter to places where there is no airport.*

herb /ûrb, hûrb/ *n.* any of various often aromatic plants used especially in medicine or as seasoning.

he•roes /hîr′ ōz/ *n. pl.* (**he•ro** *sing.*) people admired for courage, great deeds, or fine qualities. *George Washington and Abraham Lincoln are national heroes.*

he•ro•ic /hĭ rō′ ĭk/ *adj.* (**he•ro•i•cal•ly** *adv.*) **a.** having, displaying, or marked by the qualities appropriate to a hero; courageous: heroic deeds. **b.** impressive in size or scope; grand.

hes•i•tate /hĕz′ ĭ tāt′/ *v.* (**-tates, -tat•ed, -tat•ing**) **a.1.** to be slow to act, speak, or decide. **a.2.** to pause in uncertainty; waver. **b.** to be reluctant. *He hesitated to ask for help.*

hes•i•ta•tion /hĕz′ ĭ tā′ shən/ *n.* the act or an instance of hesitating.

hin•drance /hĭn′ drəns/ *n.* **a.** the act or condition of being hindered. **b.** one that hinders; impediment.

his•tor•i•cal /hĭ stôr′ ĭ kəl, -stŏr′-/ *adj.* (**his•tor•i•cal•ly** *adv.*) **a.** of, relating to, or of the character of history. **b.** based on or concerned with events in history. **c.** having considerable importance or influence in history; historic.

hon•es•ty /ŏn′ ĭ stē/ *n.* (**-ties** *pl.*) **a.** the quality or condition of being honest; integrity. **b.** truthfulness; sincerity.

hor•ri•ble /hôr′ ə bəl/ or /hŏr′-/ *adj.* **a.** causing horror; shocking; dreadful: *a horrible disease.* **b.** very unpleasant: *a horrible grating noise.*

hos•pi•ta•ble /hŏs′ pĭ tə bəl, hŏ spĭt′ ə bəl/ *adj.* **a.** cordial and generous to guests. **b.** favorable to growth and development: *a hospitable environment.*

hus•tle /hŭs′ əl/ *v.* (**-tles, -tled, -tling**) **a.** to jostle or shove roughly. **b.** *Informal.* to move hurriedly or urgently. **c.** *Informal.* to hurry along.

hy•a•cinth /hī′ ə sĭnth/ *n.* **a.** a plant, perhaps a lily, gladiolus, or iris, that, according to Greek mythology, sprang from the blood of the slain Hyacinthus. **b.** a deep purplish blue to vivid violet.

-ible a form of the suffix **-able.**

-ic a suffix that forms adjectives meaning "of or characteristic of": *allergic.*

i•den•ti•fy /ī dĕn′ tə fī′/ *v.* (**-fies, -fied, -fy•ing**) **a.1.** to establish the identity of. **a.2.** to ascertain the origin, nature, or definitive characteristics of. **b.** to associate or affiliate (oneself) closely with a person or group.

i•dle¹ /īd′ l/ *adj.* (**i•dler, i•dlest**) (**i•dle•ness** *n.*) **a.1.** not in use. **a.2.** without a job; unemployed. **b.** lazy; shiftless. **c.** lacking foundation in fact.

i•dle² /īd′ l/ *v.* (**-dles, -dled, -dling**) **a.** to pass time without working or in avoiding work. **b.** to run at a slow speed or out of gear.

i•dol /īd′ l/ *n.* **a.** an image used as an object of worship. **b.** a person or thing that is blindly or excessively adored.

ig•no•rance /ĭg′ nər əns/ *n.* the condition of being ignorant.

i•gua•na /ĭ gwä′ nə/ *n.* any of various large tropical American lizards of the family *Iguanidae,* often having spiny projections along the back. [Sp. < Arawak *iwana.*]

il•lic•it /ĭ lĭs′ ĭt/ *adj.* not sanctioned by custom or law; unlawful.

➤ **Illicit** sounds like **elicit.**

i•mag•i•nar•y /ĭ măj′ ə nĕr′ ē / *adj.* not real; happening only in the mind.

im•me•di•ate•ly /ĭ mē′ dē ĭt lē/ *adv.* without delay.

im•mense /ĭ mĕns′/ *adj.* **a.** extremely large; huge. **b.** immeasurably vast; boundless.

im•par•tial /ĭm pär′ shəl/ *adj.* not partial or biased; unprejudiced.

im•passe /ĭm′ păs′/ *n.* **a.** a road or passage having no exit; cul-de-sac. **b.** a difficult situation offering no workable escape. [Fr.: in-, not (<Lat. in-) + -passer, to pass < OFr.]

im•per•fect /ĭm pûr′ fĭkt / *adj.* not perfect; having faults or defects. *The diamond was beautiful, but the single flaw made it imperfect.*

im•pres•sion /ĭm prĕsh′ ən/ *n.* **a.** the effect, mark, or imprint made on a surface by pressure. **b.** an effect, feeling, or image retained as a consequence of experience. **c.** a vague notion, remembrance, or belief.

im•prob•a•ble /ĭm prŏb′ ə bəl/ *adj.* not believable; untrue. *It is improbable that people will travel to Mars anytime soon.*

im•prove /ĭm prōōv′/ *v.* (**-proves, -proved, -prov•ing**) to advance to a better state or quality; make better.

im•prove•ment /ĭm prōōv′ mənt/ *n.* **a.** the act or procedure of improving. **b.** a change or addition that improves.

in-¹ a prefix meaning without or not: *inaccurate.* When **in-** is followed by **l** or **r**, it becomes **il-** or **ir-** respectively. Before **b**, **m**, or **p**, it becomes **im-.**

in-² a prefix meaning in, within, or into: *inbound.* When **in-** is followed by **l** or **r**, it becomes **il-** or **ir-** respectively. Before **b**, **m**, or **p**, it becomes **im-.**

in•a•bil•i•ty /ĭn′ ə bĭl′ ĭ tē/ *n.* lack of ability or means.

ă	pat	ŏ	pot	th	**th**in
ā	pay	ō	toe	*th*	**th**is
âr	care	ô	paw, for	hw	**wh**ich
ä	father	oi	n**oi**se	zh	vi**s**ion
ĕ	pet	ou	**ou**t	ə	**a**bout,
ē	be	ōō	t**oo**k		it**e**m,
ĭ	pit	ōō	b**oo**t		penc**i**l,
ī	pie	ŭ	c**u**t		gall**o**p,
îr	p**ie**r	ûr	**ur**ge		circ**u**s

in•ad•vis•a•ble /ĭn′ əd vī′ zə bəl/ *adj.* unwise; not recommended.

in•an•i•mate /ĭn ăn′ ə mĭt/ *adj.* (**in•an•i•mate•ly** *adv.*) not having the qualities associated with active, living organisms; not animate. [Lat. *animare, animat-, < anima,* soul.]

in•ca•pa•ble /ĭn′ kā′ pə bəl/ *adj.* unable; lacking ability or strength. *We were incapable of hiking another mile.*

in•ci•den•tal•ly /ĭn′ sĭ dĕn′ tl ē/ *adv.* **a.** by chance, casually. **b.** apart from the main subject; parenthetically.

in•cog•ni•to /ĭn′ kŏg nē′ tō/ or /ĭn′ kŏg′ nĭ tō′/ *adv.* in disguise. *When they were out in public, the famous couple liked to travel incognito.*

in•con•sis•ten•cy /ĭn′ kən sĭs′ tən sē/ *n.* (**-cies** *pl.*) something that is illogical; disharmony.

in•cred•i•ble /ĭn krĕd′ ə bəl/ *adj.* too implausible to be believed; unbelievable.

in•def•i•nite /ĭn dĕf′ ə nĭt/ *adj.* not definite; unclear; vague; uncertain.

in•di•cate /ĭn′ dĭ kāt′/ *v.* (**-cates, -cat•ed, -cat•ing**) **a.** to demonstrate or point out: *indicate a route.* **b.** to state or express briefly.

in•dif•fer•ent /ĭn dĭf′ ər ənt/ or / ĭn dĭf′ rənt/ *adj.* **a.** having no particular interest or concern; apathetic: **b.** not mattering one way or the other. **c.** characterized by a lack of partiality; unbiased.

in•di•ges•tion /ĭn′ dĭ jĕs′ chən/ or /ĭn′ dī jĕs′ chən/ *n.* an upset stomach. *After eating the spicy food, I suffered with indigestion.*

in•ed•i•ble /ĭn ĕd′ ə bəl/ *adj.* unfit to be eaten; not edible.

in•el•i•gi•ble /ĭn ĕl′ ĭ jə bəl/ *adj.* not qualified for an election to an office or position.

in•fec•tion /ĭn fĕk′ shən/ *n.* invasion by microorganisms of a bodily part in which conditions are favorable for growth, production of toxins, and subsequent injury to tissue.

in•fec•tious /ĭn fĕk′ shəs/ *adj.* contaminated with disease-producing germs. *The doctor said that as long as I have a fever, I am infectious.*

in•fer /ĭn fûr′/ *v.* (**-fers, -ferred, -fer•ring**) to conclude from evidence or premises.

in•flu•ence[1] /ĭn′ floo əns/ *n.* a power indirectly or intangibly affecting a person or a course of events.

in•flu•ence[2] /ĭn′ floo əns/ *v.* (**-enc•es, -enced, -enc•ing**) to have power over; affect.

in•flu•en•tial /ĭn′ floo ĕn′ shəl/ *adj.* having or exercising influence.

in•flu•en•za /ĭn′ floo ĕn′ zə/ *n.* a contagious and sometimes serious disease caused by a virus; the flu. *Because so many students and teachers were sick with influenza, the principal had to close the school.*

in•her•i•tance /ĭn hĕr′ ĭ təns/ *n.* heritage; something inherited. *Our instinct for survival is an inheritance from many previous generations.*

in•i•tial[1] /ĭ nĭsh′ əl/ *adj.* occurring at the very beginning; first.

in•i•tial[2] /ĭ nĭsh′ əl/ *n.* (often **initials.**) the first letter or letters of a person's name or names, used as a shortened signature or for identification.

in•i•tial[3] /ĭ nĭsh′ əl/ *v.* (**-tials, -tailed, -tailled, -tail•ing, -tail•ling**) to mark or sign with initials.

in•i•ti•ate /ĭ nĭsh′ ē āt′/ *v.* (**in•i•ti•ates, in•i•ti•at•ed, in•i•ti•at•ing**) to bring a new person into a group. *A special ceremony will initiate the new members.*

in•i•ti•a•tion /ĭ nĭsh′ ē ā′ shən/ *n.* an official act of bringing a new person into a group. *The new members of the club were excited about their initiation.*

in•no•cent /ĭn′ ə sənt / *adj.* **a.** not guilty. *She claimed she was innocent of the crime.* **b.** harmless; having no bad effect: *an innocent trick.* **c.** unaware of evil. *An innocent child trusts everyone.*

in•sep•a•ra•ble /ĭn′ sĕp′ ər ə bəl/ or /ĭn′ sĕp′ rə bəl/ *adj.* cannot be parted. *The two girls are inseparable friends.*

in•sist /ĭn sĭst′/ *v.* (**in•sis•tence** *n.*) to be firm in a demand or course; refuse to yield. [Lat. *insistere*, to persist: *in-*, on + *sistere*, to stand.]

in•sis•tent /ĭn sĭs′ tənt/ *adj.* **a.** firm in asserting a demand or an opinion; unyielding. **b.** demanding attention or a response. **c.** repetitive and persistent.

in•spect /ĭn spĕkt′/ *v.* to examine carefully and critically, especially for flaws.

in•stant•ly /ĭn′ stənt lē / *adv.* at once; immediately.

in•suf•fi•cient /ĭn sə fĭsh′ ənt/ *adj.* not sufficient; inadequate.

in•sure /ĭn shoor′/ *v.* (**in•sures, in•sured, in•sur•ing**) **a.** to buy or sell insurance. **b.** to make sure, certain, or secure.

➢ **Insure** sounds like **ensure**.

in•tent /ĭn tĕnt′/ *adj.* very interested; attentive. *He was intent on finding his missing homework assignment.*

in•tent•ly /ĭn tĕnt′ lē/ *adv.* fixedly; with concentration. *She read the paper intently, to find and correct any errors.*

in•ter•mis•sion /ĭn′ tər mĭsh′ ən/ *n.* **a.** a respite or recess. **b.** the period between the acts of a theatrical performance. [Lat. *intermissio* < *intermissus*, p.part. of *intermittere*, to intermit: *inter-*, at intervals + *mittere*, to let go.]

in•ter•rupt /ĭn′ tə rŭpt′/ *v.* **a.** to break the continuity or uniformity of. **b.** to hinder or stop by breaking in upon.

in•trigue[1] /ĭn′ trēg′, ĭn trēg′/ *n.* a secret or underhanded scheme; plot. [Fr. < Ital. *intrigo* < *intrigare*, to perplex < Lat. *intricare*: *in-*, in + *tricae*, perplexities.]

in•trigue[2] /ĭn trēg′/ *v.* (**-trigues, -trigued, -trigu•ing**) **a.** to engage in intrigue; plot. **b.** to arouse the interest or curiosity of.

in•tro•duce /ĭn′ trə doos′/ or / ĭn′ trə dyoos′/ *v.* (**in•tro•duc•es, in•tro•duced, in•tro•duc•ing**) **a.** to present by name to another in order to establish an acquaintance. **b.** to present to the public for the first time. **c.** to bring forward for consideration. **d.** to provide with a beginning knowledge or first experience of something. **e.** to open or begin; preface.

in•tro•duc•tion /ĭn trə dŭk′ shən/ *n.* the first part, as of a book. *Read the chapter introduction.*

in•tro•spec•tion /ĭn′ trə spĕk′ shən/ *n.* reflection on one's own thoughts and feelings; self-inspection.

in•tro•vert[1] /ĭn′ trə vûrt′, ĭn′ trə vûrt′/ *v.* to turn or direct inward. [Lat. *intro*, to the inside + *vertere*, to turn.]

in•tro•vert[2] /ĭn′ trə vûrt′/ *n.* a person whose thoughts and interests are directed inward.

in•ven•tive /ĭn vĕn′ tĭv/ *adj.* (**in•ven•tive•ness** *n.*) adept or skillful at inventing; creative.

in•volve /ĭn vŏlv′/ *v.* **(-volves, -volved, -volv•ing)**
a. to contain or include as a part. **b.** to have as a
necessary feature or consequence; entail. **c.** to
occupy or engross; absorb.

in•volve•ment /ĭn vŏlv′ mənt / *n.* participation;
inclusion. *Writing the article required involvement
in several interviews with several people.*

ir•re•spon•si•ble /ĭr′ ĭ spŏn′ sə bəl/ *adj.* **a.** showing
no sense of responsibility or concern for
consequences; not dependable, reliable, or
trustworthy. **b.** not capable of being called to
account for one's actions.

ir•re•vers•i•ble /ĭr′ ĭ vûr′ sə bəl/ *adj.* incapable of
being reversed.

i•so•la•tion /ī′ sə lā′ shən/ *n.* **a.** the act of isolating.
b. the quality or condition of being isolated.

is•sue /ĭsh′ o͞o/ *v.* **(-sues, -sued, -su•ing) a.** to go or
come out. **b.** to circulate or distribute in an
official capacity: *issue uniforms to the players.*
c. to publish.

-ity a suffix that forms nouns meaning "a quality or
condition": *authenticity.*

-ive¹ a suffix that forms adjectives meaning "tending
toward, performing, or accomplishing something":
disruptive.

-ive² a suffix that forms nouns meaning "something
that performs or accomplishes something":
sedative.

jew•el•ry /jo͞o′ əl rē/ *n.* jewels; ornaments of gold,
silver, gems, etc.

jos•tle /jŏs′ əl/ *v.* **(-tles, -tled, -tling) a.** to come in
contact or collide. **b.** to make one's way by
pushing or elbowing. **c.** to vie for an advantage or
position.

jun•ta /ho͞on′ tə/ or /jŭn′ tə/ *n.* a group of persons
controlling a government. *After the prime minister
was forced out, a junta took control of the
government.*

ka•lei•do•scope /kə lī′ də skōp′/ *n.* a special tube
with bits of colored glass and two mirrors that
reflect a constantly changing pattern of colors
when the tube is turned and viewed through.

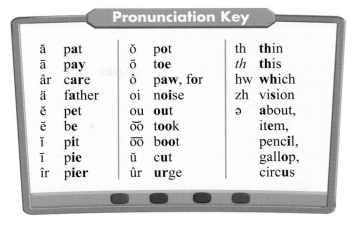

Pronunciation Key

ă	pat	ŏ	pot	th	thin
ā	pay	ō	toe	*th*	this
âr	care	ô	paw, for	hw	which
ä	father	oi	noise	zh	vision
ĕ	pet	ou	out	ə	about,
ē	be	o͝o	took		item,
ĭ	pit	o͞o	boot		pencil,
ī	pie	ŭ	cut		gallop,
îr	pier	ûr	urge		circus

key•board¹ /kē′ bôrd′, -bōrd′/ *n.* a set of keys, as on a
piano, an organ, or a typewriter.

key•board² /kē′ bôrd′, -bōrd′/ *v.* to set (copy) by
means of a keyed typesetting machine.

kneel /nēl/ *v.* **(kneels, knelt or kneeled, kneel•ing)**
to rest on bent knees. *Be careful not to kneel in
the dirt.*

knife /nīf/ *n.* **(knives** /nīvz/ *pl.*) a cutting instrument
consisting of a sharp blade with a handle.

knob /nŏb/ *n.* a rounded handle on a door, drawer,
etc. *The knob on the right of the radio controls the
sound.*

knoll /nōl/ *n.* a small rounded hill or mound; hillock.

la•bor /lā′ bər/ *n.* physical work. *Moving these stones
is hard labor.*

lab•o•ra•to•ry /lăb′ rə tôr′ ē, -tōr′ ē, lə bŏr′ ə trē,
-tə rē/ *n.* **(-ries** *pl.*) a room or building equipped for
scientific experimentation or research.

lar•i•at /lăr′ ē ət / *n.* a long rope with a running
noose for catching livestock; lasso. [Sp. *la reata:
la,* the + *reatar,* to tie again. (*re-,* again + *atar,* to
tie).]

laun•dry /lôn′ drē, län′-/ *n.* **(-dries** *pl.*) **a.** soiled or
laundered clothes and linens; wash. **b.** a place
where laundering is done.

league /lēg/ *n.* **a.** an association of states,
organizations, or individuals for common action;
alliance. **b.** an association of sports teams or clubs
that compete chiefly among themselves. **c.** a class
of competition: *out of his league.*

lei•sure•ly /lē′ zhər lē, lĕzh′ ər-/ *adv.* in an unhurried
manner; slowly.

le•o•tard /lē′ ə tärd′/ *n.* (often **leotards.**) **a.** a snugly fitting, elastic one-piece garment that covers the torso, worn especially by dancers or acrobats. **b. leotards.** tights [after Jules *Léotard* (1830–1870).]

-less a suffix that forms adjectives meaning "without or free of": *nameless.*

li•cense /lī′ səns/ *n.* a document giving official permission; a permit. *Ms. Soto obtained a pilot's license after she learned how to fly a plane.*

life•guard[1] /līf′ gärd/ *n.* an expert swimmer trained to watch over other swimmers, as at a beach or swimming pool.

life•guard[2] /līf′ gärd/ *v.* (**life•guards, life•guard•ed, life•guard•ing**) to work as a lifeguard.

light•ning /līt′ nĭng/ *n.* **a.** a large-scale high-tension natural electric discharge in the atmosphere. **b.** the visible flash of light accompanying such a discharge.

lik•a•ble /lī′ kə bəl/ *adj.* pleasing; attractive.

like•ly /līk′ lē/ *adj.* **a.** possessing or displaying the qualities or characteristics that make something probable. **b.** within the realm of credibility; plausible. **c.** apparently appropriate or suitable. **d.** apt to achieve success or yield a desired outcome; promising.

liq•ue•fy /lĭk′ wə fī′/ *v.* (**-fies, -fied, -fy•ing**) to cause to become liquid, especially: **a.1.** to melt (a solid) by heating. **a.2.** to condense (a gas) by cooling. **b.** to become liquid.

loaf /lōf/ *n.* (**loaves** *pl.*) shape of bread baked as a single piece. *We bought two loaves of rye bread.*

loy•al•ties /loi′ əl tēz/ *n. pl.* (**loy•al•ty** *sing.*) allegiances; devotions. *Our loyalties were divided between our old team and our new team.*

lux•u•ry /lŭg′ zhə rē, lŭk′ shə-/ *n.* (**-ries** *pl.*) **a.** something that is not essential but that gives pleasure and comfort. **b.** something that is expensive or hard to obtain. **c.** sumptuous living or surroundings.

-ly[1] a suffix that forms adjectives and means: **a.** characteristic of: *sisterly.* **b.** appearing or occurring at specified intervals: *weekly.*

-ly[2] a suffix that forms adverbs and means: **a.** in a specified manner: *gradually.* **b.** at a specified interval: *hourly.*

mac•in•tosh also **mack•in•tosh** /măk′ ĭn tŏsh′/ *n.* an outer garment for keeping the wearer warm and dry. *The worker on the fishing boat wore his macintosh on deck.*

mad•ras /măd′ rəs/, /mə drăs′/, or /mə dräs′/ *n.* a kind of cotton fabric made with plaid or striped designs in bright colors. *Her beautiful new skirt is made from madras.*

maes•tro /mīs′ trō/ *n.* (**maes•tros** or **maes•tri** /-trē/ *pl.*) an eminent composer, conductor, or teacher of music; a music master. *The concert sold out after people learned the maestro would be there.*

mag•nan•i•mous /măg năn′ ə məs/ *adj.* noble of mind and heart, especially generous in forgiving. [Lat. *magnanimus: magnus,* great + *animus,* soul.]

mag•nif•i•cent /măg nĭf′ ĭ sənt/ *adj.* (**mag•nif•i•cent•ly** *adv.*) **a.** splendid in appearance; grand: *a magnificent palace.* **b.** outstanding of its kind; superlative.

mag•ni•fy /măg′ nə fī′/ *v.* (**-fies, -fied, -fy•ing**) **a.** to make greater in size; to enlarge. **b.** to cause to appear greater or seem more important; exaggerate. **c.** to increase the apparent size of, especially by means of a lens.

mag•no•lia /măg nōl′ yə/ *n.* **a.** tree or shrub with large, showy, usually white or pink flowers. **b.** the flower of the magnolia. [NLat. *Magnolia,* genus name, after *Pierre Magnol* (1638–1715).]

main•tain /mān tān′/ *v.* **a.** to continue; carry on. **b.** to preserve or keep in a given existing condition, as of efficiency or repair: *maintain two cars.*

main•te•nance /mān′ tə nəns/ *n.* **a.1.** the action of maintaining. **a.2.** the state of being maintained. **b.** the work of keeping something in proper condition.

ma•li•cious /mə lĭsh′ əs/ *adj.* resulting from or having the nature of malice: *malicious gossip.* [ME *malice, malice* < OFr. < Lat. *malitia* < *malus,* bad.]

man•age /măn′ ĭj/ *v.* (**-ag•es, -aged, -ag•ing**) **a.** to direct or administer (a business, for example). **b.** to contrive or arrange. [Ital. *maneggiare* < VLat. **manidiare* < Lat. *manus,* hand.]

man•age•ment /măn′ ĭj mənt/ *n.* **a.** the act, manner, or practice of managing, supervising, or controlling. **b.** the person or persons who manage a business establishment, organization, or institution.

man•a•ge•ri•al /măn′ ĭ **jîr′** ē əl/ *adj.* executive; having to do with a manager. *The president of the company makes most of the managerial decisions.*

man•da•to•ry /măn′ də tôr′ ē/ or / măn′ də tōr′ ē/ *adj.* required or commanded by authority; obligatory. *Taking this class is mandatory.*

ma•neu•ver[1] /mə **noo′** vər, -**nyoo′**/ *n.* a physical movement or way of doing something requiring skill and dexterity.

ma•neu•ver[2] /mə **noo′** vər, -**nyoo′**/ *v.* to manipulate into a desired position or course.

man•i•cure[1] /**măn′** ĭ kyoor/ *n.* treatment of the hands and fingernails, including shaping, cleaning, and polishing of the nails. [Fr.: Lat. *manus,* hand + *cura,* care.]

man•i•cure[2] /**măn′** ĭ kyoor/ *v.* (**-cures, -cured, -cur•ing**) **a.** to care for (the fingernails) by shaping, cleaning, and polishing. **b.** to clip or trim evenly or closely.

man•i•fest /**măn′** ə fĕst/ *v.* to display; to make obvious; to show. *Her excellent project will manifest her planning and hard work.*

ma•nip•u•late /mə **nĭp′** yə lāt′/ *v.* (**-lates, -lat•ed, -lat•ing**) **a.** to operate or control by skilled use of the hands; handle. **b.** to influence or manage shrewdly or deviously. [< Fr. *manipule,* handful < Lat. *manipulus* < *manus,* hand.]

man•ner /**măn′** ər/ *n.* a style or way of doing something. *Because of her brusque manner, she sometimes offended people who didn't really know her.*

man•ner•ism /**măn′** ə rĭz′ əm/ *n.* **a.** a distinctive behavioral trait; idiosyncrasy. **b.** exaggerated or affected style or habit, as in dress, speech, or art.

man•u•al[1] /**măn′** yoo əl/ *adj.* **a.** of, pertaining to, or done by the hands. **b.** employing human rather than mechanical energy: *manual labor.*

man•u•al[2] /**măn′** yoo əl/ *n.* **a.** a small reference book, especially one giving instructions. **b.** a keyboard of an organ played with the hands.

man•u•fac•ture /măn′ yə **făk′** chər/ *v.* (**-tures, -tured, -tur•ing**) **a.** to make or process (a raw material) into a finished product, especially by means of a large-scale industrial operation. **b.** to concoct or invent; fabricate: *manufacture an excuse.*

mar•a•thon /**măr′** ē thŏn′/ *n.* a long race; an endurance contest. [*Marathon:* Greek city from which a messenger ran to Athens to announce victory.]

Pronunciation Key

ă	pat	ŏ	pot	th	thin
ā	pay	ō	toe	*th*	this
âr	care	ô	paw, for	hw	which
ä	father	oi	noise	zh	vision
ĕ	pet	ou	out	ə	about,
ē	be	oo	took		item,
ĭ	pit	oo	boot		pencil,
ī	pie	ŭ	cut		gallop,
îr	pier	ûr	urge		circus

mar•shal /**mär′** shəl/ *n.* a type of police officer who helps keep law and order. *The job of a marshal is much like that of a sheriff.*
   ➢ **Marshal** sounds like **martial**.

mar•tial /**mär′** shəl/ *adj.* having to do with the police or the military. *In basic training, the cadets learn martial arts.*
   ➢ **Martial** sounds like **marshal**.

mas•quer•ade[1] /măs′ kə **rād′**/ *n.* **a.** a costume party at which masks are worn; masked ball. **b.** a disguise or false outward show; pretense: *a masquerade of humility.* [OFr. *mascarade* < OSp. *mascarada,* poss. < Ar. *maskharah,* buffoon.]

mas•quer•ade[2] /măs′ kə **rād′**/ *v.* (**-ades, -ad•ed, -ad•ing**) **a.** to wear a mask or disguise, as at a masquerade. **b.** to go about as if in disguise; have or put on a deceptive appearance.

mas•ter•mind /**măs′** tər mīnd′/ *n.* a main person who plans a scheme or an operation. *The clever thief was the mastermind of the plan to rob the bank.*

mast•head /**măst′** hĕd/ *n.* **a.** the listing in a newspaper, magazine, or other publication of information about its staff and operation. **b.** the name of a newspaper on the first page.

max•i•mum /**măk′** sə məm/ *adj.* having the greatest amount possible. *One student achieved the maximum score on the test.*

me•an•der /mē **ăn′** dər/ *v.* to roam or wander aimlessly. *They set out to meander through the park.*

meas•ure•ment /**mĕzh′** ər mənt / *n.* **a.** the act of measuring or the process of being measured. *A gallon is a unit of liquid measurement.* **b.** the length, size, or amount of something.

me•chan•i•cal /mĭ **kăn′** ĭ kəl/ *adj.* (**me•chan•i•cal•ly** *adv.*) **a.** of or pertaining to machines or tools. **b.** acting or performing like a machine; automatic. *The speaker's delivery was mechanical.*

me•di•a /mē′ dē ə/ *n. pl.* See **medium**.

me•di•um /mē′ dē əm/ *n.* (**-dia,** *pl.*) **a.** an intervening substance through which something is transmitted or carried on. **b.** an agency by which something is accomplished, conveyed, or transferred. **c.** a means of mass communication, as newspapers, magazines, or television.

mega- a prefix meaning **a.** large: *megadose.* **b.** one million: *megahertz.*

meg•a•phone /mĕg′ ə fōn′/ *n.* a funnel-shaped device used to direct and amplify the voice.

me•lod•ic /mə lŏd′ ĭk/ *adj.* of, pertaining to, or containing melody.

me•lod•i•cal•ly /mə lŏd′ ĭ kəl lē/ *adv.* musically; in a way that is pleasant to hear.

mel•o•dies /mĕl′ ə dēz/ *n. pl.* (**mel•o•dy** *sing.*) songs; tunes. *The concert featured a wide range of old and new melodies.*

me•nag•er•ie /mə nǎj′ ə rē, mə nǎzh′-/ *n.* **a.** a collection of live wild animals on exhibition. **b.** the enclosure in which wild animals are kept. [Fr. *ménagerie* < *ménage,* ménage.]

me•ni•al /mē′ nē əl/ *or* /mēn′ yəl/ *adj.* slavish and for the benefit of others; suited to or related to a servant. *Without an education or any special skills, all the work he could find was menial.*

-ment a suffix that forms nouns and means: **a.** an action or process: *government.* **b.** a condition: *amazement.* **c.** the product, means, or result of an action: *entanglement.*

me•sa /mā′ sə/ *n.* a flat-topped elevation with one or more clifflike sides, common in the southwestern United States. [Sp. < OSp.< Lat. *mensa,* table.]

micro- a prefix meaning: **a.** small or smaller: *microcosm.* **b.** an instrument or technique for working with small things: *microscope.*

mi•cro•phone /mī′ krə fōn′/ *n.* an instrument that converts acoustical waves into an electric current, usually fed into an amplifier, recorder, or broadcast transmitter.

mi•cro•scope /mī′ krə skōp′/ *n.* an optical instrument that uses a combination of lenses to produce magnified images of small objects, especially of objects too small to be seen by the unaided eye.

mi•cro•scop•ic /mī′ krə skŏp′ ĭk/ *adj.* (**mi•cro•scop•i•cal•ly** *adv.*) too small to be seen without a microscope; extremely small.

mile•age /mī′ lĭj/ *n.* the number of miles covered. *What was the total mileage of the trip?*

mil•li•gram /mĭl′ ĭ grăm′/ *n.* a unit of measurement equal to one thousandth of a gram; abbreviated **mg.**

mim•ic /mĭm′ ĭk/ *v.* (**-ics, -icked, -ick•ing**) to copy or imitate closely, especially in speech, expression, and gesture; ape.

min•i•a•ture[1] /mĭn′ ē ə chŏŏr′, mĭn′ ə chər,/ *n.* **a.** a copy or a model that represents something in a greatly reduced size. **b.** something small of its class.

min•i•a•ture[2] /mĭn′ ē ə chŏŏr′, mĭn′ ə chər,/ *adj.* on a small or greatly reduced scale: *miniature furniture.*

mi•rage /mĭ räzh′/ *n.* **a.** an optical phenomenon that creates the illusion of water, often with upside-down reflections of distant objects. It is caused by distortions that occur as light passes between alternate layers of hot and cool air. **b.** something that is illusory or insubstantial. [Fr. < *mirer,* to look at < Lat. *mirari,* to wonder at.]

mis•chie•vous /mĭs′ chə vəs/ *adj.* **a.** playful; teasing. **b.** causing harm, injury, or damage: *mischievous falsehoods.*

mis•sion /mĭsh′ ən/ *n.* a person's calling. *Her mission in life was teaching.*

mis•sive /mĭs′ ĭv/ *n.* a letter or message.

mis•take[1] /mĭ stāk′/ *n.* **a.** an error or fault. **b.** a misconception or misunderstanding.

mis•take[2] /mĭ stāk′/ *v.* (**-takes, -took, -tak•en, -tak•ing**) to make a mistake; err.

mis•tak•en /mĭ stā′ kən/ *adj.* wrong; incorrect. *I thought that classes were canceled, but I was mistaken.*

mis•un•der•stand•ing /mĭs′ ŭn dər stǎn′ dĭng/ *n.* a failure to understand correctly. *Because of a misunderstanding, she did the wrong page for homework.*

mix-up /mĭks′ ŭp′/ *n.* a state of confusion; muddle.

mono- or **mon-** a prefix meaning "one," "single," or "alone": *monocle.*

mon•o•cle /mŏn′ ə kəl/ *n.* an eyeglass for one eye. [Fr. < Lat. *monoculus,* having one eye: Gk. *monos,* one + Lat. *oculus,* eye.]

mon•o•gram[1] /mŏn′ ə grăm′/ *n.* a design composed of one or more letters, usually the initials of a name.

mon•o•gram[2] /mŏn′ ə grăm′/ *v.* (**-grams, -grammed, -gram•ming**) to mark with a monogram.

mon•o•logue /**mŏn′** ə lôg′, -lŏg′/ *n.* **a.** a long speech made by one person, often monopolizing conversation. **b.** a long speech delivered by an actor on the stage or a character in a story or poem; a dramatic soliloquy. **c.** a continuous series of jokes or comic stories delivered by a comedian.

mo•nop•o•lize /mə **nŏp′** ə līz′/ *v.* (**-liz•es, -lized, -liz•ing**) **a.** to gain and hold a monopoly over. **b.** to dominate by excluding others: *monopolized the conversation.* **c.** to take all of; have all to oneself.

mo•nop•o•ly /mə **nŏp′** ə lē/ *n.* (**-lies** *pl.*) exclusive control by one group of the means of producing or selling a commodity or service.

mon•o•rail /**mŏn′** ə rāl′/ *n.* **a.** a single rail on which a vehicle or train of cars travels. **b.** a railway system using a monorail.

mon•o•syl•la•ble /**mŏn′** ə sĭl′ ə bəl/ *n.* a word with only one syllable. *The reporter was frustrated during the interview when she got so many answers with just a monosyllable.*

mon•o•tone¹ /**mŏn′** ə tōn′/ *n.* **a.** a succession of sounds or words uttered in a single tone of voice. **b.** sameness or dull repetition in sound, style, manner, or color.

mon•o•tone² /**mŏn′** ə tōn′/ *adj.* **a.** of, pertaining to, or characteristic of sounds emitted at a single pitch. **b.** of or having a single color.

mo•not•o•nous /mə **nŏt′** n əs/ *adj.* **a.** sounded or spoken in an unvarying tone. **b.** repetitiously dull or lacking in variety.

mo•not•o•ny /mə **nŏt′** n ē/ *n.* **a.** uniformity or lack of variation in pitch, intonation, or inflection. **b.** wearisome sameness.

mort•gage /**môr′** gĭj/ *n.* a temporary and conditional pledge of property to a creditor as security for the performance of an obligation or the repayment of a debt.

mos•qui•to /mə **skē′** tō/ *n.* (**-toes** *pl.*) any of various winged insects of which the females bite and suck blood from animals and human beings. Some kinds transmit diseases such as malaria and yellow fever. [Sp. < dim. of *mosca,* fly < Lat. *musca.*]

moth•er-in-law /**mu***th***′** ər ĭn lô/ *n.* (**moth•ers-in-law** *pl.*) the mother of one's wife or husband.

mo•ti•vate /**mō′** tə vāt′/ *v.* (**-vates, -vat•ed, -vat•ing**) to provide with an incentive or motive; impel.

mus•cle /**mŭs′** əl/ *n.* body tissue composed of fibers that tighten or loosen to move parts of the body. *The athlete was careful to stretch his muscles before the race.*

Pronunciation Key

ă	pat	ŏ	pot	th	thin
ā	pay	ō	toe	*th*	this
âr	care	ô	paw, for	hw	which
ä	father	oi	noise	zh	vision
ĕ	pet	ou	out	ə	about,
ē	be	o͝o	took		item,
ĭ	pit	o͞o	boot		pencil,
ī	pie	ŭ	cut		gallop,
îr	pier	ûr	urge		circus

mus•tang /**mŭs′** tăng′/ *n.* a wild horse of the North American plains, descended from Spanish horses. [Sp. *mesteño,* stray animal < OSp. *mesta,* association of cattle owners < Lat. *miscere,* to mix.]

mu•tu•al /**myo͞o′** cho͞o əl/ *adj.* **a.** having the same relationship to the other: *mutual friends.* **b.** directed and received in equal amount: *mutual respect.* **c.** possessed in common: *mutual interests.*

mys•tique /mĭ **stēk′**/ *n.* an aura of heightened value, interest, or meaning surrounding something, based on attitudes and beliefs that relate special power or mystery to it. [French *mystical, mystique* < Latin *mysticus.*]

nar•rate /**năr′** āt′/ or /nă **rāt′**/ *v.* (**nar•rates, nar•rat•ed, nar•rat•ing**) to tell a story. *They hired a famous actor to narrate the story in the movie.*

na•tive¹ /**nā′** tĭv/ *adj.* **a.** originating, growing, or produced in a certain place or region; indigenous. **b.** being a member of the original inhabitants of a particular place. **c.** of, belonging to, or characteristic of such inhabitants. **d.** natural; unaffected.

na•tive² /**nā′** tĭv/ *n.* **1. a.** One born in or connected with a place by birth: *a native of Scotland now living in the United States.* **1. b.** One of the original inhabitants or lifelong residents of a place. **2.** An animal or plant that originated in a particular place or region.

nec•es•sar•i•ly /nĕs′ ĭ **sâr′** ə lē/ *adv.* of necessity; inevitably.

-ness a suffix that forms nouns and means a state, condition, or quality: *rudeness.*

news•cast /nŏŏz′ kăst′, nyŏŏz′-/ *n.* a radio or television broadcast of events in the news.

news•print /nŏŏz′ prĭnt′, nyŏŏz′-/ *n.* inexpensive paper made from wood pulp, used chiefly for printing newspapers.

news•reel /nŏŏz′ rēl′, nyŏŏz′-/ *n.* a short motion picture dealing with recent news events.

news•room /nŏŏz′ rŏŏm′, -rŏŏm′, nyŏŏz′-/ *n.* a room, as in a newspaper office or a radio or television station, in which news is prepared for release.

news•stand /nŏŏz′ stănd′, nyŏŏz′-/ *n.* a shop or open booth at which newspapers and periodicals are sold.

no•ble¹ /nō′ bəl/ *adj.* (**-bler, -blest**) (**no•bly** *adv.*) **a.** superior in nature or character; exalted: *a noble ideal.* **b.** grand and stately in appearance; majestic: *noble mountain peaks.*

no•ble² /nō′ bəl/ *n.* a member of the nobility.

no•ta•ble /nō′ tə bəl/ *adj.* **a.** worthy of notice; remarkable. *Writing a book is a notable accomplishment.* **b.** prominent; distinguished. *He is a notable physicist.*

no•tice•a•ble /nō′ tĭ sə bəl/ *adj.* (**no•tice•a•bly** *adv.*) readily observed; evident.

no•ti•fy /nō′ tə fī/ *v.* (**-fies, -fied, -fy•ing**) to give notice to; inform: *notified his client.*

no•tion /nō′ shən/ *n.* **a.** a belief; opinion. **b.** a fanciful impulse; whim.

nu•mer•ous /nŏŏ′ mər əs, nyŏŏ′-/ *adj.* consisting of many persons or items.

nu•tri•tious /nŏŏ trĭsh′ əs/ or /nyŏŏ-/ *adj.* providing nourishment. *Apples are a nutritious snack.* [Latin *nutrire,* to nourish.]

ob- a prefix meaning "toward", "in front of", or "against.: When **ob-** is followed by **c, f,** or **p,** it becomes **oc-, of-,** or **op-** respectively. When it is followed by **m,** it is reduced to **o-.**

o•blig•ing /ə blī′ jĭng/ *adj.* accommodating; helpful. *The owners of the inn are very obliging toward their guests.*

ob•ser•vant /əb zûr′ vənt/ *adj.* **a.** quick to perceive; alert: *an observant traveler.* **b.** diligent in observing a law, custom, duty, or principle: *observant of the speed limit.*

oc•ca•sion•al /ə kā′ zhə nəl/ *adj.* (**oc•ca•sion•al•ly** *adv.*) occuring from time to time.

oc•cur /ə kûr′/ *v.* (**-curs, -curred, -cur•ring**) **a.** to take place; come about. **b.** to come to mind.

oc•cur•rence /ə kûr′ əns/ *n.* **a.** an act or instance of occurring. **b.** something that takes place; incident.

old-fash•ioned /ōld′ făsh′ ənd/ *adj.* **a.** of a style or method formerly in vogue; outdated. **b.** attached to or favoring methods, ideas, or customs of an earlier time.

om•e•let /ŏm′ ə lĭt / or / ŏm′ lĭt / *n.* a dish of beaten eggs cooked and folded in half over a filling of cheese, chopped meat, or vegetables. *We enjoyed a breakfast of omelet and toast.*

o•mis•sion /ō mĭsh′ ən/ *n.* something left out. *Because of an omission on the list, his name was left out of the program.*

o•mit /ō mĭt′/ *v.* (**-mits, -mit•ted, -mit•ting**) to fail to include; leave out. [ME *omitten* < Lat. *omittere: ob,* away + *mittere,* to send.]

op•por•tu•ni•ty /ŏp′ ər tŏŏ′ nĭ tē, -tyŏŏ′-/ *n.* (**-ties** *pl.*) a favorable or advantageous combination of circumstances; suitable occasion or time.

or•gan•i•za•tion /ôr′ gə nĭ zā′ shən/ *n.* **a.** the state or manner of being organized. **b.** a number of persons or groups having specific responsibilities and united for a particular purpose.

-ous a suffix that forms adjectives and means "full of" or "having": *joyous.*

out-of-date /out′ əv dāt′/ *adj.* outmoded; old-fashioned.

out•ra•geous /out rā′ jəs/ *adj.* **a.** being an outrage; grossly offensive. **b.** extravagant; immoderate; extreme.

o•val¹ /ō′ vəl/ *adj.* **a.** resembling an egg in shape. **b.** resembling an ellipse in shape.

o•val² /ō′ vəl/ *n.* an oval form or figure.

pag•i•na•tion /păj′ ə na′ shən/ *n.* the numbering of pages in a book. *We made a chart to show the pagination of the pages in the script.*

pais•ley /pāz′ lē/ *n.* a kind of fabric, often wool, covered with colorful swirled shapes. *His handsome new tie was made from paisley.*

pal•met•to /păl mĕt′ ō/ *n.* (**pal•met•tos** or **pal•met•toes** *pl.*) a small palm tree with fan-shaped leaves. *The palmetto that my grandfather planted is still growing in the backyard.*

pal•o•mi•no /păl′ ə mē′ nō/ *n.* (**pal•o•mi•nos** *pl.*) a horse with a golden or tan coat and a white or cream-colored mane and tail, thought to have been developed from Arabian stock.

par•a•chute¹ /păr′ ə shoot′/ *n.* a foldable umbrella-shaped device used to slow the fall of persons or objects from great heights.

par•a•chute² /păr′ ə shoot′/ *v.* (**-chutes, -chut•ed, -chut•ing**) to descend by means of a parachute.

par•al•lel•o•gram /păr′ ə lĕl′ ə grăm′/ *n.* a four-sided plane figure with opposite sides parallel. *A rectangle is a parallelogram.*

par•tial /păr′ shəl/ *adj.* not complete. *We saw a partial eclipse of the moon.*

par•tial•ly /păr′ shə lē/ *adv.* to a degree; not totally.

par•tic•u•lar¹ /pər tĭk′ yə lər/ *adj.* **a.** separate and distinct from others; specific. **b.** worthy of note; exceptional. [ME < *particuler* < OFr. < LLat. *particularis* < Lat. *particula,* dim. of *pars,* part.]

par•tic•u•lar² /pər tĭk′ yə lər/ *n.* an individual item, fact, or detail.

par•tic•u•lar•ly /pər tĭk′ yə lər lē/ *adv.* **a.** to a great degree; especially. **b.** with particular reference or emphasis; specifically.

pas•ser•by /păs′ ər bī′/ *n.* (**pas•sers•by** *pl.*) a person who passes by, often by chance.

pa•tient•ly /pā′ shənt lē/ *adv.* in a tolerant or understanding way; perseveringly.

pat•i•o /păt′ ē ō, pä′ tē ō′/ *n.* (**-os** *pl.*) **a.** an inner, roofless courtyard. **b.** a space for dining or recreation, usually paved, that adjoins a residence. [Sp. < OSp. < Lat. *patēre,* to be open.]

pa•tron /pā′ trən/ *n.* **a.** one who supports, protects, or champions someone or something, such as an institution, event, or cause; a sponsor or benefactor. **b.** a customer, especially a regular customer.

peace•a•ble /pē′ sə bəl/ *adj.* **a.** inclined or disposed to peace; promoting calm. **b.** peaceful; undisturbed.

pe•cu•liar /pĭ kyool′ yər/ *adj.* (**pe•cu•liar•ly** *adv.*) **a.** unusual or eccentric; odd: *peculiar behavior.* **b.1.** exclusive; unique. **b.2.** belonging distinctively or primarily to one person, group, or kind.

pen•cil sharp•en•er /pĕn′ səl shär′ pə nər/ *n.* a small mechanical device that shaves the end of a pencil into a point for writing: *I need to use the pencil sharpener to sharpen my new pencils.*

pen•i•cil•lin /pĕn′ ĭ sĭl′ ĭn/ *n.* an antibiotic used to treat a variety of infections and diseases. *The doctor prescribed penicillin to treat my earache.*

Pronunciation Key

ă	pat	ŏ	pot	th	thin
ā	pay	ō	toe	*th*	this
âr	care	ô	paw, for	hw	which
ä	father	oi	noise	zh	vision
ĕ	pet	ou	out	ə	about,
ē	be	ŏŏ	took		item,
ĭ	pit	ōō	boot		pencil,
ī	pie	ŭ	cut		gallop,
îr	pier	ûr	urge		circus

per•fec•tion /pər fĕk′ shən/ *n.* the state, quality, or condition of being perfect.

peri- a prefix meaning "around," "about," or "enclosing": *periscope.*

per•i•scope /pĕr′ ĭ skōp′/ *n.* any of several instruments in which mirrors or prisms allow observation of objects that are not in a direct line of sight.

per•mis•si•ble /pər mĭs′ ə bəl/ *adj.* that can be permitted; allowable.

per•mis•sion /pər mĭsh′ ən/ *n.* consent, especially formal consent. *With the permission of the principal, our class visited the zoo.*

per•se•cute /pûr′ sĭ kyoot′ / *v.* (**per•se•cutes, per•se•cut•ed, per•se•cut•ing**) to cause to suffer. *The bully was wrong to persecute the younger student from a different neighborhood.*

per•sist /pər sĭst′, -zĭst′/ *v.* **a.** to hold firmly and steadfastly to a purpose, state, or undertaking despite obstacles, warnings, or set-backs. **b.** to continue in existence; last. [Lat. *persistere: per-* (intensive) + *sistere,* to stand.]

per•sist•ence /pər sĭs′ təns, -zĭs′-/ *n.* **a.** the act of persisting. **b.** the quality of being persistent; perseverance; tenacity.

per•sis•tent /pər sĭs′ tənt / or /pər zĭs′ tənt / *adj.* **a.** refusing to give up. *When she knew she was right, she was persistent about not changing her mind.* **b.** enduring. *This persistent pain in my foot makes it difficult to walk.*

pho•net•ic /fə nĕt′ ĭk/ *adj.* representing the sounds of speech with a set of distinct symbols, each denoting a single sound: *phonetic spelling.*

phon•ics /fŏn′ ĭks/ *n.* (*used with a sing. verb*) **a.** the study or science of sound; acoustics. **b.** the use of phonetics in the teaching of reading.

pho•to•gen•ic /fŏ′ tə **jĕn′** ĭk/ *adj.* looking attractive in photographs. *Models who appear in advertising pictures are photogenic.*

pho•to•jour•nal•ism /fō′ tō **jûr′** nə lĭz′ əm/ *n.* presentation of a news story primarily through photographs.

pic•nic¹ /**pĭk′** nĭk/ *n.* (**pic•nick•er** *n.*) a meal eaten outdoors on an excursion.

pic•nic² /**pĭk′** nĭk/ *v.* (**-nics, -nicked, -nick•ing**) to go on or participate in a picnic.

pic•tur•esque /pĭk′ chə **rĕsk′**/ *adj.* **a.** of or suggesting a picture: *picturesque rocky shores.* **b.** strikingly expressive or vivid: *picturesque language.* [Fr. *pittoresque* < Ital. *pittoresco* < *pittore,* painter < Lat. *pictor* < *pingere,* to paint.]

pi•geon /**pĭj′** ən/ *n.* a bird with a small head, stout body, and short legs. *Some pigeons are trained to carry messages.*

plau•si•ble /**plô′** zə bəl/ *adj.* believable; true; probable. *The article in the newspaper seemed very plausible.*

pla•za /**plä′** zə/ or /**plăz′** ə/ *n.* a public square in a city or town. *The cathedral faces the plaza.* [Spanish, from Latin *platea,* broad street.]

plumb•er /**plŭm′** ər/ *n.* a person whose job is putting in and fixing sinks, pipes, and other plumbing fixtures. *We called a plumber when the basement pipes started leaking.*

pneu•mo•nia /noo **mōn′** yə, nyoo-/ *n.* an acute or chronic disease marked by inflammation of the lungs and caused by viruses, bacteria, and physical and chemical agents.

po•et•ic /pō ĕt′ ĭk/ *adj.* having to do with poetry; expressing beauty. *The poetic story brought tears to my eyes.*

po•et•i•cal•ly /pō ĕt′ ĭ kəl lē/ *adv.* in a poetic or fanciful way.

pol•y•phon•ic /pŏl′ ē **fŏn′** ĭk/ *adj.* having two or more melodies played or sung at the same time.

pos•i•tive /**pŏz′** ĭ tĭv/ *adj.* (**pos•i•tive•ly** *adv.*) **a.** characterized by or displaying certainty. **b.** admitting of no doubt. **c.** determined or settled in opinion or assertion; confident: *a positive manner.*

pos•si•bil•i•ty /pŏs′ ə **bĭl′** ĭ tē/ *n.* (**-ties** *pl.*) the fact or state of being possible. [ME < OFr. < Lat. *possibilis* < *posse,* to be able.]

post•mas•ter /**pōst′** măs′ tər/ *n.* a person in charge of the postal system. *The postmaster helps keep the mail delivery going smoothly.*

post of•fice /**pōst′** ô′ f ĭs/ or /- ŏf′ ĭs/ *n.* **a.** an office or a building where people can buy stamps and mail letters or packages. *Mail these cards at the post office.* **b.** the public department in charge of mail. *The post office employs thousands of workers.*

po•ta•to /pə **tā′** tō/ *n.* (**-toes** *pl.*) a plant native to South America and widely cultivated for its starchy, edible tubers.

po•ten•tial¹ /pə **tĕn′** shəl/ *adj.* capable of being but not yet in existence.

po•ten•tial² /pə **tĕn′** shəl/ *n.* **a.** the inherent ability or capacity for growth, development, or coming into being. **b.** something possessing the capacity for growth or development.

prac•ti•cal /**prăk′** tĭ kəl/ *adj.* **a.** able to be done, used, or carried out. *Her practical solution took care of the problem.* **b.** dealing with facts rather than theory; concrete. *Her practical approach to children is a great help.*

prac•tice /**prăk′** tĭs/ *n.* training by doing something over and over. *Playing the piano requires regular practice.*

pre- a prefix meaning "before": *precaution.* When **pre-** is followed by a vowel, it may appear with a hyphen: **pre-empt, pre•empt.**

pre•ar•range /prē′ ə **rānj′**/ *v.* (**pre•ar•rang•es, pre•ar•ranged, pre•ar•rang•ing**) (**pre•ar•range•ment** *n.*) to arrange in advance.

pre•cau•tion•ar•y /prĭ **kô′** shə nĕr′ ē/ *adj.* guarding against something in advance, especially illness. *The family took precautionary measures to stay healthy by getting flu shots.*

pre•cede /prĭ **sēd′**/ *v.* (**pre•cedes, pre•ced•ed, pre•ced•ing**) **a.** to occur before in time. **b.** to be in a position in front of; go in advance of. **c.** to preface; introduce.

pre•cious /**prĕsh′** əs/ *adj.* **a.** having a high price; costing a great deal. *Diamonds are precious jewels.* **b.** much loved; dear. *Their precious child brought happiness to the parents.* [Latin *pretium,* price.]

pre•dict /prĭ **dĭkt′**/ *v.* (**pre•dict•a•bil•i•ty** *n.*) (**pre•dict•a•ble** *adj.*) (**pre•dict•a•bly** *adv.*) **a.** to tell about or make known in advance: *predict the weather.* **b.** to foretell what will happen; prophesy.

pre•fer /prĭ **fûr′**/ *v.* (**-fers, -ferred, -fer•ring**) to choose as more desirable; like better.

pref•er•ence /**prĕf′** ər əns, **prĕf′** rəns/ *n.* **a.** the exercise of choice. **b.** the state of being preferred.

pref•er•en•tial /prĕf′ ə **rĕn′** shəl/ *adj.* of, relating to, or giving advantage or preference.

pre•ju•dice /prĕj′ ə dĭs/ *n.* **a.1.** an adverse judgment or opinion formed beforehand or without knowledge or examination of the facts. **a.2.** a preconceived preference or idea; bias. **b.** irrational suspicion or hatred of a particular group, race, or religion.

pre•mi•um /prē′ mē əm/ *n.* **a.** an unusual or high value: *put a premium on honesty and hard work.* **b.** the amount paid or payable, often in installments, for an insurance policy.

prep•a•ra•tion /prĕp′ ə rā′ shən/ *n.* **a.** the act or process of preparing. **b.** the state of having been made ready beforehand; readiness.

pre•sent•a•ble /prĭ zĕn′ tə bəl/ *adj.* that can be given, displayed, or offered.

pres•ent•ly /prĕz′ ənt lē/ *adv.* in a short time; soon.

pre•vi•ous /prē′ vē əs/ *adj.* coming before; coming earlier. *We had studied that information in a previous chapter of the book.*

pre•vi•ous•ly /prē′ vē əs lē/ *adv.* before; earlier. *I checked the paper for correct spelling; previously, I had checked all the facts.*

prin•ci•pal[1] /prĭn′ sə pəl/ *adj.* (**prin•ci•pal•ly** *adv.*) first, highest, or foremost in importance, rank, worth, or degree.

prin•ci•pal[2] /prĭn′ sə pəl/ *n.* **a.** one who holds a position of presiding rank, especially the head of a school. **b.** a main participant in a given situation.

pri•or /prī′ ər/ *adj.* preceding in time or order: a prior commitment. —*idiom.* **prior to.** *before.*

priv•i•lege /prĭv′ ə lĭj/ *n.* a special advantage, immunity, permission, right, or benefit granted to or enjoyed by an individual, class, or caste. [ME < OFr. < Lat. *privilegium,* a law affecting one person: *privus,* single + *lex,* law.]

pro-[1] a prefix meaning: **a.** favor or support. **b.** acting as; substituting for: *pronoun.* When **pro-** is followed by a capital letter, it appears with a hyphen: *pro-American.* [ME < Lat. *pro,* for.]

pro-[2] a prefix meaning "before" or "in front of": *prologue.* [< Gk. *pro,* before, in front of.]

prob•a•bly /prŏb′ ə blē/ *adv.* not for sure; most likely. *The storm will probably cause the picnic to be canceled.*

pro•ceed /prō sēd′/ or /prə sēd′/ *v.* **a.** to go forward or onward, especially after an interruption; continue. **b.** to begin to carry on an action or a process: looked surprised, then proceeded to roar with laughter. **c.** to come from a source; originate.

pro•ces•sion /prə sĕsh′ ən/ *n.* a group of persons, vehicles, or objects moving along in an orderly and formal manner, usually in a long line.

pro•fes•sion•al[1] /prə fĕsh′ ə nəl/ *adj.* engaged in a specific activity as a source of livelihood.

pro•fes•sion•al[2] /prə fĕsh′ ə nəl/ *n.* **a.** one who has an assured competence in a particular field or occupation. **b.** one who earns his or her livelihood as an athlete.

pro•fi•cien•cy /prə fĭsh′ ən sē/ *n.* competence; the state of having mastered a particular skill or process.

pro•fi•cient /prə fĭsh′ ənt/ *adj.* skilled at doing something. *The student is especially proficient at math.*

prof•it•a•ble /prŏf′ ĭt ə bəl/ *adj.* (**prof•it•a•bly** *adv.*) bringing profit or benefit. *The store had a profitable year.*

pron•to /prŏn′ tō/ *adv. Informal.* without delay; quickly. [Sp. < Lat. *promptus.*]

pro•pel /prə pĕl′/ *v.* (**pro•pels, pro•pelled, pro•pel•ling**) to cause to move forward. *The fuel will propel the rocket into space.*

prop•er•ty /prŏp′ ər tē/ *n.* (**-ties** *pl.*) **a.1.** a possession. **a.2.** possessions collectively. **b.** something to which its owner has legal title. **c.1.** a characteristic trait or peculiarity. **c.2.** a quality serving to define or describe an object or substance. **c.3.** a characteristic attribute possessed by all members of a class.

pros•e•cute /prŏs′ ĭ kyōōt′/ *v.* (**pros•e•cutes, pros•e•cut•ed, pros•e•cut•ing**) to begin and continue a legal suit against someone. *The job of some attorneys is to prosecute a person accused of breaking the law.*

pros•pect[1] /prŏs′ pĕkt′/ *n.* **a.** something expected; possibility. **b.** the location or probable location of a mineral deposit.

pros•pect[2] /prŏs′ pĕkt′/ *v.* to search for or explore (a region) for gold or other mineral deposits.

pro•vin•cial /prə **vĭn′** shəl/ *adj.* **a.** pertaining to a province. *Before we travel to Manitoba, we need to have a provincial road map.* **b.** unsophisticated; limited in outlook. *After moving from the country to a large city, she sometimes felt provincial.*

pur•pose•ful /**pûr′** pəs fəl/ *adj.* very useful. *My parents want me to grow up and have a purposeful life.*

pur•sue /pər **sōō′**/ *v.* (**-sues, -sued, -su•ing**) **a.** to follow in an effort to overtake or capture; chase. **b.** to strive to gain or accomplish. **c.** to proceed along the course of; follow.

pur•suit /pər **sōōt′**/ *n.* **a.** the act or an instance of chasing or pursuing. **b.** the act of striving. **c.** a vocation, hobby, or other activity regularly engaged in.

qual•i•fy /**kwŏl′** ə fī′/ *v.* (**qual•i•fies, qual•i•fied, qual•i•fy•ing**) to make capable or suitable for a certain position or purpose. *His good grades helped him qualify for a large scholarship.*

quar•rel•some /**kwôr′** əl səm/ or /**kwŏr′** əl səm/ *adj.* ready to disagree, argue, and fight. *The quarrelsome bully was punished for fighting with his classmates.*

ques•tion•a•ble /**kwĕs′** chə nə bəl/ *adj.* **a.** open to doubt or challenge; problematic. **b.** not yet determined or specified; uncertain.

ques•tion•naire /kwĕs′ chə **nâr′**/ *n.* a printed form containing a set of questions, especially one addressed to a statistically significant number of subjects by way of gathering information, as for a survey.

quick-wit•ted /**kwĭk′** wĭt′ ĭd/ *adj.* mentally alert and sharp; keen.

quo•ta•tion /kwō **tā′** shən/ *n.* a passage that is quoted. *The speaker used a quotation to illustrate his point.*

ra•di•ate /**rā′** dē āt′/ *v.* (**ra•di•ates, ra•di•at•ed, ra•di•at•ing**) **a.** to send out rays or waves. **b.** to issue or emerge in rays or waves. **c.** to extend in straight lines from or toward a center. **d.** to manifest in a glowing manner: *radiates warmth.*

ra•di•a•tor /**rā′** dē ā′ t ər/ *n.* a heating device with pipes through which hot water or steam is circulated to produce heat. *Our apartment has a radiator that provides heat during cold weather.*

ra•di•o broad•cast /**rā′** dē ō′ **brôd′** kăst/ *n.* a program on the radio. *We tuned in to the radio broadcast to hear the latest news report.*

rap•id[1] /**răp′** ĭd/ *adj.* (**rap•id•ly** *adv.*) moving, acting, or occurring with great speed.

rap•id[2] /**răp′** ĭd/ *n.* an extremely fast-moving part of a river.

rasp•ber•ry /**răz′** bĕr′ ē/ *n.* **a.** any of various shrubby, usually prickly plants of the genus *Rubus,* bearing edible berries. **b.** the fruit of the raspberry. **c.** a moderate to dark or deep purplish red.

ra•ven[1] /**rā′** vən/ *n.* a large bird, *Corvus corax,* having black plumage and a croaking cry. [ME < OE *hraefn.*]

ra•ven[2] /**rā′** vən/ *adj.* black and shiny.

re- a prefix meaning: **a.** again; anew: *reassemble.* **b.** back; backward: *recall.* When **re-** is followed by **e**, it may appear with a hyphen: *re-elect.*

read•i•ly /**rĕd′** ə lē/ *adv.* **a.** promptly. **b.** willingly. **c.** easily.

re•al•i•ty /rē **ăl′** ĭ tē/ *n.* (**-ties** *pl.*) **a.** the quality or state of being actual or true. **b.** the totality of all things possessing actuality, existence, or essence.

re•ap•pear /rē ə **pîr′**/ *v.* (**re•ap•pear•ance** *n.*) to come into view again.

rea•son•a•ble /**rē′** zə nə bəl/ *adj.* (**rea•son•a•bly** *adv.*) **a.** capable of reasoning; rational. **b.** not excessive or extreme; fair: *reasonable prices.*

re•ceive /rĭ **sēv′**/ *v.* (**-ceives, -ceived, -ceiv•ing**) **a.** to acquire or get something; be a recipient. **b.** *Electronics.* to convert incoming electromagnetic waves into visible or audible signals.

re•cep•tion /rĭ **sĕp′** shən/ *n.* a social gathering to receive and welcome guests, especially after a wedding. *People talked, ate, and danced at the wedding reception.*

rec•og•nize /**rĕk′** əg nīz′/ *v.* (**-niz•es, -nized, -niz•ing**) (**rec•og•niz•a•ble** *adj.*) **a.** to know to be something that has been perceived before. **b.** to know or identify from past experience or knowledge. **c.** to perceive or acknowledge the validity or reality of.

re•con•sid•er /rē′ kən **sĭd′** ər/ *v.* to consider again, especially with intent to alter or modify a previous decision.

re•cur /rĭ **kûr′**/ *v.* (**re•curs, re•curred, re•cur•ring**) to happen again; to repeat. *We didn't expect the error to recur.*

re•cur•rence /rĭ **kûr′** əns/ *n.* a repetition; a regular occurrence. *A sale at a mall is a regular recurrence.*

re•cy•cle /rē **sī′** kəl/ *v.* (**-cles, -cled, -cling**) **a.** to put or pass through a cycle again, as for further treatment. **b.** to extract and reuse (useful substances found in waste). **c.** to use again, especially to reprocess in order to use again: *recycle aluminum cans.*

re-e•lect /rē ′ ĭ **lĕkt′**/ *v.* to choose again to be in a certain position or office. *That member of Congress was not re-elected.*

re•fer /rĭ **fûr′**/ *v.* (**-fers, -ferred, -fer•ring**) (**re•fer•ral** *n.*) **a.** to direct to a source for help or information. **b.** to pertain; concern: *questions referring to yesterday's lecture.* **c.** to turn to, as for information or authority.

ref•er•ence /**rĕf** ′ ər əns, **rĕf** ′ rəns/ *n.* **a.** an act of referring. **b.** an allusion to an occurrence or situation. **c.1.** a note in a publication referring the reader to another passage or source. **c.2.** the passage or source so referred to. **d.1.** a person who is in a position to recommend another or to vouch for his or her fitness, as for a job. **d.2.** a written statement about a person's qualifications, character, and dependability.

re•gard•less¹ /rĭ **gärd′** lĭs/ *adj.* heedless; unmindful. [ME r*egarden,* to regard < OFr. *regarder: re-,* back + *guarder,* to guard, of Germanic origin.]

re•gard•less² /rĭ **gärd′** lĭs/ *adv.* in spite of everything; anyway.

re•mark•a•ble /rĭ **mär′** kə bəl/ *adj.* (**re•mark•a•bly** *adv.*) **a.** worthy of notice. **b.** extraordinary; uncommon.

re•mem•brance /rĭ **mĕm′** brəns/ *n.* **a.** the act of remembering. **b.** something remembered; reminiscence. **c.** a memento; souvenir.

rem•i•nisce /**rĕm′** ə **nĭs′**/ *v.* (**rem•i•nisc•es, rem•i•nisced, rem•i•nisc•ing**) to recall and think about past events. *At family reunions, we like to reminisce about things that happened when we were young.*

re•miss /rĭ **mĭs′**/ *adj.* **a.** lax in attending to duty; negligent. **b.** exhibiting carelessness or slackness.

re•mit /rĭ **mĭt′**/ *v.* (**re•mits, re•mit•ted, re•mit•ting**) to send money. *We had to remit the payment before they would send the order.*

Pronunciation Key

ă	pat	ŏ	pot	th	thin
ā	pay	ō	toe	*th*	this
âr	care	ô	paw, for	hw	which
ä	father	oi	noise	zh	vision
ĕ	pet	ou	out	ə	about,
ē	be	ŏŏ	took		item,
ĭ	pit	ōō	boot		pencil,
ī	pie	ŭ	cut		gallop,
îr	pier	ûr	urge		circus

---

re•mit•tance /rĭ **mĭt′** ns/ *n.* a payment or sum of money that someone sends. *The librarian told me where to send the remittance for the lost book.*

ren•dez•vous /**rän′** dā vōō′/ or /**rän′** də vōō′/ *n.* (**ren•dez•vous** /-vōōz′/ *pl.*) an appointment to meet at a certain time or place. *We had a rendezvous every Wednesday for lunch.*

rep•e•ti•tious /**rĕp′** ĭ **tĭsh′** əs/ *adj.* characterized by or filled with repetition, especially needless or tedious repetition.

re•place•ment /rĭ **plās′** mənt/ *n.* a substitute. *The actress's replacement was nervous about her performance.*

rep•li•ca /**rĕp′** lĭ kə/ *n.* **a.** a copy or reproduction of a work of art, especially one made by the original artist. **b.** a copy or reproduction.

re•quire•ment /rĭ **kwīr′** mənt / *n.* **a.** something that is required; necessity. **b.** something obligatory; prerequisite. [ME *requiren,* to require < OFr. *requere* < VLat. *requaerere* < Lat. *requirere: re-,* again + *quaerere,* to seek.]

re•search /rĭ **sûrch′**/ or /**rē′** sûrch/ *n.* systematic investigation or careful study. *The scientist's research helped prove that her theory was accurate.*

res•er•voir /**rĕz′** ər vwär′, -vwôr′, -vôr′/ *n.* **a.** a body of water collected and stored for future use in a natural or artificial lake. **b.** a large supply; reserve: *a reservoir of gratitude.* [Fr. *réservoir* < *réserver,* to reserve.]

res•i•den•tial /**rĕz′** ĭ **dĕn′** shəl/ *adj.* **a.** of, relating to, or having residence. **b.** of, suitable for, or limited to residences.

re•sign /rĭ **zīn′**/ *v.* **a.** to submit (oneself) passively; accept as inevitable. **b.** to give up (a position), especially by formal notification; quit.

res•ig•na•tion /rĕz′ ĭg nā′ shən/ *n.* the withdrawal from a job or a position.

re•sist /rĭ zĭst′/ *v.* **a.** to strive or work against; oppose actively. **b.** to remain firm against the action or effect of; withstand. **c.** to keep from giving in to or enjoying. [ME *resisten* < Lat. *resistere: re-*, against + *sistere*, to place.]

re•sis•tance /rĭ zĭs′ təns/ *n.* **a.1.** the act of resisting. **a.2.** the capacity to resist. **b.** a force that tends to oppose or retard motion.

re•sis•tor /rĭ zĭs′ tər/ *n.* a device used to control current in an electric circuit by providing resistance.

re•source•ful•ness /rĭ sôrs′ fəl nəs/, /rĭ sōrs′ fəl nəs/, /rĭ zôrs′ fəl nəs/, or /rĭ zōrs′ fəl nəs/ *n.* the ability to come up with answers to problems and with new ideas. *Forgetting to take extra food on our camping trip tested our resourcefulness.*

re•spect[1] /rĭ spĕkt′/ *v.* **a.** to feel or show deferential regard for; esteem. **b.** to relate or refer to; concern. [Lat. *respicere, respect-: re-*, back + *specere*, to look.]

re•spect[2] /rĭ spĕkt′/ *n.* **a.** a feeling of deferential regard; esteem. **b.** a particular aspect, feature, or detail.

re•spect•a•ble /rĭ spek′ tə bəl/ *adj.* worthy of respect or esteem. *My parents believe that teaching is a respectable career.*

re•spect•ful /rĭ spĕkt′ fəl/ *adj.* showing respect.

res•pi•ra•tion /rĕs′ pə rā′ shən/ *n.* the act or process of inhaling and exhaling; breathing. [ME *respiren*, to breathe again < Lat. *respirare: re-*, again + *spirare*, to breathe.]

res•tau•rant /rĕs′ tər ənt / or /-tə ränt′/ *n.* a place where meals are sold and served. *We ate dinner in a restaurant downtown.*

re•strict /rĭ strĭkt′/ *v.* to keep within limits; confine. [Lat. *restringere, restrict-*, to restrain: *re-*, back + *stringere*, to bind.]

re•stric•tion /rĭ strĭk′ shən/ *n.* **a.** the act of restricting. **b.** the state of being restricted. **c.** something that restricts; a regulation or limitation.

re•stric•tive /rĭ strĭk′ tĭv/ *adj.* confining; limiting; keeping within limits. *Riding a bicycle is hard to do in restrictive clothing.*

résumé /rĕz′ ōō mā′/ *n.* a summary, especially a brief record of one's personal history and experience submitted with a job application. [Fr. < p.part. of *résumer*, to summarize < OFr. *résumer*, to resume.]

re•trace /rē trās′/ *v.* (**-trac•es, -traced, -trac•ing**) **a.** to trace again. **b.** to go back over, as one's steps.

re•tract /rĭ trăkt′/ *v.* **a.** to take back; disavow. **b.** to draw back or in. [ME *retracten* < OFr. *retracter* < Lat. *retractare*, to handle again, freq. of *retrahere*, to draw back: *re-*, back + *trahere*, to draw.]

re•trac•tion /rĭ trăk′ shən/ *n.* the act of taking back or withdrawing something. *The retraction of her statement did not make the controversy go away.*

re•vers•i•ble /rĭ vûr′ sə bəl/ *adj.* capable of being turned backward or inside out; able to be reversed. *Jo wore her reversible coat.*

rev•o•lu•tion /rĕv′ ə lōō′ shən/ *n.* **a.1.** orbital motion about a point, especially as distinguished from axial rotation: *the planetary revolution about the sun.* **a.2.** a single complete cycle of such orbital or axial motion. **b.** a sudden or momentous change in any situation.

rev•o•lu•tion•ar•y /rĕv′ ə lōō′ shə nĕr′ ē/ *adj.* bringing about great changes; sweeping; radical. *The invention of the printing press was a revolutionary development in the world of communications.*

re•volve /rĭ vŏlv′/ *v.* (**-volves, -volved, -volv•ing**) **a.** to orbit a central point. **b.** to turn on an axis; rotate. [ME *revolven* < Lat. *revolvere*, to turn over, to roll back: *re-*, back + *volvere*, to roll.]

rhap•so•dy /răp′ sə dē/ *n.* (**rhap•so•dies** *pl.*) a kind of musical composition. *The musicians opened the performance with a lively rhapsody.*

rheu•ma•tism /rōō′ mə tĭz′ əm/ *n.* a condition that causes pain in the muscles or joints. *Doctors are seeking a cure for rheumatism.*

rhythm /rĭth′ əm/ *n.* a regular, repeated movement in which a beat or accent rises and falls or occurs steadily. *The rhythm in music is often provided by the drums.*

rhyth•mic /rĭth′ mĭk/ *adj.* (**rhyth•mi•cal•ly** *adv.*) of or related to a regular beat or accent in music. *The children clapped their hands to the rhythmic sounds of the music.*

ro•de•o /rō′ dē ō, rō dā′ ō/ *n.* (**-os** *pl.*) **a.** a cattle roundup. **b.** a competition in which cowboys display skills such as riding broncos or lassoing. [Sp. < *rodear*, to surround < Lat. *rotare*, to rotate < *rota*, wheel.]

rus•tic /rŭs′ tĭk/ *adj.* **a.** of, pertaining to, or typical of country life. **b.** simple and unsophisticated.

sab•o•tage[1] /**săb′** ə täzh′/ *n.* a deliberate attempt to defeat or hinder an endeavor. [French < *saboter*, to walk noisily, bungle, sabotage < *sabot*, sabot.]

sab•o•tage[2] /**săb′** ə täzh′/ *v.* to commit sabotage against.

sal•a•ry /**săl′** ə rē, **săl′** rē/ *n.* (**-ries** *pl.*) a fixed compensation for services, paid to a person on a regular basis. [ME *salarie* < Lat. *salarium*, money given to Roman soldiers to buy salt < *sal*, salt.]

sand•wich /**sănd′** wĭch/ or /**săn′** wĭch/ *n.* (**sand•wich•es** *pl.*) slices of bread with a filling such as meat, cheese, or spread placed between them. [After John Montagu, 4th Earl of *Sandwich* (1718–1792).]

sar•dine /sär **dēn′**/ *n.* a small or half-grown kind of food fish, often canned. *He enjoyed a snack of sardines and crackers.* [ME *sardin* < OFr. *sardine* < Lat. *sardīna* < *sarda*, a fish, < Gk. Sardō, Sardinia.]

sat•in /**săt′** n/ *n.* a smooth fabric, as of silk or rayon, woven with a glossy face and a dull back. [prob. from *Zaitun*, after a city in China.]

sat•is•fy /**săt′** ĭs fī′/ *v.* (**sat•is•fies, sat•is•fied, sat•is•fy•ing**) **a.** to please; to fill a need or desire. *You can satisfy the baby by giving her a toy.* **b.** to put an end to. *Water will satisfy my thirst.*

sax•o•phone /**săk′** sə fōn′/ *n.* a wind instrument with a single-reed mouthpiece and a usually curved conical metal tube, available in a variety of sizes. [after Adolphe *Sax* (1814–1894), its inventor.]

scen•er•y /**sē′** nə rē/ *n.* (**-ies** *pl.*) (**scen•ic** *adj.*) **a.** a landscape. **b.** the painted backdrops on a theatrical stage.

sched•ule[1] /**skĕj′** ōōl, -əl/ *n.* **a.** a printed or often written list of items in tabular form. **b.1.** a program of forthcoming events or appointments. **b.2.** a student's program of classes. **c.** a timetable of departures and arrivals.

sched•ule[2] /**skĕj′** ōōl, -əl/ *v.* (**-ules, -uled, -ul•ing**) **a.** to make up a schedule for. **b.** to plan or appoint for a certain time or date.

scho•las•tic[1] /skə **lăs′** tĭk/ *adj.* of or relating to schools; academic.

scho•las•tic[2] /skə **lăs′** tĭk/ *n.* one who is scholarly.

sci•en•tif•ic /sī′ ən **tĭf′** ĭk/ *adj.* (**sci•en•tif•i•cal•ly** *adv.*) of, relating to, or employing the methodology of science.

scrump•tious /**skrŭmp′** shəs/ *adj.* delicious. *We could hardly wait for the scrumptious meal to begin.*

se•lec•tion /sĭ **lĕk′** shən/ *n.* a collection of items to choose from. *It was hard to decide because of the large selection of items.*

self-ad•dressed /sĕlf′ ə **drĕst′**/ *adj.* addressed to oneself. *If you would like a reply, please send a self-addressed envelope.*

self-em•ployed /sĕlf′ ĕm **ploid′**/ *adj.* working for oneself, rather than for an employer.

self-es•teem /sĕlf′ ĭ **stēm′**/ *n.* pride in oneself.

self-taught /sĕlf′ **tôt′**/ *adj.* having taught oneself without formal instruction or the help of others. *Many famous people throughout history had no formal education; they were self-taught.*

sen•si•ble /**sĕn′** sə bəl/ *adj.* (**sen•si•bly** *adv.*) full of good sense; reasonable; wise. *She is too sensible to accept a ride from strangers.*

sen•sor /**sĕn′** sər/ or /**sĕn′** sôr/ *n.* a special device for detecting something, such as light, heat, or smoke. *If the battery in the smoke detector is dead, the sensor won't work.*

➤ **Sensor** sounds like **censor**.

sep•a•rate[1] /**sĕp′** ə rāt′/ *v.* (**-rates, -rat•ed, -rat•ing**) (**sep•a•rate•ly** *adv.*) **a.1.** to set or keep apart. **a.2.** to space apart; scatter. **a.3.** to sort. **b.** to become divided into components or parts.

sep•a•rate[2] /**sĕp′** ər ĭt, **sĕp′** rĭt/ *adj.* **a.** set apart from others; detached. **b.** independent. **c.** not shared; individual.

se•quen•tial /sĭ **kwĕn′** shəl/ *adj.* of or related to an order of succession. *The steps in the recipe were listed in a sequential list.*

se•ra•pe /sə **rä′** pē/ or /sə **răp′** ē/ *n.* a woolen poncho. *As the weather grew colder, he used his serape to keep warm.*

se•vere /sə vîr′/ *adj.* (**se•vere•ly** *adv.*) **a.** unsparing, harsh, or strict. **b.** causing great discomfort, damage, or distress. **c.** extremely plain in substance or style.

shelf /shĕlf/ *n.* (**shelves** *pl.*) a flat, usually rectangular structure of a rigid material, as wood, glass, or metal. It is usually fixed to a vertical surface and used to hold or store objects.

shep•herd[1] /shĕp′ ərd/ *n.* **a.** one who tends sheep. **b.** one who guides a group of people. **c.** a German shepherd dog.

shep•herd[2] /shĕp′ ərd/ *v.* to tend or guide in the manner of a shepherd.

si•er•ra /sē ĕr′ ə/ *n.* **a.** a rugged range of mountains having an irregular or serrated profile. [Sp. < Lat. *serra,* saw.]

si•es•ta /sē ĕs′ tə/ *n.* a rest or nap, usually taken after the midday meal. [Sp. < Lat. *sexta* (*hora*), sixth (hour) < *sextus,* sixth.]

sil•hou•ette[1] /sĭl′ o͞o ĕt′/ *n.* **a.** a drawing consisting of the outline of something, especially a human profile, filled in with a solid color. **b.** an outline of something that appears dark against a light background.

sil•hou•ette[2] /sĭl′ o͞o ĕt′/ *v.* (**-ettes, -et•ted, -et•ting**) to cause to be seen as a silhouette; outline. [Fr. < Etienne de *Silhouette* (1709–1767).]

sin•cer•i•ty /sĭn sĕr′ ĭ tē/ *n.* the quality or condition of being sincere; genuineness, honesty.

slight•ly /slīt′ lē/ *adv.* **a.** to a small degree or extent; somewhat. **b.** slenderly; delicately: *slightly built.*

sol•emn /sŏl′ əm/ *adj.* serious; earnest; grave: *a solemn promise.*

so•lid•i•fy /sə lĭd′ ə fī′/ *v.* (**so•lid•i•fies, so•lid•i•fied, so•lid•i•fy•ing**) **a.** to make solid, compact, or hard. **b.** to make or become strong or united.

-some a suffix that forms adjectives and means "being" or "tending to be": *burdensome.*

sought /sôt/ *v.* past tense and past participle of **seek.**

sou•ve•nir /so͞o′ və nîr′, so͞o′ və nîr′/ *n.* something serving as a token of remembrance; memento. [Fr., memory < *souvenir,* to recall < Lat. *subvenire,* to come to mind: *sub-,* under + *venire,* to come.]

spa•cious /spā′ shəs/ *adj.* **a.** providing or having much space or room; extensive. **b.** vast in range or scope: *a spacious view.*

spa•ghet•ti /spə gĕt′ ē/ *n.* a pasta made into long, solid strings and cooked by boiling.

spa•tial /spā′ shəl/ *adj.* of, pertaining to, involving, or having the nature of space.

spe•cies /spē′ shēz, -sēz/ *n.* (**spe•cies** *pl.*) **a.1.** a group of similar animals or plants that are regarded as of the same kind and that are able to breed with one another. **a.2.** an animal or plant belonging to such a group, identified by a scientific name consisting of two Latin terms. **b.** a kind, variety, or type.

spe•cif•ic /spĭ sĭf′ ĭk/ *adj.* (**spe•cif•i•cal•ly** *adv.*) **a.** explicitly set forth; definite. **b.** pertaining to, characterizing, or distinguishing a species. **c.** special, distinctive, or unique, as a quality or attribute. **d.** intended for, applying to, or acting upon a particular thing.

spec•ta•cle /spĕk′ tə kəl/ *n.* **a.** a public performance or display. **b.** an object of interest. **c.1.** something seen or capable of being seen. **c.2.** the sight of something. **d.** spectacles. glasses.

spec•tac•u•lar /spĕk tăk′ yə lər/ *adj.* of the nature of a spectacle; sensational. [Lat. *spectaculum,* spectacle < *spectare,* to watch, freq. of *specere,* to look at.]

spec•ta•tor /spĕk′ tā′ tər/ *n.* an observer of an event. [Lat. *spectator* < *spectare,* to watch, freq. of *specere,* to look at.]

spec•u•late /spĕk′ yə lāt′/ *v.* (**spec•u•lates, spec•u•lat•ed, spec•u•lat•ing**) to ponder; to reflect. *Because of the many unanswered questions, we could only speculate on an answer.*

spec•u•la•tion /spĕk′ yə lā′ shən/ *n.* **a.** contemplation or consideration of a subject. **b.** a conclusion, opinion, or theory reached by conjecture. **c.** engagement in risky business transactions on the chance of quick or considerable profit.

spite•ful /spīt′ fəl/ *adj.* filled with spite; malicious.

spon•ta•ne•ous /spŏn tā′ nē əs/ *adj.* **a.** happening or arising without apparent external cause. **b.** voluntary and impulsive: *spontaneous applause.* **c.** unconstrained and unstudied in manner or behavior.

spoon•ful /spo͞on′ fo͞ol′/ *n.* (**-fuls** *pl.*) the amount a spoon holds.

sports•cast /spôrts′ kăst′, spôrts′-/ *n.* (**sports•cast•er** *n.*) a radio or television broadcast of a sports event or of sports news.

sta•ble[1] /stā′ bəl/ *adj.* **a.** resistant to change of position or condition; not easily moved or disturbed. **b.** consistently dependable.

sta•ble[2] /stā′ bəl/ *n.* **a.** a building for the shelter and feeding of domestic animals, especially horses and cattle. **b.** a group of animals lodged in such a building. **c.** a group under common management: *a stable of writers.*

sta•ble³ /stā′ bəl/ *v.* (**sta•bles, sta•bled, sta•bling**) to put or keep in a stable.

stam•pede¹ /stăm pēd′/ *n.* **a.** a sudden headlong rush of startled animals. **b.** a sudden headlong rush of a crowd of people. [Sp. *estampida,* uproar < Prov. < *estampier,* to stamp, of Germanic orig.]

stam•pede² /stăm pēd′/ *v.* (**-pedes, -ped•ed, -ped•ing**) **a.** to move in a headlong rush. **b.** to act on impulse.

stat•us /stăt′ əs/ or /stā′ təs/ *n.* rank; professional standing. *She expected a title that reflected her high-ranking status in the company.*

steth•o•scope /stĕth′ ə skōp′/ *n.* an instrument used for listening to sounds produced within the body. [Fr. *stéthoscope:* Gk. *stēthos,* chest + Fr. *-scope,* -scope.]

stir¹ /stûr/ *v.* (**stirs, stirred, stir•ring**) **a.** to pass an implement through in circular motions so as to mix or cool the contents. **b.** to cause to move or shift slightly. **c.** to move away from a customary or usual place or position.

stir² /stûr/ *n.* **a.** a stirring or mixing movement. **b.** a slight movement. **c.** a disturbance or commotion.

stom•ach•ache /stŭm′ ək āk′/ *n.* a pain in the digestive area. *The child was crying because of a stomachache.*

stren•u•ous•ly /strĕn′ yōō əs lē/ *adv.* energetically; vigorously. *They played so strenuously that they soon were exhausted.*

strict /strĭkt/ *adj.* **a.** precise; exact. **b.** complete; absolute: *strict loyalty.* **c.** kept within narrow and specific limits: *a strict application of a law.* **d.** imposing an exacting discipline. [Lat. *strictus* < p.part. of *stringere,* to bind tightly.]

strict•ly /strĭkt′ lē/ *adv.* with firm discipline or control.

stud•y hall /stŭd′ ē hôl′/ *n.* **a.** a schoolroom reserved for study. **b.** a period set aside for study.

sub•stan•tial /səb stăn′ shəl/ *adj.* **a.** of, pertaining to, or having substance; material. **b.** ample; sustaining. **c.** considerable in importance, value, degree, amount, or extent.

sub•tle /sŭt′ l/ *adj.* **a.** so slight as to be difficult to detect or analyze; elusive. **b.** not immediately obvious.

suc•ces•sor /sək sĕs′ ər/ *n.* one that succeeds another.

suede /swād/ *n.* leather with a soft napped surface. [Fr. *suède* < *Suède,* Sweden.]

suf•fi•cient /sə fĭsh′ ənt / *adj.* as much as is needed; enough; adequate: *sufficient food for survival.*

suit•a•ble /sōō′ tə bəl/ *adj.* (**suit•a•bil•i•ty** *n.*) (**suit•a•bly** *adv.*) appropriate to a given purpose or occasion.

su•per•fi•cial /sōō′ pər fĭsh′ əl/ *adj.* **a.** of, affecting, or being on or near the surface. **b.** concerned with only what is apparent or obvious. **c.1.** apparent rather than actual or substantial. **c.2.** trivial; insignificant.

su•per•flu•ous /sōō pûr′ flōō əs/ *adj.* extra; more than is needed. *Once he had made his point, any further comments were superfluous.*

su•per•sti•tious /sōō′ pər stĭsh′ əs/ *adj.* inclined to believe in superstition.

sup•port¹ /sə pôrt′, -pōrt′/ *v.* **a.** to bear the weight of, especially from below. **b.** to hold in position so as to keep from falling, sinking, or slipping. **c.** to provide for or maintain, by supplying with money or necessities. **d.** to aid the cause of by approving, favoring, or advocating.

sup•port² /sə pôrt′, -pōrt′/ *n.* **a.1.** the act of supporting. **a.2.** the state of being supported. **b.** one that supports. **c.** maintenance or subsistence.

sur- a prefix meaning: **a.** over; above; upon. **b.** addition.

sur•charge /sûr′ chärj′/ *n.* a sum added to the original cost or amount. *The bill for our cable service included a surcharge after we moved to a new address.*

sure•ly /shōōr′ lē/ *adv.* **a.** undoubtedly; certainly. *Surely we will find a parking spot in this large lot!* **b.** with skill; in an expert way. *Slowly but surely, Bob carved a beautiful horse from the soft wood.*

sur•name¹ /sûr′ nām′/ *n.* a person's family name as distinguished from his or her given name.

sur•name² /sûr′ nām′/ *v.* (**-names, -named, -nam•ing**) to give a surname to.

sur•prise[1] /sər **prīz'**/ *v.* (-pris•es, -prised, -pris•ing) (sur•pris•ing•ly *adv.*) **a.** to encounter suddenly or unexpectedly; take or catch unaware. **b.** to cause to feel wonder, astonishment, or amazement.

sur•prise[2] /sər **prīz'**/ *n.* **a.** the condition of being surprised; astonishment. **b.** something that surprises, as an unexpected encounter, event, or gift. [ME *surprysen,* to overcome < OFr. *surprendre, surpris-: sur-,* over + *prendre,* to take < Lat. *praehendere,* to seize.]

sur•ren•der[1] /sə **rĕn'** dər/ *v.* **a.** to relinquish possession or control of to another because of demand or compulsion. **b.** to give up in favor of another. **c.** to give up or abandon: *surrender all hope.* **d.** to give oneself up, as to an enemy.

sur•ren•der[2] /sə **rĕn'** dər/ *n.* the act or an instance of surrendering. [ME *sorendren* < OFr. *surrender: sur-,* over + *rendre,* to deliver.]

sus•pect[1] /sə **spĕkt'**/ *v.* (sus•pect•ed, sus•pect•ing) **a.** to surmise to be true or probable; imagine. **b.** to have doubts about; distrust: *suspected his motives.*

sus•pect[2] /**sŭs'** pĕkt', sə **spĕkt'**/ *adj.* open to or viewed with suspicion. [Lat. *suspectare,* freq. of *suspicere,* to watch: *sub-,* from below + *specere,* to look at.]

sus•pi•cious /sə **spĭsh'** əs/ *adj.* **a.** arousing or apt to arouse suspicion; questionable: *suspicious behavior.* **b.** tending to suspect; distrustful: *a suspicious nature.* **c.** expressing suspicion: *a suspicious look.*

sym•phon•ic /sĭm **fŏn'** ĭk/ *adj.* pertaining to or having the character or form of a symphony.

sym•pho•ni•ous /sĭm **fō'** nē əs/ *adj.* harmonious.

syn- or **sym-** a prefix meaning: **a.1.** together; with: *symphony.* **a.2.** united. **b.** same; similar.

syn•chro•ni•za•tion /sĭng' krə nĭ **zā'** shən/ or /sĭn' krə nĭ **zā'** shən/ *n.* a simultaneous occurence. *The swim team presented a wonderful show of synchronization.*

syn•chro•nize /**sĭng'** krə nīz', **sĭn'-**/ *v.* (-niz•es, -nized, -niz•ing) to cause to operate with exact coincidence in time or rate. [Lat. *synchronos* < Gk. *synkhronos: syn-,* same + *khronos,* time.]

T

tan•ger•ine /tăn' jə **rēn'**, tăn' jə rēn'/ *n.* **a.** a widely cultivated citrus tree bearing edible fruit having an easily peeled deep-orange skin and sweet, juicy pulp. **b.** the fruit of the tangerine. **c.** a strong reddish orange to strong or vivid orange. [< Fr. *Tanger,* Tangier, Morocco.]

ta•ran•tu•la /tə **răn'** chə lə/ *n.* (ta•ran•tu•las or ta•ran•tu•lae *pl.*) a kind of large, hairy spider.

tea•spoon•ful /tē' spoon' fool'/ *n.* (-fuls *pl.*) the amount a teaspoon will hold.

tele- a prefix that means "distance": *telegraph.*

tel•e•gram /tĕl' ə grăm'/ *n.* a communication transmitted by telegraph.

tel•e•phone[1] /tĕl' ə fōn'/ *n.* an instrument that reproduces or receives sound, especially speech at a distance.

tel•e•phone[2] /tĕl' ə fōn'/ *v.* (-phones, -phoned, -phon•ing) to communicate by telephone.

tel•e•scope[1] /tĕl' ə skōp'/ *n.* **a.** an instrument for collecting and examining electromagnetic radiation. **b.** an arrangement of lenses or mirrors or both that gathers visible light, permitting direct observation or photographic recording of distant objects. **c.** any of various devices, such as a radio telescope, used to detect and observe distant objects by their emission, transmission, reflection, or other interaction with invisible radiation.

tel•e•scope[2] /tĕl' ə skōp'/ *v.* (-scopes, -scoped, -scop•ing) **a.** to cause to slide inward or outward in overlapping sections, as the cylindrical sections of a small hand telescope. **b.** to make shorter or more precise; condense.

tel•e•scop•ic /tĕl' ĭ skŏp' ĭk/ *adj.* (tel•e•scop•i•cal•ly *adv.*) having to do with a telescope or with being seen through a telescope.

tem•per•a•ment /tĕm' prə mənt, tĕm' pər ə-/ *n.* the manner of thinking, behaving, or reacting characteristic of a specific individual. [ME < Lat. *temperamentum* < *temperare,* to temper.]

tem•per•a•ture /tĕm' pər ə choor', tĕm' prə-/ *n.* **a.** the degree of hotness or coldness of a body or environment. **b.** an abnormally high temperature caused by illness; fever. [Lat. *temperatura,* composition < *temperare,* to mix.]

te•na•cious /tə **nā'** shəs/ *adj.* stubborn; holding fast. *He was tenacious about holding on to his opinions.*

text•book /tĕkst' book'/ *n.* a book used as a standard work for the formal study of a particular subject.

thief /thēf/ *n.* (**thieves** /thēvz/ *pl.*) a person who steals.

thir•teen-year-olds /thûr tēn′ yîr ōldz/ *n. pl.* a group of young adolescents who are thirteen years old. *They invited the whole class of thirteen-year-olds to their party.*

thor•ough /thûr′ ō/ *adj.* (**thor•ough•ly** *adv.*) **a.** exhaustively complete. **b.** painstakingly accurate or careful. **c.** completely satisfactory in all respects.

thought•ful /thôt′ fəl/ *adj.* (**thought•ful•ly** *adv.*) (**thought•ful•ness** *n.*) **a.** occupied with thought; contemplative. **b.** well thought-out; well considered. **c.** showing regard for others; considerate.

thought•less /thôt′ lĭs/ *adj.* (**thought•less•ly** *adv.*) (**thought•less•ness** *n.*) **a.** careless; unthinking. **b.** inconsiderate; inattentive.

three-fourths /thrē fôrths/ *n. pl.* three parts of something that has been divided into four equal parts. *Three quarters are three-fourths of a dollar.*

-tion a noun suffix that means "action" or "process."

tis•sue /tĭsh′ oo/ *n.* **a.** a group of cells in a plant or animal that carry out a certain function: *skin tissue.* **b.** light, soft, thin paper or cloth. *I wiped my nose with a tissue.*

to•ma•to /tə mā′ tō, -mä′-/ *n.* (**-toes** *pl.*) **a.** a plant native to South America, widely cultivated for its edible, fleshy, usually red fruit. **b.** the fruit of this plant.

to•pi•ar•y /tō′ pē ĕr′ ē/ *adj.* having to do with a bush or other plant that has been clipped or trimmed to resemble an animal or other shape. *The topiary garden was made to look like the scene in a famous painting.*

tor•na•do /tôr nā′ dō/ *n.* (**-does** or **-dos** *pl.*) a rotating column of air usually accompanied by a funnel-shaped downward extension of a cumulonimbus cloud and having a vortex several hundred yards in diameter whirling destructively at speeds up to 300 miles per hour. [Alteration of Sp. *tronada,* thunderstorm < *tronar,* to thunder < Lat. *tonare.*]

tor•pe•do[1] / tôr pē′ dō/ *n.* (**tor•pe•does** *pl.*) a cigar-shaped, self-propelled underwater projectile launched from a submarine, aircraft, or ship and designed to detonate on contact with or in the vicinity of a target.

tor•pe•do[2] / tôr pē′ dō/ *v.* (**tor•pe•does, tor•pe•doed, tor•pe•do•ing**) **a.** to attack, strike, or sink with a torpedo. **b.** to destroy decisively; wreck.

tor•ti•lla /tôr tē′ yə/ *n.* a thin, round unleavened bread, usually made from cornmeal and served hot with various toppings of ground meat or cheese. [Mex. Sp. < Sp., omelet < Sp. *torta,* cake < LLat. *torta,* a kind of bread.]

trans•mis•sion /trăns mĭsh′ ən, trănz-/ *n.* **a.1.** the act or process of transmitting. **a.2.** the state of being transmitted. **b.** something transmitted, as a voice or message. **c.1.** an automotive assembly of gears and associated parts by which power is transmitted from the engine to a driving axle. **c.2.** a system of gears. [Lat. *transmissio,* a sending across < *transmittere,* to transmit: *trans,* across + *mittere,* to send.]

trans•mit /trăns mĭt′, trănz-/ *v.* (**-mits, -mit•ted, -mit•ting**) to send from one person, thing, or place to another; convey.

trea•ty /trē′ tē/ *n.* (**trea•ties** *pl.*) an agreement between nations. *The leaders signed two treaties to end the war.*

tri•al /trī′ əl, trīl/ *n.* **a.** *Law.* the examination of evidence, charges, or claims made in a case in court. **b.** the act or process of testing, trying, or putting to the proof by actual or simulated use and experience. **c.** made, done, used, or performed during the course of a trial or trials.

tro•phy /trō′ fē/ *n.* (**-phies** *pl.*) something received as a symbol of victory or achievement, often preserved as a memento.

trop•ic /trŏp′ ĭk/ *adj.* of or relating to the region of Earth on both sides of the equator; tropical.

trop•i•cal•ly /trŏp′ ĭ kəl lē/ *adv.* in a tropical way; in a way relating to the tropics region of Earth.

turn•pike /tûrn′ pīk/ *n.* **a.** a toll road, especially a highway with tollgates. **b.** a tollgate.

tux•e•do /tŭk sē′ dō/ *n.* (**-dos** or **-does** *pl.*) **a.** a man's usually dark jacket with satin or grosgrain lapels worn for formal or semi-formal occasions. **b.** a complete outfit including a tuxedo jacket, black trousers with a stripe down the side, and a black bow tie. [After *Tuxedo* Park, New York.]

ty•phoon /tī fo͞on′/ *n.* a severe tropical storm in the western Pacific or the China Sea.

ul•ti•ma•tum /ŭl′ tə mā′ təm/ or /ŭl′ tə mä′ təm/ *n.* (**ul•ti•ma•tums** or **ul•ti•ma•ta** *pl.*) an order, proposition, or final demand; a threat; a final warning. *My parents issued an ultimatum: clean my room or else.*

un-[1] a prefix meaning "not" or "contrary to."

un-[2] a prefix meaning: **a.** reversal of action. **b.** release or removal from: *unburden.* **c.** intensified action: *unloose.*

un•ac•cept•a•ble /ŭn′ ăk sĕp′ tə bəl/ *adj.* not acceptable, especially not satisfactory or pleasing.

u•na•nim•i•ty /yo͞o′ nə nĭm′ ĭ tē/ *n.* condition of sharing or having the same views or opinions about an issue.

u•nan•i•mous /yo͞o năn′ ə məs/ *adj.* **a.** sharing the same opinions or views; being in complete harmony or accord. **b.** based on or characterized by complete assent or agreement. [Lat. *unanimus: unus,* one + *animus,* mind.]

un•as•sist•ed /ŭn′ ə sĭs′ tĭd/ *adj.* without help from anyone or anything. *They were excited when the little boy was able to walk unassisted.*

un•a•void•a•ble /ŭn′ ə voi′ də bəl/ *adj.* not able to be avoided; inevitable.

un•com•fort•a•ble /ŭn kŭm′ fĕr tə bəl, -kŭmf′ tə bel/ *adj.* **a.** experiencing discomfort; uneasy. **b.** causing discomfort.

un•con•scious /ŭn kŏn′ shəs/ *adj.* not aware of one's own thoughts and feelings. *After the accident, she was unconscious for an hour.*

un•co•or•di•nat•ed /ŭn′ kō ôr′ dn ā′ tĭd/ *adj.* **a.** lacking physical or mental coordination. **b.** lacking planning, method, or organization.

under- a prefix meaning: **a.** location below or under: *underground.* **b.** inferiority in rank or importance: *undersecretary.* **c.** degree, rate, or quantity that is lower or less than normal: *underestimate.* **d.** secrecy or treachery: *underhand.*

un•der•es•ti•mate[1] /ŭn dər ĕs′ tə māt′/ *v.* (**-mates, -mat•ed, -mat•ing**) to make too low an estimate of the quantity, degree, or worth of.

un•der•es•ti•mate[2] /ŭn dər ĕs′ tə māt′/ *n.* an estimate that is or proves to be too low.

un•e•mo•tion•al /ŭn′ ĭ mō′ shə nəl/ *adj.* **a.** not easily stirred or moved. **b.** involving little or no emotion; rational.

un•ex•pect•ed /ŭn′ ĭk spĕk′ tĭd/ *adj.* coming without warning; unforeseen.

un•for•giv•able /ŭn′ fər gĭv′ ə bəl/ *adj.* of or relating to an act that one cannot or will not forgive.

uni- a prefix meaning "one" or "single": *unilateral.*

u•ni•corn /yo͞o′ nĭ kôrn′/ *n.* a mythical horselike animal with one horn on its head. *A unicorn is a magical animal in fairy tales.*

u•ni•cy•cle /yo͞o′ nĭ sī′ kəl/ *n.* a vehicle with a single wheel propelled by pedals. *A clown in the parade was riding a unicycle.*

u•ni•form /yo͞o′ nə fôrm′/ *adj.* always the same, as in color, texture, or design.

u•ni•fy /yo͞o′ nə fī′/ *v.* (**-fies, -fied, -fy•ing**) to make into a unit; consolidate; to become unified.

u•ni•lat•er•al /yo͞o′ nə lăt′ ər əl/ *adj.* involving only one side.

un•in•ter•est•ed /ŭn ĭn′ trĭs tĭd, -ĭn′ tə rĕs′ tĭd/ *adj.* **a.** without an interest: *uninterested parties.* **b.** not paying attention.

u•nique /yo͞o nēk′/ *adj.* **a.** being the only one of its kind; sole. **b.** being without an equal. [Fr. < Lat. *unicus,* sole < *unus,* one.]

u•ni•son /yo͞o′ nĭ sən′, -zən/ *n.* an instance of agreement; concord. —***idiom.* in unison.** in complete agreement; harmonizing exactly. [OFr. < Med. Lat. *unisonus,* in unison: Lat. *unus,* one + Lat. *sonus,* sound.]

u•nite /yo͞o nīt′/ *v.* (**-nites, -nit•ed, -nit•ing**) **a.** to bring together so as to form a whole. **b.** to combine (people) in interest, attitude, or action.

u•ni•ver•sal /yo͞o′ nə vûr′ səl/ *adj.* **a.** of or relating to the entire world or all within the world; worldwide. **b.** including or relating to all members of the class or group under consideration. **c.** applicable or common to all purposes, conditions, or situations: *a universal truth.* **d.** of or relating to the universe or cosmos; cosmic.

u•ni•verse /yōō′ nə vûrs′/ *n.* **a.** all existing things, including the earth, the heavens, the galaxies, and all therein, regarded as a whole. **b.** the sphere or realm in which something exists or takes place. [ME < OFr. *univers* < Lat. *universum,* neuter of *universus,* whole: *unus,* one + *versus,* p.part. of *vertere,* to turn.]

u•ni•ver•si•ty /yōō′ nə **vûr′** sĭ tē/ *n.* (**-ties** *pl.*) an institution for higher learning with teaching and research facilities comprising a graduate school and professional schools that award master's degrees and doctorates and an undergraduate division that awards bachelor's degrees.

un•mis•tak•a•ble /ŭn′ mĭ **stā′** kə bəl/ *adj.* obvious; evident.

un•nec•es•sar•y /ŭn **nĕs′** ĭ sĕr′ ē/ *adj.* not necessary; needless.

un•rea•son•a•ble /ŭn **rē′** zə nə bəl/ *adj.* **a.** not governed by reason. **b.** exceeding reasonable limits; immoderate.

up•date /ŭp **dāt′**/ *v.* (**-dates, -dat•ed, -dat•ing**) to bring up to date: *update a textbook.*

ur•gent /**ûr′** jənt/ *adj.* (**ur•gent•ly** *adv.*) **a.** compelling immediate action; imperative: *a crisis of an urgent nature.* **b.** conveying a sense of pressing importance: *an urgent message.* [ME < OFr. < Lat. *urgens,* p.part. of *urgere,* to urge.]

use•less /yōōs′ lĭs/ *adj.* (**use•less•ness** *n.*) being or having no beneficial use; ineffective.

u•su•al /yōō′ zhōō əl/ *adj.* (**u•su•al•ly** *adv.*) **a.** such as is commonly or frequently encountered, experienced, observed, or used. **b.** habitual or customary; particular.

u•til•i•ty /yōō tĭl′ ĭ tē/ *n.* (**u•til•i•ties** *pl.*) **a.** the quality or condition of being useful; usefulness. **b.** a useful article or device. **c.** a commodity or service, such as electricity, water, or public transportation, that is provided by a public utility.

u•til•ize /yōōt′ l īz′/ *v.* (**-iz•es, -ized, -iz•ing**) to put to use for a certain purpose. [Fr. *utiliser* < Ital. *utilizzare* < *utile,* useful < Lat. *utilis* < *uti,* to use.]

va•can•cy /**vā′** kən sē/ *n.* (**va•can•cies** *pl.*) a position or office that is unfilled or not occupied. *The company wanted to hire someone to fill the vacancy.*

vac•u•um¹ /**văk′** yōōm, -yəm, -yōō əm/ *n.* (**-u•ums** or **-u•a** *pl.*) **a.** the absence of matter. **b.** a state of emptiness; void. **c.** *pl.* **vacuums.** a vacuum cleaner.

vac•u•um² /**văk′** yōōm, -yəm, -yōō əm/ *v.* to clean with or use a vacuum cleaner.

vague /vāg/ *adj.* (**vague•ly** *adv.*) **a.** not clearly expressed or outlined: *vague instructions.* **b.** not thinking or expressing oneself clearly. *She was vague about her future plans.* [OFr. < Lat. *vagus.*]

val•en•tine /**văl′** ən tīn′/ *n.* a sentimental or humorous gift or greeting card sent on St. Valentine's Day. [after St. Valentine.]

van•dal•ism /**văn′** dl ĭz′ əm/ *n.* a deliberate destruction of property. *When we found that the fence had been destroyed, we called the police to report the vandalism.* [Lat. *Vandalus,* a Vandal, prob. of Germanic orig.]

va•nil•la¹ /və **nĭl′** ə/ *n.* **a.** any of various tropical American vines of the genus Vanilla in the orchid family cultivated for its seedpods from which a flavoring agent is obtained. **b.** the seedpod of this plant. Also called vanilla bean. **c.** a flavoring extract prepared from the cured seedpods of this plant or produced synthetically.

va•nil•la² / və **nĭl′** ə/ *adj.* **a.** flavored with vanilla. **b.** basic or ordinary.

va•ri•e•ty /və **rī′** ĭ tē / *n.* (**-ties** *pl.*) **a.** the condition or quality of being various or varied; diversity. **b.** a number or collection of varied things, especially of a particular group; assortment: *brought home a variety of snacks.*

ve•hi•cle /**vē′** ĭ kəl/ *n.* **a.** a device, such as a car or sled, for carrying passengers, goods, or equipment; conveyance. **b.** a medium through which something is conveyed, transmitted, expressed, or achieved.

ver•ba•tim /vər′ **bā′** tĭm/ *adv.* corresponding word-for-word. *She was able to quote the Constitution verbatim.* [ME < Med. Lat. *verbātim* < Lat. *verbum* word.]

ver•i•fy /vĕr′ ə fī′/ *v.* (**-fies, -fied, -fy•ing**) **a.** to prove the truth of by the presentation of evidence or testimony; substantiate. **b.** to determine or test the truth or accuracy of, as by comparison, investigation, or reference: *conduct experiments to verify a hypothesis.*

ver•sa•tile /vûr′ sə təl/ *adj.* **a.** capable of doing many things well. **b.** having varied uses or serving many functions. [Fr. < Lat. *versatilis* < *versare,* freq. of *vertere,* to turn.]

vet•er•i•nar•i•an /vĕt′ ər ə năr′ ē ən, vĕt′ rə-/ *n.* a person trained and authorized to treat animals medically. [Lat. *veterinarius,* pertaining to beasts of burden, *veterinus* < *veterinae,* beasts of burden.]

vi•al /vī′ əl/ *n.* a small glass or plastic container for medicines or other liquids. *The sample of perfume came in a small vial.*

vi•cious /vĭsh′ əs/ *adj.* **a.** characterized by violence or ferocity: *a vicious storm.* **b.** savagely aggressive; dangerous: *a vicious shark.*

vic•tim /vĭk′ tĭm/ *n.* one who is harmed by or made to suffer from an act, circumstance, agency, or condition.

vig•i•lan•te /vĭj′ ə lăn′ tē/ *n.* a person who takes or favors taking law enforcement into one's own hands. [Sp., watchman, *vigilante* < Lat. *vigilāns, vigilant-,* pr.part. of *vigilāre,* to be watchful < *vigil,* watchful.]

vil•lain /vĭl′ ən/ *n.* a wicked or evil character. *When the villain appeared onstage, the audience booed.*

vi•o•lent /vī′ ə lənt/ *adj.* **a.** marked by or resulting from great physical force or rough action. **b.** severe, intense: *a violent storm.*

vi•sa /vē′ zə/ *n.* an official permission stamp allowing a traveler to enter or exit a certain country. *The officer checked my visa before allowing me into her country.*

vi•su•al /vĭzh′ ōō əl/ *adj.* (**vi•su•al•ly** *adv.*) **a.** serving, resulting from, or pertaining to the sense of sight. **b.** capable of being seen by the eye; visible. **c.** optical.

voice•less•ly /vois′ lĭs lē/ *adv.* mutely; speechlessly.

vol•ca•no /vŏl kā′ nō, vôl-/ *n.* (**-noes** or **-nos** *pl.*) **a.** a vent in the earth's crust through which molten lava and gases are ejected. **b.** a mountain formed by the materials ejected from a volcano.

war•rant /wôr′ ənt, wŏr′-/ *n.* **a.** authorization or certification; sanction, as given by a superior. **b.** justification for an action; grounds. **c.** something that assures, attests to, or guarantees some event or result; proof.

wash-and-wear /wŏsh′ ən wâr′/ or /wôsh′ ən wâr′/ *adj.* easily or quickly washed or rinsed clean, requiring little or no ironing: *wash-and-wear pants.*

well-known /wĕl′ nōn′/ *adj.* widely known; familiar or famous.

wharf /hwôrf/ or /wôrvf/ *n.* (**wharves** *pl.*) a pier or dock where ships can load and unload. *The force of the hurricane destroyed several of the seaport's wharves.*

wheel•bar•row /hwēl′ băr′ ō/ or /wēl′ băr′ ō/ *n.* a one- or two-wheeled piece of equipment with handles, used to convey small loads.

whole•sale[1] /hōl′ sāl/ *n.* the sale of goods in large quantities, as for resale by a retailer.

whole•sale[2] /hōl′ sāl/ *adj.* **a.** of, relating to, or engaged in the sale of goods in large quantities for resale. **b.** made or accomplished extensively and indiscriminately; blanket.

whole•sale[3] /hōl′ sāl/ *adv.* **a.** in large bulk or quantity. **b.** extensively; indiscriminately.

whole•some /hōl′ səm/ *adj.* healthful. *The doctor gave us advice on the importance of exercise and wholesome meals.*

wis•dom /wĭs′ dəm/ *n.* **a.** understanding of what is true, right, or lasting. **b.** common sense; good judgment.

wit•ness[1] /wĭt′ nĭs/ *n.* **a.** one who has seen or heard something. **b.** one who furnishes evidence.

wit•ness[2] /wĭt′ nĭs/ *v.* **a.** to be present at or have personal knowledge of. **b.** to provide or serve as evidence of. **c.** to testify to; bear witness.

word pro•ces•sing /wûrd′ prŏ′ sĕs′ ĭng/ *n.* a system of producing typewritten documents by use of automated typewriters and electronic text-editing equipment.

wres•tle /rĕs′ əl/ *v.* (**-tles, -tled, -tling**) **a.** to contend by grappling and attempting to throw one's opponent, especially under certain contest rules. **b.1.** to contend; to struggle. *City planners wrestle with budget cuts.* **b.2.** to strive in an effort to master: *wrestle with one's conscience.*

Using the Thesaurus

The **Writing Thesaurus** provides synonyms—words that mean the same or nearly the same—and antonyms—words that mean the opposite—for your spelling words. Use this sample to identify the various parts of each thesaurus entry.

- **Entry words** are listed in alphabetical order and are printed in boldface type.
- The abbreviation for the **part of speech** of each entry word follows the boldface entry word.
- The **definition** of the entry word matches the definition of the word in your **Spelling Dictionary**. A **sample sentence** shows the correct use of the word in context.

- Each **synonym** for the entry word is listed under the entry word. Again, a sample sentence shows the correct use of the synonym in context.
- Where appropriate, **antonyms** for the entry word are listed at the end of the entry.

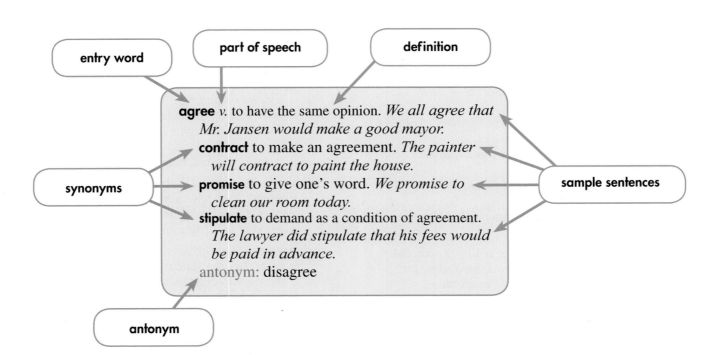

entry word | part of speech | definition

agree v. to have the same opinion. *We all agree that Mr. Jansen would make a good mayor.*
contract to make an agreement. *The painter will contract to paint the house.*
promise to give one's word. *We promise to clean our room today.*
stipulate to demand as a condition of agreement. *The lawyer did stipulate that his fees would be paid in advance.*
antonym: disagree

synonyms | sample sentences | antonym

297

accompany *v.* 1. to go along with; join in company. *I was asked to accompany my friends to the zoo.* 2. to supplement; add to. 3. to coexist or occur with.

    attend to go with. *A sore throat often will attend a cold.*

    escort to go with. *Secret Service agents escort the President to public events.*

    join to come into the company of. *Amanda will join us at the party later.*

    antonyms: desert, abandon

accomplish *v.* 1. to succeed in doing; bring to pass. 2. to reach the end of; complete. *I always accomplish what I set out to do.*

    achieve to carry out; do. *You have to work hard to achieve your goals.*

    complete to finish. *Please complete the test and hand in your papers.*

    finish to complete. *Ted must finish washing the dishes before he begins his homework.*

    fulfill to carry out; finish. *Terry will fulfill her part of the task before we finish ours.*

    succeed to do well. *Will she succeed in running a mile in three minutes?*

    antonyms: foil, thwart, frustrate

accustomed *adj.* 1. usual; characteristic; normal. *Alicia worked with her accustomed thoroughness.* 2. in the habit of. *Jack had become accustomed to sleeping late on weekend mornings.*

    characteristic distinctive. *Bob has a characteristic laugh.*

    common usual. *Political upheaval is common in that region.*

    customary usual. *The Bensons sat at their customary table.*

    familiar common. *The old town looked strangely familiar to him.*

    habitual done by habit. *Dawn is a habitual nail biter.*

    usual customary. *It is usual for the baby to take a nap at two o'clock.*

    antonyms: unaccustomed, unusual, unfamiliar, uncommon

actual *adj.* 1. existing in fact or reality. 2. current. 3. based on fact. *The book was said to be an actual account of a spy's secret missions.*

    certain sure. *I am certain that it will rain today; I read all the reports.*

    definite sure. *She was quite definite about her decision to take the job.*

    genuine real. *The expression of happiness on his face was genuine.*

    real genuine. *He was astounded to discover that the rock contained real gold.*

    tangible real; able to be touched. *Rumors and hearsay are not tangible evidence.*

    true real. *Knowing when to keep a secret is a true test of friendship.*

    antonyms: unreal, untrue, fake

adapt *v.* to adjust to a specified use or situation. *The cat was able to adapt quickly to its new surroundings.*

    accommodate to make suitable to a particular situation. *She learned to accommodate herself to the variable weather.*

    adjust to change to fit. *The seat belts adjust automatically to fit each passenger.*

    fit to adjust. *Ask the tailor at the store to fit your suit before you take it home.*

    modify to change somewhat. *George will modify the sailboat to make it lighter and faster.*

    suit to make fit. *A judge will decide how to suit the punishment to the crime.*

admiration *n.* a feeling of pleasure, wonder, and approval. *He sat looking at the painting, lost in admiration.*

    awe wonder and fear. *The view from the edge of the Grand Canyon filled them with awe.*

    delight joy; pleasure. *His delight at seeing me made me feel good.*

    esteem regard; good opinion. *He was held in high esteem by his colleagues.*

    pleasure delight; joy. *The puppy made the children squeal with pleasure.*

    regard esteem. *She was worried that the professor's low regard of her work would affect her class standing.*

    wonder feeling of amazement. *She gazed in wonder at the lights of the city spread out below her.*

    antonyms: disgust, hatred

admire *v.* 1. to regard with pleasure, wonder, and approval. 2. to have a high opinion of; esteem or respect. *I admire his ability to remain calm and competent in all situations.* See **respect.**

admission *n.* 1.a. the act of admitting or allowing to enter. 1.b. the state of being allowed to enter. 2. the right to enter; access. 3. the price required or paid for entering; entrance fee. 4. a voluntary acknowledgment that something is true. *His admission of the error helped to resolve the conflict.*

access right to enter or use. *Despite their protests, the reporters were denied immediate access to the scene of the crime.*

  admittance right or permission to enter. *The pass allowed us admittance backstage after the show.*

  entrance permission to enter. *Entrance is restricted to club members.*

  antonyms: rejection, exclusion

advantageous *adj.* affording benefit or gain; useful. *Investing money in those stocks was an advantageous move.*

  beneficial helpful; favorable. *Proper diet and exercise are beneficial to a person's health.*

  profitable having real value. *Terry worked hard to make her pet-sitting service a profitable venture.*

  rewarding satisfying. *Working as a volunteer at the hospital is a rewarding activity for Denise.*

  worthwhile having merit or value. *Bob contributed to the wildlife group because it seemed like a worthwhile cause.*

  antonyms: harmful, unfavorable, injurious, ruinous, destructive

advise *v.* 1. to offer advice to; counsel. 2. to recommend; suggest. 3. to inform; notify. *Howard always waits until the last minute to advise a person of a decision.* See **notify**.

  admonish to advise; warn. *The flight attendant had to admonish the passenger to fasten his seat belt.*

  consult to talk over. *Doris will consult with her doctor about possible treatments.*

  counsel to give advice to. *Her job is to counsel students on career choices.*

  inform to tell. *Janice must inform me that she is no longer a member of the committee.*

  notify to let know. *The bank will notify me if my account is overdrawn.*

  recommend to advise. *She would often recommend that we invest our money in stocks.*

  suggest to propose. *I suggest that we buy a house now while interest rates are low.*

agreeable *adj.* 1. to one's liking; pleasing; pleasant. 2. ready to consent or submit. *If you want to go downtown, I'm agreeable.*

  pleasant pleasing. *We had a pleasant day at the zoo.*

  pleasing pleasant. *Tom has a very pleasing personality; he gets along with everyone.*

  willing consenting. *Julio is always willing to play with the baby.*

  antonyms: disagreeable, unpleasant, unwilling, reluctant

ambitious *adj.* 1. full of, characterized by, or motivated by ambition. *The ambitious man would stop at nothing to gain fortune and power.* 2. greatly desirous; eager. 3. showing or requiring much effort.

  aspiring desiring strongly. *She is an aspiring actress.*

  desirous desiring; eager. *He is desirous of making your acquaintance.*

  eager desiring strongly. *Melinda was eager to learn to play the guitar.*

  enterprising bold; daring to take risks. *Building a treehouse was an enterprising project for the two boys.*

  antonyms: apathetic, humble, modest

apparent *adj.* 1. readily seen; open to view; visible. 2. readily understood or perceived; plain or obvious. 3. appearing as such but not necessarily so. *His ability to speak Spanish was an apparent advantage in getting the job.*

  clear easily seen. *From the third floor there is a clear view of the lake.*

  conspicuous easily seen. *The footprint by the back door was a conspicuous clue.*

  evident clear; plain. *It was evident to all but Cindy that the party was over.*

  obvious easily seen; clear. *I cannot believe that Tim could make such an obvious mistake.*

  open exposed; not secret. *The argument had not yet turned into open warfare.*

  plain easily perceived. *It was plain that there would be no picnic because of the rain.*

  antonyms: concealed, obscure, mysterious

appetite *n.* 1. a desire for food or drink. 2. a physical desire. 3. a strong wish or urge. *All of his life, Thomas Jefferson displayed an appetite for learning.*

  craving strong desire; longing. *Thanksgiving dinner satisfies my craving for turkey and cranberries for an entire year.*

  desire strong wish; craving. *After seeing the toys in the window, the children were filled with desire.*

  hunger desire for food; craving. *Hunger made him dream of steak and potatoes.*

  longing desire. *Her longing to see the child overcame her fear of being seen.*

  urge force or impulse. *Quentin resisted the urge to run away from the barking dog.*

appliance *n.* a device or instrument, especially one operated by electricity and designed for household use. *The refrigerator is a major household appliance.*

    apparatus tool for a particular use. *He hung hammers, saws, and other carpentry apparatus on the walls of his garage.*

    device something made for a particular use. *That round piece of flexible plastic is a clever device for opening jars.*

    instrument mechanical device; tool. *A surgeon uses many special instruments to perform an operation.*

    tool instrument used in doing work. *A wrench is a mechanic's tool, while a pen is a writer's tool.*

assemble *v.* 1. to bring or gather together into a group or whole. 2. to fit or join together the parts of. *It took me three hours to assemble the computer desk.*

    build to put together; construct. *Ken and his friends are trying to build a treehouse.*

    collect to gather together. *The children banded together to collect cans of food for the homeless.*

    congregate to come together in a group. *The ducks tend to congregate under the willow by the pond.*

    construct to put together; build. *My father and my brother construct houses for a living.*

    convene to gather together. *The Fifth Cell Wall Congress was to convene in Edinburgh, Scotland, last August.*

    gather to bring together. *I tried to gather all the library books into one pile.*

    antonyms: disperse, disassemble

assess *v.* to evaluate; appraise. *He must assess the situation before he decides what to do.*

    appraise to consider the value or importance of. *The judges will appraise each contestant's cooking skills.*

    calculate to estimate. *Joy wanted to calculate how many days it would take her to finish the book.*

    estimate to judge; form an opinion about. *The foreman estimated that he would need four workers to unload the truck in an hour.*

    evaluate to find out the value or importance of. *The scientist planned to evaluate the impact of pollution on the marshlands.*

    gauge to judge; estimate. *Sam could not gauge the distance between his house and mine without measuring.*

attain *v.* to gain, reach, or accomplish by mental or physical effort. *She worked hard to attain her goal of becoming a doctor.*

    accomplish to carry out; finish. *Anna can accomplish the task with great ease.*

    achieve to complete successfully. *Hard work will help you achieve your goals.*

    acquire to get; obtain. *Marcia must acquire a new swimsuit while she is in Florida.*

    obtain to gain or acquire. *How did Shirley obtain her new bicycle?*

    reach to arrive at, get to. *I could not reach a decision based on the information.*

    secure to obtain; get. *He tried to secure the position by meeting with the boss after working hours.*

    antonyms: fail, lose

attempt *n.* 1. an effort or try. 2. an attack; assault. *He feared there would be an attempt on his life.*

    effort good try. *She made an effort to finish the marathon.*

    endeavor serious effort. *He approaches every endeavor with determination.*

    enterprise bold project. *Designing and selling clothes is a risky enterprise.*

    try test; attempt. *I promised my mother I would give cooking a try.*

attentive *adj.* 1. paying attention; observant. 2. mindful of the well-being of others; considerate. *Julio was very attentive to his great-aunt.*

    alert watchful. *It is hard to stay alert when you are tired.*

    considerate thoughtful of people. *Carrying Mrs. Johnson's bags was a considerate thing for Erin to do.*

    mindful heedful; careful. *Be mindful of the traffic when you cross the street.*

    observant watchful. *It is important for a police officer to be observant.*

    thoughtful thinking of others; considerate. *Sending a sympathy card was a thoughtful gesture.*

    watchful observant; careful. *The watchful dog kept guard in the backyard.*

basis *n.* 1. a supporting element; foundation. 2. the chief component of something. 3. the essential principle. *Trust is the basis of a good partnership or any relationship.*

    foundation base. *They poured the concrete for the foundation of the new building yesterday.*

groundwork foundation. *The notes I took at the library provided the groundwork for my science report.*

boundaries *n.* something that indicates borders or limits. *The boundaries of the farm were marked by fieldstone walls.*

borders lines separating countries, states, or other areas. *We crossed the borders of ten different countries during our vacation trip in Europe.*

frontiers borders. *Sol likes to explore new frontiers.*

limits bounds. *The streets were narrow and crowded within the limits of the city.*

bravado *n.* a pretense of courage; false bravery. *The lizard's hissing and charging are really just a show of bravado.*

bluster loud talk with empty threats. *The man's bluster did not worry the police officer; she knew it did not mean anything.*

boasting overpraise of one's talents or possessions. *The two boys tried to outdo each other with their boasting of their strength and prowess.*

bombast grand, pompous language. *There were some good ideas hidden under the bombast in his speech.*

bragging boasting. *After much bragging about his town, the mayor went on to criticize the neighboring city.*

heroics melodramatic words or actions used only for effect. *Such heroics were out of place in a sensible debate.*

swaggering noisy boasting. *Susie thought that his swaggering was annoying.*

antonyms: modesty, humility

briefly *adv.* 1. in a short time. 2. to a short length or extent. *She spoke briefly before announcing the guest of honor.* See **presently.**

concisely in a few meaningful words. *They asked him to give his opinion of the situation as concisely as possible.*

shortly in a short time; in a few words. *He promised to speak with me shortly.*

succinctly concisely. *She is known for being able to state complex problems succinctly.*

antonyms: gradually, slowly, deliberately

canyon *n.* a narrow chasm with steep cliff walls, formed by running water; gorge. *The awestruck hikers looked cautiously into the mile-deep canyon.*

dell small valley with trees. *We enjoyed hiking in the dell.*

glen small, narrow valley. *In Scotland, a lake is a loch and a valley is a glen.*

gorge narrow valley between mountains. *After the rainstorm, the water rushed through the gorge.*

gully small ravine; deep ditch. *In the fall the gully was filled with leaves, branches, and other debris.*

ravine deep, narrow valley made by running water. *Do not walk in a ravine if it looks as if it might rain.*

vale valley. *In poems, a valley is often called a vale.*

valley low land between mountains. *The village was nestled in the valley between Casper Mountain and Black Mountain.*

caption *n.* a title, short explanation, or description accompanying an illustration or photograph. *The caption under the photograph identified the location as Paris, France.*

heading word or words at the beginning of a page, chapter, etc. *Read the headings to get an idea of what the chapter is about.*

title name of a picture, book, poem, etc. *The title of the book was We Struck It Rich: The California Gold Rush of 1848.*

chronic *adj.* 1. of long duration; continuing; constant. 2. prolonged; lingering, as certain diseases. 3. subject to a disease or habit for a long time. *Jay's grandmother has chronic arthritis.*

confirmed habitual. *Don had often declared that he was a confirmed cat hater.*

constant never stopping. *The constant noise kept me awake all night.*

continual without stopping. *The continual dripping of the faucet annoyed Eric.*

habitual done by habit. *Habitual shoppers should avoid the new mall.*

inveterate habitual. *Mrs. Perkins has a reputation as an inveterate busybody.*

perpetual never stopping. *The children were a perpetual source of joy to their grandparents.*

unending without end. *The stream of complaining customers seemed unending.*

antonyms: fleeting, temporary

chronicle *n.* a chronological record of historical events. *Much of our historical knowledge comes from chronicles that were kept by people of ancient times.*

account detailed statement. *The newspaper account of the fire included the names of the ten victims.*

annals history. *The association's annals are kept by the librarian.*

history account of events. *Can you tell us the history of this campaign?*

memoir record written from personal knowledge. *The teacher wrote a memoir of her days in a one-room schoolhouse.*

record written account. *Let the record show that the witness refuses to answer my questions.*

story account of an event or events. *The story of the shipwreck was the lead on the evening news.*

colleague *n.* a fellow member of a profession, staff, or academic faculty; associate. *He and a colleague at the university worked on the experiment together.*

accomplice person who helps another in a wrong act. *Terry's brother was her accomplice in the kitchen mess last night.*

ally helper; partner. *My sister has always been my ally.*

associate partner; companion. *Darryl and I were associates at the same law firm for three years.*

companion comrade; a person who shares in another's activities. *Cheryl and Alan are often dinner companions when he is in town.*

comrade partner; coworker. *He wanted to be with his comrades for the rally.*

confederate ally; partner. *The police knew that the thief had a confederate in the job.*

coworker person who works with another. *Her coworkers at the office gave her a surprise birthday party.*

partner person who invests with others in a company or business. *When Jane wanted to open a restaurant, she asked Henry to be her partner.*

combine *v.* 1. to bring into a state of unity. 2. to join (two or more substances) to make a single substance; mix. *If you combine blue paint with red paint, you will get purple paint.*

blend to mix. *Chris is careful to blend the milk and the eggs by adding the milk a little at a time.*

join to put together. *At camp we all were asked to join hands and sing songs around the fire.*

mix to put together as one. *The directions said to mix 1 cup of water, 1 cup of oil, and 1 teaspoon of ground mustard.*

unite to join together. *The thirteen colonies had to unite to fight the British.*

antonyms: divide, separate, split

comfort *v.* 1. to soothe in time of grief or fear; console. *The teacher tried to comfort the crying child.* 2. to ease physically; relieve.

console to ease; relieve. *It is hard to console someone who has lost a relative.*

relieve to reduce; ease. *A heating pad can relieve sore muscles.*

soothe to calm; quiet. *The singing and laughing helped soothe the campers' fears.*

antonyms: irritate, annoy, aggravate, embarrass, upset, burden, hamper

commence *v.* 1. to begin; start. *The debate will commence promptly at seven o'clock.* 2. to come into existence; have a beginning.

begin to start. *Open your test booklets and begin working on item one.*

inaugurate to begin officially or formally. *The completion of the transcontinental railroad served to inaugurate the era of the railroads in America.*

initiate to begin. *Carl was the one who tried to initiate reduced-price passes for senior citizens and students.*

originate to begin; come into being. *The idea for the play did originate in a writing class.*

start to begin. *Remember to always start with the first problem.*

antonyms: end, finish, terminate

commend *v.* 1. to represent as worthy, qualified, or desirable; recommend. 2. to express approval of; praise. *The coach always tries to commend the efforts of the entire team.*

applaud to praise; approve. *Jessie wanted to applaud her brother's decision to go to college.*

extol to praise. *He should extol the virtues of hard work.*

laud to praise. *The mayor was happy to laud the citizen's rescue of the drowning child.*

praise to express approval of. *My mother and father praise my desire to learn to paint.*

recommend to speak of favorably. *I recommend that you take the scenic route rather than the interstate highway.*

antonyms: blame, censure

commentary *n.* 1. a series of explanations or interpretations. 2. something that explains or illustrates. *The reporter delivered his commentary on the White House press conference.*

editorial newspaper or magazine article expressing the editor's or publisher's opinion on a topic. *The editorial in today's paper spoke out against corruption.*

essay written composition presenting the author's views. *The teacher asked us to write an essay on our role in the democratic process.*

review report offering a critical evaluation of a work. *In my book review, I discussed both the merits and flaws of the author's first-person narrative.*

companies *n.* 1. groups; gatherings. 2. business enterprises; firms. *Many companies have offices in several major cities.*

associations groups of people joined together. *Over the years Ava has belonged to many different associations.*

bands numbers of persons or animals joined together. *Long ago this region was home to many bands of outlaws.*

bodies groups of persons or things. *Congress is the largest of all our government bodies.*

businesses commercial enterprises. *Most of the businesses on Main Street have been there for thirty years.*

corporations groups of people with charters to operate businesses as separate legal entities. *Big corporations often have lobbyists who work for their interests in Washington, D.C.*

firms two or more people in business together. *Jeff has worked for three law firms since he finished law school.*

groups numbers of persons or things joined together. *Groups of children were working on different projects.*

parties groups of people joined together. *The restaurant is too small to seat parties of six or more people.*

partnerships two or more people who agree to contribute to and profit from a business. *He did not want to form any partnerships because he liked to work on his own.*

compel *v.* to force, drive, or constrain. *My parents try to compel me to explain my actions.*

coerce to force. *Ali tried to coerce the group into choosing him as the leader.*

commit to pledge. *Alicia and Joan always commit themselves to new programs of diet and exercise.*

constrain to force. *Dorothy had to constrain the dog from chasing the little rabbit.*

demand to request firmly. *I demand to see the manager of the store!*

drive to force. *The desire for success seemed to drive him to work harder than everyone else.*

force to make happen by force. *The company tried to force the man to resign his position.*

impel to force. *The approaching test date might impel Cathy to study harder.*

insist to stand firm on some issue. *The teacher often insists that the students work in groups.*

motivate to impel; move to act. *The teacher could motivate her students to read by scheduling additional reading periods.*

oblige to force. *The school will oblige its students to wear uniforms.*
antonym: coax

compete *v.* to strive or contend with another or others, as for profit or a prize; vie. *Twenty people signed up to compete in the relay race.*

contend to fight; vie. *The first five racers will contend in the first heat.*

contest to fight for; challenge. *The determined Central High team tried to contest the results of every single race today.*

dispute to fight; contest. *An underdog team from Monroe High seemed to dispute every heat.*

oppose to fight; struggle. *The coach from Jefferson will hotly oppose the decision to limit the number of entrants.*

rival to compete with. *The cheering squads must rival each other in screaming, shouting, and singing.*

vie to compete. *Earl Williamson and Guillermo Martinez will once again vie for first-place points in every race.*
antonym: support

complicate *v.* 1. to make or become complex, intricate, or perplexing. *David's arrival right after Hugh's seemed to complicate things even more.* 2. to twist or become twisted together.

confound to confuse; perplex. *Sylvia will confound you with her mastery of the game.*

confuse to mix up; bewilder. *The babble of different languages at the airport could confuse a tourist.*

perplex to puzzle; confuse. *The structure of a car's engine does perplex me.*

concentrate *v.* 1. to direct or draw toward a common center; focus. 2. to converge toward or meet in a common center. 3. to direct one's thoughts or attention. *I concentrate on going through all the problems on the test at least once.*

converge to come together to a central point. *On a warm summer day, a crowd might converge on the city park.*

focus to concentrate. *He must focus his attention on the speaker.*
antonyms: dissipate, disperse

confer *v.* 1. to bestow (an honor, for example). *The president will confer a medal on the hero.* 2. to hold a conference; consult together.

  advise to counsel. *It is good to advise the rafters to wear their life jackets at all times.*

  bestow to give. *The mayor will bestow the keys to the city on the visiting head of state.*

  consult to talk over. *The patient decided to consult with his doctor about the available treatments for his condition.*

  converse to talk. *Ed and Matt converse regularly about current events.*

  deliberate to talk over. *The jury members could deliberate their verdict for more than a week.*

  discuss to talk over. *The study group might discuss the topics they can investigate together as their semester project.*

  donate to contribute. *Millions of people donate money to the Red Cross for the emergency relief fund.*

  give to present. *The book promises to give the true story behind the political campaign last November.*

  grant to give formally. *The Spanish king would grant large tracts of land to his nobles.*

  talk to discuss. *Dan and Tom met to talk about where they would like to go on vacation.*

conscientious *adj.* thorough and painstaking; careful. *Rhonda is known at the office as a conscientious worker.* See **deliberate.**

  careful thorough; exact. *She was careful to draw the pattern to the correct size.*

  meticulous very careful about details. *Joanie keeps meticulous records of her weekly expenses.*

  painstaking exacting. *It was painstaking work to glue the vase together.*

  scrupulous very careful. *My father was scrupulous in his planning of the garden.*

  thorough very careful. *He did a thorough job of assembling the model.*

  antonyms: negligent, careless

considerable *adj.* 1. *large in amount, extent, or degree. It is of considerable importance that you listen to him.* 2. worthy of consideration; important; significant. See **substantial.**

consistent *adj.* in agreement; compatible. *His speech was consistent with his earlier remarks on pollution.*

  compatible agreeing. *The two people seemed quite compatible.*

  constant not changing. *His constant loyalty is one of his redeeming qualities.*

  faithful accurate. *She wanted to produce a replica that was faithful to the original.*

  harmonious agreeing. *We felt very comfortable among such harmonious people.*

  suitable fitting; proper. *A dress would be suitable for the occasion.*

  unwavering steady; constant. *Dogs are known for their unwavering devotion to their owners.*

  antonym: inconsistent

copies *n.* 1. imitations or reproductions of something original; duplicates. 2. specimens or examples of printed text or pictures. *At least twenty copies of the lithograph were sold at the art gallery.*

  carbons copies made with carbon paper. *The files were filled with carbons of letters the manager had sent to the salespeople.*

  duplicates exact copies. *You should always keep duplicates of business letters.*

  facsimiles exact copies. *The autographs of the presidents were very good facsimiles of the originals.*

  imitations likenesses. *Even the art experts found it hard to tell the real paintings and the imitations apart.*

  replicas copies. *Charlie likes to build replicas of old sailing vessels.*

  reproductions copies. *The company makes reproductions of eighteenth-century American furniture.*

  transcripts copies. *To apply for the job, I had to send transcripts of my high school and college records.*

  antonym: originals

copy *v.* 1. to make a copy of. 2. to follow as a model or pattern; imitate. *It is wrong to copy from someone else's paper.*

  duplicate to make a copy of. *Can you duplicate this material by tomorrow?*

  reproduce to make a copy of. *This machine can reproduce a letter in two seconds.*

correction *n.* 1. the act or instance of correcting. *I had to make a correction in my paper.* 2. something offered or substituted for a mistake or fault.

  alteration a change. *An author can make an alteration in the manuscript.*

  amendment a change for improvement. *At his request, she made an amendment in the article.*

  improvement a change for the better. *Everyone agreed that the new title was an improvement over the old one.*

revision a change; alteration. *Kay got annoyed when the publishers asked for dozens of revisions in the copy.*

courtesy *n.* 1. polite behavior; gracious manner or manners. *My mother always insisted that we treat others with courtesy.* 2. a polite gesture or remark.

civility polite behavior. *Civility is essential if you have a job in which you deal directly with customers.*

consideration thoughtfulness for others. *She showed consideration for her elderly neighbor by carrying his grocery bags up the stairs.*

manners polite ways of behaving. *Good manners require that you write a "Thank-you" note after you receive a gift.*

politeness good manners; polite behavior. *He is known for his charm and politeness.*

thoughtfulness consideration. *Kim's thoughtfulness made a difficult time a little easier for the children.*

antonyms: rudeness, incivility, thoughtlessness

defect *n.* 1. the lack of something necessary or desirable for completion or perfection; deficiency. 2. an imperfection; fault. A defect in the wiring caused the fan to overheat and short out.

blemish flaw. *The water spot was the only blemish on the table's polished surface.*

deficiency lack of something necessary or desirable. *Scurvy is caused by a deficiency of vitamin C in the diet.*

failing fault; weakness. *One of my failings is an inability to speak in public.*

fault flaw that spoils perfection. *A fault in the plaster caused the wall to collapse.*

imperfection fault. *The imperfection in the china cup was so tiny that it could not be seen without a magnifying glass.*

shortcoming fault; flaw. *Great-aunt Sarah is quick to point out one's shortcomings while ignoring one's virtues.*

deliberate *adj.* 1. done or said on purpose; intentional. 2. careful and thorough in deciding or determining. *He weighed all the factors before making a deliberate choice.* See **conscientious.**

careful done with thought and effort. *Arlene wants to do a careful job of restoring the water-damaged painting.*

cautious very careful. *She is cautious about the toys she gives to the baby.*

intentional done on purpose. *The insult was intentional; he knew what he was saying.*

methodical done according to a plan. *Dale approached each task in a methodical way.*

premeditated planned beforehand. *The attorney contended that the crime was premeditated.*

purposeful having an aim or intent. *She moved forward with a purposeful air.*

thorough very careful. *He was very thorough in cleaning up after the flood.*

antonyms: unintentional, haphazard, careless

deliver *v.* to take to the intended recipient. *Dan delivers groceries after school.*

convey to take from one place to another. *Airplanes convey mail across the country.*

transfer to move from one place to another. *Trucks are generally used to transfer goods from one city to another.*

deluxe *adj.* particularly elegant and luxurious; sumptuous. Ted chose the deluxe sedan over the standard one.

comfortable giving comfort. *The down coat is soft, warm, and comfortable.*

luxurious very comfortable and beautiful. *The Waldorf-Astoria is a luxurious hotel.*

rich elegant; expensive. *Velvet and satin are rich materials.*

sumptuous magnificent; rich. *The cruise ship provides five sumptuous meals every day.*

antonyms: uncomfortable, poor

demonstration *n.* 1. the act of making evident or proving. 2. conclusive evidence; proof. 3. an illustration or explanation, as of a theory or product, by practical application. *Dave made extra money by giving demonstrations of vacuum cleaners.* 4. a public display of group opinion, as by a rally or march.

display showing; exhibit. *In the display, the jewelry was arranged by color.*

exhibition display; public show. *There are art exhibitions every summer weekend in the village square.*

presentation offering; exhibition. *One critic had seen at least fifteen different presentations of that play.*

descend *v.* 1. to move from a higher to a lower place. 2. to come down from a source; derive. *Paul is descended from an old New England family.*

drop to let fall; cause to fall. *I tried not to drop the glass pitcher on the kitchen floor.*

fall to drop down. *Every autumn the leaves fall from the trees.*

plunge to jump down. *The swimmer took a running start and plunged into the pool.*

sink to fall slowly. *The ship began to sink after it hit an iceberg.*

antonyms: ascend, rise, soar, climb

diagram *n.* 1. a plan, sketch, drawing, or outline designed to demonstrate or explain how something works or to clarify the relationship between the parts of a whole. *He drew a diagram of his idea for a new lamp on the back of a paper napkin.* 2. a chart or graph.

chart information in lists, pictures, tables, or diagrams. *The chart in the science book shows the life cycle of a wood tick.*

depiction drawing; painting; description. *His depiction of a Canada goose was very lifelike and natural.*

figure picture; drawing; illustration. *Figure A shows the parts of an internal combustion engine.*

graph diagram showing the relationship between two quantities. *You can draw a graph showing the increase in the company's profits over the last ten years.*

illustration picture, diagram, or map used to explain or decorate. *The illustration on page 42 shows one of Georgia O'Keeffe's flower paintings.*

representation likeness; picture. *Alicia was upset because she felt that the representation of her face was unflattering.*

disappointment *n.* the act, condition, or feeling of not satisfying a hope, desire, or expectation. *Andy felt a pang of disappointment when he realized that the bicycle he wanted to buy was gone.*

chagrin feeling of humiliation. *Much to her chagrin, Connie could not remember the words to the song.*

frustration feeling caused by being thwarted. *The baby howled in frustration when he could not reach the toy.*

antonyms: satisfaction, fulfillment

disastrous *adj.* causing widespread destruction and distress. *Hurricane Hugo's sweep across the mainland had disastrous results for thousands of people.*

calamitous causing misery. *The region had been hit by a series of calamitous fires.*

destructive causing ruin. *The recent earthquake in California was not as destructive as the one in 1906.*

dreadful terrible. *The state of the city after the typhoon was dreadful.*

ruinous bringing ruin. *The stock market crash was ruinous to his career.*

antonyms: beneficial, useful

dismiss *v.* 1. to discharge, as from employment. 2. to direct or allow to leave. *The general will dismiss the troops.* 3. to discontinue consideration of; drop.

discard to throw away. *Paul had to discard his old track shoes.*

discharge to let go. *The doctor said he would discharge the patient in two weeks.*

reject to throw out as useless. *You can't reject all the bananas because a few have brown spots.*

release to let go. *Dana will release the trout into the river.*

distract *v.* to cause to turn away from the original focus of attention or interest; divert. *The television can distract her from her studies.*

divert to turn aside. *The interruption will divert their attention from his red face.*

fluster to confuse. *Don't fluster Mrs. Conners by singing off-key.*

upset to disturb. *Please don't upset the children by mentioning the lost puppy.*

antonyms: concentrate, attend

drastic *adj.* 1. taking effect violently or rapidly. 2. quite severe or radical in nature; extreme. *The boss took drastic steps to curb excessive spending.*

extreme more than usual. *I thought the decision to ban all imports of fruit from that country was extreme.*

radical extreme. *Giving up his job as a stockbroker and going to work as a laborer represented a radical change for Bob.*

ruthless cruel. *The ruthless dictator imposed heavy taxes on the people.*

severe strict; harsh. *The company placed severe restrictions on access to the computer.*

stringent severe; strict. *Vanessa protested the more stringent curfew rules.*

antonyms: relaxed, indulgent, lenient

dynamic *adj.* characterized by vigor and energy; forceful. *Jackson has a dynamic personality.*

active energetic; busy. *Clara took an active role in establishing the social center.*

energetic active; vigorous. *She did the housework in her usual energetic fashion.*

forceful strong; vigorous. *His forceful manner can be overwhelming at times.*

intense vigorous; extreme. *December is a time of intense activity for merchants.*

vigorous active; forceful. *Even at ninety-one, George was the most vigorous dancer in the group.*
antonyms: languid, passive, sluggish

education *n.* 1. the knowledge or skill obtained or developed by a learning process. 2. the field of study that is concerned with teaching and learning. *Jesse plans to major in education in college and become a first-grade teacher.*
  instruction lessons; teaching; education. *Ed had to have forty hours of classroom instruction and eighty hours of flight time before he could get his pilot's license.*
  learning knowledge. *Thomas Jefferson was a man of wide and varied learning.*
  schooling instruction; education. *Formal schooling may end when you leave school, but education is a lifelong process.*
  training practical instruction. *Josie completed her nurse's training at a hospital in her hometown.*
  tuition teaching; instruction. *The quality of the tuition at the state university is very high.*
  antonyms: illiteracy, ignorance

effect *n.* 1. something brought about by a cause or agent; result. 2. the way in which something acts upon or influences an object. 3. something that produces a specific impression or supports a general design or intention. *The sound effects in the movie really made you think you were on a safari in Africa.*
  consequence result; effect. *He did not want to face the consequences of his rudeness.*
  force power to influence or control. *He delivered the opening address at the political convention with force and passion.*
  intent meaning; significance. *She was puzzled by the intent of the question.*
  meaning intent; significance. *I had to read the card three times before I finally grasped its meaning.*
  outcome result; consequence. *The reporters waited outside the courtroom to hear the outcome of the trial.*
  power influence; right. *The courts have the power to award custody of a child to either parent in a divorce case.*
  result something that is caused. *The result of the fight was a bloody nose.*
  antonym: cause

elegant *adj.* 1. characterized by or exhibiting either (a) refinement and grace in movement, appearance, or manners, or (b) tasteful richness in form, decoration, or presentation. *Ann gave an elegant dinner for the visiting politician and his entourage.* 2. excellent.
  graceful pleasing in movement, form, or proportion. *Angela is a graceful ballet dancer.*
  stylish fashionable. *Henry's new apartment was modern and very stylish.*
  antonyms: crude, ugly, tasteless

eliminate *v.* 1. to get rid of; remove. 2.a. to leave out or omit from consideration; reject. 2.b. to remove from consideration by defeating, as in a contest. *His opponent tried to eliminate Tony in the first heat.*
  exclude to leave out. *The tougher requirements will exclude any student who has not had a recent physical.*
  expel to drive out. *Blowing air into the tube will expel the liquid trapped inside.*
  omit to leave out. *The list of cast members did mistakenly omit Anna's name.*
  reject to refuse; throw out. *Levon decided to reject the possibility that he might not be chosen for the school play.*
  remove to get rid of. *A careful inspection will remove all suspicion from the employee.*
  antonyms: include, accept

embarrass *v.* 1. to cause to feel self-conscious or ill at ease; disconcert. *She turned bright red at his question when he meant to embarrass her.* 2.a. to beset with difficulties. 2.b. to hinder; impede. 3. to complicate.
  annoy to disturb; trouble. *Don't annoy your classmates, please.*
  confuse to mix up; bewilder. *Driving on the left side of the road in England did confuse me.*
  trouble to disturb. *Jim's reckless behavior does trouble his sister.*
  vex to trouble; annoy. *Sean did not mean to vex the professor with his questions.*
  antonyms: comfort, console

encourage *v.* 1. to inspire with hope, courage, or confidence; hearten. 2. to give support to; foster. 3. to stimulate. *My mother always encourages me to do the best I can in everything I try.*
  promote to contribute to; further. *Proper food, adequate sleep, and moderate exercise will promote good health.*
  support to favor; lend strength. *Alice supports Ben's decision to try out for the soccer team.*

urge to push forward. *Jamie urged me to run for class president.*
antonyms: discourage, daunt, depress, intimidate, dissuade, prevent, obstruct

endurance *n.* the act, quality, or power of withstanding hardship or stress. *Pioneers must have great endurance to begin new lives in forbidding places.*
perseverance determination to achieve a purpose. *Dana won a scholarship with hard work and perseverance.*
persistence refusal to give up. *Alex has the persistence of a bull terrier.*
stamina strength to endure. *Athletes need physical stamina to last through a game.*
tenacity stubbornness. *Owen finished the marathon on tenacity alone.*
antonyms: weakness, cowardice

examination *n.* the act of inspecting, observing, or analyzing, or the state of being inspected, observed, or analyzed. *After careful examination of the store, the police officer concluded that two people were involved in the robbery.*
inquiry search for information. *Shortly after beginning the inquiry, the police arrested two possible suspects in the Riverside district.*
inspection careful examination. *A close inspection revealed that the robbers had worn gloves.*
investigation detailed search or examination. *Several detectives were assigned to the robbery investigation.*
scrutiny close study or examination. *All store employees were kept under close scrutiny after a series of robberies.*

exclusive *adj.* not divided or shared with others. *The club was very exclusive; members had to be voted in by other members.*
single for only one. *That victory was the single most important event in her life so far.*
sole for only one person or group. *The grant gave him the sole right to mine the land for all ores.*
antonyms: general, common

excuse *v.* 1.a. to apologize for. 1.b. to seek to remove the blame from. 2.a. to grant pardon to; forgive. *The manager was able to excuse the worker's tardiness the first time.* 2.b. to make allowances for; overlook. See **forgive.**

exhibition *n.* a display for the public, as of art objects, industrial achievements, or agricultural products. *The exhibition at the museum featured paintings by Monet.* See **demonstration.**

expertise *n.* 1. expert advice or opinion. 2. specialized knowledge or skill. *We need his expertise in furniture restoration.*
knowledge familiarity with a subject. *Her knowledge of horticulture helped make her garden a showplace.*
skill expertness. *It takes skill to be able to paint a portrait.*
specialty special profession, trade, field, etc. *Dwayne's specialty is sixteenth-century English poetry.*
technique special method or system. *Jennie's technique for separating eggs is different from mine.*

facsimile *n.* an exact copy or reproduction, as of a document. *The letter was a good facsimile of the original.* See **copies.**

faculty *n.* 1. a special ability or skill. *Jimmy has an amazing faculty for remembering names and faces.* 2. a body of teachers as distinguished from their students.
ability skill at doing something. *She has a remarkable ability to juggle five tasks at once.*
aptitude talent; ability. *My mother thinks I have an aptitude for music because I can hum tunes after I hear them once.*
capacity ability. *That teacher encourages her students' capacity for hard work.*
competence ability. *I have always envied my brother's competence in math.*
knack special skill. *Mia has a knack for making friends easily.*
skill ability to do something. *It takes skill to wrap a present the way she does.*
talent special ability. *Juan has a talent for training horses.*
antonyms: inability, incapacity, ineptness, weakness, incompetence

far-fetched *adj.* strained or improbable. *The idea the stone could be turned into gold was a little far-fetched.*
bizarre odd or fantastic. *Elly's costume was a bizarre combination of Little Red Riding Hood and a rock star.*
curious odd or strange. *You can sometimes find very curious things at a garage sale.*
strange odd or unusual. *Animals will often exhibit strange behavior before an earthquake occurs.*
unusual rare. *It is unusual for Mr. Simon to be seen without a tie.*

antonyms: typical, normal, everyday, ordinary, average, natural

fatigue *n.* 1. physical or mental weariness resulting from exertion. *Fatigue made it difficult for her to concentrate on the test.* 2. tiring effort or activity; labor.

> **exhaustion** extreme fatigue. *Many of the runners had to drop out of the marathon because of exhaustion.*
>
> **lassitude** weariness. *The disease is characterized by weight loss and lassitude.*
>
> **tiredness** weariness. *Monica's tiredness finally wore off after many relaxing days at the cottage.*
>
> **weariness** tiredness. *Weariness and hunger eventually drove the children into the house.*
>
> antonyms: energy, vigor, enthusiasm

ferocious *adj.* 1. extremely savage; fierce. 2. marked by unrelenting intensity; extreme. *On Friday the Northeast was crippled by a ferocious blizzard.*

> **cruel** causing pain. *It is cruel to laugh at someone in pain.*
>
> **fierce** savage; wild. *The fierce bear was protecting her cubs.*
>
> **savage** fierce; cruel. *A mistreated dog can become savage.*
>
> **violent** forceful; severe. *The battle was brief but violent.*
>
> **wild** savage. *It was rumored that a wild man lived in the mountain forest.*
>
> antonyms: tame, calm, mild

fluent *adj.* 1. having facility in the use of language. *Melanie is fluent in three languages.* 2.a. flowing effortlessly; polished. 2.b. flowing smoothly; graceful.

> **flowing** moving smoothly. *Her flowing poetry is much admired by the students in her classes.*
>
> **glib** speaking too smoothly. *Abby offered a glib reason for her tardiness.*
>
> **polished** smooth; refined. *After weeks of practice, his speaking style had become easier and more polished.*
>
> **smooth** even; polished. *The experienced politician made a smooth transition from the difficult issue to a safer one.*
>
> **voluble** talkative. *He is known as a voluble speaker who can easily talk for an hour.*
>
> antonyms: terse, silent, curt

forgive *v.* to excuse for a fault or offense; pardon. *I hope Cathy will forgive me for forgetting her birthday.*

> **absolve** to declare free from blame. *The council might absolve him of any connection with the embezzlement.*
>
> **acquit** to declare not guilty. *The jury can acquit the defendant.*
>
> **excuse** to pardon; forgive. *If you will excuse me, I have to leave to make a telephone call.*
>
> **pardon** to make allowance for. *Grandmother will certainly pardon your behavior if you apologize to her.*
>
> antonyms: blame, condemn, censure

gracious *adj.* 1. characterized by kindness and warm courtesy. *The gracious hostess made sure that her guests enjoyed the dinner.* 2. characterized by charm and beauty; graceful. 3. characterized by elegance and good taste. See **elegant.**

> **benevolent** kind; charitable. *It was a benevolent gesture to give money to the children's home.*
>
> **benign** kind; gracious. *Her benign face encouraged people to trust her.*
>
> **charming** pleasing; attractive. *They thought the small boys were charming.*
>
> **courteous** thoughtful; polite. *The courteous girl gave her seat on the bus to the blind man.*
>
> **graceful** pleasing. *She rejected the invitation in a graceful manner.*
>
> **kind** friendly; gentle. *He was kind to the new child in the class.*
>
> antonyms: ungracious, unkind, discourteous, impolite, rude

guarantee *v.* 1. to assume responsibility for the debt, default, or miscarriage of. 2. to assume responsibility for the quality or execution of. 3. to give a guarantee for. *The moving company guaranteed that the furniture would be delivered Friday.*

> **ensure** to make sure or certain. *Elena knew her grades and test scores would ensure her a place at the university.*
>
> **pledge** to give one's word; promise. *Dan and Tom each pledge to give up smoking for a month.*
>
> **promise** to give one's word; pledge. *His parents promise to take him to a baseball game for his birthday.*
>
> **secure** to make sure or certain. *The team members did everything they could to secure a victory.*
>
> **warrant** to promise. *The building contractor warrants that construction of all his buildings will last for fifty years.*

hesitate *v.* 1.a. to be slow to act, speak, or decide. 1.b. to pause in uncertainty; waiver. 2. to be reluctant. *He seemed to hesitate to ask for help.*
  delay to postpone; stop for a while. *Snow will delay the flight to Chicago for five hours.*
  falter to waver; hesitate. *Despite the long years of training, Carmen's resolution to become a doctor never faltered.*
  fluctuate to vary; waver. *Prices on the stock market fluctuate with every little rumor.*
  pause to stop for a while. *Debbie paused in her speech and looked straight at the audience for a moment.*
  vacillate to move one way and then another. *During the campaign the politician seemed to vacillate on the major issues.*
  waver to be uncertain or undecided. *Jane and I waver between voting "No" and voting "Yes" on the referendum.*
  antonyms: resolve, determine, decide, continue

hindrance *n.* 1. the act or condition of being hampered or obstructed. 2. one that hinders; impediment. *Her younger sister was a hindrance to our secret meeting.*
  hitch obstacle. *The dinner party proceeded without a hitch.*
  impediment obstacle. *They refused to allow any impediment to block their marriage.*
  obstacle something in the way. *She overcame every obstacle on her way to recovery from the operation.*
  obstruction something in the way. *Receiving permission is not an obstruction to our plan to go fishing.*
  antonyms: help, aid, support

honesty *n.* 1. the quality or condition of being honest; integrity. 2. truthfulness; sincerity. *Mr. Parker is known for his honesty in dealing with his customers.*
  candor frankness in giving views or opinions. *Jason made his statement with more candor than his mother was comfortable with.*
  frankness openness in giving thoughts. *Tanya said with great frankness that she did not like the new outfits.*
  integrity honesty; sincerity; uprightness. *Integrity is an important quality in a politician or anyone else in public life.*

  sincerity honesty; freedom from deceit. *Thank-you notes should be written with as much sincerity as possible.*
  truthfulness honesty, sincerity. *The story of George Washington and the cherry tree tells about the value of truthfulness.*
  antonyms: dishonesty, insincerity

hustle *v.* 1. to jostle or shove roughly. 2. informal. to move hurriedly or urgently. 3. informal. to urge forward; hurry along. *Streams of shoppers tried to hustle through the department store aisles.*
  bustle to hurry busily. *People often bustle about in preparation for a party.*
  hasten to speed; hurry. *The extra hours in the library certainly can hasten the completion of my report.*
  hurry to move too quickly. *We must hurry or we will miss the bus!*
  scramble to move hurriedly. *People had to scramble to get places in line.*
  scurry to hurry. *The children had to scurry to put their toys away before dinner.*
  scuttle to run; scurry. *We watched the crab scuttle across the sand and into the grass.*

idle *adj.* 1.a. not in use. 1.b. without a job; unemployed. 2. lazy; shiftless. *Susan likes to stay really busy; she is rarely idle.*
  indolent not liking to work. *He led an indolent life, always expecting others to do the work.*
  lazy not active. *Tom was too lazy to mow the lawn.*
  sluggish moving slowly. *The river was sluggish on the warm summer day.*
  antonyms: active, busy, energetic, industrious

immediately *adv.* without delay. *When the call came, she left immediately.*
  directly at once. *Be sure to come home directly after the game.*
  instantly at once. *He knew instantly that he had come to visit at a bad time.*

immense *adj.* 1. extremely large; huge. 2. immeasurably vast; boundless. *The universe is so immense that its size is impossible for us to comprehend.*
  extensive large; far-reaching. *He was promised extensive powers in the new government in return for his contribution.*
  great large; big. *A great mountain range stretched for many miles.*

huge large; very big. *The national debt is a huge amount of money.*

vast great; immense. *Millions of years ago, vast oceans covered much of what is now land.*
antonyms: small, tiny, minute

impartial *adj.* not partial or biased; unprejudiced. *My mother was impartial in dealing with my brother and me.*

  fair just; honest. *Amy got more than her fair share of the apple.*

  just right; fair. *Making us each pay half the cost was a just decision.*

  unbiased fair; not prejudiced. *There is no such thing as an unbiased opinion.*

  unprejudiced without prejudice; fair. *It is important for a judge to be unprejudiced.*

improve *v.* to advance to a better state or quality; make better. *Dan knows that he needs to improve his reading skills.*

  progress to develop; move ahead. *A baby will progress from crawling to walking.*

  reform to make better. *Dorothea Dix worked to reform the prison system in the nineteenth century.*
antonyms: ruin, deteriorate, decline, regress

incredible *adj.* too implausible to be believed; unbelievable. *The book told the incredible story of a man who survived for forty-five days in the desert.* See **remarkable.**

indicate *v.* 1. to demonstrate or point out. *He drew a line on the map to indicate a route.* 2. to state or express briefly.

  demonstrate to show or prove. *Can you demonstrate the accuracy of your pitching?*

  signify to mean or denote. *What does this dotted line on the map signify?*

insist *v.* to be firm in a demand or course; refuse to yield. *Cesar tried to insist that he was not the one who left the windows open.* See **compel.**

inspect *v.* to examine carefully and critically, especially for flaws. *I need to inspect the new car thoroughly.*

  examine to look at carefully. *The collector needed to examine the stamp with a magnifying glass.*

  investigate to examine; search. *The insurance company tried to investigate the cause of the fire.*

  scrutinize to examine carefully. *It made me uncomfortable to have so many people scrutinize my work.*

instantly *adv.* at once; immediately. *Casey instantly realized that she had said the wrong thing.* See **immediately.**

interrupt *v.* 1. to break the continuity or uniformity of. 2. to hinder or stop by breaking in upon. *Please do not interrupt me when I am talking on the telephone.*

  cease to stop. *The laughter will cease the minute the lights go out.*

  discontinue to put a stop to; give up. *They found it necessary to discontinue that line of clothing.*

  intrude to force in. *Why does Amy intrude on people's private conversations?*

  suspend to stop for a while. *It was necessary for workers to suspend traffic on the bridge while they cleared the wreckage from the accident.*
antonym: continue

jostle *v.* 1. to come in contact or collide. 2. to make one's way by pushing or elbowing. *We tried to jostle through the crowd in the stadium.* 3. to vie for an advantage or position.

  collide to crash together. *We saw the two cars collide at the busy intersection.*

  crowd to push; shove. *Excited fans will crowd past the guards onto the field.*

  elbow to move through by pushing. *The running back elbowed his way through the defensive line to make a touchdown.*

  push to move forward forcefully. *He needed to push his way to the front of the line.*

  shove to push roughly. *The big boy might shove the little children out of his way.*

knoll *n.* a small rounded hill or mound; hillock. *The house was built on the top of the knoll.*

  dune mound of sand. *The children chased each other up and down the dune.*

  hill raised portion of earth. *The old car had a hard time making it up the hill.*

  hillock little hill. *He was completely winded, even though he had only climbed a hillock.*

  mound small hill. *The pitcher returned to the mound for the final inning.*

L

league *n.* 1. an association of states, organizations, or individuals for common action; alliance. 2. an association of sports teams or clubs that compete chiefly among themselves. 3. a class of competition. *Harry is a good golfer, but he is not in the same league as the professionals.*
> **alliance** a joining together of people, groups, or nations for some purpose. *In World War II the United States was part of an alliance with western European nations against Germany and Italy.*
> **association** group of people joined together for some purpose. *The bankers' association offers scholarships for qualified students.*
> **coalition** alliance for a special purpose. *The different political parties in the country formed a coalition because no one party commanded a majority of the votes.*
> **compact** agreement. *The compact between the two nations ended the twenty-year war.*
> **confederation** a joining together in an alliance. *The confederation of the colonies was necessary to ensure their protection against larger nations.*
> **covenant** agreement between people or groups. *The temperance groups urged people to sign covenants to stop drinking.*
> **organization** group of people united for a purpose. *Kathleen belongs to several social organizations in her neighborhood.*
> **union** group united for a special purpose. *The environmental groups proposed a union to combine their forces.*

likable *adj.* pleasing; attractive. *She is one of the most likable girls in school.*
> **agreeable** pleasing. *His agreeable manners make him a popular guest at parties.*
> **attractive** inspiring liking; pleasing. *He made me a very attractive job offer.*
> **congenial** agreeable. *The visit was more congenial than she thought it would be.*
> **pleasing** pleasant. *Tad has a pleasing personality; everyone likes him.*
> **popular** liked by many people. *Angela was voted the most popular girl in her class.*
> antonyms: unpopular, disliked, disagreeable, obnoxious

M

magnificent *adj.* 1. splendid in appearance; grand. *The king lived in a magnificent palace.* 2. outstanding of its kind; superlative.
> **brilliant** splendid. *He was dazzled by the brilliant gleam of the jewels.*
> **excellent** superior; better than others. *He was awarded a grant for his excellent work in biochemistry.*
> **exquisite** lovely. *The flower arrangements on the tables were exquisite.*
> **gorgeous** splendid. *The shop was filled with gorgeous dresses.*
> **grand** beautiful in appearance; high in quality. *Dora felt very shy when she saw the grand surroundings.*
> **imposing** impressive due to size or appearance. *At six feet, six inches and 280 pounds, the governor was an imposing figure.*
> **impressive** able to have an effect on the mind and feelings. *The world-renowned doctor delivered an impressive speech.*
> **outstanding** important; beyond others. *She was offered several scholarships because of her outstanding student academic record.*
> **splendid** grand. *Cinderella was invited to a splendid ball at the palace.*
> **superb** grand; first-rate. *The production of the play was really superb.*
> **superior** excellent; better than others. *Eddie makes a superior apple pie.*
> **superlative** above others; supreme. *The Book of Kells is a superlative example of illuminated manuscript.*
> antonyms: poor, sordid, squalid, ugly, dull, plain, insignificant, common, inferior

magnify *v.* 1. to make greater in size; to enlarge. 2. to cause to appear greater or seem more important; exaggerate. 3. to increase the apparent size of, especially by means of a lens. *The scientist used the microscope to magnify the bacterium.*
> **amplify** to enlarge; expand. *The city editor told the reporter to amplify the important points in his story on the mayoral campaign.*
> **augment** to make larger in size or number. *She will augment her education classes by taking two for no credit.*
> **enlarge** to make larger in size. *They tried to enlarge the photograph to make it easier to see the faces of the criminals.*

exaggerate to make something more than it is. *He did exaggerate when he said he traveled four thousand miles a week!*

glorify to make something more wonderful than it is. *Sheila tends to glorify all dogs.*

increase to make larger in number or power. *The profits may increase twofold in the next two years.*

overstate to exaggerate. *I think he overstated his ability to climb sheer rock walls.*
antonyms: diminish, decrease, shrink, downplay, understate

manage *v.* 1. to direct or administer (a business, for example). 2. to contrive or arrange. *He did manage to get an invitation to the exclusive party.*

administer to direct. *Both teachers were needed to administer the test this morning.*

arrange to plan. *How did you arrange to get two tickets on such short notice?*

conduct to direct. *They conduct all of their business by telephone.*

contrive to plot; scheme. *Elly contrived to get the seat next to the guest of honor.*

control to direct. *Shawn and Mike control the company's purchasing.*

devise to plot; scheme. *He must devise a way to make the fake jewels look like real ones.*

direct to guide; control. *The supervisor will direct the activities of the department.*

handle to direct. *Mr. Gomez will handle the introduction of a new computer system.*

plot to plan. *Chris had to plot how she would get into the hotel unseen.*

scheme to plot; plan. *They always scheme to get what they want without having to work for it.*
antonyms: mismanage, disarrange

menagerie *n.* 1. a collection of live wild animals on exhibition. 2. the enclosure in which wild animals are kept. *The roadside menagerie featured a coyote, a bear, a rattlesnake, and a prairie dog.*

circus traveling show of people and animals. *Al thought it would be exciting to be a clown in the circus.*

collection group of things belonging together. *The zoo has an outstanding collection of primates.*

zoo place where animals are kept. *In zoos today vanishing species of animals are preserved.*

miniature *adj.* on a small or greatly reduced scale. *My mother collects miniature furniture for her dollhouse.*

diminutive very small. *The gymnast was diminutive next to the football player.*

minute very small. *Microorganisms are so minute that they can be seen only through a microscope or other magnifier.*

small little; not big. *A toy poodle is a small dog.*

tiny very small. *A Yorkshire terrier is a tiny dog.*

wee very small. *My grandfather likes to tell stories of the days when he was a wee lad in Ireland.*

mistake *n.* 1. an error or fault. 2. a misconception or misunderstanding. *I made a wrong turn by mistake.*

blunder foolish mistake. *I made a second blunder when I mispronounced her last name.*

error incorrect action. *I did not have time to correct the error I made on my math test.*

miscalculation wrong estimate. *Because of my miscalculation, we missed the airplane.*

mix-up *n.* state of confusion; muddle. *Connie's inability to remember names and faces caused many mix-ups.*

chaos great disorder and confusion. *The early morning thunderstorm caused chaos on the expressways.*

mess difficulty. *He is known for his ability to clean up other people's messes.*

mistake misunderstanding; error. *I made a lot of mistakes in my speech because I was nervous.*

problem difficulty; things to be worked out. *Despite problems with the car, the weather, and the hotels, we enjoyed our trip to New York.*

monotonous *adj.* 1. sounded or spoken in an unvarying tone. 2. repetitiously dull or lacking in variety. *The landscape was a monotonous brown.*

dull tiresome; boring. *It was hard to stay awake through the dull movie.*

humdrum dull. *He thought he had a humdrum existence as a grocer.*

tedious long; tiring. *Packing and unpacking boxes is a tedious chore.*

tiresome tiring; boring. *Long car trips are often tiresome.*

uniform not varying. *All the clothes were a uniform color.*

unvaried all alike. *She longed to escape the round of unvaried tasks.*
antonyms: interesting, amusing, diverting

motivate *v.* to provide with an incentive or motive; impel. *His mother used a special treat to motivate Tim to finish his assignment.* See **compel.**

impel to cause to act. *The approaching deadline will impel her to work late.*

incite to urge on. *He was accused of trying to incite a riot at the rally.*

induce to lead on; persuade. *They used an ad to induce him to try a new kind of shampoo.*

influence to use power to urge on. *He tried to influence the judge's decision in the trial.*

spur to urge on. *Opposition only served to spur the movement to greater efforts.*

stimulate to spur on. *Preschools are designed to help stimulate a child's development.*

mutual *adj.* 1. having the same relationship to the other. 2. directed and received in equal amount. 3. possessed in common. *Our mutual interests include baseball and fishing.*

common joint; held by all alike. *It is a common belief that colds can be caused by cold weather.*

interchangeable able to be exchanged. *The drill I gave Dad for his birthday has interchangeable bits.*

reciprocal on both sides. *The two countries have had a reciprocal trade agreement since 1855.*

antonyms: single, singular

noble *adj.* 1. superior in nature or character; exalted. 2. grand and stately in appearance; majestic. *Many western travelers have been inspired by the noble mountain peaks of the Rockies.*

august majestic. *The judge seemed to her a wise and august personage.*

exalted raised high in power, honor, or rank. *The followers paid homage to their exalted leader.*

lofty grand. *He often expresses lofty sentiments in his poetry.*

majestic grand; stately. *She strolled into the room with a majestic air.*

stately dignified; grand. *England has many beautiful, stately mansions.*

sublime raised high in feeling, thought, or language. *Calvin was awestruck when he first saw the sublime coastal landscape.*

notify *v.* to give notice to; inform. *The lawyer had to notify his client that the trial was set to begin December 12.* See **advise.**

acquaint to let know. *She asked if someone could show her around and acquaint her with the building's layout.*

advise to inform. *Police officers are required to advise people of their rights.*

apprise to let know. *The tax accountant must apprise his clients of changes in the tax laws that would affect their returns.*

inform to tell. *I intended to inform the clerk that her rude behavior would be reported to the manager at once.*

notion *n.* 1. a belief; opinion. 2. a fanciful impulse; whim. *I got this notion that I would learn to play the harmonica.*

concept notion; idea. *The football coach discussed the concept of fair play.*

idea belief; opinion. *I had a great idea for a costume for the party.*

theory opinion; idea. *David has a theory about the best way to train a dog.*

thought what one thinks. *The essay is supposed to reflect your thoughts on the school elections.*

occurrence *n.* 1. an act or instance of occurring or happening. 2. something that takes place; incident. *The accident at that intersection was the fifth such occurrence this year.*

affair happening. *His graduation party was a wild affair.*

appearance a coming into sight. *The appearance of too many white blood cells in the blood sample alarmed the doctor.*

circumstance event; fact. *Getting the first place in line was a fortunate circumstance.*

event happening. *The opening of the Berlin Wall was a major historical event.*

incident event; happening. *She dismissed the fall as a minor incident.*

omit *v.* to fail to include; leave out. *The newspaper inadvertently omitted the telephone number in our classified ad.* See **eliminate.**

organization *n.* 1. the state or manner of being put together into an orderly, functional, structured whole. *She worked a long time on the organization of the office.* 2. a number of persons or groups having specific responsibilities and united for a particular purpose. See **league.**

arrangement ordered parts. *The arrangement of the furniture was intended to make the room wheelchair-accessible.*

design arrangement of color and details. *The design on the tablecloth was burgundy and blue paisley.*

pattern arrangement; design. *The child used a pencil to connect the pattern of dots.*

plan design; scheme. *We made a plan for the vegetable garden.*

scheme coordinated things or parts. *I wanted the color scheme for the bedroom to be blue and white.*

structure arrangement of parts. *The plot provides the structure of the story.*

system parts forming a whole. *The lightning knocked out our telephone system.*

outrageous *adj.* 1. being an outrage; grossly offensive. 2. extravagant; immoderate; extreme. *Steven's behavior at the party was outrageous.*

disgraceful bringing shame. *The child's conduct at the day camp was simply disgraceful, according to the counselor.*

excessive too much. *The management took steps to curb the excessive amount of talking in the theater.*

extravagant going beyond reasonable limits. *The actress is given to making extravagant gestures and movements.*

shameful bringing disgrace. *Aunt Hetty thought it was shameful that Uncle Dick was seen playing billiards in town.*

shocking very offensive. *The official showed a shocking lack of concern for the victims of the fire.*

antonyms: modest, sober, sedate, moderate, reasonable

particular *adj.* 1. separate and distinct from others; specific. 2. worthy of note; exceptional. *That discovery was of particular importance because it advanced cancer research.*

distinct definite. *Candace got the distinct impression that Larry was avoiding her.*

extraordinary unusual. *The Voyager missions provided extraordinary pictures of Jupiter and Saturn.*

individual separate; particular. *Each artist expresses an individual vision in his or her work.*

noteworthy remarkable. *Abby's dedication to her job is noteworthy.*

special singular; exceptional. *Jack's special hen laid golden eggs.*

specific particular; definite. *I had no specific reason for wanting to go there.*

unusual uncommon; rare. *It is unusual to see a canary this far north.*

antonyms: general, common, ordinary

peculiar *adj.* 1. unusual or eccentric; odd. *The man muttered to himself and exhibited other peculiar behavior.* 2.a. exclusive; unique. 2.b. belonging distinctively or primarily to one person, group, or kind.

bizarre odd. *Are you going to work in that bizarre outfit?*

eccentric odd. *Great-aunt Agatha liked to be thought of as eccentric; she said it meant she was interesting.*

odd strange. *What seems odd to one person may seem perfectly normal to another person.*

strange odd. *It seems strange to me that Allison left without saying good-bye.*

uncommon unusual. *A comet streaking through the sky is an uncommon sight.*

antonyms: usual, common, ordinary

picturesque *adj.* 1. of or suggesting a picture. 2. strikingly expressive or vivid. *Charles Dickens is noted for the picturesque language he used to describe Victorian London.*

colorful exciting; interesting. *Years at sea had made him a colorful character.*

graphic picture-like; vivid. *His graphic description made the picture really come alive for me.*

interesting attention-holding. *The baby found the mobile very interesting.*

scenic having beautiful scenery. *Vermont is crisscrossed by scenic highways.*

striking attention-getting. *The scenery along Highway 1 is particularly striking.*

vivid lively; interesting. *The vivid tale enthralled the children.*

antonyms: uninteresting, dull

prefer *v.* to choose as more desirable; like better. *Barbara Ann likes baths; I prefer showers.*

choose to take one thing over another. *Which candidate did the voters choose?*

elect to choose; select. *I elected to wait until tomorrow to do the laundry.*

favor to approve; prefer. *Clay seemed to favor the Cortland apples over the Red Delicious apples.*

pick to choose; select. *Why did you pick that particular puppy?*

select to choose. *After trying on ten sweaters, Joe selected the navy blue one.*

antonyms: exclude, dislike

premium *n.* an unusual or high value. *My parents always put a premium on honesty.*

bonus something given in addition to what is expected. *The workers were given a bonus of $100.*

prize a reward won in competition. *Helen won first prize in the spelling bee.*

reward something given for special behavior or service. *Lee offered a $10 reward for information on the missing cat.*

presently *adv.* in a short time; soon. *Presently Dwayne will leave for school.* See **briefly.**

shortly in a short time. *Mr. Anderson will see you shortly.*

soon in a short time. *My father said that dinner would be ready soon.*

antonym: later

prior *adj.* preceding in time or order. *She turned down my invitation, saying she had a prior commitment.*

earlier before this time. *My earlier proposal was rejected.*

first coming before all others. *Anita took her first trip to Spain last summer.*

preceding coming before. *The preceding television program was sponsored by a national foundation.*

previous coming before. *He had seen that man on a previous occasion.*

privilege *n.* a special advantage, immunity, permission, right, or benefit granted to or enjoyed by an individual, class, or caste. *Mark always considered it a privilege to work for the senator.*

advantage something favorable or beneficial. *His height was an advantage in playing basketball.*

benefit advantage. *One of the benefits of this job is the opportunity to travel.*

franchise privilege or right granted to a particular person or company. *He was given the franchise to sell plastic doilies in the Midwest.*

immunity exemption from something. *The witness was offered immunity from prosecution if she would testify.*

permission consent to do something. *I had to have my parents' permission to go on the field trip.*

prerogative special right or privilege. *It is a person's prerogative to make up his or her own mind.*

right something that is due to a person. *A democracy guarantees certain rights to all its citizens.*

pursue *v.* 1. to follow in an effort to overtake or capture; chase. *The police had to pursue the car thief to the state line.* 2. to strive to gain or accomplish. 3. to proceed along the course of; follow.

chase to go after; to catch. *Every morning the cat would chase the squirrel around the backyard.*

follow to pursue. *The bears follow the fish up the river and catch them near the dam.*

hunt to look for. *Cheryl likes to hunt through every store in town for the perfect gift for her mother.*

search to look for. *I will search the whole house until I find my black glove.*

seek to look for. *Let's play a game; you hide and I will seek you.*

stalk to pursue carefully. *We watched the fox quietly and patiently stalk the field mouse.*

trace to follow; trail. *Computer records can be used to trace missing people.*

track to follow; trail. *Lee was able to track Henry to the record store at the mall.*

antonyms: avoid, desert, escape, retreat

questionable *adj.* 1. open to doubt or challenge; problematic. *Joey's choice of outfit was questionable at best.* 2. not yet determined or specified; uncertain.

debatable not decided. *Whether we will go on vacation this year is debatable.*

doubtful open to question; uncertain. *I was doubtful about Serena's ability to sing at such a large gathering.*

dubious uncertain. *Charlie has a dubious future as an artist.*

uncertain doubtful. *She was uncertain about whether they had met before.*

antonyms: certain, sure, positive

quick-witted *adj.* mentally alert and sharp; keen. *Sally is quick-witted in a crisis; she always knows what to do.*

bright quick-witted; clever. *Joe had the bright idea of gluing the lamp back together again.*

clever smart; intelligent. *The clever baby can put the puzzle pieces together.*

intelligent quick to learn and understand. *Apes are intelligent animals.*

antonyms: stupid, dumb, slow, dim-witted

reasonable *adj.* 1. capable of reasoning; rational. 2. not excessive or extreme; fair. *That particular store has very reasonable prices.*

logical able to reason. *Abby always plans her projects in a logical, step-by-step fashion.*

moderate not extreme. *David has a moderate lifestyle and lives well within his means.*

rational able to reason; sensible. *Was it the act of a rational human being to eat four pepperoni pizzas?*

sane normal; rational. *Off the football field, he behaves like a sane person.*

sensible having good sense. *The only sensible course was to apologize and leave as quickly as possible.*

antonyms: unreasonable, illogical, irrational, intolerable, unsound

remarkable *adj.* 1. worthy of notice. 2. extraordinary; uncommon. *Mary has a remarkable facility for learning foreign languages.*

extraordinary very unusual. *Donald's grandmother lived to the extraordinary age of 106.*

incredible unbelievable. *It seems incredible to me that she could do such a thing.*

notable important. *The annual charity ball is a notable event of the season.*

rare unusual. *An eclipse of the moon is a rare occurrence.*

uncommon unusual. *Chester is an uncommon cat; he can open and close doors.*

unusual not usual. *It is unusual for Annie to stay at work past five o'clock.*

antonyms: common, usual, ordinary

replica *n.* 1. a copy or reproduction of a work of art, especially one made by the original artist. 2. a copy or reproduction. *He was noted for his replicas of well-known sculptures.* See **copies.**

requirement *n.* 1. something that is required; necessity. 2. something obligatory; prerequisite. *A requirement of the course is a paper on an aspect of American foreign policy.*

claim something demanded. *After the accident several people filed claims with the insurance company.*

demand something claimed. *Tony's schedule of sports and activities puts many demands on his time and energy.*

necessity something wanted. *Qualified accountants were a necessity for the company.*

requisite something needed. *Love and attention are requisites for babies.*

resign *v.* 1. to submit (oneself) passively; accept as inevitable. 2. to give up (a position), especially by formal notification; quit. *Mr. Mores decided to resign from his job as a salesman to go back to school.*

abandon to give up completely. *Sheila had to abandon the attempt to haul the box upstairs by herself.*

abdicate to give up; resign. *A king may abdicate his throne.*

cede to give up. *The farmer had to cede his land to the state for a highway.*

forego to give up; do without. *I must forego butter and sour cream on my baked potato.*

quit to give up. *Jay quit his after-school job to join the chess club.*

relinquish to give up; let go. *I reluctantly relinquished my request for the last piece of pie.*

renounce to give up; do without. *Cynthia had to renounce her claim on the grand prize.*

submit to yield. *The king occasionally submitted to the wishes of his wife.*

surrender to give up; yield. *The knight was able to force his opponent to surrender.*

yield to give up. *We yield the right-of-way at this intersection.*

resist *v.* 1. to strive or work against; oppose actively. 2. to remain firm against the action or effect of; withstand. 3. to keep from giving in to or enjoying. *I had to resist the temptation to yell back at the rude cabdriver.*

assail to attack. *She tried to assail the speaker's claim that no one wanted the pollution laws enforced to their full extent.*

attack to begin fighting. *The politician began to attack her opponent's position on income tax increases.*

oppose to fight against. *The student council will oppose the plan to limit access to the gym after school hours.*

rebuff to reject. *He tried to rebuff the notion that he had done anything improper.*

refrain to hold back. *Sue decided to refrain from telling George that he was right.*

withstand to hold out against. *We feared the house might not withstand the fierce wind.*

respect *v.* 1. to feel or show deferential regard for; esteem. *My family has always respected my need for privacy.* 2. to relate or refer to; concern.

admire to think highly of. *Cecil admired her ability to remember the minute details of every contract.*

esteem to think highly of. *I esteem her opinion; she is often right.*

honor to think highly of; respect. *The professor's students honored her in a special farewell dinner.*

revere to honor; respect. *Native American cultures revere the land and its resources.*

venerate to revere; respect. *They venerated their ancestors and their homeland.*

antonyms: dislike, hate, loathe, abhor, detest

revolve *v.* 1. to orbit a central point. *Earth revolves around the sun.* 2. to turn on an axis; rotate.

circle to move in a ring. *The dog spied the cat and began to circle the tree.*

orbit to move in a path around a heavenly body. *There are dozens of satellites that orbit Earth.*

roll to turn over and over. *The dog rolled the ball back to the child.*

rotate to move in a circle. *When you turn the handle, the wheels rotate.*

spin to turn around. *If you twist it just right, the top will spin for five minutes.*

turn to rotate. *Every time the mobile turned, the baby smiled and giggled.*

rustic *adj.* 1. of, pertaining to, or typical of country life. *Built to look like a rustic barn, the house would have fit in better in the country.* 2. simple and unsophisticated.

country of the country. *Their country ways included being friendly to strangers and helpful to everyone.*

plain simple; uncomplicated. *The plain clapboard house could be clearly seen from miles away.*

rural in the country. *Many people prefer the quieter rural life.*

simple plain; natural. *They enjoyed the simple pleasures of farm life.*

unsophisticated simple; natural. *Some city people regard country life as unsophisticated.*

antonyms: urban, city, sophisticated

salary *n.* a fixed compensation for services, paid to a person on a regular basis. Dave receives a 5 percent increase in salary every year.

earnings money earned. *The government requires that you report your earnings.*

income money from work, investments, etc. *They could live very well on their combined incomes.*

pay money for work. *When she left the company to start her own, she had to take a cut in pay.*

wages money for work. *Angie receives the wages from her part-time job every Friday afternoon.*

souvenir *n.* something serving as a token of remembrance; memento. *Tess bought a picture made of seashells as a souvenir of her Florida trip.*

keepsake something kept in memory of the giver. *The gold flower charm was a keepsake from her friend Stacy.*

memento reminder; remembrance. *The shelves in Dana's room are filled with mementos of her travels.*

remembrance souvenir; keepsake. *The portrait in the hall was a remembrance from her grandmother's house.*

reminder something to help one remember. *He kept the smooth stone as a reminder of the river trip.*

spacious *adj.* 1. providing or having much space or room; extensive. 2. vast in range or scope. *The huge windows offer a spacious view of the surrounding mountains.*

ample roomy; large. *The day-care center is ample enough for one hundred children.*

capacious roomy; large. *Troy needs a capacious storage place for his collection of model trains.*

extensive large. *He planned an extensive addition to the house.*

huge very big. *The living room in the new house is huge.*

vast immense. *The city covers a vast amount of land.*

antonyms: crowded, cramped, small

spectacular *adj.* of the nature of a spectacle; sensational. *The view from the top of the tower is spectacular.* See **magnificent.**

stampede *v.* 1. to move in a headlong rush. 2. to act on impulse. *The storm caused the cattle to stampede to the river.*

flee to run away. *Amy wanted to flee, but her feet felt too heavy to move.*

frighten to drive away by scaring. *The big dog will frighten the cats away.*

panic to lose control through fear. *I always panic when I am in a small space.*

scare to frighten away. *The forest fire began to scare away the campers.*

stationary *adj.* 1.a. not moving. 1.b. not capable of being moved; fixed. *A building is a stationary object.* 2. unchanging.

inactive not active. *The broken leg kept him inactive all summer.*

motionless not moving. *The cat sat motionless, watching the birds on the patio.*

antonyms: active, energetic

strict *adj.* 1. precise; exact. 2. complete; absolute. 3. kept within narrow and specific limits. *Judge Dawson is known for his strict application of the law.* 4. imposing an exacting discipline.

accurate correct; exact. *The clock kept very accurate time.*

exact correct; accurate. *She was careful to take the exact amount of medicine.*

inflexible rigid; unyielding. *She tends to be inflexible on matters of money.*

precise correct; accurate. *The floor plan was drawn using precise measurements.*

rigid not changing. *Mr. Porteous is very rigid in his views on punctuality.*

severe stern; harsh. *We have had five severe winters in a row.*

stern firm; hard. *His stern face indicated that we were in terrible trouble.*

stiff not easily bent. *The man felt stiff and uncomfortable around children.*

unyielding not giving way. *Doris has an unyielding desire to become a dancer.*

antonyms: inexact, inaccurate, imprecise, flexible, yielding, compliant

substantial *adj.* 1. of, pertaining to, or having substance; material. 2. ample; sustaining. 3. considerable in importance, value, degree, amount, or extent. *He owes the IRS a substantial sum of money.*

actual existing; real. *As it turned out, the actual event was not as frightening as she had feared it would be.*

ample more than enough. *We have ample time to plan our next tour.*

considerable much; important. *I put a considerable amount of time and effort into my paper on children's literature.*

firm solid; hard. *Jeff stood firm against the pushing of the excited crowd.*

important having significance or value. *Getting a driver's license is an important event in a teenager's life.*

material physical. *The material world mattered to her more than the spiritual.*

real existing; actual. *The real reason they left is that they did not want to see him.*

significant important. *The visit was significant because it was the first time he had met his in-laws.*

sizable large. *Grandfather placed a sizable portion of turkey on my plate.*

solid firm; hard. *After the earthquake, the citizens could no longer depend on having solid ground under their feet.*

stable firm; steady. *Even with the extra weight on it, the platform remained stable.*

antonyms: insubstantial, immaterial, trivial, minor, insignificant, unstable, unsound, unimportant

sufficient *adj.* as much as is needed; enough; adequate. *The castaways had sufficient food to survive for several weeks on the island.*

adequate as much as is needed. *He was provided with adequate food and hotel accommodations.*

ample as much as is needed. *Five dollars is ample money for lunch.*

enough as much as is needed or wanted. *Does she have enough money with her to pay for the theater tickets?*

satisfactory adequate; good enough. *We agreed upon a satisfactory amount for a weekly allowance.*

antonyms: insufficient, inadequate

support *v.* 1. to bear the weight of, especially from below. 2. to hold in position so as to keep from falling, sinking, or slipping. *Denise struggled to support the ladder that Harold was climbing on.*

bear to hold up. *The roof could not bear the weight of that many men.*

sustain to hold up. *The bridge's towers help to sustain the weight of many vehicles.*

antonyms: drop, demolish, crush

surrender *v.* 1. to relinquish possession or control of to another because of demand or compulsion. 2. to give up in favor of another. 3. to give up or abandon. *After the opposing team got a fourth touchdown in the first quarter, we surrendered all hope of victory.* 4. to give oneself up, as to an enemy. See **resign.**

capitulate to surrender. *I will capitulate now only if you promise me a rematch next week.*

relinquish to give up. *Prince John was made to relinquish his claim to the crown.*

yield to give up. *He was forced to yield to the stronger wrestler.*

antonyms: win, defeat, conquer, vanquish, triumph, succeed

thieves *n.* people who steal. *The thieves left dozens of fingerprints in the house.*

bandits robbers or thieves, usually a group. *According to legend, Robin Hood and his men were bandits who lived in Sherwood Forest.*

burglars people who enter buildings to steal. *Dead bolts and alarm systems can help deter burglars.*

muggers people who attack and rob people. *Muggers will hesitate to attack several people traveling together.*

pickpockets people who steal from people's pockets. *In Oliver Twist, Fagin was the leader of a gang of pickpockets.*

robbers people who take things by force. *The police caught the robbers when they tried to sell the stolen merchandise.*

thoroughly *adv.* 1. exhaustively, completely. 2. painstakingly, accurately. 3. satisfactorily, completely. *After reading every book she could find on koalas, Sue was thoroughly familiar with the animal.*

carefully in an exacting way. *Zia dug around the roots of the plant carefully before transplanting it.*

completely entirely. *Jack was completely exhausted after working sixteen hours at his computer.*

entirely completely. *Whether we go on or turn back is entirely up to you.*

totally wholly; entirely. *The village was totally destroyed by the volcanic eruption.*

thoughtfulness *n.* regard for others; consideration. *She showed her thoughtfulness by sending cards to her friends on all kinds of occasions.* See **courtesy.**

tornado *n.* a rotating column of air usually accompanied by a funnel-shaped downward extension of a cumulonimbus cloud and having a vortex several hundred yards in diameter whirling destructively at speeds up to 300 miles per hour. *The tornado that hit our town last spring uprooted trees and overturned mobile homes.*

cyclone tornado. *In The Wizard of Oz, a cyclone picked up Dorothy's house and carried it to Oz.*

twister informal name for a tornado. *Ellen lives in a part of the country where twisters are very common.*

waterspout tornado occurring over a body of water. *The people on the boat stared in amazement at the huge waterspout twirling on the horizon.*

whirlwind windstorm in which the air whirls around violently. *The whirlwind picked up all the leaves and debris and pulled them up into the air.*

transmit *v.* to send from one person, thing, or place to another; convey. *It is easy to transmit a cold from one person to another.*

carry to take from one place to another. *She will carry the baby to the car.*

convey to carry from one place to another. *Trucks convey goods across the country.*

dispatch to send off for a reason. *The colonel will dispatch a messenger to carry important information to headquarters.*

forward to send on. *The post office will forward her letters to her new address.*

send to cause to go from one place to another. *If you misbehave once more, the principal may send you home.*

transfer to move from one place to another. *My mother got transferred every two years when I was growing up.*

transport to carry from one place to another. *Buses were used to transport the children to the summer camp.*

underestimate *v.* to make too low an estimate of the quantity, degree, or worth of. *Tom and Joe always underestimate the amount of time they need to spend studying for the math tests.*

belittle to make seem less. *I belittle my writing because it does not seem good enough to take seriously.*

depreciate to devalue; lessen. *An appliance begins to depreciate as soon as it leaves the store.*

underrate to put too low a value on. *I think the coaches underrate Ed's pitching ability.*

undervalue to put too low a value on. *People tend to undervalue the importance of fiber in their diet.*

unexpected *adj.* coming without warning; unforeseen. *The invitation to the grand ball was unexpected.*

abrupt sudden. *The conversation came to an abrupt halt when Joey mentioned that he had his pet snake with him.*

sudden happening without warning. *Anna was hit by a sudden gust of wind.*

surprising causing astonishment. *Why do you find it so surprising that I can play the piano without being able to read music?*

unanticipated not thought of beforehand. *Sharon is experiencing some unanticipated side effects from the chemotherapy.*

unforeseen not known beforehand. *The tremendous demand for tickets was unforeseen by the new theater owners.*
antonyms: expected, foreseen, anticipated, gradual

uninterested *adj.* 1. without an interest. *They were uninterested parties in the lawsuit.* 2. not paying attention.

inattentive paying no attention. *I must apologize for being inattentive during the council meeting.*

indifferent having no interest. *Jason loved the movie, but Jane was indifferent.*

unconcerned not interested. *He seemed unconcerned about his own safety.*
antonym: interested

unique *adj.* 1. being the only one of its kind; sole. 2. being without an equal or equivalent. *The study tour was a unique opportunity to see Russia.*

alone with nothing more. *Money alone cannot guarantee happiness.*

only sole. *Andy is an only child.*

peerless unequaled. *Dave's peerless performance on the court brought the spectators to their feet.*

singular only one. *The signing of the treaty was a singular event in the course of Western European history.*

sole one and only. *She was the sole support of her mother and her brothers.*

unequaled no equal. *The Great Barrier Reef is a place of unequaled beauty.*
antonyms: common, usual

unite *v.* 1. to bring together so as to form a whole. 2. to combine (people) in interest, attitude, or action. *The neighbors needed to unite to fight street crime.*

associate to connect. *I associate red hearts with Valentine's Day.*

blend to mix together completely. *Have you ever tried to blend oil and water?*

combine to join things together. *The teacher combines kindness with firmness in handling her class of preschoolers.*

compound to mix; combine. *The scientist tried to compound several elements in her most recent experiment.*

connect to join; link. *The diagram showed Part A connected to Part G.*

couple to join together. *Dad will couple the car and the trailer.*

fuse to blend. *The fire can fuse the coins into a single mass.*

incorporate to add or blend. *Remember to incorporate the new information in your weekly report.*

join to combine. *We should join forces with our neighbors to fight the zoning changes.*

link to join; connect. *He did not want his name linked with the plan.*
antonyms: separate, sever

urgent *adj.* 1. compelling immediate action; imperative. 2. conveying a sense of pressing importance. *The caller left an urgent message.*

immediate without delay. *The Red Cross can bring immediate aid to the victims of natural disasters.*

imperative necessary; urgent. *It is imperative that we find the missing key.*

insistent demanding attention. *The dog's insistent barking warned the family of uninvited guests.*

pressing needing immediate attention. *After the storm, our most pressing need was fresh batteries.*
antonyms: unimportant, insignificant, trivial

usually *adv.* 1. commonly or frequently encountered, experienced, observed, or used. 2. habitually or customarily; particularly. *The baby usually takes a nap every day at about two o'clock.*

commonly generally. *Children commonly start school at the age of five.*

frequently often. *I frequently use my lunch hour to run errands.*

generally most of the time. *Claudia is generally able to handle any kind of domestic problem.*

ordinarily generally. *Juan ordinarily attends computer classes on Saturday.*

regularly in a fixed manner; habitually. *Exercising regularly is an important part of a healthy lifestyle.*
antonyms: rarely, infrequently, seldom

vague *adj.* 1. not clearly expressed or outlined. *The vague instructions made it hard to know how to put the kit together.* 2. not thinking or expressing oneself clearly. *She was vague about her future plans.*

dim not distinct. *The lighting in the room was too dim for me to see her face clearly.*

indefinite not clear. *The precise date of the exam is indefinite.*

obscure not clear. *Tina found the meaning of the poem obscure.*

uncertain indefinite. *He sounded uncertain when Jan asked him what his plans for the summer were.*

unsure uncertain. *Leon is unsure of his future with the company.*

antonyms: clear, definite, specific

verify *v.* 1. to prove the truth of by the presentation of evidence or testimony; substantiate. 2. to determine or test the truth or accuracy of, as by comparison, investigation, or reference. *A good scientist will conduct numerous experiments to verify a hypothesis before publishing a new theory.*

prove to show to be right and true. *You will have to prove your theory.*

substantiate to establish by evidence. *The insurance agent had to see the damage to substantiate our claim.*

antonyms: disprove, refute, invalidate

versatile *adj.* 1. capable of doing many things competently. 2. having varied uses or serving many functions. *That versatile tool can be used as a hammer, a screwdriver, or a wrench.*

adroit having skill with the body or the mind. *No matter what the question, she was adroit in providing answers.*

all-around able to do many things. *Jean is a good all-around student; she handles all her subjects equally well.*

competent able. *She is a competent driver.*

dexterous having skill with the hands or the mind. *Maria is dexterous from years of playing the piano.*

diverse varied; different. *The people at the convention were a diverse group.*

diversified varied. *His diversified interests meant that he did not spend much time on any one activity.*

multifarious many, varied. *For multifarious reasons, she had to drop out of the play.*

skillful having skill. *He is a skillful electrician.*

sundry several; varied. *He finally finished the report after sundry excuses.*

well-known *adj.* widely known; familiar or famous. *J.P. Thatcher is well-known in literary circles.*

celebrated much talked about. *Joe was eager to get the autograph of the celebrated actress.*

famous noted; acclaimed. *Janice is famous for her apple pies.*

renowned famous. *The renowned pianist is playing a concert on Saturday night.*

antonyms: unknown, obscure, modest

witness *v.* 1. to be present at or have personal knowledge of. 2. to provide or serve as evidence of. 3. to testify to; bear witness. *Mrs. Garson witnessed the robbery that took place on First Street last Tuesday.*

notice to see or detect. *Kate noticed that the fish seemed to prefer the dried flakes.*

observe to see. *Matt could observe that the birds preferred the cracked corn.*

Index

A

accent mark, 65, 141. *See also* **stress mark**

adjectives, 36, 85, 90, 94, 96–100, 126, 127, 170, 204–209, 226, 232, 235

adjective suffixes, 56, 70–75, 96–101, 120, 121, 232

adverbs, 88, 89, 90–95, 120, 204–209, 235

advertisement, writing, 41

analogies, 16, 22, 28, 40, 54, 72, 116, 122, 130, 148, 160, 186, 192, 212

analyzing word parts, 21, 97

answer questions, 34

antonyms, 56, 97, 100, 147, 211, 214

argument (persuasive) writing
  editorial, 17, 241
  paragraph, 99, 111, 219
  persuasive essay, 165
  speech, 61

art and spelling. *See* **spelling across the curriculum**

assessment
  review, unit, 45–47, 83–85, 121–123, 159–161, 197–199, 235–237
  standardized test practice, 48–49, 86–87, 124–125, 162–163, 200–201, 238–239
  words for, 44, 82, 120, 158, 196, 234

B

base words, 70–75, 90–95, 170, 214. *See also* **word roots/ origins**

dictionary form, 97, 129
  identifying, 58, 64, 70, 108, 150, 170, 220, 226
  prefixes and, 42, 52–57, 82, 83, 134–139, 166–171
  suffixes and, 27, 52–57, 58–63, 64–69, 70–75, 82, 83, 84, 90–95, 96–101, 103, 108–113, 120, 121, 122, 150, 204–209, 220

biographical sketch, writing, 35, 207

C

categorizing words, 18, 27, 36, 62, 65, 77, 85, 103, 115, 129, 132, 191, 229, 237

closed compounds, 14, 32–37, 44, 46

closed syllables, 20, 44

comma, use, 51, 89, 127, 165, 203, 241

commands. *See* **imperative sentences**

commonly confused words, 178–183, 196, 198

compound words, 14–19, 32–37, 44, 46

consonants. *See also* **letters and sounds**
  digraphs, 30
  double consonants, 38–43, 44, 47, 108–113
  silent consonants, 76–81, 112
  special spellings,
    /ch/, 30
    /j/, 42, 74, 106, 150, 184
    /k/, 184
    /r/, 80
    /s/, 42, 74, 80, 150, 184
    /sh/, 30, 74, 106, 184

    /th/ (as in *they*), 106
    /z/, 74
    /zh/, 106, 184
  suffixes and, 90–95, 108–113
  syllable division, 20

context clues, 16, 22, 28, 34, 40, 45, 46, 54, 60, 66, 68, 72, 78, 92, 98, 104, 110, 116, 121, 130, 136, 142, 148, 154, 156, 168, 174, 180, 186, 192, 198, 212, 218, 224, 230

coordinating conjunctions, 164–165

cross-curricular activities. *See* **spelling across the curriculum**

D

descriptive writing
  observation report, 89
  paragraph, 143, 213, 225

dialogue, writing, 93

dictionary skills,
  accent mark, 65, 141
  entry word, 97, 103, 129, 167, 205
  etymology, 59, 91, 135, 147, 185, 223
  guide words, 167
  homographs, 24
  homophones, 179
  inflectional endings, 39, 129
  informal language, 115
  multiple-meaning words, 27, 191
  parts of speech, 21, 33, 97
  plural forms, 129
  pronunciation, 15, 65, 77, 103, 141, 208
  respellings, 15, 65, 77, 103, 141, 208
  run-on entries, 97, 205

slang, 115
stress mark, 65, 141
suffixes, 97
syllables, 15, 20, 26, 65
understanding meaning, 115, 191
digraphs
consonant digraphs, 30
drafting, 17, 23, 29, 35, 41, 51, 55, 61, 67, 73, 79, 89, 93, 99, 105, 111, 117, 127, 131, 137, 143, 149, 155, 165, 169, 175, 181, 187, 193, 203, 207, 213, 219, 225, 231, 241
dropping final e (when adding suffixes), 64–69, 70–75, 96–101, 120, 121

E

editing, 17, 23, 29, 35, 41, 51, 55, 61, 67, 73, 79, 89, 93, 99, 105, 111, 117, 127, 131, 137, 143, 149, 155, 165, 169, 175, 181, 187, 193, 203, 207, 213, 219, 225, 231, 241
editing checklist, 51, 89, 127, 165, 203, 241
editorial, writing, 17, 241
electronic resources/dictionary, 17, 23, 29, 35, 41, 51, 55, 61, 67, 73, 79, 89, 93, 99, 105, 111, 117, 127, 131, 137, 143, 149, 155, 165, 169, 175, 181, 187, 193, 203, 207, 213, 219, 225, 231, 241
e-mail, writing, 127
Netiquette, 127
endings. See inflectional endings; suffixes
eponyms, 140–145, 158, 160
etymology, 42, 59, 91, 135, 147, 185, 223
expository (informative/explanatory) writing
advertisement, 41

biographical sketch, 35, 207
e-mail, 127
letter, 137
news story, 23
outline, 175
paragraph, 29, 67, 169, 193, 231
summary, 203

F

fine arts and spelling. See spelling across the curriculum
folktale, writing, 73
foreign words/phrases, 114–119, 184–189
French, words from, 59, 184–189, 196, 198
frequently misspelled words, 102–107, 122, 146–151, 158, 160

G

genre. See argument writing; descriptive writing; informative/explanatory writing; narrative writing
grammar, usage, and mechanics
adjectives, 36, 90, 94, 96, 126, 127, 170, 204–209, 226, 232, 235
adverbs, 88, 89, 90–95, 120, 204–209, 235
conjunctions, 164, 165
nouns, 24, 39, 50, 59, 64, 65, 94, 126, 128–133, 159, 202, 203, 226, 232
parts of a sentence, 50–51
parts of speech, 21, 33, 97, 232
prepositions/prepositional phrases, 202, 203
pronouns, 50, 126, 202, 203, 208
subject-verb agreement, 240, 241
subject/predicate, 50–51
verbs, 24, 39, 50, 59, 64,

65, 94, 99, 226, 232, 240
Greek prefixes, 166–171
Greek roots, 59, 172–177, 196, 197

H

handwriting models, 244–245
high-frequency words, 246–248
homographs, 24
homophones, 178, 179
hyphenated compounds, 32–37, 44, 46

I

identifying misspelled words in context, 17, 23, 29, 35, 41, 51, 55, 61, 67, 73, 79, 89, 93, 99, 105, 111, 117, 127, 131, 137, 143, 149, 155, 165, 169, 175, 181, 187, 193, 203, 207, 213, 219, 225, 231, 241
inferences, 16, 22, 28, 34, 40, 54, 60, 66, 68, 72, 78, 83, 84, 91, 92, 98, 104, 110, 115, 116, 130, 142, 148, 154, 168, 173, 176, 180, 186, 192, 197, 198, 199, 206, 211, 217, 218, 224, 226, 230, 235
inflectional endings, 39, 70–75, 108–113, 189
informal language, 115
informative/explanatory (expository) writing
advertisement, 41
biographical sketch, 35, 207
e-mail, 127
letter, 137
news story, 23
outline, 175
paragraph, 29, 67, 169, 193, 231

J

journal. See Spelling Journal
journal entry, writing, 55

L

language arts and spelling. *See* **spelling across the curriculum**
Latin prefixes, 42, 134–139, 153, 158, 159, 166–171, 196, 197, 217, 222–227, 234, 236
Latin roots, 42, 59, 91, 135, 147, 152–157, 158, 161, 190–195, 196, 199, 216–221, 223, 228–233, 234, 236, 237
letters, writing, 137

M

making inferences, 16, 22, 28, 34, 40, 54, 60, 66, 68, 72, 78, 83, 84, 91, 92, 98, 104, 110, 115, 116, 130, 142, 148, 154, 168, 173, 176, 180, 186, 192, 197, 198, 199, 206, 211, 217, 218, 224, 226, 230, 235
math and spelling. *See* **spelling across the curriculum**
meaning, 15, 18, 21, 27, 33, 36, 39, 53, 56, 59, 65, 68, 71, 74, 77, 80, 84, 91, 94, 97, 100, 103, 106, 109, 115, 118, 121, 129, 132, 135, 141, 144, 153, 156, 167, 170, 173, 176, 179, 182, 185, 188, 191, 194, 197, 198, 205, 211, 214, 217, 220, 223, 226, 229, 232
mechanics. *See* **grammar, usage, and mechanics**
multiple-meaning words, 27
mystery, writing, 51, 187

N

narrative writing
dialogue, 93
folktale, 73
journal entry, 55
mystery, 51, 187
paragraph, 105, 117, 149, 181
passage, 155
short story, 131

tall tale, 79
Netiquette. *See* **e-mail message**
news story, writing, 23
noun suffixes, 56, 62, 64–69, 70–75
nouns, 24, 39, 50, 59, 64, 65, 94, 126, 128–133, 159, 202, 203, 226, 232

O

observation report, writing, 89
open compounds, 32–37, 44, 46
open syllables, 26, 44
oral and written language. *See* **answer questions; dictionary skills; phonics skills; proofreading; reading skills; writing skills**
outline, writing, 175

P

paragraphs
argument (persuasive), 99, 111, 219
descriptive, 143, 213, 225
informative/explanatory (expository), 29, 67, 169, 193, 231
narrative, 105, 117, 149, 181
parts of speech, 21, 33, 97, 232. *See also specific parts of speech*
passage, 155
patterns
spelling patterns,
consonants (*see* **consonants**)
double consonants, 38–43, 44, 47, 108–113
silent consonants, 76–81, 82, 85, 112
schwa sound, 114
in last syllable
/shəl/, 210–215, 234, 235

/shəs/, 210–215, 234, 235
silent letters
pronunciation and spelling, 76–81, 112
silent consonants, 76–81, 82, 85, 112
silent e and suffix, 58–63, 64–69, 70–75, 82, 83, 84, 90–95, 96–101, 120, 121
vowels
long vowels, 18, 26–31, 44, 46, 114
short vowels, 20–25, 44, 45
structural patterns
compound words, 14–19, 32–37, 44, 46
Greek roots, 172–177
Latin roots, 42, 190–195, 216–221, 228–233
plurals, 128-133, 158, 159
prefixes, 21, 42, 52–57, 82, 83, 134–139, 166–171, 222–227
suffixes, 52–57, 58–63, 64–69, 70–75, 82, 83, 90–95, 96–101, 108–113, 120, 121, 122, 204–209
personal spelling journal. *See* **Spelling Journal**
persuasive (argument) writing
editorial, 17, 241
paragraph, 99, 111, 219
persuasive essay, 165
speech, 61
phonics skills. *See also* **consonants; dictionary skills; sounds; vowels**
analyzing word parts, 21
digraphs
consonant digraphs, 30
using syllables, 102 (*see* **syllables**)
word building, 36

word structure, 103, 182 (*see* word structure)

plurals, 128–133, 158, 159

possessives, 132

predicate, 50, 89. *See also* simple predicate

prefixes
ad-, 42, 134–139, 158, 159, 217
base word and,
bi-, 166–171
com-, 42, 222–227
con-, 156
contra-, 217
de-, 156, 184
dis-, 57, 156
duo-, 166–171, 196–197
en-, 21
ex-, 21, 156, 184, 191, 217
extro-, 217
Greek, 166–171, 196, 197
im-, 21, 184
in-, 21, 97, 191
inter-, 191
intro-, 217
Latin, 134–139, 158, 159, 166–171, 196, 197, 217, 222–227, 234, 236
mono-, 166–171, 196–197
re-, 56, 156
trans-, 21, 191
un-, 57, 97
unus- (uni-), 166–171, 191, 196–197

prepositions/prepositional phrases, 202–203

prewriting, 17, 23, 29, 35, 41, 51, 55, 61, 67, 73, 79, 89, 93, 99, 105, 111, 117, 127, 131, 137, 143, 149, 155, 165, 169, 175, 181, 187, 193, 203, 207, 213, 219, 225, 231, 241

pronouns, 50, 126, 202, 203, 208

pronunciation
French words, 184–189
Spanish words, 118
spelling and, 15
suffixes and, 58, 108–113, 120, 122, 208
syllables and, 15, 103, 108–113

proofreading, 17, 23, 29, 35, 41, 51, 55, 61, 67, 73, 79, 89, 93, 99, 105, 111, 117, 127, 131, 137, 143, 149, 155, 165, 169, 175, 181, 187, 193, 203, 207, 213, 219, 225, 231, 241
marks for, 17, 23, 29, 35, 41, 51, 55, 61, 67, 73, 79, 89, 93, 99, 105, 111, 117, 127, 131, 137, 143, 149, 155, 165, 169, 175, 181, 187, 193, 203, 207, 213, 219, 225, 231, 241

publishing, 17, 23, 29, 35, 41, 51, 55, 61, 67, 73, 79, 89, 93, 99, 105, 111, 117, 127, 131, 137, 143, 149, 155, 165, 169, 175, 181, 187, 193, 203, 207, 213, 219, 225, 231, 241

punctuation. *See specific kinds of punctuation*

R

reading skills,
analogies, 16, 22, 28, 40, 54, 72, 116, 122, 130, 148, 160, 186, 192, 212
answer questions, 34
antonyms, 56, 97, 100, 147, 211, 214

categorizing words, 18, 27, 36, 62, 65, 77, 85, 103, 115, 129, 132, 191, 229, 237

complete the sentence/ paragraph, (*see also* context clues)

context clues, 16, 22, 28, 34, 40, 45, 46, 54, 60, 66, 68, 72, 78, 92, 98, 104, 110, 116, 121, 130, 136, 142, 148, 154, 156, 168, 174, 180, 186, 192, 198, 212, 218, 224, 230

making inferences, 16, 22, 28, 34, 40, 54, 60, 66, 68, 72, 78, 83, 84, 91, 92, 98, 104, 110, 115, 116, 130, 142, 148, 154, 168, 173, 176, 180, 186, 192, 197, 198, 199, 206, 211, 217, 218, 224, 226, 230, 235

synonyms, 21, 22, 27, 28, 33, 39, 40, 53, 66, 71, 91, 94, 97, 100, 106, 109, 136, 138, 147, 153, 161, 173, 174, 185, 205, 206, 211, 214, 217, 220, 229

word meaning, 15, 18, 21, 27, 28, 33, 36, 39, 53, 56, 59, 65, 68, 71, 74, 77, 80, 84, 91, 94, 97, 100, 103, 106, 109, 115, 118, 121, 129, 132, 135, 141, 144, 153, 156, 167, 170, 173, 176, 179, 182, 185, 188, 191, 194, 197, 198, 205, 211, 214, 217, 220, 223, 226, 229, 232

related words, *See* synonyms

review, unit, 45–47, 83–85, 121–123, 159–161, 197–199, 235–237

review words. *See* assessment

revising, 17, 23, 29, 35, 41, 51, 55, 61, 67, 73, 79, 89, 93, 99, 105, 111, 117, 127, 131, 137, 143, 149, 155, 165, 169, 175, 181, 187, 193, 203, 207, 213, 219, 225, 231, 241
roots. *See* **word roots/origins**
rules
    spelling (*see* **patterns**)

S

schwa sound, 114
    /shəl/, 210–215, 234, 235
    /shəs/, 210–215, 234, 235
    in final syllable, 210–215, 234, 235
science and spelling. *See* **spelling across the curriculum**
sentences
    complex sentence, 165
    compound sentence, 165
short story, writing, 131
silent letters
    pronunciation and spelling, 76–81, 112
    silent consonants, 76–81, 82, 85, 112
    silent e, 58–63, 64–69, 70–75, 82, 83, 84, 90–95, 96–101 (*See also* **suffixes, dropping final e in endings**)
    suffixes and, 58–63, 64–69, 70–75, 90–95, 96–101
simple predicate, 50
simple subject, 50
slang, 115
social studies and spelling. *See* **spelling across the curriculum**
sorting words,
    adjectives, 90, 95, 204, 209
    adverbs, 90, 95, 204, 209
    commonly confused words, 178, 183
    compound words, 14, 32, 37, 44

double consonants, 38, 43, 44, 108–113
eponyms, 140, 145, 158, 160
French words, 184, 189
frequently misspelled words, 102, 107, 122, 146, 151, 158, 160
Greek roots, 172, 177
Latin roots, 152, 157, 190, 195, 216, 221, 228, 233
long vowels, 26, 31, 44, 46
plural nouns, 128, 133
prefixes, 52, 57, 134, 139, 166, 171, 222, 227
short vowels, 20, 25, 44, 45
silent consonants, 76, 81
silent e, 58, 63, 64, 69, 70, 75
Spanish words, 114, 119, 123
suffixes, 52, 57, 58, 63, 64, 69, 70, 75, 96, 101, 108, 113, 204, 209, 210, 215
toponyms, 140, 145, 158, 160
sound. *See also* **patterns; spelling patterns**
    beginning, 30
    consonants (*see* **consonants**)
    schwa sound (*see* **schwa sound**)
    silent letters
        silent consonants, 76–81, 112
        silent e and suffix, 58–63, 64–69, 70–75, 82, 83, 84, 90–95, 96–101
    vowels (*see* **vowels**)
speech, 61
spelling across the curriculum
    fine arts, 95, 189, 209
    health, 81, 151
    language arts, 19, 69, 75, 119, 145, 171
    mathematics, 37, 57, 139, 177, 227
    science, 31, 63, 107, 183, 233
    social studies, 43, 113, 133, 157, 215
    technology, 25, 101, 195, 221

Spelling Dictionary, 15, 20, 21, 26, 27, 33, 39, 59, 65, 77, 91, 97, 103, 115, 129, 135, 141, 147, 167, 170, 179, 185, 191, 205, 223
Spelling Journal, 17, 23, 29, 35, 41, 55, 61, 67, 73, 79, 93, 99, 105, 111, 117, 131, 137, 143, 149, 155, 169, 175, 181, 187, 193, 207, 213, 231
spelling patterns. *See* **patterns, spelling patterns**
standardized test practice, 48–49, 86–87, 124–125, 162–163, 200–201, 238–239
stress mark, 65, 141
structural patterns. *See* **patterns**
subject, 50, 89. *See also* **simple subject**
subordinating conjunctions, 164–165
suffixes
    -able, 70–75, 82, 96–101, 220
    -al, 194
    -ance, 56, 70–75
    -ary, 194
    -ate, 194
    -ation, 64–69, 70–75, 220
    base word and, 27, 52–57, 58–63, 64–69, 70–75, 82, 83, 84, 90–95, 96–101, 103, 108–113, 150, 214, 220
    -ence, 108–113
    -ful, 56
    -ible, 96–101, 220
    -ive, 232
    -less, 56, 57
    -ly, 57, 63, 90–95, 120, 121, 204–209, 234, 235
    -ment, 62, 63
    -ness, 56, 57, 63
    -ous, 63, 194
    silent e and, 58–63, 64–69, 70–75, 82, 83, 84, 90
    -some, 56
    -tion, 64–69, 70–75, 194, 220
summary, 203
syllabication. *See* **syllables**

syllables, 102
  dictionary skills for, 15, 20, 26, 65
  double consonants and, 108–113
  open and closed, 20, 26, 44
  pronunciations and, 15
  schwa sound in final, 210–215, 234, 235
  short/long vowels and, 18, 20, 23–26, 44–46
  silent consonants and, 112
  stressed and unstressed, 24, 108–113, 208
synonyms, 21, 22, 27, 28, 33, 39, 40, 53, 66, 71, 91, 94, 97, 100, 106, 109, 136, 138, 147, 153, 161, 173, 174, 185, 205, 206, 211, 214, 217, 220, 229

tall tale, writing, 79
thesaurus, using, 53, 71, 94, 109, 153, 173, 211, 217, 229. See also **Writing Thesaurus**
toponyms, 140–145, 158, 160
Transfer
  Assess for Transfer, 44, 82, 120, 158, 196, 234
  Spelling Journal, 17, 23, 29, 35, 41, 55, 61, 67, 73, 79, 93, 99, 105, 111, 117, 131, 137, 143, 149, 155, 169, 175, 181, 187, 193, 207, 213, 231
troublesome words. See commonly confused words; frequently misspelled words

usage. See grammar, usage, and mechanics
use context clues. See context clues

use the dictionary. See dictionary skills
use the thesaurus. See thesaurus, using

verbs, 24, 39, 50, 59, 64, 65, 94, 99, 226, 232, 240
vocabulary skills
  analogies, 16, 22, 28, 40, 54, 72, 116, 122, 130, 148, 160, 186, 192, 212
  analyzing word parts, 21, 97
  antonyms, 56, 97, 100, 147, 211, 214
  applying foreign words/phrases, 114–119, 184–189
  categorizing words, 18, 27, 36, 62, 65, 77, 85, 103, 115, 129, 132, 191, 229, 237
  compound words, 14–19, 32–37, 44, 46
  context clues, 16, 22, 28, 34, 40, 45, 46, 54, 60, 66, 68, 72, 78, 92, 98, 104, 110, 116, 121, 130, 136, 142, 148, 154, 156, 168, 174, 180, 186, 192, 198, 212, 218, 224, 230
  eponyms, 140–145, 158, 160
  homographs, 24
  homophones, 178, 179
  informal language, 115
  multiple-meaning words, 27
  slang, 115
  synonyms, 21, 22, 27, 28, 33, 39, 40, 53, 66, 71, 91, 94, 97, 100, 106, 109, 136, 138, 147, 153, 161, 173, 174, 185, 205, 206, 211, 214, 217, 220, 229
  toponyms, 140–145, 158, 160
  word building, 36
  word families (See word families)
  word history, 59, 91, 135, 141, 147, 185, 223

word meaning, 15, 18, 21, 27, 33, 39, 53, 56, 59, 65, 68, 71, 74, 77, 80, 84, 91, 94, 97, 100, 103, 106, 109, 115, 118, 121, 129, 132, 135, 141, 144, 153, 156, 167, 170, 173, 176, 179, 182, 185, 188, 191, 194, 197, 198, 205, 211, 214, 217, 219, 220, 223, 226, 229, 232
  word roots (see word roots/origins)
  words, 18, 27, 62, 103, 115, 129
  word structure (see word structure)
  working with syllables (see syllables)
vowels
  long vowels, 18, 26–31, 44, 46, 114
  short vowels, 20–25, 44, 45

word analysis, 21, 97. See also analyzing word parts
word building, 36
word categorization. See categorizing words
word families. See also **patterns, spelling patterns**
  identifying base words, 58, 64, 70, 108, 150, 170, 220, 226
word groups, 18, 27, 36, 62, 65, 77, 85, 103, 115, 129, 132, 191, 229, 237. See also categorizing words
word histories, 42, 59, 91, 135, 141, 147, 185, 223
word hunts
  fine arts, 95, 189, 209
  health, 81, 151
  language arts, 19, 69, 75, 119, 145, 171
  mathematics, 37, 57, 139, 177, 227

science, 31, 63, 107, 183, 233
social studies, 43, 113, 133, 157, 215
technology, 25, 101, 195, 221
word meaning. *See* meaning mastery; reading skills; vocabulary skills
word roots/origins, 170. *See also* foreign words/phrases
eponyms, 140–145, 158, 160
French, 59, 184–189, 196, 198
Greek, 59, 166–171, 172–177, 196, 197
Latin, 42, 59, 91, 134–139, 147, 152–157, 158, 159, 161, 166–171, 190–195, 196, 197, 199, 216–221, 222–227, 228–233, 234, 236, 237
Middle English, 59, 147
obsolete, 59
Old English, 59
prefixes and, 56, 57, 134–139, 152–157, 166–171 (*see also* **prefixes**)
Spanish, 114–119, 123
suffixes and, 56, 57, 58–63, 96–101, 120, 121, 122 (*see also* **suffixes**)
toponyms, 140–145, 158, 160
word sorts. *See* sorting words
word structure. *See also* patterns, structural patterns; phonics skills
base words (*see* base words)
compound words, 14–19, 32–37, 44, 46
homographs, 24
homophones, 178, 179
letter substitution, 182
plurals, 128–133, 158, 159
syllables (*see* syllables)
word study, 18, 24, 30, 36, 42, 56, 62, 68, 74, 80, 94, 100, 106, 112, 118, 132, 138, 144, 150, 156, 170, 176, 182, 188, 194, 208, 214, 220, 226, 232
words. *See also* **base words**; word building
analyzing, 21, 97
categorizing, 18, 27, 36, 62, 65, 77, 85, 103, 115, 129, 132, 191, 229, 237
commonly confused, 178–183, 196, 198
compound, 14–19, 32–37, 44, 46
frequently misspelled, 102–107, 122, 146–151, 158, 160
identifying, 58, 64, 70, 108, 150, 170, 220, 226
Word Swap, 47
Writer's Workshop. *See also* writing skills
argument (persuasive) writing, 165, 241
descriptive writing, 89
identifying conjunctions, 164–165
identifying modifiers: adjectives, 126–127
identifying modifiers: adverbs, 88–89
informative/explanatory (expository) writing, 127, 203
narrative writing, 51
parts of a sentence, 50–51
prepositions, 202–203
subject-verb agreement, 240–241
writing process, 242–243. *See also* **drafting; editing; prewriting; publishing; revising; writing skills**
writing skills. *See also* **Writer's Workshop**
advertisement, 41
argument (persuasive) prompts, 17, 61, 99, 111, 165, 219, 241
biographical sketch, 35, 207
descriptive prompts, 89, 143, 213, 225
dialogue, 93
editorial, 17, 241
e-mail, 127
folktale, 73
informative/explanatory (expository) prompts, 23, 29, 35, 41, 67, 127, 137, 169, 175, 193, 203, 207, 231
journal entry, 55
letter, 137
mystery, 51, 187
narrative prompts, 51, 55, 73, 79, 93, 105, 117, 131, 149, 155, 181, 187
news story, 23
observation report, 89
outline, 175
paragraph, 29, 67, 99, 105, 111, 117, 143, 149, 169, 181, 193, 213, 219, 225, 231
passage, 155
persuasive essay, 165
proofreading (*see* proofreading)
short story, 131
speech, 61
summary, 203
tall tale, 79
Writing Thesaurus, 297–322

Credits

Photography: Cover images top and bottom left © Zaner-Bloser, top right © iStockphoto.com/Jan Pietruska, bottom right © iStockphoto.com/klosfoto; p. 9 © Blend Images/Alamy; p. 10 top © George C. Anderson Photography; p. 10 bottom © 2001–2009 Smart Technologies ULC. All rights reserved; p. 11–13 © George C. Anderson Photography; p. 19 © Don Ryan/AP Images; p. 25 © Hulton-Deutsch Collection/Corbis; p. 31 © Library of Congress Prints and Photographs Division [LC-DIG-ppmsca-13269]; p. 37 © Scott Boehm/Getty Images; p. 43 © Alfredo Dagli Orti/Corbis; p. 57 © age fotostock/SuperStock; p. 63 © BIOS/Photolibrary; p. 69 © NASA-JPL; p. 75 © Superstock; p. 81 © Time & Life Pictures/Getty Images; p. 95 © Alabama Department of Archives and History; p. 101 © E.M. Pasieka/Science Photo Library/Corbis; p. 107 © Hiroshi Watanabe/Getty Images; p. 113 © Greg Kock/USFWS; p. 119 © James Nesterwitz/Alamy; p. 133 © Library of Congress Prints and Photographs Division [LC-DIG-nclc-03765]; p. 139 © Classic Image/Alamy; p. 145 © Joe Clark/Tetra Images/Corbis; p. 151 © Bettmann/Corbis; p. 157 © Bill Bachman/Alamy; p. 171 © Library of Congress Prints and Photographs Division [LC-USZ62-31799]; p. 177 © Mary Kate Denny/PhotoEdit; p. 183 © IndexStock/SuperStock; p. 189 © PR Newswire/AP Images; p. 195 © Nivek Neslo/Getty Images; p. 209 © Kyodo/AP Images; p. 215 © Blaine Harrington III/CORBIS; p. 221 © Alex Bramwell/Alamy; p. 227 © North Wind Picture Archives/Alamy; p. 233 © Todd Reese/Alamy